WESTERN[...]

0   50   100   200 km

Names or locations of battles are printed in red

LOWER CANADA

French R.

Lake Nipissing

St. Lawrence River

Montreal

St-Jean

Richelieu R.

Cornwall

Prescott   Ogdensburg

Plattsburg

Ottawa River

Georgian Bay

Penetanguishene

Lake Simcoe

Nottawasaga R.

Kingston

Sackets Harbor

Lake Champlain

VERMONT

UPPER   CANADA

York

LAKE ONTARIO

Oswego

Burlington Heights

NIAGARA PENINSULA
See enlargement on back endpaper

Buffalo

NEW   YORK

Albany

MAS

Thames R.

Port Dover

Port Talbot

agwood
4

Moraviantown
1813
tham

Long Pt.

LAKE ERIE

CONN

Hudson River

PENNSYLVANIA

Pittsburgh

Delaware River

New York

NEW

Susquehanna River

Philadelphia

JERSEY

MARYLAND

Baltimore

Potomac R.

Patuxent R.

Bladensburg
1814

Washington

DELAWARE

Chesapeake Bay

ATLANTIC

OCEAN

VIRGINIA

1983.

Merry Christmas John,

I hope you enjoy this book.
It's really about time you reflected
on important events in world history!

all my love,

Mary Jane, x.o.

The
War of 1812
Land Operations

Canadian
War Museum
Historical Publications

Previous titles in the series

[1] *Canada and the First World War*, by John
Swettenham. Canadian War Museum, Ottawa, 1968.
Bilingual.

[2] *D-Day*, by John Swettenham. Canadian War
Museum, Ottawa, 1969. Bilingual.

[3] *Canada and the First World War*, by John
Swettenham. Based on the Fiftieth Anniversary
Armistice Display at the Canadian War Museum.
Ryerson, Toronto, 1969. Published in paperback,
McGraw-Hill Ryerson, 1973.

[4] *Canadian Military Aircraft*, by J.A. Griffin. Queen's
Printer, Ottawa, 1969. Bilingual.

5. *The Last War Drum: The North West Campaign of
1885*, by Desmond Morton. Hakkert, Toronto, 1972.

6. *The Evening of Chivalry*, by John Swettenham.
National Museums of Canada, Ottawa, 1972. French
edition available.

7. *Valiant Men: Canada's Victoria Cross and George
Cross Winners*, ed. by John Swettenham. Hakkert,
Toronto, 1973.

8. *Canada Invaded, 1775-1776*, by George F. G.
Stanley. Hakkert, Toronto, 1973. French edition
available.

9. *The Canadian General, Sir William Otter*, by
Desmond Morton. Hakkert, Toronto, 1974.
Bilingual.

10. *Silent Witnesses*, by John Swettenham and
Herbert F. Wood. Hakkert, Toronto, 1974. French
edition available.

11. *Broadcast from the Front: Canadian Radio Overseas
in the Second World War*, by A. E. Powley.
Hakkert, Toronto, 1975.

12. *Canada's Fighting Ships*, by K. R. Macpherson.
Samuel Stevens Hakkert & Co., Toronto, 1975.

13. *Canada's Nursing Sisters*, by G. W. L. Nicholson.
Samuel Stevens Hakkert & Co., Toronto, 1975.

14. *RCAF: Squadron Histories and Aircraft, 1924-1968*,
by Samuel Kostenuk and John Griffin. Samuel
Stevens Hakkert & Co., Toronto, 1975.

15. *Canada's Guns: An Illustrated History of Artillery*,
by Leslie W. C. S. Barnes. National Museums of
Canada, Ottawa, 1979. French edition available.

16. *Military Uniforms in Canada, 1665-1970*, by Jack L.
Summers and René Chartrand, and illustrated by
R. J. Marrion. National Museums of Canada,
Ottawa, 1981. French edition available.

17. *Canada at Dieppe*, by T. Murray Hunter. Balmuir,
Ottawa, 1982. French edition available.

*For further information on these titles, please write to the
Canadian War Museum, National Museum of Man,
National Museums of Canada, Ottawa   K1A 0M8*

1. Major General Sir Isaac Brock, administrator of the province and commander of the British and Canadian forces, Upper Canada, 1811–12

The War of 1812

Land Operations

George F. G. Stanley

Canadian War Museum
Historical Publication No. 18

Macmillan of Canada
in collaboration with the
National Museum of Man
National Museums of Canada

Canadian Cataloguing in Publication Data
Stanley, George F. G., 1907–
The War of 1812: land operations

Issued also in French under title:
La guerre de 1812 : les opérations terrestres

Bibliography: p.
Includes index
ISBN 0-7715-9859-9

1. Canada—History—War of 1812—Campaigns
and battles.* 2. United States—History—
War of 1812—Campaigns and battles.
I. National Museum of Man (Canada). II. Title.
FC442.S73   971.03'4   C83-098595-6
E359.85.S73

SCC Catalogue No. NM95-16/18E

Design by Maher and Murtagh

Macmillan of Canada
A Division of Gage Publishing Limited
in collaboration with the
Canadian War Museum
National Museum of Man
National Museums of Canada

Printed in Canada

Gu cuimhne dhiadhaidh air mo shinn-sheanair
GEORGE FRANCIS GILLMAN STANLEY
1806–1901
a bha a lathair cath
Crysler's Farm
nuair bha e na giullan beag
's e tarraing uiste do'n na saighedearan a bha leòinte.

Fois shiòrruidh gu robh aig anam

Contents

Foreword • xv
Preface • xvii

THE BACKGROUND

1 The Declaration of War • 3
2 The United States • 11
3 British North America • 49

1812

4 The Detroit Frontier • 83
5 The Niagara Frontier • 117

1813

6 The Erie Frontier • 143
7 The Niagara Frontier • 167
8 Moraviantown • 201
9 Montreal • 225

1814

10 Western Upper Canada • 271
11 Lundy's Lane • 299
12 The British Offensive • 333
13 The Castine Expedition • 357

THE RESTORATION OF PEACE

14   The Treaty of Ghent • 381
15   Conclusion • 403

APPENDICES

I   Honours and Awards • 421
II   Canadian Uniforms • 427
III   Regiments and Other Units • 429
IV   The Medical Services • 433

Notes • 435
Bibliography • 461
Illustration Credits • 469
Index • 473

Maps

The Treaty of Greenville, 1795
• 22 •

Vote on the Declaration of War
House of Representatives, 4 June 1812
• 40 •
Senate, 17 June 1812
• 41 •

The St. Lawrence Frontier, 1812
• 77 •

The Detroit Frontier, 1812
• 92 •

Detroit, 1812
• 100 •

The Niagara Frontier, 1812
• 123 •

The Battle of Queenston Heights, 13 October 1812
• 128 •

The Western Region, 1812–1814
• 149 •

The Siege of Fort Meigs, 1–5 May 1813
• 152 •

The Attack on Fort Stephenson, 1 August 1813
• 159 •

Fort Astoria, 1813
· 164 ·

The Capture of York, 27 April 1813
· 171 ·

Dearborn's Invasion of the Niagara, 1813
· 181 ·

Harrison's Invasion of Upper Canada, 1813
· 205 ·

The St. Lawrence Frontier, 1813
· 227 ·

The Attack on Sackets Harbor
· 236 ·

Hampton's Invasion of Lower Canada, 1813
· 248 ·

The Battle of Crysler's Farm
· 262 ·

Western Upper Canada, 1814
· 277 ·

The Battle of Chippawa, 5 July 1814
· 314 ·

The Battle of Lundy's Lane
· 320 ·

The Raid on Washington, 17–28 August 1814
· 339 ·

Plattsburg, 11 September 1814
· 347 ·

The Penobscot Bay Expedition
· 371 ·

Eastern Canada–United States Boundary, 1798–1842
· 389 ·

Boundary—Passamaquoddy Bay, 1818
· 397 ·

Maps drawn by William Constable

Foreword

I am honoured to have been asked to write the foreword for George Stanley's latest book. As a cadet at the Royal Military College of Canada in Kingston, I benefited from his vast knowledge of Canada's military history and, incidentally, developed a particular interest in the subject of this work. The publication of this critical study of the War of 1812 will enable a wide audience to draw on Dr. Stanley's scholarship and enjoy a rousing account of an important episode in North American history.

The War of 1812 began one hundred and seventy years ago. During the conflict many errors in tactics and strategy were made. Dr. Stanley has not only succeeded in presenting a detailed history of this, the last war to be fought on Canadian soil, but has also discerned lessons that are relevant to us today.

The war had a profound effect on both Canada and the United States. Formerly foes, the two countries have since been allies for many years. Dr. Stanley's account of the war—its origins, incidents and aftermath—illuminate the subsequent histories of both nations. Readers can look forward to an entertaining as well as an educational experience. I wholeheartedly recommend Dr. Stanley's study to the history buff and general reader alike.

General Ramsey M. Withers, CMM, CD

Preface

Six years ago, in 1976, the late John Swettenham of the Canadian War Museum in Ottawa asked me to write a book on the Canadian War of 1812. He had in mind a two-volume publication, one dealing with the land operations and the other with the naval war on the Great Lakes and the Atlantic. The first was to be my responsibility; the second would be undertaken by Dr. Alec Douglas, Director of History, National Defence Headquarters. Both John Swettenham and I were aware that a number of twentieth-century historians, Canadian and American, had written about the war, including my former colleague in the Canadian Army Historical Section, the late J. M. Hitsman. Even a few British historians had published books on the subject, notably Sir Charles Lucas, although, generally speaking, the War of 1812 has never attracted much attention in Britain, neither while it was being fought nor since.

I accepted the Museum's invitation, not only because I had spent a considerable portion of my life writing military history and believed I might have something to say about the War of 1812 that would interest modern-day enthusiasts of military history, but also because I had, as a boy, listened to tales of the war told me by my father, who had had them from his grandfather. My great great grandfather, Matthew Wyn Stanley, formerly of the 24th Regiment of Foot, had settled at Mille Roches, in Upper Canada, and was a member of Captain David Sheek's company, 1st Regiment Stormont Militia, a unit that took part in the fighting along the St. Lawrence front. Some of the tales I listened to so intently may have strayed over the boundaries of historical accuracy, but they stimulated an interest in the War of 1812 that I have not lost to this day.

But do I have anything new to add to what Hannay, Lucas, Cruikshank, Adams, Wood, Burt and Hitsman, to name only a few, have already said about the war? Perhaps not in terms of factual data, but possibly in terms of emphasis. Canadians and Americans have tended to see the war in General Staff terms and to locate it in Upper Canada. That is natural enough. The actual battles are the most exciting aspect of military history, and most of the battles of the War of 1812 were fought in Upper Canada or on neighbouring American territory. However, as I see the war, it was a contest that extended from sea to sea, from Halifax to Astoria. That is why I have devoted more space to operations in the western and Atlantic regions than historians have usually done in the past. I have also placed more emphasis on logistics. This does not mean that I have written a logistical history of the war; someone else will have to do that. It does mean that I have tried to point out the significance of logistical factors in the field operations. After all, are not logistics as important in determining victories and defeats as are the manoeuvres of companies and regiments or the courage and timidity of individuals?

Because there will be another volume dealing with naval operations, freshwater and saltwater, I have only touched on that side of the War of 1812, but I have been careful to indicate where and how naval actions influenced the course of the war on land. I have written nothing about the American operations against the Indians in the South, and have referred only in passing to the British attack at New Orleans. My object has been to write the history of the Canadian war as seen from the standpoint of the inhabitants of British North America. The southern war has no particular relevance for Canadians, simply because they were not involved.

The book is not long. In making certain that I did not overburden it with detail or dialogue, I followed a rule familiar to all fishermen: events of no special significance, like small fish, should be returned to the waters. What I included I have drawn, in large measure, from contemporary sources, both in manuscript and published.

A word about the illustrations. Of previous accounts of the War of 1812, only Lossing's *Pictorial Field-Book*, first published in 1868, contains as many illustrations. Included here are views of fortifications and depictions of battles, many of them contemporary, as well as portraits of participants—British, Canadian, Indian, American, soldiers and politicians alike. The Canadian War Museum was able to supply photographs of regimental colours, muskets, medals and drums from its collection, but, for the rest, Fred Gaffen and I were obliged to range widely, from Halifax to Ottawa, to Toronto, to Fort Malden, and south to New York and Washington. I am most grateful to all those institutions that provided us with prints and to the National Museums of Canada and Macmillan of Canada for generously publishing so many of them.

A work of academic research that reaches publication is in the nature of a team effort, and I am grateful to every person who helped me by providing books, documents or access to documents, and by giving me permission to reproduce illustrations in their possession. By listing names I run the risk of omitting, through oversight, someone who should be included, and I apologize if I have overlooked anyone. But first, an acknowledgement of a personal nature. I could never have written this book without the silence of the study. My thanks to my spouse. She kept the door closed—most of the time. I am also grateful to her for undertaking the demanding chore of reading proof. To Fred Gaffen of the Canadian War Museum go my sincere thanks. He not only served as my research assistant, but he diligently and thoroughly checked all references, quotations, ranks, names and titles, and did so with good spirit at all times. The generosity with which he gave time and effort to detecting textual errors could not have been greater. To Viviane Appleton of the Publishing Division of the National Museums of Canada, who acted as my editor, I express my gratitude for her meticulous examination of the text, illustrations and bibliography, and for the improvements that followed. Both Mrs. Appleton and Mr. Gaffen went beyond the usual line of a publisher's duty in order to bring this book to its present form.

Others whose assistance in various ways I am happy to acknowledge include Anne Brown, John Elting, Harrison Bird, the late John Spurr, Laurie Stanley, Dr. J. C. Medcoff, René Chartrand, Dr. Alec Douglas, Dr. William Dudley, Brereton Greenhous, Ross W. Irwin, Ludwig Kosche, Paul Marshall, Dr. Desmond Morton and Dr. William E. Taylor, Jr. I should especially like to thank Lee Murray and his staff at the Canadian War Museum for their help. I am also grateful for the cooperation extended by the Public Archives of Canada, the Public

Archives of Nova Scotia, the Public Archives of Ontario, the Massey Library (Royal Military College of Canada), the National Library of Canada, and the libraries of Brown University, the University of Maine (Orono), Mount Allison University, the Department of National Defence, and the Canadian War Museum.

Finally, I should like to acknowledge that any errors that may appear in the text, appendices, bibliography or references are, like the opinions expressed in this book, my own responsibility.

George F. G. Stanley

Frosty Hollow, New Brunswick
St. Ninian's Day, 1981

The Background

1

The Declaration of War

ON 13 MAY 1812, Congressman John Harper of New Hampshire wrote to Senator William Plumer of the same state:

> The great question will undoubtedly be taken early in June. The President will probably send an important and very argumentative message to Congress. A manifesto will be brought forward by the Committee of Foreign Relations and a declaration that 'war exists' between the United States and the crown of Great Britain and its dependencies.[1]

Harper was right in his guess, if guess it was. On 1 June a message from James Madison, fourth president of the United States, was read to the members of Congress behind closed doors—"very argumentative", as Harper said it would be. It contained a lengthy list of grievances and charges against Great Britain, irritants that an independent nation could not ignore. The message did not, in so many words, call for a declaration of war, but the President's hint was obvious: "I am happy in the assurance that the decision will be worthy [of] the enlightened and patriotic councils of a virtuous, a free and a powerful nation."[2] That war was what the chief executive wanted became clear in the manifesto that followed the message on 3 June. Drafted by James Monroe, secretary of state, and presented by John C. Calhoun, acting chairman of the House Committee on Foreign Relations, the manifesto called upon "the free-born sons of America" to follow "the Lord of Hosts" and do battle "in a righteous cause".[3] The next day the House of Representatives voted for war 79 to 49.

3

Although the House deliberated in secret session, there was talk of war in every coffee-house and on every street corner. Augustus John Foster, the British minister in Washington, knowing that war was imminent, sent a hurried letter to Halifax by HMS *Tartarus*, warning the Governor of Nova Scotia that the House of Representatives had voted for war and that he saw no reason to believe that it would not be endorsed by the Senate. In public, however, he adopted the stance that there would be no breaking of the peace. When asked if he would be interested in selling his horses, he replied that he had no intention of parting with them or moving: in fact he was going ahead with plans to purchase an icehouse for the ensuing winter.

War did not immediately follow the vote in the House of Representatives. There were prolonged arguments in the Senate, where on 12 June a vote ended in deadlock, 16 to 16. But the "War Hawks" were unyielding. They claimed that theirs was the voice of patriotism, and after several amendments and much talking the war resolution carried on 17 June by a vote of 19 in favour and 13 against. It was the anniversary of Bunker Hill. For the moment there was no official announcement. That same evening, Augustus Foster attended Dolley Madison's drawing-room. He found the President "ghastly pale" and disposed to talk only about Lord Selkirk, Russia and "the British successes in Spain".[4] On 18 June the secret declaration of war, together with the senate amendments, was referred back to the House of Representatives, and on that day a formal document committing the United States to war with Great Britain received Madison's "wandering" signature. Twenty-four hours later the President issued a wordy proclamation exhorting the people of the United States to support the administration's actions and thereby secure for themselves "a speedy, a just and an honorable peace".[5] Madison's political opponents called it "Mr. Madison's War".

AS SOON AS the news of war became official, on 19 June, express riders set out for all parts of the United States, to the seaports and to the western frontier. By accident or bad management, the messengers to the Ohio Valley carried only a simple instruction to the commanding general to hurry forward to Detroit so as to be ready to invade Canada; the actual declaration of war went by postal service and arrived six days later. In Nova Scotia, the warning from Augustus Foster was confirmed on 27 June, when HMS *Belvidera* limped into Halifax harbour,

2. James Madison, fourth president of the United States, 1809–17

having been badly mauled by an American squadron in a surprise attack on the high seas. On Lake Ontario the American brig *Oneida* had anticipated the outbreak of war by seizing three schooners beating up the lake towards Kingston;[6] but after the news of war became public knowledge, Dunham Jones of Pointe-au-Baril (Maitland), with a detachment of militia in row-

5

boats, turned the tables on several American schooners trying to escape into Lake Ontario, overtaking them at the head of the Thousand Islands near Elizabethtown (Brockville), capturing two and forcing the others back downriver to Ogdensburg. At Fort George, Major General Isaac Brock was informed of Madison's declaration of war while dining with the enemy, for the officers of the 41st Regiment of Foot, whose guest he was, were at that moment engaged in entertaining their American counterparts from across the river at Fort Niagara. In a manner reminiscent of the eighteenth century, the officers continued their meal, concluding with expressions of hope that the exchange of hospitalities might be resumed when hostilities should end.[7]

Lieutenant Charles Frédéric Rolette of the Provincial Marine at Fort Malden, on the Detroit River, was less courteously inclined on the morning of 2 July. Catching sight of an American schooner, *Cuyahoga*, making her way up the far side of the river towards Detroit, he set out in pursuit in a longboat with a dozen sailors, "all well armed with sabers and pick-axes"[8] and followed closely by a canoe bearing another French Canadian, Thomas Verchères de Boucherville, and several Indians. The schooner, carrying a number of bandsmen, a cargo of medical stores, and baggage belonging to the officers of Brigadier General William Hull's army, hove to on Rolette's demand and allowed the Canadians to board her. "My friend Rolette then ran up the British flag", wrote Boucherville, "and ordered the band to play 'God Save the King'."[9] This was the first intimation the American troops on their way to Detroit had that war had actually broken out. The capture of *Cuyahoga* was serious for the Americans, not so much because of the loss of a few musicians and bags of clothing, but because of the seizure of medical stores that could not easily be replaced and, above all, of the Commanding General's personal and official correspondence with Washington, including nominal rolls of the men under his command.

Farther north, the news of war reached the British garrison at St. Joseph Island before their American counterparts at Fort Michilimackinac learned of it. Isaac Brock had already considered moving against Michilimackinac, but, having been warned by his commander-in-chief, Sir George Prevost, to restrain any aggressive inclinations, he limited his orders to Captain Charles Roberts at St. Joseph Island to act according to his best judgment.[10] Roberts understood the mind of his com-

3. 10th Royal Veteran Battalion, 1812

mander in Upper Canada, and, acting on his own initiative, set out with a small force of regulars (old men of the 10th Royal Veterans) and militia, along with some 400 Indians, in the North West Company vessel *Caledonia* and a fleet of canoes, for the American position at the entrance to Lake Michigan. In the early hours of 17 July, Roberts landed to the north of the American fort. Dragging a small cannon to a commanding height and placing his men in position to assault the fort, he presented the enemy with the news of war and a demand for their immediate surrender. Outnumbered, threatened by artillery and caught completely by surprise, the Americans capitulated. Their soldiers became prisoners but the civilians were allowed to return to American territory. Ordnance ammunition, provisions and furs (classified conveniently as public property), a fort far better than the miserable station on St. Joseph Island, and the enthusiasm of the western Indians, ready to wield their tomahawks in the British interest, were the fruits of success—a bloodless victory and a rich haul for Roberts, and for Brock a justification of his "offence-is-the-best-defence" approach to the war.

On the Atlantic Coast there were no surprises or rich hauls: there everybody and everything remained quiet, at least for the time being. In New Brunswick, news of war reached Fredericton through the agency of friendly Indians. In Maine, as soon as the people of Eastport learned from Washington of the change in their relationship with the inhabitants of the British provinces, they called a public meeting to decide upon the proper course of action. The decision was to take no action at all. Eastporters would refrain from any show of hostility towards the British, "discountenance all depredations" and "preserve a good understanding with the inhabitants of New Brunswick".[11] Major General Martin Hunter and his successor as military and civil head of New Brunswick, Major General George S. Smyth, were both disposed to reciprocate this pacific gesture. If nothing else, it would give them time to repair the dilapidated fortifications of Saint John, St. Andrews and Fort Cumberland (Fort Beauséjour), and to organize and find arms for the provincial militia. It would also enable them to stockpile foodstuffs imported from the United States, and that might be the most important benefit of all. Hunter, therefore, just prior to his departure from Fredericton, wrote to the British prime minister, Lord Liverpool, assuring him that

> the Eastern States are very averse to a war. . . . Mr. Madison and his party, being alarmed that he will not be re-elected in October as president, has taken the rash step of declaring war as the only chance of remaining in power.[12]

In Halifax, war was not unexpected, but when the state of hostilities became official the editor of the *Nova-Scotia Royal Gazette* wrote on 1 July, "The madness which has for many years pervaded the European continent has at length reached this hemisphere, which is now to be visited by war and all its horrors." He had no doubt in his mind who was to blame for the war and on which side God would lend his arm. "It is consoling to reflect", he wrote, "that Great Britain has hitherto been providentially supported" and that "these colonies, under the wing of their Parent State, have attained their present growth and prosperity", and that, in consequence, "every man, as he values the blessings he enjoys", would be prepared to "rally round his Parent Oak, and by his exertions to defend his family and his fire-side" would prove himself "worthy of that flock from whence he sprung". A more belligerent editorialist in Montreal wrote on 13 July in the *Gazette*:

> At length, fellow-subjects, the dreadful crisis has arrived that stamps us a conquered people or inspires our hearts with patriotic enthusiasm in support of our liberty, our constitutional rights, our altars and our homes. An infatuated enemy has declared an unjust war against us; a war not founded upon the broad basis of real injuries sustained, but whose foundation is discovered to have been delineated by the contaminating finger of the arch-usurper, Napoleon.

2

The United States

THE HALIGONIANS and the Montrealers may have seen the outbreak of war between the United States and Great Britain in
June 1812 as the product of James Madison's political ambitions
or the sinister manipulations of Napoleon Bonaparte. But
neither explanation indicated much knowledge of history or
understanding of the nature of the relationship between the two
powers during the previous generation. The fundamental cause
of the war went back fully thirty years, to the dynamic
struggle that had seen Great Britain humiliated, her military
power defeated in battle, and her political authorities forced
to recognize the transformation of her rebellious colonies into
a new political entity, separate from and independent of the
mother country. For the British, defeat in 1783 had been bitter,
and they had remained slow to accept the full implications of
the American success or the full significance of American independence. For the Americans, military and political victory had
been sweet. But while they gained in self-assertiveness, they did
not acquire self-assurance and self-confidence. Both would come
in time, but that time had not yet arrived in 1812. To Americans, feeling their way in the world of nation-states, freedom
to choose their own course of action, political or economic,
knowing that they would not have to yield to outside pressures,
was the true substance of independence. Nothing can erode a
sense of nationhood more than constantly giving in to the
demands of powerful neighbours; and nationhood was the over-
riding concern of the leaders of American opinion between 1783

11

and 1812. It was unfortunate that, during the same years, Great Britain found herself involved in a life-and-death struggle in Europe and, for reasons of self-defence, perhaps even self-preservation, disposed to ignore the susceptibilities of her former colonials in North America. In simple terms, callousness in Britain and oversensitivity in the United States were the twin legacies of the American Revolutionary War; they were, in consequence, the fundamental forces behind the renewal of that struggle in 1812. History and geography, rather than pique or caprice, underlay the posturings and polemics that preceded the shooting in 1812. The Americans, of course, readily convinced themselves that they were fighting for valid principles, at least principles they believed to be valid, principles that would have to be upheld by fighting if they could not be affirmed by other means. More mature in their approach to war, the British simply maintained that they were fighting for the defence of their empire.

THE WAR OF THE REVOLUTION between Great Britain and the Thirteen Colonies ended with the signing of a formal treaty of peace in Paris on 3 September 1783. The treaty stopped the gunfire, but it did not achieve peace in the sense of mutual tolerance and friendly understanding. Too many unsettled issues were left to rankle in British and American memories. There were, for instance, those Americans whose loyalties had remained with the Crown, some of whom had actively taken up arms on behalf of Great Britain. During the war these "Loyalists" had been regarded as pariahs by the rebels who controlled the state governments. They had been barred from exercising their civil rights; they could not collect debts, claim legal protection from slander and assault, hold land or remain in the professions. Freedom of speech and of travel were denied them. Some were hanged and others exiled, imprisoned or herded into concentration camps. George Washington referred to them as "abominable pests of society",[1] and John Adams was for hanging all who offered opposition to the Revolution. Whig hoodlums ransacked their houses, insulted their women and subjected their men to degrading brutalities. When the representatives of Parliament and Congress met in Paris to talk terms of peace, they recognized that something should be done about the abused Loyalists. It was only simple justice that they should be compensated for their losses and treated with some consideration: hence the undertaking by Congress that it would "recommend" to individual state governments that they cease their persecutions, offer monetary payment for confiscated Loyalist properties, and permit individual Loyalists to return home for a period of twelve months to settle their personal affairs without fear of molestation or retribution. This was the substance of article V of the Treaty of Paris. Unfortunately, Congress had no means of forcing the states to carry out promises made on their behalf; the Constitution provided no means whereby the central government could coerce the states to fulfil international obligations imposed by the Treaty of Paris. The result was that the treatment accorded the Loyalists after the signing of the peace treaty was, if anything, even harsher and more brutal than it had been before. That is the explanation for the migration to British North America of thousands of American Loyalists, many of them embittered by their treatment in the new United States, and most of them filled with hatred towards the Revolution and everything associated with it.

There was little Great Britain could do for the Loyalists that was not done in the way of providing them with a refuge, in both the maritime and the upper provinces. Great Britain was not ready to go back to war; perhaps a little political pressure would be effective, such as declining to carry out some of its obligations under the Treaty of Paris. Admittedly there were other reasons for the British refusal to return the western Great Lakes posts, extending from Michilimackinac to Oswego, but the Loyalist issue at least provided moral justification for what might otherwise have been looked upon in both countries as a matter of commercial self-interest.

Perhaps a more compelling explanation of why the British did not immediately recognize the boundary settlement agreed upon in 1783 was the desire to forestall an Indian war. When Great Britain's Indian allies learned that the British had agreed to surrender all territorial claims south of the Great Lakes, including the lands claimed by the Six Nations and other Indians, they were incensed. Joseph Brant declared that they had been "sold" to Congress and that they would have to "defend their own just rights or perish in the attempt".[2] Sir John Johnson, the British superintendent of Indian Affairs, never positively said so, but when he met the Indians at Niagara to explain the terms of the Treaty of Paris, he left them with the impression that Great Britain had surrendered none of the Indians' claims to their traditional homelands. To keep the Indians quiet, Colonel John Butler, Brigadier General Allan Maclean and the governor of Canada, Sir Frederick Haldimand, all strongly urged the British government not to withdraw British garrisons from the western posts. As long as the Indians could see British troops in these forts, it would be difficult for the Americans to persuade them that the British had betrayed or abandoned them. Better, from the British standpoint, to risk the unlikely renewal of hostilities by the war-weary Americans over the issue of the western posts than to risk an almost certain vengeful attack by the disillusioned Indians. Perhaps Haldimand's fears were exaggerated. Certainly there was reason to believe that the Six Nations were tired of fighting; but it was significant that the Ohio Indians continued to fight against the Americans, hoping to stem the tide of white settlers moving into the Ohio Valley. The Americans replied with punitive expeditions led by Josiah Harmar in 1790 and Arthur St. Clair in 1791. Both met with disaster. Finally, in 1794, Anthony Wayne dealt the Indians a telling blow at Fallen Timbers. No British troops took part in this fighting but, because British troops remained in the forts and because British traders operating out of these forts furnished the Indians with ammunition, a lasting suspicion was produced in American minds that their old antagonists, the British, were prompting Indian resistance for their own selfish territorial motives.

In the end the British gave up the posts, not because they felt morally obliged to do so or because they were prepared to abandon the Indians, but because of developments in Europe. Fearing that the United States might join the Armed Neutrality League, a pressure group of northern European countries demanding that Great Britain relax her rigid interpretation of neutral trading rights, the British government agreed to enter into negotiations with the United States to try to settle outstanding differences. The resulting treaty, named after the American negotiator, John Jay, chief justice of the United States Supreme Court, was concluded in 1794. Both nations agreed that the old irritants, such as the Maine–New Brunswick boundary and the payment of old debts, should be referred to arbitration, and that the British garrisons should withdraw from the western posts within a reasonable period of two years. It was not the kind of treaty to cause great rejoicing among Americans, but the Federalist senators saw some good in it—the return of the posts—and Alexander Hamilton and George Washington were prepared to support it. And so it was ratified in June 1795.

Jay's Treaty tended to remove some of the heat from British–American relations, and none too soon. In the year before Jay's mission to London, Great Britain and France had gone to war with one another, and Americans were wondering if they were under any moral or legal obligation to assist France. Presumably such obligations had been acquired when the United States entered into a mutual assistance agreement with France in 1778, during the Revolutionary War. The French had lived up to their side of the bargain, sending troops and ships to North America to help the United States defeat Great Britain. That the French contribution had played a notable part in the American victory was never at issue. Now the question was whether the United States should take up arms with Great Britain once again, this time to help revolutionary France. There were many people in the United States who thought they should. They looked upon the new, revolutionary France with satisfaction; here was a country following the United States' lead in throwing off the shackles of the rule of kings. Great Britain, as a continuing monarchy, was the enemy of all republics. People who thought in these terms looked to Thomas Jefferson, that aristocratic democrat who was later to serve as third president of the United States. They were the people who went about the country organizing republican clubs, singing French songs and talking enthusiastically about liberty, equality and fraternity. Opposed were those repelled by the French Revolution and its violence, who frankly admitted that they hoped the British would prevail over their antagonists. These were conservative people, many with strong economic ties to Great Britain. Broadly speaking, they were adherents of the governing party, the Federalists, who argued that, since France had declared war against Great Britain, France was the aggressor state and therefore not entitled to assistance from the United States. In any event, the Federalists argued, the original treaty had been made with the Crown of France and now the Crown lay bleeding in the basket below the guillotine. There had never been any treaty of mutual assistance with the French Republic.

For the moment, the Federalists held the upper hand. In outfitting French privateers in American ports and trying to enlist American support for a French expedition against Spanish Louisiana, "Citizen" Edmond Genêt, the French minister to Washington, went beyond his diplomatic duties, thereby alienating many Americans, even those with pro-French sympathies. When in 1796, Pierre Adet, Genêt's successor, urged American voters to throw the Federalists out of office and substitute republicans, and American representatives in Paris were given an insolent brush-off because they would not pay the bribes required by Charles Maurice de Talleyrand, minister of foreign affairs under the Directoire, opinion in the United States became generally hostile to France. Even the Francophile Jefferson could find little good to say about those he had once admired. In 1800, however, relations were patched up with Napoleon Bonaparte, the one-time Jacobin and still republican who had become First Consul of France. Thus, three years later, when Napoleon needed funds for his continuing war against Great Britain and he offered the United States Louisiana, an area extending from the Gulf of Mexico to the Hudson's Bay Company territories, the American government accepted. And why not? The price was right: $15 million, probably the best real-estate bargain in all history. French stock rose; and Jefferson moved into the White House.

With the Louisiana Purchase of 1803 came a shift in American foreign policy, not towards strengthened friendship with France, but most certainly away from friendly relations with Great Britain. This shift was a byproduct of the war between Great Britain and France, which was becoming yearly more and more economic in character. With France dominating most of the European landmass and Great Britain controlling the sea lanes, there was no easy way one country could defeat the other in decisive military contest. However, each could strike blows at the other's economy. France could attempt to keep British ships from trading with any continental nation; Britain could try to keep French ships from leaving any continental ports. As a result of this economic stand-off, neutral shipping took over the trade that French and British ships had once enjoyed. That is why the number of commercial vessels on the high seas sailing under neutral, that is American, registry greatly increased after 1803. Indeed, almost the whole of the carrying trade of Europe passed to American ships.[3] It was this development that brought Great Britain into conflict with the United States, for Britain was determined to prevent France from receiving goods from or sending goods to any part of the world, regardless of whose ships carried them; the United States was equally determined to retain the profits of acting as Europe's carrier. As compromise appeared impossible, the memories of old grievances revived, and with them new clashes at sea.

There was, for instance, the seizure of the *Essex*, an American vessel that loaded a cargo in Spain (a French ally), landed it in the United States, paid the duties, and then, laden with the same cargo, set sail for Spain's colony, Cuba. The owners of the *Essex* argued that this was a legal "broken voyage", that once the goods reached the United States they became, technically, American and therefore not subject to seizure. The Lords Commissioners of Admiralty decided otherwise: the goods were Spanish and never intended for the United States, and the voyage was a "continuous voyage" between two enemy ports. They saw it as an attempt by American shipowners to contravene the British blockade. Then there was the case of the British vessel *Leander*, which fired several shots at the coastal schooner *Richard* off Sandy Hook, damaging the American vessel and decapitating the helmsman. Again, in June 1807, the British ship *Leopard* fired three broadsides into the USS *Chesapeake* to compel her to heave to and submit to a search for deserting British sailors. Subsequently the British authorities expressed regret, but did so in a manner little calculated to smooth ruffled eagle feathers. The American people reacted with indignation and fury, and there were loud demands for war against the insolent British. President Jefferson, calmer than the tavern jingoes who clamoured for war, prudently avoided a call to arms, contenting himself with a proclamation barring British ships of war from American rivers and harbours.

Meanwhile, the British government continued its restrictions on international trade. In May 1806, George III, by Order in Council, declared a commercial blockade of the coast of France from the Elbe to Brest, forbidding any neutral vessel to enter a port within these limits unless it carried the products of its own country or those of Great Britain. Napoleon replied with a decree, issued in Berlin six months later, placing the British Isles under a similar commercial blockade. The British went one better, in January 1807, with an Order in Council forbidding any neutral vessel to trade between two ports in the possession of France or her allies. Still a third Order in Council followed in November, stating that every port from which British ships were excluded would be closed to neutral vessels unless they first stopped at a British port and took out a licence to trade. A month later Napoleon responded with a decree from Milan, ordering the confiscation of any neutral ships that submitted to Great Britain's right of search.

17

4. American cartoon caricaturing the 1813 Embargo Act, symbolized by a terrapin because the Federalists had called Jefferson's earlier embargo act "a terrapin policy". The anagram is embargo spelled backwards.

Faced with a situation that could not help but have a depressing effect on American trade, Thomas Jefferson had the choice of fighting, submitting to the pressures of Great Britain and France, or abandoning the ocean altogether. The first two he rejected for political reasons. The third he chose to attempt. He therefore adopted a series of retaliatory measures, beginning in 1806 with the Non-Importation Act, which forbade the importation into the United States of a long list of specified British goods. This Act he dropped after six months, substituting the Embargo Act, which closed United States ports to all foreign trade and commerce.

It is open to question how deeply the Orders in Council and the Berlin and Milan decrees touched the lives of ordinary American citizens, particularly those living in commercial and maritime centres such as Boston and New York. To most citizens these measures seemed remote and not particularly significant. What the Europeans did on the other side of the ocean was less bothersome than it was baffling. There were therefore no violent demonstrations, no loud protests, no political confrontations against either the Orders in Council of the British or the decrees of the French. It was otherwise when Jefferson imposed his Embargo Act. This did affect ordinary citizens and they reacted strongly; few laws in American history have been so unpopular. Since legal trade was prohibited, smuggling became widespread, particularly in those regions close to the Canadian frontier. So bitter was the feeling in northern New York that soldiers sent to enforce the Act were either threatened, as they were in Ogdensburg, or ostracized, as they were in Sackets Harbor. Augustus Sacket, the collector of customs at Sackets Harbor, resigned his appointment, as the Secretary of the Treasury wrote to Jefferson, "from fear, or at least from a wish not to lose his popularity".[4] Hart Massey was appointed to succeed Sacket, but he too was unable to put an end to smuggling. Writing to the Secretary of the Treasury he complained that at Ogdensburg many merchants had entered into a combination "not to entertain, nor even suffer" a military force to be stationed there, adding:

> Their threats are handed out that if I or any other officer should come there again, they will take a rawhide to them, which they declare they have prepared for that purpose. These threats don't terrify me. I only mention them to let you know their unprincipled determination. . . . My life and the lives of my deputies are threatened daily; what will be the fate of us, God only knows.[5]

It was scarcely reassuring to the authorities that Jacob Brown, the leading militia officer in the vicinity, constructed a road from Brownville to Collins Landing—known as the Embargo, or Smuggler Brown's, Road—to facilitate the transport of potash to boats waiting on the St. Lawrence to carry the forbidden cargo to Montreal.

In 1809 the embargo was lifted and the Non-Intercourse Act was passed. This Act forbade American trade with Great Britain and France, or with their colonial possessions, but it did offer to suspend the prohibition for either country should that country be willing to revoke its offensive orders or decrees. That was as far as Jefferson felt he could go. Whatever the average American might think of the policy of using economic measures for political purposes, the administration held it to be the only way short of war to defend the national honour and the independence of the United States. When honour is rated highly, to be deprived of honour is worse by far than to be deprived of funds.

In addition to the economic pressure imposed on the United States by Great Britain and France—but principally Great Britain, as the only country capable of enforcing its blockade—there was the particularly irritating business of impressment. Naval service had always been tough, demanding and brutal, and the navy had long been compelled to find its recruits in the streets and taverns or wherever they could be seized by force. But with the increased American merchant-marine traffic, impressed sailors in Britain's Royal Navy were inclined to desert and pick up a sailing post on an American trading vessel. One of the attractions was that wages on board the American vessels trebled in the four years after 1803.[6] Men slipped over the bulwarks or failed to return from shore leave when their vessels were in or near American ports. To recover these deserters, the Royal Navy took the liberty of searching American merchant vessels and seizing the delinquents; if they took a few Americans, well, it was just a case of mistaken identity.

Was the right of search and impressment a vital issue to either Great Britain or the United States? It should be kept in mind that at no time did Britain ever claim any right to impress American seamen, only the right to recover British subjects. Neither did the Americans ever argue that they could legally protect British deserters by granting them American citizenship. It was still difficult, in the early nineteenth century, for a man to divest himself of his nationality. As far as Great Britain was concerned, wartime necessity knew no law, certainly no law of naturalization. What was important about the impressment issue was not the legality of search and impressment, but Britain's disinclination to pay due attention to the sensitivities of the Americans, to appreciate that what British naval officers were doing, if not strictly illegal at that time, could be interpreted as insulting to the national pride and national honour of a country scarcely a generation old. Americans, at the same time, were disposed to see in the actions of British captains not the acts of men in desperate need of sailors but of arrogant Britishers ignoring the independent status of the United States. There is little doubt that, had Congress been in session at the time of the *Chesapeake* affair, an Anglo-American war might have resulted from the intemperate action of an insensitive officer who was, in fact, in the wrong. An international crisis! All for the sake of four men, three of whom turned out to be Americans; the fourth, an Englishman, was subsequently hanged at the yardarm in Halifax in full view of the assembled sailors and curious onlookers from the town. Yet, London waited for years to make an apology. It was this kind of contemptuous indifference on the part of the British Foreign Office that irritated Jefferson and Madison long after the incident should have been forgotten.

WHATEVER IMPACT "Free Trade and Sailors' Rights" may have had in the Atlantic states, the dominant reason for the war psychosis in the western regions of the United States was the conviction that the British in Canada were behind the continued opposition of the Indian peoples to the western advance of American settlement. Americans had always had an Indian fixation, ever since the days when Abenaki and Micmac war parties raided the frontier settlements of New England and New York during the days of the French regime. But it was not only the French who had employed Indians against the Americans; the successors to Frontenac in the Château Saint-Louis in Quebec, Guy Carleton and Frederick Haldimand, had done the same thing during the American Revolutionary War. A few Indians had followed John Burgoyne; others had followed Colonel Barrimore St. Leger and ambushed the American general, Nicholas Herkimer, at Oriskany (N.Y.). Still others had joined forces with Butler's Rangers and had carried out raids in New York (Cherry Valley and German Flatts) and Pennsylvania (Wyoming Valley). Had not the British given that notorious Mohawk, Joseph Brant, a commission in their army? What about those raids on the western frontier prompted by British Indian agents, such as Alexander McKee and Henry Hamilton, the "hair-buyer", at Detroit? The Treaty of Paris was to have brought peace to a harried land, but the Indians had kept on fighting until finally routed by "Mad" Anthony Wayne at Fallen Timbers and forced to accept the Treaty of Greenville in 1795. Was not that the work of British traders and Indian agents?

Of course it had not been the traders and the agents who had kept the Indians on the warpath. The Indians were fighting a losing battle, admittedly, but the battle was theirs, fought to live on the lands and in the ways that traditionally had been theirs. The constant pressure exerted by the inexorable westward march of white settlement is what kept the Indians fighting. However, the Americans could see in continued Indian resistance only the sinister hand of British agents. American lives

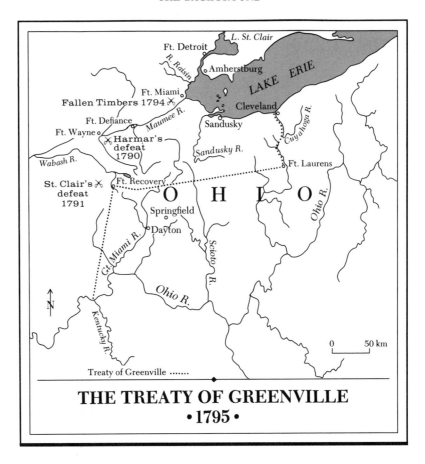

THE TREATY OF GREENVILLE
• 1795 •

were being extinguished by "savages" carrying British muskets and firing British ammunition, provided from the stores of British-held forts on American soil. "The bitterness thus engendered in the United States was poisoning the American attitude and working for a renewal of the war against Britain" is how a historian familiar with both Canadian and American history saw it.[7]

The Treaty of Greenville—scarcely a treaty since it was imposed by Wayne upon the defeated Indians rather than negotiated with them—drew a boundary line between Indian and American territory, south from Lake Erie along the Cuyahoga, then west (south of the sources of the Sandusky and the Wabash), and south again to the Ohio at a point west of the Great Miami River. All lands to the south and east of the line were to be opened to American settlement; all those to the north and west were to belong to the Indians. Those who sympathized with the Indians were inclined to think of the Treaty of Greenville as deceitful and iniquitous, but it must be admitted that a period of peace followed, and lasted for a few years, until American infiltration into the Indian territories once more prompted a violent reaction. It was because the treaty did produce a cessation of hostilities that the British cut down on their gifts to various Indian nations. Sir James Craig, reporting to London from Lower Canada, wondered whether the "diminution of the establishment" of the Indian Department "as well as very considerable reduction in the usual supplies" had not "lessened and almost destroyed" the influence of the Department over the western Indians.[8]

Because of its declining influence, the British Indian Department was in no position to encourage the Indians to take up arms again. That the Indians ever contemplated doing so was owing to rumours that the United States might declare war as a reply to the broadsides the *Leopard* hurled at the *Chesapeake* on 22 June 1807. The Atlantic might be far away, but it was not long before the Indians knew what had happened off Cape Henry, and knew too of the verbal violence that ensued between Great Britain and the United States. The Indians would have liked to see war break out, if only because it would mean that the British would again provide them with help, help in the form of men as well as guns and ammunition. The Americans were quick to sense the change in the Indian attitude and declared that the British were pushing the Indians to fight. According to Lieutenant Colonel Jasper Grant, the British officer commanding on the Detroit frontier:

> Great apprehensions are expressed at Detroit by the Governor and principal officers there of an attack from the Indians and they industriously spread a report that the Indians are instigated by the British officers at Amherstburg. A law has been passed at Detroit, for that colonial privilege is allowed the Governor, requiring the aid of all subjects to assist in erecting works, etc., for the defence of the place. The inhabitants in consequence have been called in from the distance of 30 miles to contribute in labour. . . . I have had information given me from a most respectable person at this side that the Governor of Detroit declares, if an Indian fires a hostile shot in Detroit or in the territory, he will treat the Canadians with the utmost severity.[9]

Governor William Henry Harrison was thoroughly, perhaps one might say easily, convinced, because he wanted to be, that the British were encouraging the Indians and that they were using Lolawauchika, the Prophet, as their "vile instrument".[10] James Madison told the British minister in Washington that he

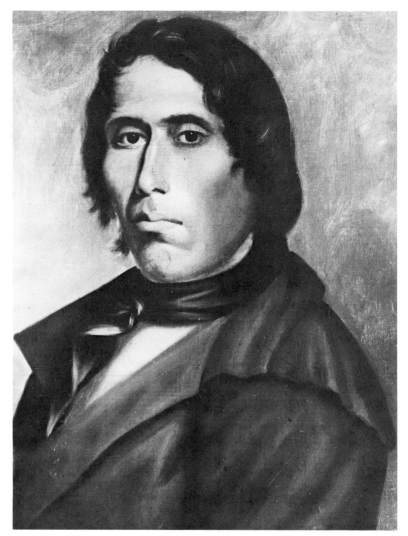

5. *This portrait may be a likeness of Tecumseh, the Shawnee chief*

had what, in effect, he did not have, namely "irrefragible proof" that the British were back at their old tricks in Ohio and the Indiana Territory.[11] Poor John Thomas, who resided on the Grand River in Upper Canada, took a journey to Tennessee in 1809 and found the local people so incensed that he had difficulty doing any business with them. "I am afraid of a war with the U.S.", he wrote, and went on:

> You may expect my immediate return before any stroke can be made on either side. Goods begin to sell very high here. I fear I shall not

6. Lolawauchika, the Prophet, Tecumseh's brother

be able to get a bill on New York, as business begins to slacken and merchants are distrustful of a war and its consequences.[12]

Not wily British agents, but outspoken Indian chiefs, the Shawnee brothers—Tecumseh (Leaping Panther) and Lolawauchika (Loud Mouth)[13]—were the men responsible for the growing Indian threat on the western frontier. Both were men of great influence. Their father had been killed by American frontiersmen and the two brothers had fought at Fallen Timbers. Both rejected the surrender of land under the Greenville Treaty and both hated the Long Knives, as much for their duplicity as for their strength. That was the extent of their similarities, for otherwise the two men were a study in contrast. Tecumseh was tall, handsome, proud, courageous and reliable; his brother was scrawny, ugly, blind in one eye, epileptic and perhaps a little mad. Tecumseh was the more powerful orator, the greater warrior and the more influential politician; Lolawauchika was the prophet, the man who dreamed wild dreams and experienced supernatural revelations, the earthly voice of the Great Spirit. He supplied the mysticism necessary to give strength and meaning to his older brother's politics. In Tecumseh's mind, an Indian should never, as Jefferson urged, become a farmer or a rancher and integrate himself into the white man's economy and way of life; he should, instead, hold fast to his Indian heritage, remain a hunter and live as his ancestors had lived before him on the lands he had inherited from them. Tecumseh's plea was the eternal plea of all great Indian leaders, a plea that has been heard throughout the centuries, ever since the white man came to North America.

As Tecumseh went from one Indian nation to another, presenting his arguments with an eloquence that has become legendary, his supporters began to gather in their huts and tipis on the Tippecanoe River, a tributary of the Wabash. It was a beautiful part of the country, destined to become one of the world's great corn-growing areas. It happened also to be one of the regions coveted by the Americans, despite its being well within the area designated as Indian territory by the Treaty of Greenville. Taking advantage of Tecumseh's absence in the autumn of 1809, Governor Harrison of the Indiana Territory entered into a dubious deal with several chiefs, none of them Shawnee, for the surrender of some 3 million acres of land in the Wabash country. Tecumseh was furious. His own people had not been consulted, and the whole arrangement violated the Indian concept of common ownership. Both he and his brother denounced the Indians who had given Harrison what it was not in their power to give and swore vengeance against them. Harrison, thinking Lolawauchika to be the more influential (or perhaps the weaker) figure, invited him to Vincennes to discuss what was euphemistically called a "treaty". But it was Tecumseh, not the younger brother, who went to see the American governor. When asked if he would enter the governor's house, Tecumseh declined: "Houses are built for you to hold councils in, Indians hold theirs in the open air." When the invitation was repeated, "Your father requests you to sit by his side",

Tecumseh answered, with a sarcasm overlaid with dignity, "My father! The sun is my father, and the earth is my mother, and I will recline on her bosom."[14] It was a reply that set the tone of the meeting. Correctly polite, neither Harrison nor Tecumseh would yield to the other's arguments and importunities. With reluctant respect, Harrison reported to Washington:

> If it were not for the vicinity of the United States, he [Tecumseh] would, perhaps, be the founder of an empire that would rival in glory Mexico or Peru. No difficulties deter him. For four years he has been in constant motion. You see him to-day on the Wabash, and in a short time hear of him on the shores of Lake Erie or Michigan, or on the banks of the Mississippi; and wherever he goes he makes an impression favorable to his purposes. He is now upon the last round to put a finishing stroke to his work.[15]

It was not Tecumseh who brought on the encounter between the Indians and Harrison's soldiers at Tippecanoe on 7 November 1811. The battle took place while the Shawnee chief was absent, visiting the western tribes. But it was a direct sequel to the Vincennes meeting. As Harrison had watched the Indians depart, he had felt frustrated and angry and had considered the possibility of using force to expel that gang of malcontents gathered at the Prophet's town. After all, he had the interests of his own people to look after, and they were peppering him with requests to chase the Indians away. Moreover, President Madison had sent him reinforcements of regular troops under Colonel John Boyd, a career soldier who had fought in India as an officer in the army of the Nizam of Hyderabad. Madison did not tell Harrison to attack the Indians; he simply told him to use his discretion, with the result that the Governor of Indiana assembled a small army, numbering about 900 men, the majority of them militia, and set out for the Indian country. After building a blockhouse on the Wabash (which was "christened" Fort Harrison with a bottle of whisky, much to the distress of at least one soldier, who muttered that "water would have done just as well"),[16] he moved slowly to the Indian position on the Tippecanoe. The Indians knew he was coming; he had already ordered them to disperse to their own tribes and threatened them with punishment if they did not return the horses they had stolen. But they preferred to remain and fight. Encamped not far from the Prophet's town, Harrison was attacked by the Indians in the early hours of 7 November on the front and two flanks of his position. It was dark and rainy, and a few of the Americans were killed in the confusion, but as daylight crept over the eastern horizon the figures of the attackers became more clearly defined and Harrison was able to use his better-disciplined forces to advantage. In the end the Indians were defeated. While his adversary had been in the thick of the fighting, Lolawauchika had stood on a nearby hill invoking his magic powers to bring victory; that neither his chants nor his incantations brought results was, according to Lolawauchika, because his wife had approached the fire while he was mixing his charms, thus rendering them ineffective. Tippecanoe was not a long battle; before the day was very far advanced the sharp conflict was over and the Indians had fled, leaving 38 warriors dead on the field.[17] When Harrison moved into the Prophet's town he found it deserted. With no military or political justification for remaining there, Harrison's troops collected as much corn and beans as they could carry, burned the rest, and, bearing their wounded with them, returned via Fort Harrison to Vincennes. He could not have realized it then, but Harrison had just taken his first step towards the presidency of the United States.

Tecumseh returned to find his brother's town in ruins and the plans for a vast Indian confederacy shattered. Everything had failed because of a battle he had wished to avoid. What now was to be done? Perhaps he should go to Washington to see Madison. Harrison was agreeable, but would not let Tecumseh take with him an escort of Indian warriors suitable to his rank. And so the Indian chief, despite overtures from Brigadier General William Hull, went to Amherstburg, where in May 1812 he told the story of Tippecanoe to his old acquaintance, Matthew Elliott of the British Indian Department. Later, in June, he pledged his loyalty to George III. War had come again to the West.

Was it simply because the Americans feared and disliked the Indians that they pursued them for generations on the western frontier? And was it because of British persuasion, bribes and sweet-talk that the Indians fought back so tenaciously? Or were the Indians seen as obstacles in the way of American expansion because they would not readily cede the land that the American farmers wanted—good land, agricultural land, free land? And would not the Indians, aware of what white settlement would do to their traditional patterns of culture, be prepared to fight to keep them? If the Indian wars continued after the Treaty of Paris and again after the Treaty of Greenville, and after a whole series of treaties during the nineteenth century, was it not because of the Americans' insatiable appetite for land, an appetite that carried political America from the Atlantic to the Pacific? Was not this insatiable appetite for land one of the factors behind the warmongering of western-American politicians such as Henry Clay, and behind the strategic emphasis placed by the American military authorities upon the acquisition of Upper Canada during the War of 1812? There was, in fact, a coincidence of interest between the Indians and the Canadians, a coincidence of interest that explains why they so frequently fought together, side by side. Both stood in the way of American expansion.

THE SUGGESTION that the declaration of war by the United States in 1812 might have been inspired, in part at least, by imperialistic motives has never been popular with Americans generally. And yet the evidence exists that the incorporation of Canada into the American union was among the aims of the men who dominated Congress in 1812. It was not a new idea. It had motivated Congress and the men who followed Richard Montgomery and Benedict Arnold to Quebec in 1775. Thomas Jefferson was only one of many who confidently expected to welcome Canada into the American union at that time. Despite Montgomery's death, Arnold's failure and the retreat of the Americans before the forces led by Guy Carleton and John Burgoyne in 1776, the idea of military conquest was not abandoned. With the entry of France into the Revolutionary War on the side of the United States, the project was revived. Perhaps, with the help of the French, Americans might be able to do what they had not been able to do by themselves. In 1778 an elaborate plan of operations was adopted by Congress, involving military strikes at Detroit, Niagara, Oswego and Montreal; meanwhile a French fleet would sail up the St. Lawrence against Quebec and repeat the exploits of Wolfe in 1759. That these operations never took place was owing to George Washington's fears that the French, once more established at Quebec, would find too many reasons for remaining there and refuse to yield Canada to the fledgling American republic. Later, during the war, Washington changed his mind and talked about an offensive against Canada, in 1780 and 1781, if only to complete the business left unfinished in 1775–76. But these operations never got beyond the talking stage. In any event, the talkers would have a chance when the future of Canada was discussed at the Paris peace conference.

In Paris, Benjamin Franklin brought up the question of the cession of Canada by Great Britain, such action by the British to be the pledge of peace between their country and the United States. Franklin had been one of the commissioners Congress sent to Canada at the time of the Montgomery invasion, and had spent some time in Montreal; it was there he developed the plan of annexing Canada, a plan he never wholly abandoned. Two of Franklin's co-negotiators in Paris, John Adams and Henry Laurens, indulged in the same sweet dreams. For one brief moment the British representative, Richard Oswald, almost succumbed to Franklin's winning ways, but when the treaty was signed the terms did not put Canada within the boundaries of the United States. The Americans did, however, obtain a good slice of Canadian territory. The Ohio Valley, a region historically part of Canada and linked geographically and economically with the St. Lawrence River system and Montreal, was wrenched from Canada and incorporated into the United States. This was done even though the British were still in military possession of the area.[18]

The *Chesapeake* affair once more brought the question of Canada's future to the fore in view of the possibility of war between Great Britain and the United States. The latter, possessing no navy of any significance, lacked the means to take revenge on Britain other than by attacking Canada. In a mood of irritable frankness, Jefferson told the French minister, General Louis-Marie Turreau, "If the English do not give us the satisfaction we demand, we will take the Canadas,. . .we shall have the Floridas, we shall no longer have any difficulties with our neighbours."[19] David Montagu Erskine, the British minister in Washington, was aware of the President's anger and hastened to inform the Foreign Secretary in London that American military plans called for two armies, one to defend New Orleans and the other to take the offensive against Canada and Nova Scotia, "a favourite project with the Democratic Party". In another letter Erskine wrote:

> I know that a strong idea prevails that the militia of the adjacent states aided by a large volunteer force would be sufficient to take possession of Upper Canada, and that an attack might be afterwards made with the aid of a regular force upon the fort of Quebec.[20]

He added that the attack might possibly come the following summer and warned the governor of Canada, Sir James Craig, to be on his guard against surprise. There was some substance to Erskine's warning. The governors of several American states had been told to ready their quotas for a winter campaign against Canada, and guns, ammunition and camp equipage had been ordered to rendezvous points near the Canadian frontier. Craig responded by urging the War Office to send him 12 000 regular troops.[21]

Here, then, was the War of 1812 foreshadowed in 1809. In the years following, the more bellicose members of Congress focused their attention on Canada. This was particularly true of the western members. According to one American historian, "By the end of the spring of 1812, the whole frontier country from New Hampshire to Kentucky was insisting that the British must be expelled from Canada."[22] Joseph Desha of Kentucky argued in the House of Representatives that nothing the United States might do to preserve peace would avail as long as "the British have Canada or a Nova Scotia on the continent of America", and told his colleagues, "You must remove the cause if you expect to perform the cure."[23] Henry Clay advocated the same course of action, to strike at Great Britain through Canada. Clay was not the first, nor was he the last, to urge the conquest of Canada. It was, after all, the only way the United States could effectively challenge Great Britain, in view of British naval superiority on the Atlantic Ocean. To suggest that Clay and those who favoured operations against Canada were thinking of Canada simply as a tactical objective— a hostage, as it were, for the good conduct of the British government—is to misunderstand their real motivation. Let it be recalled that Clay himself subsequently wrote to his friend Thomas Bodley, in 1813:

> It has ever been my opinion that if Canada is conquered it ought never to be surrendered if it can possibly be retained. Relations and connexions will take place which ought not to be broken, in the event of its conquest.[24]

He added his belief that the government in Washington was

> sensible of the advantages which will accrue from the possession of Canada, you may be well assured; and that it will get all it can in making a peace, its desire of fame, to say nothing of its love of country, affords a sufficient guarantee.

Clay and Desha were not alone in pushing for military operations against Canada. It was widely advocated in the American press, particularly in newspapers beyond the Alleghenies.

It was interjected into the debates in Congress. William Burwell, who, having once been Jefferson's secretary, was believed to have direct access to the wisdom of the political philosopher of Monticello, said, "The expulsion of the British from Canada has always been deemed an object of the first importance to the peace of the United States."[25] Of course, he would not go to war deliberately to conquer Canada, but he would not hesitate to seize that country should war come. A distinction more of cause than of effect! Felix Grundy and John Rhea of Tennessee spoke in similar terms, and Richard M. Johnson of Kentucky declared that "the waters of the St. Lawrence and the Mississippi interlock in a number of places, and the great Disposer of Human Events intended these two rivers should belong to the same people."[26] Johnson was not the only one with direct access to the intentions of God. John Harper of New Hampshire also spoke for Him, although not with the same certainty:

> North of the Great Lakes a population of four millions may easily be supported. And this great outlet of the northern world [the St. Lawrence River] should be at our command for our convenience and future security. To me, sir, it appears that the Author of Nature has marked our limits, in the south by the Gulf of Mexico, and on the north by the regions of eternal frost.[27]

Not to be outdone, Henry Clay remarked, "I am not for stopping at Quebec or anywhere else. I would take the entire continent."[28] Small wonder that the eloquent and choleric John Randolph, who did not want war, did not like the warmongers and hated Napoleon Bonaparte, cried in the House of Representatives:

> Sir, if you go to war, it will not be for the protection of, or defence of, your maritime rights. Gentlemen from the North have been taken up to some high mountain and shown all the kingdoms of the earth; and Canada seems tempting in their sight. . . . Agrarian cupidity, not maritime right urges the war. Ever since the report of the Committee on Foreign Relations came into the House, we have heard but one word—like the whip-poor-will, but one eternal monotonous tone—Canada! Canada! Canada![29]

Randolph might have added—he was the outspoken kind of man to have done so—that free trade and sailors' rights and the Indian excitements on the western frontier were but irritants, that the basic motives prompting the Madison administration's declaration of war in June 1812 were to satisfy national honour and to acquire control over Canada—in brief, pride and acquisitiveness.

7. John Randolph, the outspoken opponent of the War Hawks

JAMES MADISON was not likely to have signed the declaration of war on 18 June had he not had the support of strong men in Congress. The President was a man who preferred to be pushed rather than to lead. He was not a man cast in the heroic mould. He was not a man of decision. John C. Calhoun was probably right when he said of Madison, "Our President, tho a man of amiable manners and great talents, has not I fear those commanding talents which are necessary to control those about him."[30] Not a man, certainly, to become a great war leader.

Madison came to the presidency in 1809. He was a loyal Jeffersonian and had been for eight years Jefferson's right-hand man. As president he inherited all the international problems to which his mentor had found no real solution. British frigates

8. Henry Clay, one of the principal War Hawks. This portrait is considered to be "the best ever painted of Mr. Clay in his prime".

still roved the seas searching and seizing, and Napoleon still confiscated foreign vessels in French ports. Madison began well by entering negotiations with the British representative at Washington, David Montagu Erskine. And for a while it looked as if the two men might find a basis for agreement in an American offer to relax its trade ban should Great Britain exempt American ships from the operations of the Orders in Council. This promising arrangement fell through, however, when it was repudiated by the British foreign secretary, George Canning, and when Erskine was replaced in Washington by the much less sympathetic Francis James Jackson. Of the latter a contemporary wrote, "His temper was not mild, nor were his manners conciliatory, his integrity and talents were unquestioned, but no proof had yet been disclosed of his prudence."[31] Discovering for himself the annoyance aroused in official circles by British naval policy, Jackson explained it as merely the result of the malevolent influence of "every sort of artifice of misrepresentation and of falsehood which the American democrat or the French partisan could devise for the purpose".[32] With the *Chesapeake* affair still an abrasive factor in Anglo-American relations and with French influence making headway in Washington, it is obvious why Jackson's stay in the United States capital was brief.

The mid-term Congressional elections in 1810 brought about a decisive acceleration in the drift towards war. Much to everybody's surprise, the election resulted in a dumping of many of the older members and the introduction into the House of Representatives of a coterie of angry young men, intellectually vigorous, determinedly anti-British, irate because of impressment, search and seizure, convinced that the British were deliberately inciting the western Indians, and deeply distrustful of the Federalists. Above all, they were out of patience with the old leaders, the men who had guided Jefferson and Madison, the veterans of the Revolutionary War and the members of the Society of the Cincinnati. They themselves were mostly young men, "with their pin-feathers yet unshed, the shell still sticking upon them—perfectly unfledged, though they fluttered and cackled on the floor", as Josiah Quincy, the Massachusetts Federalist, described them.[33] Few of them had passed their thirty-fifth birthday. Chief among them was Henry Clay, who, although only thirty-four years of age, had already spent some years in the Kentucky legislature, where anti-British feeling ran high over the Indian issue. Others who supported him, the men who were known as the "War Hawks", were Richard M. Johnson of Kentucky, John C. Calhoun of South Carolina, William Rufus King of North Carolina (all of whom later occupied the office of vice-president of the United States), Langdon Cheves and William Lowndes of South Carolina, Felix Grundy of Tennessee, Peter B. Porter of New York, and John Harper of New Hampshire. They were, all of them, hungry for power and for war. It seems unlikely that American voters opted consciously for war in 1810; in all probability they simply voted for a change. But they got both. For the War Hawks succeeded in seizing control of Congress and in giving American government policy the push towards belligerency that Madison, by himself, would never have provided.

*9. John C. Calhoun, one of the War Hawks from the southern
states*

The new Congress had scarcely met, in November 1811, when
the War Hawks made their first successful tactical moves. Henry
Clay was elected Speaker of the House of Representatives,
Langdon Cheves became chairman of the Ways and Means
Committee, and Peter B. Porter took over the presidency of the
all-important House Committee on Foreign Affairs. These three
appointments made it possible for the War Hawks to direct the
course of the debate, control the government purse and shape
American policy in foreign affairs. This became obvious when
Porter presented his committee's first report to the new House.
With little or no leadership from the President, but with editorial

guidance from James Monroe, Porter prepared a document calling upon the United States to take the steps necessary to defend itself against international rapine and robbery and to
expand its regular and volunteer military establishment. "A
pretty bold development" was how the French minister, Louis
Sérurier, described Porter's report.[34] "The Rubicon is passed",
noted Felix Grundy, who, speaking in support of the report,
declared that America was bound by duty and honour to defend the nation's right to export, fulfil her pledge to France,
and put an end to the British policy of "setting on the ruthless
savage to tomahawk our women and children".[35] And, of
course, to add Canada to the Union to offset the acquisition
of Louisiana and the Floridas, and thus preserve a sectional
balance between the northern and the southern states. Johnson,
Lowndes and Harper all spoke in the same vein, Harper ending with the threat, "I feel no hesitation in saying the present
session will not be closed without an *arrangement*, or an actual *war*, with Britain."[36] In the Senate, William Giles reinforced these inflammatory remarks, calling for a military
establishment of 25 000 regulars and the early invasion of
Canada.

The young hotspurs did not have it all their own way. Most
of the Federalists in and out of Congress were opposed to a war
with Great Britain and suspicious of what they considered to
be the pro-French policy of the administration. John Randolph,
for instance, criticized, sneered and poked fun at the arguments
of the War Hawks. Using all the rhetorical tricks he was noted
for, Randolph denounced the territorial imperialism of his opponents. Was it the British, he asked, or "our own thirst for
territory, our own want of moderation" that drove the Indians
"to desperation". Turning to European affairs, he condemned
the government for its subservience to Napoleon Bonaparte, the
man "who had effaced the title of Attila to the 'Scourge of
God'."[37] The debate went on for weeks. "Why, Captain Cook
would have sailed around the world before you get through
this", said Randolph in January 1812.[38]

The early weeks of 1812 witnessed a new and wholly unexpected development. Late in January a strange man, "thick-
set", with "monstrous thick legs" and "little hair on his head",
came to see James Madison.[39] He called himself the Comte
Édouard de Crillon, claimed aristocratic French ancestry and
presented impeccable credentials. He was, in fact, a charlatan,
a bankrupt French gambler by the name of Paul-Émile

Soubiron. Nevertheless, he gained the confidence of Senator Richard Brent of Virginia and, through him, entry to political and diplomatic circles in Washington. Then it emerged that he had valuable papers for sale, documents that would prove the perfidious depths to which British policy had descended— nothing less than copies of letters written by a spy sent by the governor of Canada, Sir James Craig, to incite Federalist Americans in New England to resist their government and, "in concert with a British force", detach the northeastern United States from the Union. That was how Madison described John Henry's mission to Congress. What had actually happened was that Craig, at the time of the *Chesapeake* crisis, had sent the former Irish journalist, now living in Canada, to the United States to feel the pulse of American opinion, to find out what Americans were thinking and saying about Great Britain, and to determine whether, in the event of war, the Federalists "would look up to England for assistance or be disposed to enter into a connexion with us".[40] When the crisis was over, Henry's mission ended. That it became public knowledge three years later was because Henry considered he had not been sufficiently reimbursed for his services to Craig. Falling in with the spurious French count, he employed him to sell the papers to the United States government. Crillon professed to believe that he could obtain more for them, but was content to accept $50 000. Just how the money was finally divided is not clear, but it would appear that Crillon received another $21 000 from Monroe and that Henry did not do too badly for himself. In any event, Henry could always console himself with the thought that he had helped bring on a war and thereby earned a dubious place in history.

Madison sprang the news of the Henry papers on Congress in March. The War Hawks were delighted. Here was something they could stuff down the throats of the anti-war party. At first the Federalists were silent, but after reading the Henry papers they refused to attach any importance to the letters, pointing out that the money paid Crillon had never been authorized by Congress.

> The Henry papers, bought and sold,
> And paid for with the nation's gold.[41]

Despite jeers and jingles, the Henry letters did damage the credibility of the Federalist party. Citizens sympathetic to the peace party became inclined to see more significance in Henry's role than was warranted, and believed that anybody who would consort with spies was not to be trusted. Joseph Desha made a telling point when he asked:

> Can any American . . . doubt the propriety of ousting the British from the continent, or hesitate in contributing his portionable part of the expense which will necessarily be incurred in the laudable undertaking?[42]

The government's answer was unequivocal. Troops were ordered to the Canadian frontier, stores were built up at Albany, and artillery was sent to New York.

Josiah Quincy subsequently suggested that the reason Madison no longer held back on the war issue after April was that he made a deal with the War Hawks for their support in the forthcoming presidential election; without their backing his chances of re-election would be slight. Whether the charge is true or not is debatable. The likelihood is that, by June, Madison felt definitely committed to war. The tragedy is that, on 16 June, two days before Madison signed the war declaration, a new British foreign secretary, Viscount Castlereagh, announced in London that the Orders in Council were being revoked. Admittedly, they constituted only one of the several British provocations that Madison used to justify his action, but had the conciliatory British gesture come a few weeks earlier Madison might possibly have withheld his signature from the decisive document committing his country to war. A delay of this nature would have suited Madison's temperament. After all, had he been a decisive leader, he might well have gone to war earlier. Perhaps he held back because of timidity, or because summer would be the best season for military campaigning, or because his country was not ready for a major war, or perhaps because he was alarmed at just how divided his nation was on the issue.

Few countries have entered a war with as much internal dissension as there was in the United States in 1812. The nation was split not only by party and philosophy, but by region as well. The northern seaboard states, conceivably the most concerned with maritime issues, such as Massachusetts (including Maine), Rhode Island, Connecticut, New York and New Jersey, rejected the appeal of free trade and sailors' rights as a *casus belli* and generally opposed the war. In April, a Federalist, Caleb Strong, was elected governor of Massachusetts, and in May he forwarded a state petition to Congress urging that peace be preserved.[43] The states remote from the smell and taste of

VOTE ON THE DECLARATION OF WAR
•HOUSE OF REPRESENTATIVES, 4 JUNE 1812•

Majority Vote "No"	Yes	No	Majority Vote "Yes"	Yes	No
Massachusetts (incl. Maine)	6	8	New Hampshire	3	2
Rhode Island	0	2	Vermont	3	1
Connecticut	0	7	Pennsylvania	16	2
New York	3	11	Maryland	6	3
New Jersey	2	4	Virginia	14	5
Delaware	0	1	North Carolina	6	3
	11	33	South Carolina	8	0
			Georgia	3	0
			Ohio	1	0
			Kentucky	5	0
			Tennessee	3	0
				68	16
			Total	79	49

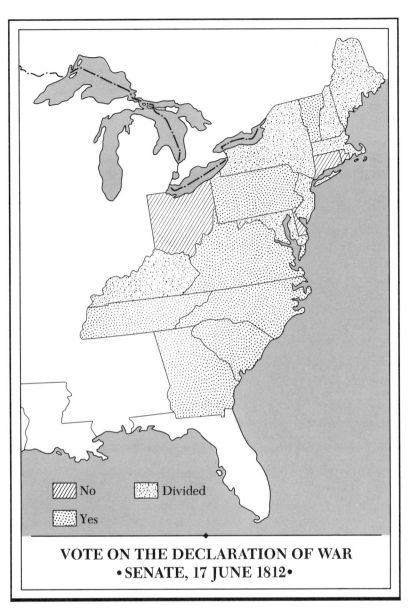

VOTE ON THE DECLARATION OF WAR
•SENATE, 17 JUNE 1812•

Legend:
- ▨ No
- ▧ Divided
- ▨ Yes

Majority Vote "No"	Yes	No
Rhode Island	0	2
Connecticut	0	2
Delaware	0	2
Ohio	0	1

Majority Vote "Yes"		
Vermont	1	0
Pennsylvania	2	0
Virginia	2	0
North Carolina	2	0
South Carolina	2	0
Georgia	2	0
Tennessee	2	0
	13	7

Divided States	Yes	No
New Hampshire	1	1
Massachusetts (incl. Maine)	1	1
New York	1	1
New Jersey	1	1
Maryland	1	1
Kentucky	1	1
	6	6
Total	19	13

10. *Caleb Strong, the Federalist anti-war governor of Massachusetts*

salt water, such as Kentucky, Tennessee and Ohio, adopted a bellicose stance, suggesting that their basic concern was with the Indian question. The southern states—Georgia, Maryland[44] and the Carolinas—were the most belligerent of all, although neither the Indian problem nor the impressment issue seems to have been of direct concern to any of them. Pennsylvania may be included with the western states because of its frontier on Lake Erie. Like Ohio and Kentucky, it was concerned about the Indians and with the desirability of expelling the British from Upper Canada.

In the Senate the majority for war was smaller than in the House of Representatives, partly because state representation in the Senate was limited to two members each and did not depend on the size of the state population. Here the voting by states followed much the same pattern as it did in the House of Representatives, although it is interesting to find that both Kentucky and Massachusetts split their votes evenly.

To explain the strength of the war party in the southern states is not simple. Some have suggested that southern bellicosity was aimed at acquiring northern support for their successful seizure of West Florida in 1810 and for George Matthews's ill-planned, badly managed attempt to do the same in East Florida in 1811. Other historians suggest that the real explanation lies in the economic discomfort suffered by the cotton- and tobacco-growing states as a result of the British Orders in Council, which made it impossible for Americans to export these crops to their principal markets in Europe.[45] Contemporary opinion provides a different and somewhat simplistic explanation. The people of the western and southern states enjoyed a relative immunity from the possibility of a counter-invasion by the British, and were prepared to take advantage of it. War with Great Britain would, in all probability, be waged on the northern frontiers of New York and New England, not on the banks of the Mississippi or on the Atlantic shores south of the Potomac. And if, by any chance, war did come to these regions, fighting Indians and Spaniards would not present the same frightening problems as fighting British regulars.

IF AMERICANS were not politically united in favour of war in 1812, neither were they militarily prepared. At sea they had no ships of the line, no vessels that could offer any serious challenge to the Royal Navy. For this Jefferson must take full responsibility, as he was not prepared to spend money on building up the United States navy. In his view, any war at sea would simply take the form of blockade and raid, with the British doing the blockading and the Americans the raiding. Thus, the United States would not require battleships; what would be wanted was fast vessels, the hit-and-run kind, and privateers that would be financed by private interests and impose no serious strain upon the Treasury. Such an attitude towards naval operations was not unreasonable for anyone who saw war with Great Britain as a land operation, with Canada as the objective. What the United States would need was soldiers, not sailors. But not necessarily regular soldiers; militia were capable of doing the job. Thus, while the War Hawks were meeting to plan the new states to be carved out of British North America, Henry Clay was boasting that the Kentucky militia alone could place Upper Canada and Montreal at the feet of Congress; John Calhoun was assuring Congress that he believed that "in four weeks from the time that a declaration of war is heard on our frontiers the whole of Upper and a part of Lower Canada will be in our possession";[46] and ex-President Jefferson was writing to Tadeusz Kosciuszko to tell him the United States would soon strip Great Britain of all her North American territory.

The minuteman tradition, the idea that the militia was the bulwark of the American defence structure, was the military legacy of Jefferson. Jefferson did not believe regular troops had any place on the American scene. Regular armies, as he had seen them in Europe, he considered inefficient and corrupt, the instruments of kings and tyrants—useful enough to guard arsenals, police the frontier and build roads, but not to be trusted with the essential tasks of national defence.[47] During the Jefferson regime, militiamen were required to report annually and to keep themselves armed and ready for an emergency. They were expected to assemble on muster or training days fully equipped. In 1803, for instance, Congress set aside the sum of $1 500 000 to equip 80 000 men to be ready to march "at a moment's notice". Four years later, another Act authorized the president to accept 30 000 volunteers. And in 1803 an additional $200 000 was added to the original vote. In December 1808—this, of course, was the period of the *Chesapeake* crisis—a committee of Congress debated a bill to raise a volunteer force for two years, but it was defeated in the Senate. The fact was that, despite Jefferson's prestige, Congress was not very interested in national defence. From time to time, individual state governments might be persuaded to do something for their militia forces, but, broadly speaking, the American approach to the armed forces was consistently casual, at least until 1810. During the intervening years, the most important contribution made by the army was in non-military activities such as the expedition carried out by Captain Meriwether Lewis and Lieutenant William Clark to the Pacific between 1804 and 1806, and the explorations by Lieutenant Zebulon Pike in the Southwest from 1805 to 1807.

As the war clouds began to gather on the horizon, interest in military matters quickened. In his presidential message of 1811, Madison drew attention to the dispatch of regulars and militia to cope with a menacing situation brought about by "a fanatic of the Shawnese tribe", and recommended that the government be authorized to fill vacancies in the regular force and recruit volunteers "whose patriotic ardor may court a participation in urgent services".[48] He also felt it would be useful to give some attention to the military academies, including West Point. The President even had something to say on the navy, suggesting that materials be stockpiled in anticipation that the United States would "resume, maintain and defend the navigation of the high seas".[49] Some newspapers scoffed at the idea of enlarging the army, but Major General Andrew Jackson of the Tennessee militia responded by addressing a stirring appeal to his officers and men to offer their services to the regular army. During the debate on Peter B. Porter's foreign policy report, the changing attitude towards the armed forces became even more apparent, with the acceptance by Congress of proposals to recruit up to a total of 35 000 regulars plus 50 000 volunteers. Suggestions that the navy be built up to twelve 74-gun ships and twenty frigates, however, ran afoul of the historic opposition to a permanent sea force, the indifference to naval matters in the inland states, and the distaste of the Federalists for increased taxes. Thus, when the secretary of the Treasury, Albert Gallatin, presented his estimates of war costs, Congress was thrown into a panic.[50] War was so much more expensive than the members of Congress had expected it to be. As a result, the naval programme was cut back and a bill to arm and classify the militia soundly defeated. Congress was apparently prepared to go in two directions—towards declaring war and away from providing the means to pursue it. With truth as well as bitterness Madison wrote to Jefferson that, "to enable the Executive to step at once into Canada", Congress had provided "after two months delay" for a "regular force requiring twelve months to raise it, and, after three months, for a volunteer force, on terms not likely to raise it at all for that object".[51] The editor of the semi-official *National Intelligencer* of Washington reminded Congress that,

> the sword being drawn, the scabbard must be thrown aside. . . . To refuse to follow up this step by the adoption of the necessary defensive or preparatory measures would be to measure back the ground they have trod, and could only lead to humiliating defeat or degradation in the eyes of the world.[52]

In addition to increasing the number of recruits, steps were taken to fill appointments at the command and staff levels. Senior appointments were the president's prerogative. His problem was whether to choose older men with war experience, or

11. Dr. William Eustis, United States Secretary of War,
April 1809–December 1812

younger men whose military experience had been limited to
peacetime duties or occasional encounters with Indians. To find
men who had seen active service meant, of course, to draw upon
the Revolutionary War veterans, but few remained, by this time,
who had ever served actively at anything above junior com-
missioned rank. Nevertheless, it was upon this group that Madison relied. Henry Dearborn, who had been with Benedict
Arnold before Quebec in 1775, was named "First Major General" of the United States army and charged with responsibil-

ity for the land operations against Canada. Thomas Pinckney became "Second Major General" and was sent to the southern states. Below them were the brigadier generals, Wade Hampton, Peter Gansevoort and James Wilkinson, a professional officer of whom it was said that he never won a battle and never lost a Court of Enquiry. The new brigadiers included Joseph Bloomfield, James Winchester and William Hull, the last-named being the governor of Michigan Territory. Dearborn and Hull, two New Englanders, were expected to moderate some of the resentment felt in that region against the war itself. Other senior officers included Harrison of Tippecanoe fame, Alexander Smyth, and Stephen Van Rensselaer commanding the militia of the state of New York. Regimental officers were recommended largely by members of Congress; rewards handed out to political retainers was what John Randolph called this practice.

At the top of the hierarchy was the secretary of war, Dr. William Eustis of Massachusetts, an ardent republican who, when Madison became president, took over his appointment from General Dearborn, who had filled the position in the Jefferson years. Eustis, however reputable he may have been as a physician and however successful as a politician, was as incompetent in his appointment as was his colleague in the Navy Department, Paul Hamilton. That he was allowed to remain there for so long can only be attributed to Madison's loyalty to his political comrades. However, when it is remembered that the secretary of war and eight clerks were expected to carry out the duties of chief of the general staff, quartermaster general and commissary general, as well as supervisor of pensions, Indian Affairs and Land Warrants, one may be inclined to forgive him some of his sins of omission, if not those of commission.

3

British North America

IN 1812, when faced with an unwelcome invasion by the armed forces of the American republic, British North America was a thinly populated land, extending from the island of Newfoundland on the east to the Hudson's Bay Company territories and Indian lands on the west. Unlike the United States of America, it was not a unified country, merely a collection of separate colonies, united only through their colonial relationship with Great Britain. Another fifty-five years would elapse before the idea of a federal union became a Canadian reality. Accurate statistics are not available to determine the origins or the numbers of people who lived in the colonies at that time, but it is estimated that New Brunswick had a population of about 25 000 in 1803, and Nova Scotia some 65 000 in 1805. In Upper Canada the population was approximately 77 000 in 1811, and is believed to have reached 95 000 by 1814. Lower Canada is said to have had 335 000 people by the same year. In all probability, there would not have been more than 500 000 colonists in the whole of British North America, nearly all of them living in scattered settlements, which grew sparser the farther west one went and which were all located just north of the American frontier. At the same time, the population of the United States was 6 million.

In the maritime region, the people were largely of New England, Scottish, English and French origin. Among them were numerous Loyalists, particularly in New Brunswick, where many disbanded Loyalist soldiers had been settled at the end of the Revolutionary War. Lower Canada was predominantly French Canadian; in fact, the French-speaking population of the province constituted over half the population of British North America. Upper Canada, where most of the fighting was to take place, contained a large American population. Loyalist refugees formed a substantial part of this group, although in the years following the original Loyalist migration a steady stream of American immigrants moved across the Niagara River into Upper Canada. They came, in part, in response to an invitation issued by Lieutenant Governor John Graves Simcoe in 1792, and in part because there were still families in the United States that had Loyalist sympathies and found continued residence in the Republic intolerable, especially after the outbreak of anti-British and pro-French demonstrations in the United States during the French Revolution in 1793 and 1794. The largest group of Americans who settled in Upper Canada, however, came later, some because they found land cheaper in Upper Canada, some because of the Indian troubles on the American frontier, and others because of the economic impact of the Embargo Act. Michael Smith, an articulate American immigrant in Upper Canada, wrote in 1814:

> I . . . moved with my family to the province of Upper Canada, in order to obtain land upon easy terms (as did most of the inhabitants now there) and for no other reason. I had not long remained in the province till I discovered that the mildness of the climate, fertility of the soil, benefit of trade, cheapness of the land, morals of the inhabitants, and equality of the government so far exceeded my former expectations, and the expectations of the public in general, that I deemed it my duty to make known the same, especially when I considered that there were many thousands of my fellow citizens of the United States who were without land.[1]

Because nobody counted the immigrants who came north to Upper Canada prior to the War of 1812, we have nothing positive to go on except a contemporary estimate of 500 families annually.[2] Michael Smith, for instance, expressed the opinion that four-fifths of the total Upper-Canadian population was of American origin and, of these, one in four was a Loyalist or of Loyalist descent.[3] How many of these Americans had taken the oath of allegiance he did not know, nor did he hazard a guess as to how many of them would stay loyal to George III in the event of hostilities developing between Great Britain and the United States.

The uncertainty regarding the loyalty of Americans living in Canada was a source of concern to both the provincial authorities and the inhabitants of British origin, for the early years of the nineteenth century were a time when friction between the two countries was growing and war was always a threatening possibility. Lieutenant Governor Francis Gore drew attention to this particular problem as early as 1806. After stating that some of the American immigrants, such as the Quakers and Pennsylvania Dutch, were proving to be "peaceable and industrious settlers", Gore pointed out that there were, unfortunately, "a considerable number" of others who had obviously come to Upper Canada as "adventurers" and had brought with them "the very worst principles of their own Constitution . . . and from what I have experienced, even during my very short residence here, endeavour to oppose and perplex His Majesty's Government."[4] Hugh Gray, an Englishman who spent several years in Upper Canada, wrote in praise of the enterprise and initiative of the American settlers; but Richard Cartwright, who had been in the province much longer, expressed the opinion that steps should be taken to halt the Americanization of the country and urged that more "men of tried loyalty" should be induced to come to Upper Canada "to discountenance that affectation of equality so discernible in the manner of those who come to us from the American republic".[5] There was some justification for the fears of Loyalists and the British settlers in the province concerning the loyalty of the Americans. At least, this is the inference to be drawn from the remarks of Christian Schultz, who wrote in 1810 that he found at Fort Erie, Niagara* and Kingston "a determined partiality towards the United States and a decided and almost avowed hostility to the British Government" following the *Chesapeake* affair. Describing the new American settlers, he wrote, "They never seek to disguise their sentiments in public, but express themselves with as much freedom as you would do at the Theatre or Tontine Coffee-House."[6]

WELL BEFORE WAR became a reality, Major General Isaac Brock, commanding the troops in Upper Canada, realized that the imbalance in the population between the Loyalists and the immigrants from the United States might well lead to serious problems. He hoped, however, that his hand would be strengthened by his being sworn in as president of the Council and administrator of the province in October 1811, when Sir Francis

---

*Although named Newark by Lieutenant Governor Simcoe in 1792, the community reverted to its previous name, Niagara, in 1798 and was renamed Niagara-on-the-Lake in 1906.

Gore was to leave for England to look after his personal affairs. To possess both political and military power would greatly simplify the situation, for most military problems were inextricably intertwined with political problems, particularly those relating to the financing of the war, recruiting, martial law, aliens, and *habeas corpus*. Problems such as these could more effectively be dealt with by a single authority than by two separate bodies.

On 3 February 1812, Brock met his first legislature. He spoke quietly to the members in patriotic terms and expressed his confidence in the loyalty of the people and the militia. Then he requested the legislature to adopt measures necessary to improve the training of the militia, to suspend *habeas corpus* should that drastic action be necessary, to control aliens, and to offer rewards for the apprehension of deserters. He also made it clear that he believed that the Assembly and the Council should insist upon an oath of allegiance, abjuring fidelity to any foreign power. Simple affirmations of fidelity of the kind required by Simcoe were not enough. "If I succeed in all this," he wrote, "I shall claim some praise, but I am not without my fears."[7] Indeed, Brock was something less than successful. The bill requiring the oath of abjuration was lost by the deciding vote of the chairman, and the bill for the suspension of *habeas corpus* by a small majority. The Assembly did, however, vote moneys to recover deserters, and gave Brock funds to train the militia. The rejection of the abjuration oath and the *habeas corpus* bill showed Brock that he was not going to have it all his own way. He saw this as strong evidence of the "truly alarming" political clout of the large number of American sympathizers[8] in the province, whose representatives in the legislature, including Joseph Willcocks, led the opposition to his restrictive measures. Brock expressed his disappointment in a letter to the adjutant general, Edward Baynes. The reply he received offered sympathy and cold comfort. Baynes wrote that Sir George Prevost,

> well versed in the fickle and intractable disposition of public assemblies, feels more regret than disappointment. He has a very delicate card to play with his House of Assembly here, who would fain keep up the farce of being highly charmed with his amiable disposition and affable manners.[9]

After the official declaration of war in June, Brock immediately called for another meeting of the legislature. On 27 July the members assembled in the little frame parliament building at York (Toronto). Brock realized that the prospects for unanimity in their deliberations were not bright. The members of the Long Point militia, for instance, had been reluctant to turn out for their own reasons, and the magistrates were equally reluctant to do anything about them—this in a region of the province where he had not anticipated any trouble. Brock wondered if Hull's rapid advance into Canada had thrown the civil authorities as well as the people of the province into a panic and nobody had any faith in the likelihood of stopping him. "Legislators, magistrates, militia officers", Brock wrote, were so "sluggish and indifferent" that they neglected to perform duties that might place them in a bad light with the United States military authorities; accordingly, "The artful and active scoundrel is allowed to parade the country without interruption and commit all imaginable mischief."[10] These were Brock's words to Baynes shortly after the legislative session began. He added, "They are so alarmed of offending that they rather encourage than repress disorders and other improper acts" because "they dread the vengeance of the democratic party, they are such a set of unrelenting villains." To counteract the effect of a threatening proclamation issued by Brigadier General Hull at Sandwich (Windsor), on 13 July 1812, Brock replied with his own proclamation stating:

> Our enemies have indeed said that they can subdue the country by a proclamation, but it is our part to prove to them that they are sadly mistaken, that the population is determinedly hostile, and that the few who might be otherwise inclined will find it to their safety to be faithful.[11]

When he addressed the two houses of the legislature in York, Brock gave no indication of his uneasiness. He expressed his confidence in the people of the province and urged the legislature to move with "unanimity and despatch". But this was too much to expect. The pro-American faction, protesting their deep concern about civil rights, again turned down Brock's request for power to suspend *habeas corpus* and to impose "a partial exercise of martial law concurrently with the ordinary course of justice". They would not even give him the moneys left over from previous appropriations. Brock described the Assembly in these words: "A more decent House has not been elected since the formation of the province."[12] Yet he could get nothing from them, and so he prorogued the legislature on 3 August. Immediately following prorogation, the Executive Council expressed their conviction that the military commander might properly proclaim and exercise martial law on authority given him by the governor general.[13] Brock therefore discussed the question with Sir George Prevost, in an exchange of letters, and on 12 August the Governor General offered it as his opinion that, "as the martial law you propose declaring is founded upon the King's Commission" and in an extreme case, such as an invasion, "whatever power is necessary for carrying the measure into effect must have been intended to have been given you by the commission", consequently "the power of assembling Courts Martial and of carrying the sentence into execution is included in the authority for declaring martial law."[14] Prevost also stated that since officers of the militia were themselves subject to martial law, he believed "they may sit upon Courts Martial with officers of His Majesty's Regular Forces." It was not an authoritative statement; Prevost made that clear when he added, "Upon both these points I desire not to be understood as speaking decisively—extreme cases must be met by measures which, on ordinary occasions, would not perhaps be justified." At least it gave Brock the powers he believed necessary, but that he had been unable to extract from the legislature. In the end, the Commander's assumption of dictatorial powers was to prove the salvation of the province.

AMERICAN SETTLERS sought to immigrate not only into Upper Canada, but into Lower Canada as well, and for the same reasons. They settled in the Eastern Townships in the vicinity of Missisquoi Bay, along the shores of the Saint-François River and Lake Memphremagog, and in the township of Hemmingford in the county of Huntingdon. Just as the Upper-Canadian Loyalists looked upon American immigration with a certain distaste, so too did the French Canadians of Lower Canada view it with a jaundiced eye. They did not like the Americans. They regarded them as aggressive, acquisitive, guilty of sharp practices, and lacking in respect for authority. What was most alarming, however, was the possibility that the newcomers might eventually swamp the local French-speaking population and take over control of the province. Were there not, already, 5000 of them settled in the Eastern Townships by 1805?[15] Was Lower Canada already on the way to becoming "an American province", as D.-B. Viger, a member of the legislature, suggested? After a century and three quarters, it is easy to say that Viger's fears were groundless, but there was enough evidence at the time to give them a semblance of plausibility; for this was the kind of advice that the Francophobe chief justice,

*12. Sir George Prevost, governor general of the Canadas and
commander-in-chief of the forces, 1812–15*

Jonathan Sewell, himself American-born, was passing on to the
governor-in-chief, Sir James Craig. In a memorandum on the
advisability of uniting Upper and Lower Canada, which Sewell
prepared for Craig and which the Governor passed on, with
his endorsement, to the British prime minister, Lord Liverpool,
was the emphatic statement that it was "indispensably necessary
to overwhelm and sink the Canadian population by English
Protestants". Sewell added, "If to people the country with such
characters is to incur a risk, the risk incurred will be less than
that which we must incur by suffering the Province to remain

13. King's Colour of the 1st Battalion Embodied Militia, Lower Canada. Embodied 8 May 1812, the unit was engaged at Châteauguay, 26 October 1813.

in its present state."[16] Which was simply another way of saying, better an American Canada than a French Canada.

American immigration was not the only issue alienating Craig from the people of Lower Canada. Initially, Craig had been sent to North America in 1807 because the British government believed that the deteriorating international situation might lead to war and that it would be best to have a military man in Canada as governor, particularly one like Craig who, because he had served in Canada as a junior officer in John Burgoyne's army in 1776, was presumably familiar with campaigning in the region where war was likely to be fought again. But Craig's rigidity of mind, his personality, his disposition to listen to men like Sewell and Herman Ryland rather than to any French Canadians, and his inability to accept the necessity of political compromise alienated the very people he would have had to defend. So little did Craig trust the French Canadians that British soldiers were told to disperse "any three citizens seen

14. Regimental Colour of the 5th Battalion Canadian Militia, Lower Canada. Embodied 21 September 1812, it was subsequently redesignated the Canadian Chasseurs and fought at Plattsburg, 11 September 1814.

speaking together in the streets of that city [Quebec]".[17] Small wonder that the situation became so tense and the Governor's temper so frayed that Craig begged to be relieved of his appointment. And none too soon. Craig had lost all credibility as the man to defend Canada. Moreover, the War Hawks were in the ascendant in Washington and war was now a probability rather than a possibility.

Craig's successor in 1811 was another military officer, a French-speaking Swiss, Sir George Prevost, who held the rank of lieutenant general in the British army. Prevost had served as military governor of St. Lucia and had proved his ability to conciliate the French population of that Caribbean island. In 1808, he had been appointed lieutenant governor of Nova Scotia. It was from that posting that he was transferred to Quebec.

Promptly discarding Sewell and Ryland as political advisers, Prevost set out, not just to conciliate, but to recognize the French Canadians for what they were—the dominant racial group in Lower Canada, strongly conscious of their own identity and in no mood to be submerged by an imported American or English population.

When Sir George met his legislature in February 1812, he encountered not an uncooperative alien American assembly like that of Upper Canada, but a cooperative French-Canadian one. Like Brock in York, Prevost in Quebec began by warning his listeners of the need for vigilance and the desirability of adopting measures "effectually to participate in the defence of their country against a regular invasion".[18] Despite an obvious inclination to warm over their complaints against Prevost's predecessor, Craig, the legislators, under the impact of the new governor's amiability, agreed to the embodiment for ninety days' training of 2000 unmarried men between the ages of 18 and 25 and, in the event of invasion, an extension of their time of service to one year. It was, in effect, a measure of conscription beyond anything Brock had ventured to suggest in Upper Canada. The only limitation imposed by the Quebec Assembly was that no militiaman should be compelled to enlist in a British regular regiment. It was as good a response, if not better, than the Administrator of Upper Canada had been able to report, although Prevost, like Brock, was not given a free hand to curb civil liberties.

Then, on 24 June, came the news of war. The Lower-Canadian authorities acted quickly. Americans were given notice to quit the city of Quebec by 1 July, and to be out of the district by the third. A few days later the time limit was extended to fourteen days. At the same time an embargo was placed upon shipping, and an emergency session of the legislature was summoned to meet the Governor on 16 July. This time all the members of the Assembly were in good temper. Not only did they authorize the use of Army Bills to meet the immediate expenses of the war, they approved the policy of expelling American aliens. The only measure they were prepared to challenge was the imposition of martial law. When the conscription law was imposed there was some resistance by young men in Pointe-Claire, Lachine and Sainte-Geneviève, apparently because they were unaware that the law had been adopted by the Assembly; after an exchange of shots and the arrest of the ringleaders, the starch went out of the protesters and the

POLICE.

WHEREAS authentic intelligence has been received that the Government of the United States of America did, on the 18th instant, declare War against the United Kingdom of Great Britain and Ireland and its dependencies, Notice is hereby given, that all Subjects or Citizens of the said United States, and all persons claiming American Citizenship, are ordered to quit the City of Quebec, on or before TWELVE o'clock at Noon, on WEDNESDAY next, and the District of Quebec on or before 12 o'clock at noon on FRIDAY next, on pain of arrest.　　　　ROSS CUTHBERT,
　　　C. Q. S. & Inspector of Police.

The Constables of the City of Quebec are ordered to assemble in the Police Office at 10 o'clock to-morrow morning, to receive instructions.

Quebec, 29th June, 1812.

15. Police order to American citizens to leave Quebec

16. Regimental Colour of the Canadian Fencible Infantry. In 1803 the regiment was authorized to be recruited in Great Britain for service in North America. It was disbanded after a mutiny by the Scottish Highlanders, but was not removed from the establishment. Later the unit was recruited in British North America and served during the war.

embodiment of the Lower-Canadian militia regiments went ahead without overt opposition.[19] In Lower Canada, as in Upper Canada, the response towards the enrolment of recruits for military service against the Americans was marked more by apathy than by opposition or enthusiasm. That nothing more serious developed than the encounter at Lachine was a tribute to Prevost; even more was it an indication of the influence of the Roman Catholic hierarchy, which was prepared to give its full support to the war effort.

THE WAR did not catch the British military authorities in Canada wholly unprepared. Great Britain had kept regular regiments in garrison in the British North American provinces ever since

17. *Belt plates of the 1st Battalion Embodied Militia, Lower Canada; the 49th Regiment of Foot; the Régiment de Watteville; and the 104th Regiment of Foot.*

the end of the American Revolutionary War, and compulsory militia service was an expected part of the life of every physically fit young or middle-aged man in every province. Provincial regular regiments had also been recruited in each of the provinces, including the Royal Nova Scotia Regiment, the King's New Brunswick Regiment, the Royal Canadian Volunteers, and the revived Queen's Rangers of Revolutionary War fame. These regiments were disbanded in 1802, at the time of the peace of Amiens. The peace proved to be only a brief breathing period, however, and when war was resumed between Great Britain

18. Drum of the Nova Scotia Regiment of Fencible Infantry

and Napoleonic France, the provincial units were revived in Newfoundland, Nova Scotia, New Brunswick and Lower Canada as fencible corps. In previous wars, Great Britain had raised military units for purely local defence and called them fencible units. In North America, however, the men enrolled in the fencible regiments undertook to serve anywhere in North America, and one of them, the New Brunswick Fencibles, volunteered to serve as a line regiment. The offer was accepted by the War Office in London, and the regiment was given the designation of the 104th Regiment of Foot in 1811. At the same time, another New Brunswick fencible regiment was recruited. Immediately prior to the American declaration of war two more

19. A British infantry officer's shako

provincial corps were organized: the one in Upper Canada carried the name of the Glengarry Light Infantry, to commemorate the Glengarry Fencibles who came to Canada under the leadership of the Reverend Alexander Macdonell after their disbandment in Scotland; the other, in Lower Canada, a French-Canadian unit, was known as the Provincial Corps of Light Infantry or, more popularly, the Voltigeurs.

When Sir George Prevost arrived in Quebec in 1811 to assume the post of governor-in-chief, he had under his command a force of something over 10 000 British regular troops and provincial regulars. Of this number, about half were troops belonging to Sir John Coape Sherbrooke's subordinate command in Nova

Scotia "and its dependencies". In Upper Canada, Major General Isaac Brock had some 1200 officers and men scattered about in various posts in the province, and in Lower Canada were some 4000 regular troops. As far as the militia was concerned, it had a potential strength of 86 000. Of these, 11 000, of whom "it might not be prudent to arm more than 4000", were in Upper Canada, 60 000 were in Lower Canada, "ill-armed and without discipline", 11 000 were in Nova Scotia, of whom 6000 had been issued with muskets, and 4000 were in New Brunswick, all of them lacking arms and training. The militia in Cape Breton and Prince Edward Island did not amount to any number "deserving to be noticed".[20] Not an impressive force, except on paper, and yet the militia was not a force to be ignored. That was why, when he met his legislature, Prevost felt that he had achieved something when he persuaded Assembly members to authorize the enrolment of 2000 militiamen for ninety days' training. Brock had to rest content when his none-too-helpful Assembly authorized him to form flank companies from each of the sedentary militia regiments and train them for six days a month; about 2000 men were enrolled for this training. Unlike the militia in the United States, provision existed in the Militia Acts of both Upper and Lower Canada authorizing the use of the militia of one province in the other, "when the same shall actually be invaded or in a state of insurrection".[21] Thus, Prevost could take into account the militias of both provinces when making plans for the defence of the country.

IT IS IMPOSSIBLE to ignore the native peoples when considering the manpower Canada might draw upon for its defence in 1812. Indians had taken part in Canada's wars ever since the day in 1609 when Champlain led a band of Algonquins, Hurons and Montagnais to the lake that was to bear his name. It was almost a matter of tradition; more particularly, it was a matter of mutual self-interest. The Indians always identified Americans with the pressures of settlement and Canadians with the freer life of hunting, trapping and trading furs. They did not appreciate that in Canada, too, this life would ultimately yield to settlement. The War of 1812 was what one historian has called "the final episode in the long struggle between settlement and the fur trade in the region of the Great Lakes".[22] Because this was true, the Indians and fur traders had no choice but to take part in the war and to throw their weight on the side of the two Canadas. There could be no neutrality when the futures of Indian and fur trader alike were at stake. That is why the fur-trading fraternity of the North West Company not only offered Prevost the services of their ships and men on the St. Lawrence and the Great Lakes, but urged him to employ Indians against the American invaders, and offered to provide stores at moderate prices to the British Indian Department. Brock was aware of the sympathetic attitude of the fur trade, for as early as February 1812 he wrote the red-haired Scottish fur trader, Robert Dickson, in Wisconsin:

> As it is probable that war may result from the present *state of af-fairs*, it is very desirable to ascertain the degree of cooperation that you and *your friends* might be able to furnish in case of such an emergency taking place.[23]

That the Americans expected the northwestern Indians, as well as Tecumseh and the southwestern tribes that had fought at Tippecanoe, to join the British is clear from a letter written by Brigadier General Hull to the secretary of war in Washington:

> I have every reason to expect in a very short time a large Body of Savages from the North whose operations will be directed against this army. They are under the influence of the North and South West Companies, and the interest of the Companies depends on opening the Detroit River this summer. . . . It is the opinion of the officers and the most respectable gentlemen from Mackinac that the British can engage any number of Indians they may have occasion for, and that including the Engagés of the North West and South West Companies, two or three thousand will be brought to this place in a very short time.[24]

Hull was not far wrong. Dickson replied to Brock's query on 18 June, the very day Madison signed the declaration of war, assuring the commander in Upper Canada of the services of the western Indians, and after sending a number of them to Amherstburg, he himself set out with bands of Sioux, Winnebagos and Menominis for the British post on St. Joseph Island. They arrived in time to take part in Captain Roberts's capture of Michilimackinac.

Brock did not experience the same degree of success in enlisting the services of the Six Nations. A century and more of fighting had made them weary of war. After the Revolution, Joseph Brant threw away his tomahawk in favour of diplomatic argument, and when war came in 1812 the nations of which he had once been the acknowledged leader held aloof. Influenced by the American Indian agent, Erastus Granger, those Iroquois Indians who had elected to live in the United States strongly supported neutrality and sent messengers to the Grand River Reserve to persuade their Canadian brothers to do likewise. Alarmed by the threats embodied in Hull's proclamation of a "war of extermination" and "one indiscriminate scene of desolation" at the "first stroke of the tomahawk",[25] the Grand River Indians found no difficulty in deciding upon a course of non-intervention. After all, they were not under the same pressures as Tecumseh's people and saw no reason why they should become involved in a war from which they could gain little and stood to lose much. They agreed that there would be no objection to individual Indians joining the British forces, but as a corporate body they would do nothing. Other efforts were made to encourage the Iroquois to enlist but, in July, John Norton reluctantly informed Captain Peter Chambers, whom Brock sent to conduct the Indians and militia to Detroit, that "40 or 50 men would be the utmost he could promise himself from the Grand River tribes."[26] The Mohawks of Caughnawaga adopted a similar posture, and from it they would not budge. Prevost might call them "old women . . . not worthy to be called warriors";[27] he might even threaten to cut off the government issue of presents, but the Iroquois of Lower Canada, like those of Upper Canada, merely adopted an attitude of wait and see. It did not augur well for the enlistment of other tribes, for the Iroquois of the Grand River and Caughnawaga reserves were the Indians who had been longest in association with the European settlers and the most committed in years gone by to fighting the Americans.

IF BRITISH NORTH AMERICA, Upper and Lower Canada in particular, was weak in manpower, it was also weak in economic resources, wealth, the sinews of war. In this respect it was far less capable of fighting a war than the United States of America, where the Revolution had led, not to economic collapse, but to growth and development, to new corporate ventures, and to a determination to assert America's economic as well as political independence. Military and political success seems to have stimulated a spirit of enterprise and a determination to exploit the interior of North America without interference from London. Moreover, the retaliatory policies of Thomas Jefferson —non-intercourse and embargo—, even if they had adversely affected the export of foodstuffs, cotton and tobacco, did stimulate the growth of manufacturing by protecting American manufacturers from normal foreign competition. As shipping

20. Major John Norton, one of the leaders of the Six Nations Indians. He fought at Queenston Heights and Lundy's Lane.

profits dwindled, northern merchants diverted more and more of their capital into industrial ventures. Not that this was a matter of deliberate government policy, for the Jefferson party was essentially dominated by agricultural interests; rather was it a result of the long-drawn-out quarrel with Great Britain. Post-Revolution economic growth had the effect of providing the United States with a stronger industrial base than that existing in Canada.

For the most part, Canadians, whether they lived in Upper or Lower Canada, were farmers. Not particularly good farmers, for their emphasis was on the subsistence family farm rather than on large-scale agriculture.[28] Wheat was the principal crop, as it required less labour and brought the highest return. Oats, barley and peas were less popular, and hemp, despite government assistance and an assured market in Great Britain, never caught on in the Canadas. In the early days of the colony of Upper Canada, cattle, hogs and sheep were imported from the United States, but after 1800 these were produced locally in sufficient numbers to occasionally permit a small export trade. Normally, however, Canadian meat suppliers were unable to satisfy local demand. A byproduct of agriculture was distilling, transforming good Canadian wheat into a poor, if popular, Canadian whisky. With the closing of the Baltic by Napoleon, British-American lumber took the place of Baltic lumber in the British market. This brought money to the colonies, but lumbering tended to draw people away from agriculture, just at the time the country needed farm produce to feed the considerable influx of men during the War of 1812. And because local militiamen were needed to supplement the regulars, even fewer farm labourers were available to produce food. The feeding of the troops, the sailors, and the Indians fighting on the British side presented a major problem to the military commissariat throughout the two and a half years of the war, simply because Canadian agriculture was not geared to a war economy. This inevitably led to greater reliance upon produce, particularly meat, smuggled across the frontier from New York, Vermont and the New England states, the areas of the United States most opposed to the declaration of war in 1812. Shortly after war was declared, Prevost asked that George McLean, a clerk in the commissariat, be assigned the job of procuring beef from Vermont; and in Ogdensburg, David Parish kept a steady supply of cattle and sheep moving across the river to Fort Wellington.

In 1811 the harvest in the two Canadas was good. There was an adequate supply of flour and grain, not only for home consumption, but also for distilling and for seed. In the spring of the following year, however, the snow remained long on the ground and considerable time elapsed before the farmers could get on the land. With the ever-present danger of an early autumn frost injuring the slow-maturing varieties of grain then available, the chances of a crop failure in 1812 were great. Although there was enough flour on hand to last until the early months of the next year, what happened after that would depend on what the crops were like in 1813. As for meat, there was invariably a shortage of home-grown beef, but deficiencies in this essential item were made good by imports from the United States and Great Britain as well as from Ireland, where the cattle industry had been geared to feeding the Duke of Wellington's troops fighting in the Spanish peninsula. The declaration of war in North America, however, changed the complexion of the provisions problem. After June 1812, it was no longer just a matter of feeding the local population, but one of providing rations for the large numbers of soldiers, sailors, militiamen and Indians likely to become involved. Provisioning became a twofold problem of availability and sufficiency. Inventories were taken and contracts let for flour, salt-meat and rum, hopefully in quantities sufficient to last until the spring of 1813. And with the prospect of poor crops in the Canadas, steps were taken to conserve supplies, prohibit exports and restrict the amount of grain given over to distilling.[29] With the mobilization of the militia, a number of farm labourers were taken out of food production; hence the need for farm leave, as granted by Brock to many militiamen in the autumn of 1812. And as the demand for foodstuffs and forage increased—for the horses of the dragoons and the animals that pulled the wagons had likewise to be fed—so too did prices. On 2 June 1812, flour sold at $10.50 a barrel, in December at $16.00, and in June 1814 at $25.00. The explanation? Profiteering, government demand and scarcity. These were the problems that faced William Henry Robinson, the commissary general, who arrived in British North America in 1810 to take charge of the commissariat in "all the provinces and islands under the military command of Governor General Sir James Craig".[30] First, Robinson reorganized the commissariat in Nova Scotia, and in September 1811 he took charge at Quebec. He remained as commissary general throughout the war.

Another serious area of shortage was in clothing, especially for men in the militia and fencible regiments. In Upper Canada the inhabitants of York were asked to subscribe funds to provide the flank companies of the York militia with shoes, stockings and shirts.[31] On the Detroit frontier the problem was solved by providing the militia with castoffs from the regulars, an improvisation, incidentally, that misled General Hull into believing that they were regular troops. In time, supplies of clothing and accoutrements were forwarded to Canada from Great Britain.

Uniforms were not the only need: camp equipage, guns, muskets, barrack stores, medical supplies and, of course, specie

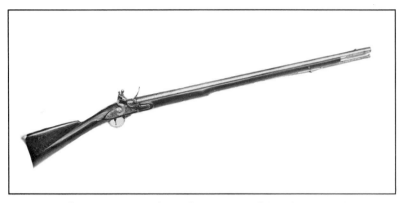

*21. An India Pattern musket, the type used by the Canadian mili-
tia in Upper Canada during the War of 1812. Though shorter
and with fewer brass furnishings, these muskets were of the same
calibre as the Tower musket used by the regular troops.*

with which to pay the contractors and the troops were all
required.[32] Everything was in short supply, even paper, tape,
black lead pencils, black ink powder, erasing knives, penknives,
sealing wax, and all materials "for sending despatches". Few,
if any, of the needed items could be obtained in Canada, even
when the government's credit was good, which was not always
the case. And all of it had to be brought across the ocean at
great expense. It cost £2000 to transport six 32-pounder cannons from Montreal to Kingston and double that amount to
move forty 24-pounders in 1813. Perhaps the largest single sum
was the £12 000 spent to carry the frame of the British frigate
Psyche from Quebec to Kingston.[33] But whatever the cost, the
supplies and reinforcements had to be kept moving over the long,
thin line of communications stretching some 6500 km from
England to Quebec to Montreal to Kingston to York to Amherstburg. That line was the vital artery through which flowed the
lifeblood of Canada's defence. Were it to be blocked or severed,
the country would choke and die.

The enemy, of course, provided the main threat to the line
of communications. But there were problems, other than those
presented by American raiding parties, that were essentially for
staff officers rather than fighting officers to solve: such problems
as the climate, the lack of suitable means of transport, and the
inadequate roads. About the climate, nobody could do anything
except curse. Severe frosts could close the harbour at Quebec
and force the diversion of late-arriving convoys; heavy rains
could transform the roadways into impassable quagmires. Lack

of river boats and wagons could lead to costly delays, and the absence or nature of the roadways could impose problems of great magnitude in the movement of goods and men, as occurred in 1813 and 1814, when the 104th Regiment of Foot and a body of seamen destined for Great Lakes service were compelled to march overland, in dead of winter, from Fredericton and Saint John to Kingston in Upper Canada.[34]

Generally speaking, the vessels from England docked at Quebec or William Henry (Sorel). Trans-shipment was by schooner or by John Molson's steamboat *Swiftsure*, which was chartered by the military authorities on a voyage basis. *Swiftsure* was capable of carrying 400 men and a load of light stores, such as clothing and camp equipage, and is said to have carried a total of 8000 men during the war. Bateaux were also used between Quebec and Montreal, but were more frequently used on the upper St. Lawrence. At Montreal the stores were unpacked, moved to Lachine and placed on board river bateaux, smallish flat-bottomed craft capable of carrying from 3 t to 4½ t and, in a good wind, of covering 50 km a day. In order to surmount the Split Rock and Lachine rapids, the bateaux were unloaded and dragged upstream until the rocks were passed and the cargoes could be reloaded. Further portaging was necessary at the Long Sault and Mille Roches rapids. It was arduous, backbreaking work.

Prior to the outbreak of war, proposals had been put forward that the bateaux service be brought under military control, but it was not until October 1812 that the special Corps of Canadian Voyageurs was embodied. It was commanded by William McGillivray of the North West Company—an organization that, as we have noted, had a certain self-interest in the war. The Voyageurs did not prove particularly amenable to discipline. McGillivray's Métis son, Joseph, described them:

> They could not be got to wear socks. . . . They presented a curious contrast to the unchangeable countenances and from the well-drilled movements of the British soldiery . . . [but] from their superior knowledge of the country were able to render material service during the war.[35]

In the spring of 1813, the Canadian Voyageurs were disbanded and a new corps, the Provincial Commissariat Voyageurs, directed by two senior officers of the commissariat, Isaac Clarke and John Finlay, were organized to take the place of the Nor'Westers. The Voyageurs service was never popular, however, and in 1814 it was suggested that men should be drafted

22. *William McGillivray and family. A senior partner in the North West Company, McGillivray commanded the Corps of Canadian Voyageurs in 1812.*

from the embodied militia to man the boats on the St. Lawrence.[36]

Transportation was not all a matter of water transport, but water did possess certain advantages over land transport. It was quicker, and the craft used could carry more men and heavier weights than could horse-drawn wagons. Water transportation was seasonal, however, and roads were therefore essential for winter. The road between Quebec and Montreal was the best in the Canadas. After all, it had been in existence since before the end of the French regime. But there was, unfortunately, no continuous road above Montreal to Kingston, York and beyond. There were some sections that were satisfactory, but others were little better than trails, filled with such obstacles as tree stumps and large stones, or even swampy ground that was negotiable only when covered with a wooden corduroy surface. There was apparently a stagecoach service between Kingston and Montreal as early as 1808, but it operated only in winter, when the ground was firm. Two years later a regular courier service began. According to George Heriot, the road served for horses, but was in no way suitable for wheeled vehicles. In February 1813, the Reverend John Strachan, who had lived in Cornwall as well as Kingston and knew the country well, reported to Lieutenant Colonel Ralph Henry Bruyères, the officer commanding the Royal Engineers, that the 110 km between Cornwall and Elizabethtown (Brockville) were in "very good shape" but, of the 55 km between Elizabethtown and Kingston, 15 were "tolerable" and the remaining 40 would "require much labour".[37] "Yet the soil is good for roads," Strachan observed, "and if well cleared out in the first place, the sun and air will make the road." Perhaps he was a little too optimistic, for that section of the road had an uneven rocky base and had already absorbed several weeks' labour on the part of the Leeds militia without showing any noticeable improvement. Captain Andrew Gray of the Quartermaster General's Department believed that Penoyer's Road, between Cornwall and Montreal to north of the Front Road, would be shorter and more suitable for military purposes—a view, incidentally, that was unacceptable to the warlike cleric, who urged that efforts would be better expended in improving the Front Road between Cornwall and Coteau-du-Lac.

Regardless of the condition of the Upper-Canadian roads and, for that matter, many of the Lower-Canadian roads as well, the fact that wagons, horses and oxen were in short supply made their use for transport of limited value for military purposes. Interestingly enough, sleighs were in greater supply than wagons, but since their capacity was less than that of the normal farm wagon and they could be employed only in winter, they were not of much use to the armed services. Their main value, along with that of wagons, was to commanders requiring transport for short distances; when moving men and heavy

23. Road between Kingston and York in the condition it was in fifteen years after the war ended

supplies long distances, recourse was invariably had to sailing craft and bateaux, despite their exposure to attack by vessels operating out of the American naval station at Sackets Harbor.

What the two Canadas offered, then, by way of economic strength to oppose the invaders was an under-populated upper province with few urban centres of any significance, except perhaps Kingston, few industries, a scattered population of farmers, and a number of isolated sawmills and gristmills that almost alone were of any military significance to the Americans since they were the principal sources of flour for the British and Canadian armed forces, and a lower province of greater strength numerically but of low agricultural productivity. In brief, a country unable to meet its own needs in peacetime and dependent upon imports from Great Britain, Ireland, and the nation that now proposed to attack it. A remote and isolated country, as far as Europe was concerned, with a long, thin line of communications extending across the North Atlantic, the St. Lawrence and Lakes Ontario and Erie, with all the enormous costs that distance and various modes of transportation imposed. A country in which every kind of military and naval store, every bolt of canvas, every rope, every gun, every tent, every item required to equip the regulars and the militia had to be imported and moved by water and roads exposed to easy interception by the enemy. Not a country that would be easy to defend under the most favourable conditions; under those that did prevail, a country that seemed to justify the confident assumptions of Henry Clay and his bellicose colleagues in Washington. Or so it must have seemed, to both the Americans and the Canadians in 1812.

IN CONTEMPLATING the eventuality of another American war, British military authorities never considered any strategy other than a defensive one for British North America. In large measure, British military thinking was dictated by Great Britain's own heavy commitment in the war against Napoleon Bonaparte in Europe and the consequent inability of the War Office to detach large numbers of regular troops for any contest on the continent of North America. It was obvious that to defend the long, exposed and vulnerable frontier of British North America would require more men than the British army could, at that time, afford. In consequence, British strategy would be limited to defending the two really vital positions in North America—Quebec and Halifax. Lord Castlereagh drove this point home as early as 1807. In his secret instructions to Sir James Craig, the governor-in-chief, he stated that

> there are only two Capital Objects which could fully repay the Expence and Danger of an [American] Expedition. One, the seizure of the Town and Harbour of Halifax in Nova Scotia, which could deprive His Majesty's Fleets of the most important Naval Station in the North American Continent; the other the capture of the Fortress of Quebec, which would place them in the Sovereignty of His Majesty's Canadian Possessions.[38]

The policy of concentrating upon Halifax and Quebec, justifiable as it may have appeared to the strategic planners, led to the neglect of all other British North American fortifications, which included the works on St. Joseph Island and at Amherstburg, Niagara and York. At none of these positions was there a formidable structure, anything capable of withstanding a serious attack. Canada's so-called forts were little more than depots and barracks, with earthworks and stockades, and, in the case of the fort at York, even these were missing. The approaches to Montreal were also neglected; the defences at Île aux Noix, Saint-Jean and Chambly were all allowed to fall into a state of ruinous decay. Small wonder that Prevost, in his report to Lord Liverpool on 18 May 1812, said:

> In framing a general outline of co-operation for defence with the forces in Upper Canada, commensurate with our deficiency in strength, I have considered the preservation of Quebec as the first object, and to which all others must be subordinate. Defective as Quebec is, it is the only post that can be considered as tenable for a moment, the preservation of it being of the utmost consequence to the Canadas, as the door of entry for that force the King's Government might find it expedient to send for the recovery of both or either of these provinces, altho' the pressure of the moment in the present extended range of warfare might not allow the sending of that force which would defend both. Therefore, considering Quebec in this view, its importance can at once be appreciated.[39]

Halifax presented no problems; it could be defended by the Royal Navy, with which the United States, with its scanty naval forces, was not likely to try conclusions. That, then, left Quebec the priority location in the defence of North America.

But even if Quebec and Halifax were British North America's best-fortified positions, not even a government as remote as that in London could, with equanimity, contemplate the abandonment of Upper Canada without a blow being struck in its defence. Accordingly, when war was declared in June 1812, Prevost did take steps to protect Montreal and to maintain the line of communication between Lower and Upper Canada. Troops, supported by artillery, were dispatched at once to positions south of Montreal to hold the line between Saint-Jean and La Prairie. They were placed under the command of Major General Francis de Rottenburg, the Swiss-born hussar officer. This area, incidentally, remained throughout the whole war the principal area of concentration of the armed forces in Lower Canada. At the same time a military headquarters was estab-

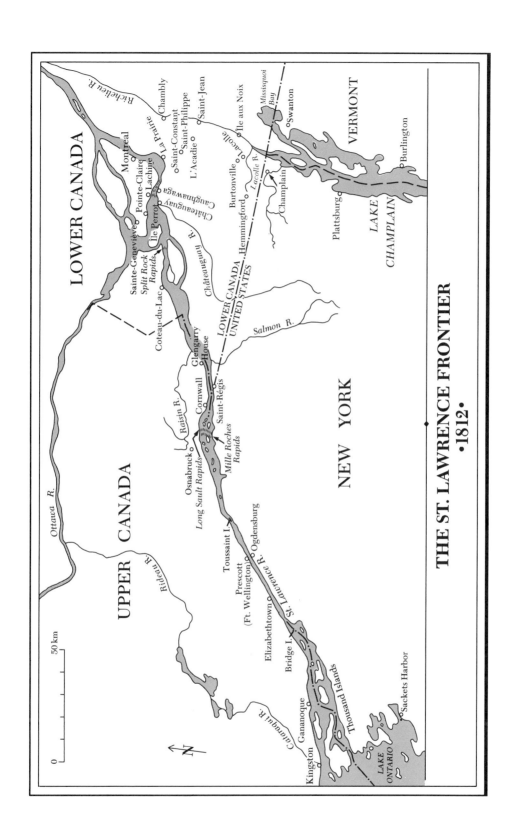

THE ST. LAWRENCE FRONTIER
•1812•

24. *Coteau-du-Lac, Lower Canada, on the St. Lawrence River near Montreal*

lished at Prescott, opposite the American town of Ogdensburg, terminus of the only direct road to the interior of New York State, and arrangements were made for the construction of a stockade and the placing of suitable guns. This was the beginning of Fort Wellington. Staging points were established along the river to provide relays for the bateaux convoys, and detachments of militia from Leeds, Grenville, Stormont and Glengarry counties were stationed at places where the river was narrow or there were rapids.

In January 1813, Lieutenant Colonel Bruyères visited some of these militia posts. Coteau-du-Lac he considered "a most essential and important position", which needed a blockhouse. The Raisin River region was defended by 100 men of the Glengarrians in "a very slight and miserable barracks", with other detachments at Glengarry House, directly opposite the mouth of the Salmon River. Both were positions badly in need of strengthening. Cornwall was occupied by 150 men of the Stormont militia, who were "very miserably accommodated" in the courthouse, "which causes discontent and some have deserted".[40] In some instances, militia detachments occupied newly constructed blockhouses, such as the one at Osnabruck,

20 km above Cornwall, which had been built in a rough manner by the militia who occupied it and which needed an abatis. Other blockhouses were constructed at points farther up the river, including "Little Gibraltar" on Bridge Island (Chimney Island) in the Thousand Islands. Additional protection was afforded the St. Lawrence by stationing several gunboats at Prescott and Kingston. Kingston itself was protected by a temporary structure on Point Henry and by five blockhouses encircling the town and harbour. Batteries were also placed on Point Frederick, Murney Point and Snake Island, comprising mortars, howitzers, guns and carronades. In 1813 some fifty pieces of ordnance guarded the terminus of the St. Lawrence line, manned by 127 gunners.[41] Although communication was generally by boat, dispatches could be sent by road by means of small detachments of dragoons stationed at staging points along the Front Road.

All of these initial measures were purely defensive in character, in accordance with the instructions received from London. But Isaac Brock did not have the kind of temperament to remain inactive while on the defensive. Although admitting the strategic importance of Quebec, he could not help but think of the political and military dividends that would accrue to Upper Canada should a successful thrust be made across the American frontier. After all, the initial response from the Loyalist regions of the province, the Niagara peninsula and the Scottish counties along the St. Lawrence above Montreal had been good. In those areas the militia had turned out in satisfactory numbers, and, despite the shortage of military equipment, even of muskets, militiamen were anxious to strike a blow at the Yankees. They had little in the way of training and even less in fighting experience, but they were products of a rural economy and knew how to handle small arms, and some were former soldiers. Brock, however, kept them in hand, if only because he was himself restrained by the cautious Prevost. But he let Rolette and Roberts slip the leash, the one to seize *Cuyahoga* on her way to Detroit, and the other to capture Michilimackinac, much to the delight of the Indians and the fur traders. There was no doubt that Prevost was not displeased by the news of these minor actions, but he did not modify the instructions he sent to Brock on 10 July:

> Our numbers would not justify offensive operations being undertaken, unless they were solely calculated to strengthen a defensive attitude—I consider it prudent and politic to avoid any measure

which can in its effect have a tendency to unite the people in the American States. Whilst dissension prevails among them, their attempts on these Provinces will be feeble; it is therefore our duty carefully to avoid committing any act which may, even by construction, tend to unite the Eastern and Southern States, unless by its perpetration we are to derive a considerable and important advantage.[42]

In August, Brock gained that "considerable and important advantage" by a daring offensive action that gave an unexpected twist to the whole war.

1812

4

The Detroit Frontier

WHILE THE QUESTION of war was still being debated in the United States, Major General Henry Dearborn set out for Albany, to establish his headquarters in the vicinity. It was a good, central location, with roads leading north along Lake Champlain to the Lower-Canadian frontier and Montreal, and west towards Sackets Harbor and Buffalo. Dearborn's task was to draft a scheme of operations and to organize the troops that would constitute his Northern Army. As far as the operations plan was concerned, he produced something simple and uncomplicated, reflecting the character of the man himself. The main line of advance of the Northern Army would be, as Craig and Prevost had foreseen, along the traditional invasion route used by Amherst in 1758 and 1759, and by Richard Montgomery in 1775, with Montreal as the ultimate objective. Three other corps would enter Canada at the same time from other directions, by way of Detroit, the Niagara region and Sackets Harbor. The Detroit movement would, if successful, deter the Indians from supporting the British and force the latter to abandon western Upper Canada or find themselves isolated and left to fight alone in the western wilderness. The Niagara and Sackets Harbor attacks would serve to tie down the bulk of General Brock's army or force it to retire; in any case, it would be cut off from the lower St. Lawrence by the capture of Montreal. With Upper Canada and Montreal both under American control, there would be time and opportunity for a descent of the river and a reversal of the decision that had cost Montgomery his life in 1775. A couple of smashing victories were all that was needed.

Dearborn had still another important responsibility, to make arrangements for the defence of the coastline of New England. For this task, he intended to use the militias of the several New England states, though New England was the part of the country that had been most outspoken in its opposition to the war with Great Britain. Nevertheless, Dearborn set out for Boston. Here he learned, to his distress and annoyance, that he was not going to receive the kind of cooperation he had hoped for, from either Massachusetts or Connecticut. Madison had expected as much and had taken counsel with his legal advisers. They had told him that he could summon any militia for active duty, either through the state governors or on his own authority as president of the United States. A law of 1795 gave him the power to do so whenever the United States was in "imminent danger of invasion". Accordingly, on 12 June, Madison formally requested the New England governors to provide Dearborn with the men he required for the defence of the sea coast. At first there was no reply. Then it came. Neither the President nor the Major General had produced evidence to the effect that the United States was in "imminent danger of invasion". War did not necessarily imply, nor did the fact that there were British ships of war cruising off the coast mean, that the country was in imminent danger. Replies such as these may have constituted what Madison thought they were, seditious sophistry, but they left no doubt in Dearborn's mind that neither Caleb Strong of Massachusetts nor Roger Griswold of Connecticut was going to provide him with any troops; and the Rhode Islanders were clearly disposed to follow the example of the two larger New England states. In fact, all New Englanders shared the view expressed by the editor of the *Connecticut Courant* when he urged state militiamen to rally to their state governments, "to which they are indebted for not being . . . dragged out of the state to fight Indians, or die before the walls of Quebec".[1] Both Dearborn and Madison knew what this near-rebellion would mean to their military plans, and Madison wrote to Jefferson complaining that the intrigues of the New Englanders had "so clogged the wheels of the war" that he feared "the campaign will not accomplish the object of it." Their opposition was particularly unfortunate because enlistments were not going well with the regulars or the volunteers, leaving the United States "dependent for every primary operation on militia, either as volunteers or draughts for six months".[2]

25. "First Major General" Henry Dearborn

Late in July, Dearborn returned to his Albany headquarters. Here he experienced another shock. Not only had he failed to find the troops he wanted to man the coastal defences, but at Albany he found that he had no more than 1200 men available to carry out his grandiose scheme of capturing Montreal. Volunteers were not offering themselves at a rate that would build up his force to the numbers required to proceed with the plans prepared earlier. Nor were sufficient armaments available to achieve the purpose for which the men were being raised. If Dearborn were ever to take Montreal, he would require a lot more men than were already enrolled, and the longer he delayed in advancing towards Canada, the more British and Canadian troops the Americans would face in their advance into Upper Canada from Detroit and the Niagara area.

Then came a further reason for delay. It took the form of a communication from Sir George Prevost. Perhaps the American government would accept the British repeal of the offensive Orders in Council as justification for resuming talks with

Great Britain. This had been the tenor of a dispatch that Prevost had received from London; as anxious for a peaceful settlement as his political chiefs, Prevost approached Dearborn to suggest an armistice while the politicians got together for talks. Dearborn, like Prevost, was ready to turn the fighting over to the politicians, and so he welcomed the suggestion of an armistice. But Madison, having opened hostilities, was not anxious to halt them and start another fruitless round of talks. At his request therefore the secretary of war, Dr. William Eustis, wrote in haste to Dearborn to the effect that the President found nothing in the British message to warrant any relaxation in the American war effort, that he was anxious for the Commanding General to "proceed with the utmost vigor in his operations" and to lose not a moment in "gaining possession of the British posts at Niagara and Kingston, or at least the former".[3]

Dearborn dragged his heels, however. Any time he could gain that was free of hostile enemy action would help him get needed supplies to the Niagara frontier and Sackets Harbor. In any event, he was still determined to proceed with his original plan. He would put together an army of 5000 to 6000 regulars and militia and "push towards Montreal at the same time that our troops on the western frontier of this state strike at Upper Canada".[4] The truce therefore continued until 29 August. It had served Prevost's purpose as well as Dearborn's, although Prevost had no need to prolong it. He had gained the information he required in the first few days. When Prevost sent his adjutant, Colonel Edward Baynes, to see Dearborn, Baynes kept his eyes open. In fact, he could not have helped seeing all he did, since he was given a guided tour of the American positions. On his return Baynes reported that the Americans had 430 untrained militia at Plattsburg, 225 regulars and about 40 militia at Burlington, 400 Vermont militia at Swanton, and 600 regulars at Albany, in all between 1700 and 2000 men[5]—still a far cry from the 6000 Dearborn deemed necessary for an offensive against Montreal. But Baynes saw what Madison and Eustis failed to see—Dearborn's lack of energy and any appreciation of the realities of the military situation.

During the weeks following the termination of the armistice, small detachments of Americans showed an initiative that had not yet spilled over onto the headquarters of the Northern Army. In September a group of American riflemen and militia carried out a surprise raid from Sackets Harbor under the command of Captain Benjamin Forsyth, making their way down the St. Lawrence among the Thousand Islands and landing at Gananoque, about 30 km below Kingston. It was the last convoy staging-point on the St. Lawrence line of communication between Montreal and the Upper-Canadian naval base. The militia defenders fired a volley and then decamped, leaving the raiders free to seize some sixty muskets with ammunition and to burn a small storehouse containing flour and beef. A few days later another group of Americans, with a gunboat and a Durham boat, this time from Ogdensburg, endeavoured to intercept a British convoy moving up the St. Lawrence protected by a military escort commanded by Lieutenant James FitzGibbon of the 49th Regiment. Owing to the timely warning given by a man who slipped away from Toussaint Island when the Americans landed there, the militia rallied, and in a sharp exchange of shots the Americans came off second best. They lost their Durham boat and several men, and barely managed to escape with their gunboat. The British also suffered several casualties, but their bateaux succeeded in moving out of range, reaching Kingston without further molestation. A month later, on 21 October, 200 American soldiers from Brigadier General Joseph Bloomfield's command at Troy attacked the Indian village of Saint-Régis, located on the boundary line between Upper Canada and New York state, near Cornwall. They surprised the picket, killed several of the defenders and took the remainder prisoner. They also captured a British flag, which was subsequently presented to the people of New York in a ceremony at Albany; it was the sole trophy captured by any member of Dearborn's army in 1812.

Finally, the lethargic Dearborn was stirred into action. He had, over the months, succeeded in making the Northern Army the largest of the armies operating against Canada in 1812, but he had never led it into action and it was getting late in the season. He still seemed mesmerized by the idea of two or more armies operating simultaneously, and, while waiting at Albany, had seen both Hull and Van Rensselaer go down to defeat without securing a foothold in Canada. His last hope now was to launch his attack while Brigadier General Alexander Smyth at Buffalo was crossing the Niagara above the Falls. On 8 November, Dearborn wrote Eustis to tell him that the Albany section of the army was at last moving north to join Brigadier General Bloomfield at Plattsburg, but that Bloomfield would have to take command owing to Dearborn's rheumatism. Thus, Bloomfield was to have the honour as well as the responsibility

26. *Private of the Provincial Corps of Light Infantry (Voltigeurs),*
1812–13

of carrying Montreal and holding it during the winter of
1812–13. But Bloomfield proved to be in even poorer health
than Dearborn, and so, rheumatism and all, Dearborn was compelled to carry out the strategy he had devised.

The fact that the Americans were on the move was not
unknown to Major Charles-Michel d'Irumberry de Salaberry
of the Voltigeurs, who commanded the cordon of posts just north
of the frontier from his headquarters at Saint-Philippe (-de-
Laprairie). As soon as the news was confirmed, Salaberry sent

two companies of Voltigeurs under Captain Joseph-François Perrault, together with 300 Indians under Captain Dominique Ducharme of the Indian Department, to reinforce the men of the 1st Battalion Embodied Militia posted at Lacolle. After a fatiguing march over heavy, swampy ground, they arrived early in the afternoon of the same day at Burtonville. Here they took up a defensive position about a mile from the Lacolle River. With them were a few Algonquins and Abenakis and a few Voyageurs under Captain William McKay of the North West Company. Salaberry himself arrived later with the remainder of the Voltigeurs and members of the Voyageurs Corps under Lieutenant Colonel William McGillivray and with volunteer Chasseurs from Châteauguay, Saint-Constant, Saint-Philippe and L'Acadie.

The Americans moved into Champlain on 19 November, and there they halted. The Canadians were expecting a determined assault, but nothing happened, at least not for some time. Then, in the early hours of 20 November, the American force started across the river. It was still dark when the Indians and the militia began firing their flintlocks, but some of the Americans who had succeeded in getting across the river mistook each other for Canadians in the morning mist, with the result that they killed several of their number and wounded others before discovering the error. They had had enough. The Americans retired to Champlain, and Dearborn made his way back to Plattsburg as quietly as possible, haunted by the memory of the ignominious retreat of 1776. His invasion of Canada was never anything more than a reconnaissance in force, and even as that it was a failure. It had occupied several days but had got nowhere near Montreal. In a spirit of dismay mingled with disgust, Dearborn confessed to the Secretary of War:

> I had anticipated disappointment and misfortune in the commencement of the war, but I did by no means apprehend such a deficiency of regular troops and such a series of disasters as we have witnessed.[6]

He wrote to Madison at the same time, suggesting that he be permitted "to retire to the shades of private life, and remain a mere interested spectator of passing events".[7] Had Madison not held Dearborn in high personal regard, he would have accepted the proposed resignation at once, perhaps even adding that Dearborn had done little else than act as an "interested spectator".

27. Brigadier General William Hull, who surrendered Detroit on 16 August 1812

SEVERAL MONTHS elapsed after Dearborn's appointment as senior major general before he fully appreciated the fact that his command included the Niagara and Sackets Harbor fronts as well as the Lake Champlain–Lower Canada front.[8] There was never any doubt in his or any other officer's mind, however, that the Detroit front and command of the North Western Army were solely the responsibility of William Hull. Hull was on his own, being responsible only to the secretary of war and, in some obscure fashion, to Return J. Meigs, the governor of Ohio. Three of the regiments making up Hull's force were provided by Meigs from the state militia and were officered by men holding their commissions from Ohio, notably Duncan Mc-

Arthur, James Findlay and Lewis Cass. Each of these men carried the state rank of colonel, and therefore outranked the regular officer, Lieutenant Colonel James Miller of the 4th Regiment of Infantry, an unfortunate situation that made it difficult for Hull to delegate any authority over the Ohio regiments to Miller. When Hull referred the question to Eustis for an opinion, the good doctor replied simply, "No doubt is entertained that your military experience will enable you to preserve harmony between the regulars and the militia."[9] The question of rank continued to rankle, however, and the relationship between the regulars and the state militia composing Hull's army was not improved when Hull had to call upon Miller's men to suppress an incipient mutiny in Dayton before setting out for Fort Detroit. "By G——d, Sir," said Hull to Miller, "your regiment is a powerful argument. Without it I could not march those volunteers to Detroit."[10]

March they did, through the rain, their long pack-train and cattle herd struggling over the muddy roads,[11] to the Shawnee village, Solomon's Town, to Fort McArthur on the Scioto River, and on to Fort Findlay, where on 26 June General Hull received the message from Eustis urging him to press on with all possible speed to Detroit, but with no definite word that war had been or was going to be declared. In accordance with his instructions, Hull struggled on, past Fort Portage and through the Black Swamp, finally pitching his camp near Wayne's old battlefield at Fallen Timbers. From there on the terrain was easier and the going less difficult for the wagons and the horses. At Frenchtown (Monroe), on the River Raisin, Hull encountered Cyrenius Chapin and arranged with him for the use of his schooner *Cuyahoga* to carry the sick, the bandsmen, the officers' baggage and the General's papers. Once relieved of this impedimenta, it would be much easier for the army to make speed to Detroit. There was still no news of war, and morale was low. One of the men taking part, J. H. Campbell, wrote to his friend, Thomas Worthington:

> Congress has received 10,000 curses from the volunteers for one provision in the law calling for volunteers, viz., allowing 160 acres of land to those soldiers who fall in battle. . . . Says the soldier, "Who the devil would turn out to get himself killed for 160 acres of land." Many wished every member of Congress had 160 acres of land stuffed up his —— instead of receiving $6 per day.[12]

Then, on 2 July, Hull finally learned that the country was at war. Unfortunately for him, that was the day the enterpris-

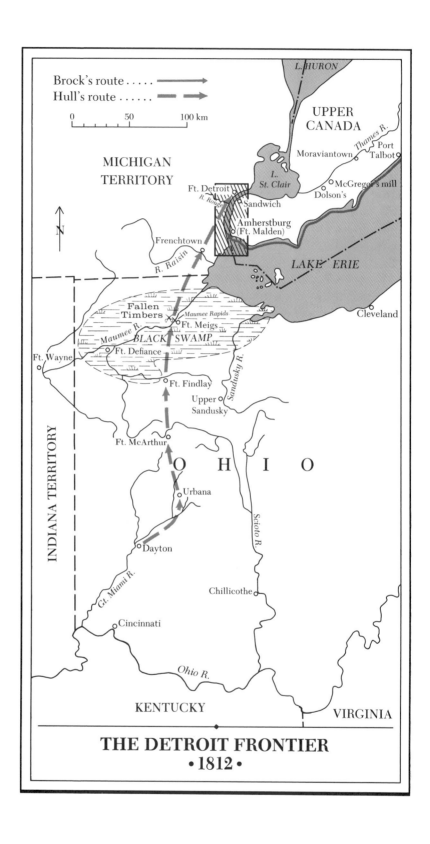

0   50   100 km

L. HURON

UPPER
CANADA

MICHIGAN
TERRITORY

Moraviantown   Port
                    Talbot
Thames R.

McGregor's mill

Ft. Detroit
R. Rouge   Sandwich
                    Dolson's

L.
St. Clair

N

Amherstburg
(Ft. Malden)

LAKE ERIE

Frenchtown

R. Raisin

Cleveland

Fallen
Timbers   Maumee Rapids
            Ft. Meigs
Maumee R.   BLACK SWAMP
Ft. Wayne

Ft. Defiance

Sandusky R.

Ft. Findlay

Upper
Sandusky

Ft. McArthur

O   H   I   O

INDIANA TERRITORY

Urbana

Dayton

Scioto R.

Chillicothe

Gt. Miami R.

Cincinnati

Ohio R.

KENTUCKY

VIRGINIA

THE DETROIT FRONTIER
•1812•

ing Rolette seized the *Cuyahoga*. For the moment there was nothing Hull could do but hurry onward as quickly as possible, expecting every moment to be attacked by the Indians. Finally, on 5 July, he arrived at his destination. Once there, whether hopeful or merely naive, he sent a flag of truce to Fort Malden asking for an exchange of prisoners and the return of the captured baggage. The British commander, Lieutenant Colonel Thomas St. George, blindfolded Hull's envoy before allowing him into the fort, listened to his request, and sent him away empty-handed.

For several days Hull and his men rested in Detroit. The fort, built during the Revolutionary War, was located on a slight rise of land, about 230 m from the river. It was a quadrangular structure, with corner bastions and barracks within the walls, occupying nearly a hectare of land. It was equipped with over forty pieces of brass or iron ordnance in various calibres and amply stocked with ammunition. About 90 men were in garrison when Hull arrived. These men were made available to Hull, together with detachments of Michigan militia posted at the River Raisin and in other parts of Michigan Territory. All told, Hull's force numbered something over 2000. In front of the fort was the town, a small settlement established by the Canadian French in 1701, with a population largely descended from the original French settlers. In 1812 it contained about 150 buildings and probably 800 people. It was surrounded by a picket fence, 4 m high, with loopholes for small arms.[13] In the dry dock on the River Rouge was *Adams*, a naval vessel mounting fourteen guns but at that time undergoing repairs and therefore never a factor in Hull's operations.

The day after arriving at Detroit, Hull held a council with the local Indians, urging them to observe strict neutrality. On the ninth he held a council with his field officers. Examining the supply situation, he not unexpectedly discovered that there were shortages of flour and meat but more than adequate supplies of whisky and soap. (If cleanliness is next to godliness, the garrison at Detroit must have been godly men, indeed, if not exactly sober.) Then Hull read to his officers the latest orders from Eustis. They were to the effect that,

> Should the force under your Command be equal to the Enterprize, consistent with the Safety of your own post, you will take possession of Malden and extend your conquests as circumstances may justify.[14]

93

28. A view of the Detroit waterfront from the direction that Brock approached the fort after landing his force near the River Rouge

At the same time, however, Eustis reminded Hull that "an adequate force cannot soon be relied on for the Reduction of the Enemies forces below you." This meant simply that the Niagara offensive and Dearborn's operations were not proceeding with the hoped-for celerity and that Hull need expect no help from those quarters. But the fact that the western army was on its own did not worry Cass and McArthur; those fire-eaters were anxious for action. Writing to a friend while still at Dayton, Cass expressed the view that Hull was "not our man. . . . He is indecisive and irresolute, leaning for support upon persons around him."[15] McArthur felt the same way, saying in a private letter, "I have every reason to believe that fifty men would have taken possession of the town and country around it, without the loss of a man", if only Hull had acted immediately.[16]

There was a great deal in what McArthur and Cass said. Like Hull, they knew that the western regions of Upper Canada contained a high percentage of Americans who might be inclined to look with sympathy upon the presence of American troops; and Hull must have suspected, if he did not know, that Lieutenant Colonel St. George's force at Fort Malden could not have numbered many more than 300 regulars and what militia could be persuaded to join them. Therefore, the Americans had good reason for crossing the Detroit River to Sandwich and establishing a base on Canadian soil. Not only would the psychological impact be considerable, but the stores at Fort Malden would be a welcome addition to their own, and, with guns on both sides of the river, Hull could interdict the passage of armed vessels from either Lake Erie or Lake Huron.

Still, it was Hull's nature to be cautious. His reply to Eustis warned the Secretary of War, "I do not think the force here equal to the reduction of Amherstburg—You therefore must not be too sanguine."[17] And so he went ahead with his plans at his own pace. In his hands was a list of 108 pro-American Canadians living in western Upper Canada upon whom he could rely for help against their adopted country. That is why he prepared a proclamation to be circulated to Canadian residents as soon as the American army should set foot on Canadian soil. It was a bombastic document, reflecting the flamboyant style and personality of Lewis Cass rather than the pedantic prose and cautious approach of William Hull. The proclamation[18] called upon the people of Upper Canada to exchange British "tyranny and oppression" for the blessings of American liberty, promised full protection for life and property, and invited Canadian participation in the invasion if the people were so inclined. That Hull was directing his appeal to a population he believed to be sympathetic to the United States is clear from the references to independence and liberty, to the historic fact that "many of your fathers fought for the freedom and independence we now enjoy", to the strength of family ties with the United States, and to a common heritage. Because they were Americans, the people of Upper Canada should hail the arrival "of an army of friends". The proclamation continued, "You will be emancipated from tyranny and oppression" and "restored to the dignified station of freemen." But it contained an ominous warning too. Unquestionably there would be a few Loyalist Tories in the province, men stubbornly determined not to consult their own best interests. They would have to take the consequences of their ill will: "You will be considered and treated as enemies and the horrors and calamities of war will stalk before you." That was letting them off easy. For those who had the temerity to join the Indians, "The first stroke of the tomahawk" would be "the signal for one indiscriminate scene of desolation". The following words were underlined in the original manuscript: "No white man found fighting by the side of an Indian will be taken prisoner." The choice, then, was to accept the Americans and enjoy "peace, liberty and security", or reject them and suffer "war, slavery and destruction".

The date set for the actual landing on Canadian soil was 10 July. But the rumour of an Indian attack on Detroit, which produced consternation, confusion, and a certain amount of indiscriminate shooting resulting in the wounding of one of the American officers, forced a delay of one day. On the eleventh, there was another delay, this time because some of the Ohio men refused to cross the river; they were, after all, militia and not required to serve outside the United States. But it was not just a constitutional matter. Some of the reluctant dragons were British deserters; they knew what would happen to them should they be taken prisoner by the British. Finally, after appeals and excuses from duty, on 12 July, under cover of gunners standing by with lighted matches ready to set down a barrage, the first wave of American troops crossed the Detroit River in small boats. Others followed. But there was no opposition. Nobody made any effort to stop them from landing or forming up their regiments or beginning a slow, cautious advance towards Sandwich. Even in the village there were no shots, no shouts, no opposition. Hull had set foot in Canada unopposed, and the Americans were now in possesion of their first conquest in Upper Canada. A camp was set up on the old Indian reserve, and Hull moved into Colonel James (Jacques) Baby's red brick house, in front of which he hoisted an American flag.[19] Some of the soldiers took copies of the proclamation and set out to find Canadians who might be interested in them. Captain James Sloan's light cavalry also took copies with them when they set out to seize provisions in the region of the Thames River. By 14 July, the Americans had erected breastworks around their camp and assumed a defensive posture, ready to resist any attack by Lieutenant Colonel St. George and his Fort Malden garrison. American foraging parties extended their activities as far as McGregor's mill and Dolson's on the Thames River and secured much-needed supplies of flour to replenish the rapidly diminishing stocks in Detroit. What was still more significant, their progress had persuaded a small number of pro-American settlers—"traitors", loyal Canadians not unfairly called them—to come to Hull's camp to offer their services to the American general. They were Ebenezer Allan, Andrew Westbrook and Simon Zelotes Watson, all of whom were to play important, if nefarious, roles in the events of the next three years. Watson,

29. Colonel James (Jacques) Baby, who commanded the militia in the Western District during the war

at this time, undertook to raise a so-called "Canadian" cavalry unit and to distribute Hull's proclamation in the townships of Delaware and Westminster in western Upper Canada. Even the Indians were influenced by Hull's threatening words and met in council at Brownstown to consider suggestions of neutrality. Most of the tribes represented at Amherstburg were present, but Tecumseh was conspicuous by his absence. Under such circumstances, Hull wrote in an optimistic vein to Eustis on 19 July, more sanguine than he had been since his initial appointment to command. These July days were, indeed, the high point of his military career in 1812.

SETTLEMENT was not as far advanced on the Canadian side of the Detroit River as in the territory belonging to the United States. The original French community dated from 1747, but not until the treaty following the American Revolutionary War drew the boundary line down the middle of the river in 1783 did the Canadian community assume a separate identity. Admittedly, British troops remained in Detroit for a few more years, but plans went ahead for the establishment of two towns and a fort on the Canadian side of the river. When, under the terms of Jay's Treaty, the British marched out of Detroit, they had only to cross the river; there, during 1796 and 1797, work went ahead on a quadrangular fort, complete with bastions, and on a townsite known as Amherstburg, opposite Bois Blanc Island. Several miles to the north, another town was established along the river, opposite and south of the American post at Detroit, and given the name of Sandwich. Of the two Canadian communities, Amherstburg was, and remained for some years, the larger and more significant location, owing to the presence of the fort and the military garrison.[20]

The soldiers who garrisoned Fort Malden at Amherstburg were members of the 41st Regiment of Foot. After service in Ireland and the West Indies, the regiment had come to Canada in 1799, where its companies were scattered among several Upper-Canadian posts. The strength of the Fort Malden garrison was no more than 300 men. The officer commanding the troops was Captain Adam Muir, and the commandant of the post was Lieutenant Colonel Thomas St. George of the 63rd. In addition to the regulars and an indeterminate number of militia, St. George had some 400 Indians as well as the officers and men of the Provincial Marine, whose vessels on Lake Erie— the sloop *Queen Charlotte*, the brig *General Hunter* and the schooner *Lady Prevost*—were based on Amherstburg. Several privately owned vessels were also located there, including the North West Company vessels *Nancy* and *Caledonia* and three small craft of little note, *Eleanor*, *Thames* and *Dover*.

As soon as Hull had settled comfortably in Detroit, St. George concentrated all his available men at Amherstburg. He realized that it would be an error to disperse his forces by trying to defend the whole of the Detroit River line. In any event, what

30. *Amherstburg and Fort Malden in 1813, with General Henry Procter and Tecumseh in the left and right foreground. The vessels are the* Queen Charlotte *in the channel and* General Hunter *in the background.*

he would have to defend would be his communications along Lake Erie to Turkey Point. From there to the head of Lake Ontario was an easy march or ride. Thus, both Fort George and York could be reached by way of Lake Erie. That is why St. George ignored the line of the Detroit and Thames rivers, and why he left Sandwich unprotected, making no attempt to halt Hull's invasion at the water's edge on 12 July. He believed it would be sufficient to keep a close watch on Hull's activities, and for that purpose sent a small roving picket to the vicinity of the bridge over the Canard River. On 16 July a probing attack by Cass outflanked the British picket, which fired several volleys and withdrew, except for two sentinels, one of whom was killed and the other taken prisoner. Cass would have liked to push on to Fort Malden, but he was brought up short by Hull with a reminder that the Canard River was some 20 km from Sandwich, the base camp, and thus not readily reinforceable should the British decide to take aggressive action against him. This was not the kind of support Cass wanted from Hull, but the commanding general was right. St. George did reinforce

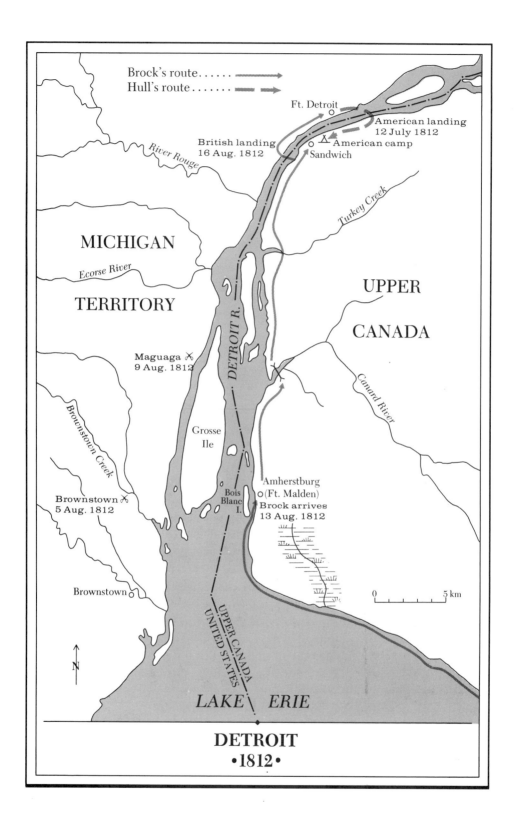

Brock's route...... →
Hull's route....... ⇢

Ft. Detroit

American landing
12 July 1812

British landing
16 Aug. 1812

American camp

River Rouge

Sandwich

Turkey Creek

MICHIGAN

Ecorse River

TERRITORY

UPPER

CANADA

DETROIT R.

Maguaga ⚔
9 Aug. 1812

Canard River

Grosse
Ile

Brownstown Creek

Bois
Blanc
I.

Amherstburg
(Ft. Malden)
Brock arrives
13 Aug. 1812

Brownstown ⚔
5 Aug. 1812

Brownstown ○

UPPER CANADA
UNITED STATES

0   5 km

N

LAKE ERIE

DETROIT
•1812•

his position with regulars and Indians, forcing both Cass and McArthur to withdraw, but not before Cass, against Hull's orders and McArthur's judgement, brought up some of his men and a gun to fire a few useless shots at the British. It was a pointless protest and a rather childish gesture of defiance. Several days later, on 24 July, a small party of Menomini Indians from Green Bay ambushed a party of Americans from Sandwich who had planned to prepare their own ambush not far from the Canard River bridge.

Meanwhile, Hull was becoming concerned about his lack of supplies, and on 21 July recrossed the Detroit River, leaving McArthur in charge at Sandwich. He was still worried about the Indians. Hoping to win their neutrality if not their friendship, he had planned to hold a council, but lacked the necessary provisions to feed them. Perhaps he should wait until the corn crop had been harvested, when there would be plenty to eat. Meanwhile, supplies were on the way to Detroit from Urbana—300 cattle and 70 pack horses, each of the latter carrying 90 kg of flour. These provisions had been provided by his good friend, Governor Meigs, and were in charge of a local attorney from Chillicothe, Captain Henry Brush. It was now early August, and Brush could be no farther away than the River Raisin, a distance of about 60 km. Brush knew that Hull badly needed the provisions he was transporting, but he also knew that the Indians from the British side were watching every road leading into Detroit. He therefore sent word to Hull asking for men to strengthen his escort to enable him to bring the supplies safely through the danger zone. Accordingly, on 4 August, Hull ordered Major Thomas Van Horne, an Ohio militia officer, to return from Sandwich, gave him a few mounted men and 150 Ohio militia, and sent him to join Brush.

What was apparently not known to Brush or Van Horne was that the Indians, having already intercepted messengers from Hull, were quite well aware of everything that was going on. When they brought word to the newly appointed commander at Fort Malden, Colonel Henry Procter, that a convoy of provisions was *en route* to Detroit, he ordered Captain Muir, with 100 men of the 41st, a few militia, and a handful of Indians under Tecumseh, to cross the river and intercept Van Horne's party. Muir's men prepared an ambush as soon as they landed, and waited. As Van Horne moved to the ford over Brownstown Creek, the Indians—24 of them, accompanied by Matthew Elliott's son Alexander, who was dressed as an Indian—opened fire. According to one of the British volunteers who formed part of the Fort Malden garrison, Van Horne had thrown out no skirmishers, nor had he detailed an advance guard to give warning to his main body. When the shooting started, Van Horne's mounted men wheeled about and never stopped galloping until they were back in Detroit. The infantry had no choice but to seek refuge in the woods, all, that is, except the 17 dead and the 2 men who were taken prisoner and tomahawked by the Indians to revenge the death of Chief Logan, the only Indian killed in the engagement. What was important to the British was not only the dispersal of Van Horne's relief column but also the capture of the mail from Detroit, which the fleeing escort abandoned and Tecumseh handed over to the British authorities. By the time Procter had finished reading the complaints, criticisms and personal details contained in the letters, he knew more about the conditions prevailing in Hull's army, and its morale, than did the General himself.

Had the Hull of Detroit been the young man who led the bayonet charge at Stony Point on the Hudson during the Revolutionary War, he would have taken immediate revenge by attacking Amherstburg; indeed, he did think briefly along these lines, but only briefly. Instead, he began to wonder about pulling out of Canadian territory altogether. Perhaps he should concentrate upon opening and strengthening his line of communication with Brush, not only because he needed Brush's provisions but also because he needed a secure line of retreat, should retreat become necessary. Therefore, on the night of the seventh and the morning of the eighth of August, on Hull's orders, the humiliated American troops made their way back across the Detroit River. They had been in Canada for thirty days and had done nothing but distribute copies of Hull's proclamation.

It was not just the drubbing that the Indians had given Van Horne at Brownstown on 5 August that discouraged Hull. It was the news that the British had captured Michilimackinac without firing a shot and that reinforcements were on the way to Amherstburg from the Niagara region. Meanwhile, there was still the matter of those provisions. What was he going to do about them? Would not the Indians be waiting for the dispatch of another relief column? There was really no question about it; the provisions would have to be brought to Detroit, and by Miller's regulars rather than by the Ohio militia.

On the morning of Saturday, 9 August, Indian scouts reported to the British troops still on the American side of the river that a strong column of cavalry and infantry had moved out of

Detroit. Muir did not have time to send for cannon from Fort Malden. He would have to hurry if he was to prepare an ambush. The site chosen was near the small Indian village of Maguaga (Monguagon in American accounts of the war), about 5 km distant. Young John Richardson, who was present as a volunteer, wrote the following description:

> The road along which we advanced was ankle-deep with mud, and the dark forest waving its close branches over our heads left no egress to the pestilential exhalations arising from the naked and putrid bodies of horses and men killed of Major Horne's detachment, which had been suffered to lie unburied beneath our feet.[21]

With Muir were a number of Indians in full war-paint. Everything was done in silence. No noise came from the moccasins of the Indians, and heavy grass deadened the sound of the soldiers' boots. When the ambush site was selected, Muir's men followed the example of the Indians and threw themselves down on the ground to wait. Then, just before the Americans put in an appearance, Muir was joined by a detachment of grenadiers and light infantry of the 41st, just arrived from the Niagara frontier and none too familiar with Indian tactics. Suddenly there was a shot. The Americans had arrived, but this time they had been expecting an encounter and, shedding their knapsacks, they formed a line of battle. Glancing to their right, the newly arrived British troops saw moving figures, and, believing them to be Americans attempting to outflank the British position, opened a hot fire—into a group of their own Indians who had become detached from the main body in the woods. The Indians returned the fire with equal spirit. In the confusion of fighting in conditions unfamiliar to men accustomed to stand-up volleys, order and discipline began to disappear among the British regular soldiers, and the superior numbers of the enemy began to tell. When the recently arrived reinforcements began to withdraw, Muir's now thoroughly confused men followed, as Richardson put it, "at the double quick, yet without being followed by the enemy, who suffered us to gain our boats without any further molestation".[22] Thomas Verchères de Boucherville, who was wounded, spent the night hiding in the grass but managed to escape the next day by means of a raft. Unwilling to go back into the woods for their knapsacks, the Americans spent the night in a cleared area, in the pelting rain, and remained there until they were joined by McArthur the following day. Then the combined forces of Miller's regulars and Cass's militia, although they ought to and probably could have pushed on to the River Raisin, followed the orders of their now nervous and apprehensive general and returned to Detroit.

The Americans, whose losses totalled 18 killed and 64 wounded as against a British loss, as reported by Procter, of 6 killed and 21 wounded, had accomplished nothing. They had failed in their basic purpose. They had put a dent in the British–Indian blockade of Detroit, but they had not broken it. Hull obviously would have to have assistance, or he would have to move his whole force out of Detroit if he were to survive. More than ever it seemed unlikely that he would be able to remain in Detroit. And this only a month after he had landed his troops, without opposition, on the soil of Upper Canada.

During this time General Brock had been busy at Fort George, unable to free himself from the red tape of governmental matters and arrangements for calling out the militia. There was also the legislature to meet, and Hull's proclamation to answer, neither of which he could afford to ignore. Above all, he would have to show a determined countenance to the people of Upper Canada as well as to the American public. In the document Brock prepared at York will be found the usual patriotic phrases, as fitting in our own day as they were in his—reference to the "unprovoked declaration of war" by the enemy, the rejection of "slavery" by all British peoples, the "liberality of the government", and the "loyalty" of Canadians to the Crown.[23] But Brock added a few more sentences, more apt then than now, images of a conquered Canada being turned over to Napoleon Bonaparte by the United States as "the stipulated reward for the aid offered to the revolted colonies, now the United States". He also addressed some of his remarks to the Indians, reminding them of Hull's threats and assuring them that they had "equal rights with all other men to defend themselves and their property when invaded, more especially when they find in the enemy's camp a ferocious and mortal foe using the same kind of warfare which the American commander affects to reprobate". Finally, Brock recalled to each Canadian freeholder that he was, by deliberate choice, "bound by the most solemn oaths to defend the monarchy as well as his own property". He continued, "To shrink from that engagement is a treason not to be forgiven." Perhaps the shrewdest point of all was the reference to Napoleon, who aroused in Anglo-Canadians as well as Englishmen the greatest depths of distrust, fear and even hatred of any man in the nineteenth century. British memories went back beyond the American Revolution, even, to the century-long struggle between France and Great Britain over the fate of North America. In peacetime, appeals to patriotism in high-flown terms generally arouse little positive response, but to the people of that day Brock's words sounded dignified and manly, and to the Loyalists and their descendants they constituted a stirring call to arms. But in western Upper Canada, with its American background, his words were greeted with indifference and apathy, particularly by the several militia regiments in the London region.

Early in 1812, efforts had been made to reorganize the London region in anticipation of war with the United States. Colonel Thomas Talbot was named the senior officer of the district; the regimental commanders included Joseph Ryerson and Robert Nichol of the two Norfolk regiments, and Henry Bostwick and Mahlon Burwell commanding the Oxford and Middlesex regiments. Some of the men in the ranks of these regiments were a "turbulent and refractory" lot; Nichol went so far as to describe his regiment as "little better than a legalized mob, the officers without respectability, without intelligence and without authority, and the men without any idea of subordination".[24] But then Nichol always was a sour individual. Burwell's regiment was weak in numbers and dispersed, owing to the scattered nature of the Middlesex population. Here was material ripe and ready for the kind of propaganda contained in Hull's proclamation, which was being distributed by the renegade, Simon Zelotes Watson, whom Nichol referred to as "a most infamous rascal". This view was shared by General Brock, who, writing to Prevost on 26 July, remarked that "the enemy's cavalry" were

> led by one Watson . . . a desperate character. This fellow had been allowed to parade with about 20 men of the same description, as far as Westminster, vowing as they went along the most bitter vengeance against the first characters of the province.[25]

To help clear up matters in Delaware Township, Brock sent a small detachment of the 41st under Captain Peter Chambers, with what militia he could collect. Chambers was embarrassed by the refusal of many of the militiamen he approached to move away from their homes; not even the Long Point militia, as James Baby from Sandwich discovered while *en route* to the legislative session in York, would march with Chambers, at least not until the Six Nations would commit themselves to the British cause. Despite these and other disappointments, Brock maintained a bold countenance, though he wrote privately, "I still

105

mean to try and send a force to the relief of Amherstburg, but almost despair of succeeding."[26]

As soon as the legislative session was over, Brock made a dash for the Detroit frontier. He received something of a fillip when the York militia offered to fight for him in any part of the province, and when Lieutenant Colonel John Macdonell, the Attorney General, offered to serve the General as his aide wherever and for as long as required. It turned out to be a lifetime engagement, for Macdonell, like Brock, was killed at Queenston Heights. At Port Dover, Brock received further encouragement when he found the flank companies of the Norfolk militia ready to join him, along with several militia officers, including Lieutenant Colonel Nichol, whom he appointed quartermaster general of militia. Brock was therefore in a good mood when he and his men embarked on a windy, wet 8 August. At Port Talbot he picked up a few more loyal militia. Brock's little fleet of "twelve sails of all kinds", which Macdonell stated "was in so bad a state that we are constantly delayed",[27] was too small to carry the men who now made up the reinforcing force destined for the Detroit frontier. Other boats had to be found, and all did not arrive the same day. It was 13 August when Brock himself landed at Amherstburg. In all, the reinforcements numbered some 350 militia, 60 regulars of the 41st Regiment of Foot who had sailed directly from Fort Erie and arrived a week earlier, in time to take part in the battle of Maguaga, and 20 Indians under Jean-Baptiste Cadot. Bostwick's and Ryerson's company of militia had also preceded the General, and when he arrived he found them busy constructing a masked battery, whose existence, it was hoped, would come as a surprise to the enemy. At Amherstburg, Brock and Tecumseh met, probably for the first time, and each was impressed by the other. "This is a man", Tecumseh said on meeting Brock.[28] Or so the legend goes.

Immediately upon his arrival at the fort, Brock examined the various papers taken from the *Cuyahoga* and at Brownstown. Then, having learned everything there was to be known about the numbers and the attitudes of Hull's troops, their low morale, their discontent, their dissatisfaction with their commanding officer, their fear of the Indians, he decided to attack as quickly as possible. Repairs had already been effected to the bridge over the Canard River, and batteries had been erected at Sandwich, directly opposite Detroit and less than 2 km from the American position. All of this had been done under cover of the guns of the *Queen Charlotte*, which had moved upstream for the purpose. Then, on 15 August, having hurried to Sandwich with all his available men, Brock drafted a summons to Hull to surrender, which he sent to Detroit by his two aides, John Macdonell and Major John B. Glegg, under a flag of truce. Hull, vacillating and dispirited as he was, nevertheless had the courage to reply, "I am prepared to meet any force which may be at your disposal, and any consequences which may result from any exertion of it you may think proper to make", although he weakened the impact of this show of determination by disclaiming responsibility for Cass's attack on the picket at the Canard bridge on 16 July or for the burning of any private buildings.[29] Then, Brock unveiled his guns and the bombardment of Detroit began. Verchères de Boucherville, his wound fairly well healed, was "deeply impressed". It was his first experience of cannons and mortars. "The balls were fired by our artillery stationed opposite Detroit and they fell like hail upon the town", he wrote. "The bombardment became ever fiercer; not for a single instant did the explosion of shells above and within the fort cease. The terrific din was increased by the howls of the savages, impatient to take part in the combat."[30] Despite Brock's statement in his report on the battle that the Americans returned his cannon fire in a "spirited manner", the evidence of those present, like Boucherville and Richardson, suggests that it was half-hearted at best. Richardson called it "languid".

Brock had never really believed that Hull would give in without fighting. He had therefore drawn up plans for an assault, to be launched at first light the next morning. During the night, the British guns kept up a desultory fire, but with the first show of dawn they began again "with unabated spirit".[31] The assault force had been assembled early, and in the "soft August sun" just rising over the horizon the troops embarked, the Indians in their canoes, the soldiers, regulars and militia in their boats, and the field artillery on scows. There was not a breath of wind and the crossing was effected in half an hour. Covering fire came from the Sandwich batteries and from the guns of the *Queen Charlotte*.

Brock's landing-place was about 5 km south of Fort Detroit. By the time all his men were ashore he had, ready to hurl themselves upon the enemy, no more than 330 regulars, 400 militia and 600 Indians, the Indians being under the command of Tecumseh and the Indian agent Matthew Elliott. This number did not, of course, include the Provincial Marine, the men row-ing or handling the landing craft, the gunners at Sandwich, or the reserve that Brock must have maintained on the Canadian side of the river. Once the attacking force was assembled, it began to move forward by sections, with intervals between them so as to give a visual impression of greater numbers. When the British column came within 2.4 km of the fort, it could see ahead, astride the road to Detroit, two large 24-pounder cannons, each with its crew standing ready with lighted fuses. But no indecision appeared in the British ranks. Marching on, they closed the gap to 1.2 km. At that point, Brock ordered the whole force to wheel to the left through an open field and an orchard; then, facing to their front, they were ready for the assault, led by Brock and Tecumseh. Meanwhile, the Sandwich guns kept up a steady cannonade upon the town and the fort, with devastating effect. As an example of precision gunnery, or pure luck, one British shell, penetrating an embrasure, burst in the officers' mess, killing no fewer than four occupants and spattering their brains over the walls. One of the victims was Lieutenant Porter Hanks, the unfortunate young officer who, only a few short weeks before, had surrendered Fort Michilimackinac to Captain Charles Roberts. At that moment, just as Brock was riding forward over a small rise in the ground that sheltered his troops, in order to reconnoitre Hull's position at close range, he learned that a flag of truce had been sent from the fort. Macdonell and Glegg went at once to inquire its meaning, Glegg galloping back to Brock to tell him the exciting news that the American general was prepared to talk terms of surrender. For another hour the troops stood idly about, their arms piled, wondering what the outcome of the negotiations would be. Then a horseman emerged from the gate of the fort, riding at full speed. His message—the capitulation would proceed. The "fall-in" was sounded, and the whole body of Brock's army moved forward through the trees and fields outside the stockade towards the gate of Fort Detroit. "As we approached", wrote John Richardson, "and beheld the numerous cannon frowning from their embrasures, it was impossible to avoid feeling mingled surprise and congratulation that so formidable a post should have been the fruit, apparently, more of a party of pleasure than of war."[32]

A guard of honour of one officer and forty men was detailed and told to take formal possession of the fort. As this group marched over the drawbridge, they suddenly discovered themselves in the midst of a sullen, hostile group of Ohio militia.

Since occupying the fort before the garrison had withdrawn was contrary to the conditions of the capitulation, the British guard, which included both regulars and militia, marched back over the drawbridge and waited until the garrison completed the evacuation. The formal occupation was then carried out in correct form; the Stars and Stripes was lowered and a Union Jack hoisted in its place. Sentinels were posted around the ramparts, and young John Richardson, armed with a musket taller than himself, was given the honour of mounting guard at the flagstaff. Not yet sixteen, he felt very proud of himself as he strutted martially up and down in front of the few dirty and dejected Americans who remained within the walls of the stockade. From across the river he could hear shouts of "Long live the King" and the sound of the band playing "Rule Britannia". Meanwhile Verchères de Boucherville watched the Indians break open the kegs of liquor. Soon they were in varying states of drunkenness, some riding through the streets in the carriages of American officers, others lying in the dust at the side of the road. It was a "disgusting spectacle",[33] and scarcely seven o'clock in the morning.

HULL WAS AN UNHAPPY MAN, and a hungry one. Captain Brush's provisions train had been stuck at the River Raisin, unable to move for fear of an Indian attack, and Hull wondered about sending an escorting party to help him make it through to Detroit. While Brock was planning his attack, Hull summoned McArthur and Cass and instructed the two Ohio colonels to force their way out of Detroit and join up with Brush. But McArthur had other matters on his mind. He and Cass and a number of Ohio men, dissatisfied with Hull's leadership, were intriguing to get rid of their commanding officer.

Two days before, on 12 August, a petition had been circulated "requesting the arrest or displacement of the General" and the transfer of command to "the eldest of the colonels, McArthur". Subsequently this had been followed by a round robin, bearing no fewer than eighty signatures, agreeing to seize Hull to deprive him of his command and defend Detroit "at all hazards".[34] The Ohio clique had also written to Governor Meigs, asking him to hurry to Detroit with reinforcements because Hull was talking vaguely about capitulation. It would appear that Hull was not unaware of the conspiracy against him, but, fearing that arresting the ringleaders would precipitate a mutiny, he decided to get them out of the fort by giving them the task of acting as escort to Brush's provisions train.[35] Not wishing to defy the General outright, McArthur and Cass rode off with 350 men late on 14 August. On the fifteenth, Hull sent an urgent message ordering the two colonels to return at once, a message they received on the same night. Neither Cass nor McArthur made any real effort to comply or to hurry to Hull's assistance. That is why neither officer was at Detroit when Brock crossed the river with his troops in the early hours of the sixteenth. They heard the bombardment—they were, after all, only a few kilometres away—but did not choose to communicate with Hull, contenting themselves with sending a few mounted men to find out what was going on upriver. As soon as they learned that Detroit had surrendered, they withdrew several kilometres and allowed their men to rest and eat an ox before returning to Detroit to surrender.[36]

Meanwhile, worried about the havoc wrought by the British bombardment, fearing for the safety of the civilians in his charge, alarmed at the desertion of a number of Michigan militia and concerned about the possibility of an Indian massacre, Hull was ready to give up. He extracted from Macdonell and Glegg promises that private persons and property would be respected and that, by including McArthur and Cass in the terms of the surrender, there would be no attack made against them or their men by British Indians. He could not, however, get the two British officers to concede the honours of war. Moreover, all soldiers (excluding the Michigan militia, who had never become part of the federal force) were to be considered as prisoners of war, and all military and public stores were to be turned over to the British authorities. Cass, after another childish if dramatic gesture, that of publicly breaking his sword, and McArthur, after vowing vengeance against Hull, submitted to the surrender terms; Brush, however, took to his heels, leaving a blockhouse to be burned and supplies to be pillaged by the Indians.[37]

One of the little ironies of history is that Brock's capture of Detroit occurred during the armistice that General Dearborn had concluded with Sir George Prevost. Had Hull's command not been independent of Dearborn's, he would presumably have been informed of the truce and given the opportunity to reinforce his army and replenish his provisions. He might, conceivably, have been spared the humiliation of surrender!

Following the surrender, Hull and most of his men were taken by vessel to Montreal as prisoners of war, to be held until exchanged. Some of the married officers and their wives were paroled at Fort George. The Ohio militiamen were allowed to make their way back to their own state. Some of the larger guns were sent across the river to Amherstburg, but the brasses that the Americans had taken from Burgoyne at Saratoga in 1777 were sent to Quebec.

While a prisoner at Fort George, Hull wrote a long letter to Dr. Eustis.[38] He forwarded the articles of capitulation and blamed his defeat largely on the Indians, who, after Hanks's surrender of Michilimackinac, had joined the British forces in great numbers, from "north from beyond Lake Superior, west from beyond the Mississippi, south from the Ohio and Wabash, and east from every part of Upper Canada". He named Tecumseh, Marpot, Logan, Walk-in-the-Water, Split Log and others who, as the principal leaders "under the entire influence and direction of the British commander, enabled him totally to obstruct the only communications which I had with my country". Hull also advanced other explanations for his miserable showing at Detroit: the poor quality of his troops, the lack of provisions and medicines, the exposed position of the fort. All of these were contributing factors; but had Hull been less inclined to attribute his defeat to secondary causes he might well have cited the indecision and delays of Dr. Eustis himself and of the administration generally, the failure to see the importance of naval control of Lake Erie, the inadequate arrangements for the commissariat. Instead of expressing his gratitude to Cass and McArthur, those military politicians, Hull might have pointed out the ill effects of their personal disloyalty, and he might have spoken of his own weakness, the declining energies of an old man. At least, it should be said of Hull that he surrendered Detroit, not through personal fear, but for reasons of humanity, and that he atoned for his weakness by being condemned to death by his military peers. He was the scapegoat for the failures of others as well as his own in a war that Henry Clay considered would be a mere matter of marching. It was to Madison's credit that the sentence passed on Hull was commuted. His country already owed him much for his services during the Revolutionary War. Poor Hull had attempted just one war too many.

IN ADDITION TO DETROIT, Hull's command included Fort Dearborn and Fort Wayne, the former located on the Chicago River close by the southern shores of Lake Michigan, the latter on the banks of the Maumee River. Both of these forts were located in the heartland of the Indian country, but Fort Dearborn was the more remote. Although defended by two blockhouses and a stockade and garrisoned by fifty-four men commanded by Captain Nathan Heald, Fort Dearborn was not a position of any real military strength. Essentially it was a trading post, with a few resident traders and Canadian voyageurs. Outside the fort, in the surrounding country, were numerous Indians, principally Potawatomi and Winnebagos; both nations sympathized with Tecumseh's concept of an Indian federation and had taken part in the fighting at Tippecanoe. Concerned about the isolation of Fort Dearborn, General Hull had sent a message to Heald telling him of the declaration of war and the invasion of Canada and ordering him to distribute "all the United States property contained in the fort and in the government factory or agency among the Indians in the neighbourhood", and to evacuate the fort. Unfortunately, Hull could not go to Heald's assistance should he be required. Some of the people in the fort favoured immediate abandonment; others thought that it should be defended. For the moment Heald did neither, but he did take the precaution of dumping the fort's liquor in the river and destroying all arms and ammunition surplus to the needs of the garrison. By the time he had done this, news had reached the Indians from Tecumseh that Michilimackinac had fallen to the British and that Hull was in the process of withdrawing from Canada. Thus, when Heald did decide to abandon Fort Dearborn, the Indians were sufficiently stimulated by the hope of success that they promptly attacked the retreating column. The fighting was short and bloody, and Heald finally surrendered to the Potawatomi chief, Blackbird, who later joined Procter's force in Upper Canada. The survivors of the fight were divided among their captors, but some of them were eventually restored to their families and friends.

The Indians burned the fort, feeling that this action would go some way towards wiping out the memories of Tippecanoe.[39] To the Indians it seemed obvious that Tecumseh had been right in tying his Indian federation to the fortunes of the British and Canadians, and right, too, in joining the British side in the War of 1812. But what the Potawatomi did not realize was that the sacking of Fort Dearborn was conducted without the prior knowledge of General Brock and might not have been approved by the civil authorities of Upper Canada.

31. Mrs. Heald resisting attack during the evacuation of Fort Dearborn

WHEN HULL marched off to Detroit in the spring of 1812, he carried with him not only the good wishes of all westerners but also promises of further help. Ohio, the Indiana Territory, Kentucky and Tennessee were all committed to Hull's success and to the maintenance of a clear line of communication through the Indian territory to the army base at Detroit. This presented few problems as long as Hull's star was in the ascendant and his men were moving into Canada. The Indians on the frontier were prepared to remain relatively quiet, though of course they were playing the game of wait and see which side would come out on top. As the summer months and Hull's chances of a dramatic or lasting success faded, the Indians became more active on the frontier, and in September, after Hull had surrendered, they undertook a series of frontier raids whose timing and location suggest direction from higher up, probably by Tecumseh: Pigeon Roost Creek, 3 September; Fort Harrison, 4 September; Fort Madison, 5 September; and Fort Wayne, 6 September.[40]

The War Hawk country was aroused, and steps were taken to strengthen the armed forces of the western states. William

Henry Harrison, the hero of Tippecanoe, recommended the erection of a number of posts along the Illinois and the reinforcement of Fort Wayne; Ohio embodied 1200 militia and placed them under Brigadier General Edward Tupper; and the Governor of Kentucky organized ten regiments and offered to place them in the service of the United States. The secretary of war, William Eustis, also acted, authorizing another Revolutionary War relic, Brigadier General James Winchester, to raise a force of regulars to march to Detroit. Winchester was also instructed to add a strong contingent of Kentuckians to his establishment. But the Kentuckians did not want Winchester; they did not like him and were reluctant to serve under him. The man they wanted was Harrison, who, in addition to commanding the Indiana militia by virtue of his role as governor, also held the rank of major general in the Kentucky militia. And Harrison wanted them. He therefore made haste with his militiamen to relieve Fort Wayne before Winchester could arrive there with his federal troops. Harrison won. Blackbird had made several rather indifferent attacks on Fort Wayne, but when Harrison approached he pulled away. Harrison thus became the man of the hour in the western states. Even Madison in Washington was impressed and offered him a federal commission as a brigadier general. But that was not what Harrison wanted; to accept Madison's commission would still leave him below Winchester in seniority, and, although publicly he protested his willingness to turn over his command to Winchester, behind the scenes he pulled hard on the political strings that would bring him command of the North Western Army. Action, rather than argument, was characteristic of the man, and in the end he got what he wanted. Harrison obtained his command directly from Madison, and with it instructions to march to the Detroit River and recover the post that Hull had so supinely surrendered. Ultimately this was what Harrison would do, but for the time being he had other more immediate problems to solve. The 10 000-man strength of his army existed largely on paper, short-term enlistments were expiring, new recruits were needed, artillery had to be found, logistical arrangements had to be concluded to keep the supplies and ammunition moving, and the autumn rains were beginning to immobilize transport and even to render cartridges useless. For the moment, then, Harrison had to content himself with sending Winchester down the Maumee River to the rapids, where the British had established themselves after Captain Brush's precipitate withdrawal following the fall of Detroit. There the Americans would sit out the winter, until operations could resume in the spring.

Meanwhile, the British at Amherstburg had not remained inactive. Procter had taken possession of the American camp at Frenchtown on the north bank of the River Raisin, and had carried out a personal reconnaissance as far as the Maumee Rapids. Then, in order to cement the Indian alliance, he resolved to send troops in the direction of Fort Wayne. Given a force numbering 1000 men, half of whom were Indians, and a few pieces of ordnance, Adam Muir, since 14 August brevet major, was told to establish a firm position on the Maumee, an order easier to give than to carry out. It was the time of year when water was low in the rivers, making the manhandling of the boats, as one of the volunteers put it, "tedious to the last degree".[41] At Fort Defiance the British disembarked and continued their journey overland. On 25 September, as they were advancing, a few of Muir's Indian scouts encountered several Americans in the woods. Pretending to be friendly, the Indians discovered that Winchester's force, totalling 2500 men, was not far distant. Once in command of this important intelligence, the Indians promptly killed the unfortunate Americans, and hurried back to report what they had discovered. Obviously, under the circumstances, no further move against Fort Wayne was feasible; Muir therefore decided to take up a defensive position and await the approach of Winchester's men at a ford the Americans would have to use in their advance. When the Americans did not appear, Muir began to wonder if they had found their dead scouts and had elected to bypass the ford in order to catch him in the rear. The British officer therefore pulled his men back another step, to the site of old Fort Defiance, then in a state of "utter ruin and dilapidation". Here Muir took up a position that the Americans would find difficult to pass undetected. From information received from a prisoner taken by the Indians, it became clear that Muir's assessment of the situation had been correct. Winchester's men had discovered the bodies of the slain scouts, but instead of advancing had set about building wooden breastworks and awaited attack. The whole object of his expedition having thus been thwarted, and seeing no further justification for remaining on the Maumee with a force like Winchester's cautiously pursuing him, Muir decided to return to Amherstburg. He had spent three weeks manhandling boats and guns through primeval forests, all to no purpose.

Still, Muir had proved one thing: he knew how to handle his men. He had offered battle on several occasions and manoeuvred his troops with speed. He had lost neither man nor gun, and had adapted successfully to the wild nature of the country and to the wild nature of the undisciplined force he commanded. Muir's expedition was, in fact, one of the few during the War of 1812 that offered opportunity for manoeuvre, an art once highly regarded as the true test of military competence.[42] But few people in Upper Canada were aware of or cared much about what was happening in the hinterland of Lake Erie; all eyes were now focused on the events taking place along the Niagara River. As far as Amherstburg was concerned, all that Verchères de Boucherville could find of importance to note in his journal was the receipt in December of an order "to have the hoods of our great coats edged with black".[43] What would an army do, even in war in the wilderness, without dress regulations?

5

The Niagara Frontier

WHEN THE PLANS were drafted for the invasion of British North America in 1812, Dearborn's and Hull's independent commands were regarded as the major American armies, and Lower Canada and western Upper Canada as the principal areas of operations. The central region, the Niagara River area, was considered of secondary importance, in terms of both command and strategy, a region of feint or diversion. When Dr. William Eustis, the secretary of war, wrote on 26 June to Major General Dearborn, then at Albany, he emphasized the need to move on Montreal. There was to be a show of force in the direction of the Niagara region or Kingston, but no emphasis was placed upon operations in the central theatre. This was confirmed in Dearborn's mind when a month later, on 20 July, Eustis wrote again telling him to "make such arrangements with Governor Tompkins as will place the militia detached by him" in "Niagara and other posts on the lake under your control".[1] Later there was still another letter, this one dated 1 August, telling the First Major General that he should "make a diversion" in favour of Brigadier General Hull, "at Niagara and Kingston as soon as may be practicable".[2] Dearborn had not to this time taken the Niagara region at all seriously, and it came as something of a shock on 3 August to realize that it was, in fact, one of his areas of responsibility and that he should do something about it, if only to relieve the pressure on Hull at Detroit. He therefore authorized the dispatch of 1000 militia to the Niagara frontier, and requested Stephen Van Rensselaer to take command there.

117

Van Rensselaer was not an officer of any military distinction. His principal qualifications would appear to have been his descent from one of the original New York patroons and his general officer's commission in the New York State militia, an appointment he had received from the governor of the state. But it was not intended that Van Rensselaer's command should be limited to militia. His force was therefore strengthened with such regular troops as could be found for the purpose, and throughout the summer regular soldiers trickled into the Niagara area, including two companies of artillery under Winfield Scott and some 1650 regular infantry under Brigadier General Alexander Smyth. All told, Van Rensselaer seems to have had under his command, in addition to Smyth's regulars at Buffalo and another 1350 regulars in garrison at Fort Niagara, about 2650 militia from various parts of New York State. By early October the troops were assembled, strung out along the Niagara River from Buffalo to Fort Niagara.

The Army of the Center, as Van Rensselaer's force became known, was neither well trained nor well disciplined, nor was its morale particularly good. At least, this is the inference to be drawn from Van Rensselaer's letter to the governor of New York, Daniel D. Tompkins, to whom he wrote on 31 August:

> Alarm pervades the country and distrust among the troops. They are incessantly pressing for furloughs under every possible pretence. Many are without shoes; all clamorous for pay. Many are sick.[3]

If the troops under his command did not inspire Van Rensselaer with hope and self-confidence, neither did his senior officer, Dearborn, who wrote after the Hull debacle:

> From the number of troops which have left Montreal for Upper Canada, I am not without fear that attempts will be speedily made to reduce you and your forces to the mortifying situation of General Hull. . . . If such an attempt . . . should be made previous to the arrival of the principal part of the troops destined to Niagara, it will be necessary for you to be prepared for all events, and to be prepared to make good a secure retreat as the last resort.[4]

In these circumstances, the Prevost–Dearborn armistice could only have been regarded as a blessing, despite Madison's disapproval of the truce negotiations. During the armistice every effort was made to hurry men to Van Rensselaer's command, and vessels were concentrated at Sackets Harbor to become the nucleus of an American lake-fleet. On 17 September, Dearborn was still writing in pessimistic terms, telling Van Rensselaer to

32. *Major General Stephen Van Rensselaer commanded the American invasion force at Queenston Heights in 1812*

assume "the best face that your situation admits", so that "the enemy may be induced to delay an attack". With the early part of the letter couched in defeatist terms, it must have been hard for Van Rensselaer to take too seriously the injunction that "at all events we must calculate on possessing Upper Canada before winter sets in."[5] Certainly, neither Dearborn nor Hull had made much of a contribution to the realization of this aim.

On 13 October, Dearborn sent another letter to the general officer commanding the Army of the Center. This time he wrote

119

to express the hope that Van Rensselaer would "embrace the first practicable opportunity for effecting a forward movement".[6] That, of course, was just what Van Rensselaer was planning to do. Smyth's regulars had arrived at Buffalo on 29 September, and early in October Lieutenant Jesse Elliott from Sackets Harbor, with a party of American sailors and soldiers, had pulled off a daring coup, seizing two British vessels on Lake Erie—the North West Company's *Caledonia* and the sloop *Detroit*, formerly *Adams*, an American ship that the British had captured at Detroit and that was commanded by Lieutenant Charles Rolette of the Provincial Marine. The loss of these two vessels was a serious matter for General Brock. He was always aware of the importance of maintaining a strong naval presence on the lakes and watched with concern the attempts the Americans were now making to build a fleet on Lakes Ontario and Erie. The loss was also an embarrassment to Colonel Henry Procter, for he had planned to use the two vessels to carry rations to Amherstburg. Provisions were always a problem on the Detroit front, and Brock had warned Procter to "husband your pork, for, I am sorry to say, there is but little in the country."[7]

Meanwhile, Van Rensselaer was making his plans for the invasion of Canada. He could not afford to wait much longer or, as he put it to Dearborn, "all the toil and expense of the campaign" would "go for nothing; and worse than nothing, for the whole" would be "tinged with dishonor". Moreover, the troops had become elated over Elliott's exploit and were demanding "orders to act"; otherwise they would "go home".[8] Van Rensselaer thought first of pushing one column of troops across the Niagara River to attack Queenston, and conveying a second column by boat across the mouth of the Niagara River to attack the British headquarters at Fort George. That this move against Fort George, one that was used with success in 1813, was not attempted in 1812 was clearly Smyth's fault. A regular officer, an aspirant for the chief command on the frontier and a stiff-necked, supercilious Virginian, Smyth was not disposed to take orders from a New Yorker, a militiaman and a Federalist, whose heart was never really in the war. On arrival at Buffalo, he did not do Van Rensselaer, his superior officer, the courtesy of calling on him in person to discuss operational plans but wrote him a letter that the proud patroon regarded as impertinent:

> I have been ordered by Major General Dearborn to Niagara, to take command of a brigade of United States troops and directed, on my arrival in the vicinity of your quarters, to report myself to

you, which I now do. I intended to have reported myself personally, but the conclusions I have drawn as to the interests of the service have determined me to stop at this place for the present. From
the description I have had of the river below the Falls, the view
of the shore below Fort Erie, and the information received as to
the preparations of the enemy, I am of opinion that our crossing
should be effected between Fort Erie and Chippewa. It has, therefore, seemed to me proper to encamp the United States troops near
Buffalo, there to prepare for offensive operations. Your instructions
or better information may decide you to give me different orders,
which I will await.[9]

When asked by Van Rensselaer to name a date for a council
of officers, Smyth simply procrastinated. As army commander,
Van Rensselaer therefore decided to proceed with his own plans,
and on 10 October resolved to attack at dawn the next morning. Boats were prepared and the assault force, troops of the
6th Infantry under Captain John Machesney and militia under
Lieutenant Colonel Solomon Van Rensselaer, the commanding
officer's aide and cousin, marched to the ferry landing at
Lewiston. The night was stormy, rain was falling, and heavy
mud made all movement difficult. When the American troops
finally reached the point of embarkation, they discovered to
their consternation that the officer in charge of the boats, a
Lieutenant Sim, had disappeared in the leading bateau with
all the oars of the other boats. He had slipped downstream,
abandoned his own craft and disappeared into the night. Van
Rensselaer would have been glad to hold a council of war, but
the attitude of his officers was that there should be as little delay
as possible in proceeding with the planned operation. The men
were simply marched back to their cantonments to await a second attempt in forty-eight hours.

When darkness fell on 12 October, the assault force, composed of 300 volunteers under Solomon Van Rensselaer and 300
regulars under Lieutenant Colonel John Chrystie of the 13th
Infantry, moved to the embarkation point. This time, oars and
boats were ready. At his headquarters, General Van Rensselaer
waited anxiously, but not despondently. He had, all told, 6000
men, and he had good intelligence of the British, their numbers
and their position. He had, moreover, placed a battery on
Lewiston Heights to cover the landing on the Canadian shore.
At 0300 hrs on the thirteenth, the first wave of assault troops
went aboard, and began to row across the swirling waters of
the Niagara River towards Queenston. In the darkness three
of the boats lost their way or were caught by the current and

forced downstream. The others, after a ten-minute struggle with the violent eddies of the river, landed and discharged the troops, and immediately rowed back to the American side, for there were too few boats to accommodate all the men of the army; they were going to have to make the Niagara crossing in relays.

ISAAC BROCK was always sensitive to developments along the Niagara River. In the first days of the war he had talked of a sudden surprise attack on Fort Niagara, of the kind that Roberts had carried out against Michilimackinac, but Prevost discouraged offensive action, and Brock had to content himself with calling out the flank companies and arranging for the defence of the river line. Colonel Henry Procter was placed in charge of the troops along the length of the river, the provincial cavalry and the car brigade were called out, and the commissariat was ordered to provide rations and fuel for those on duty. The companies of the 41st Regiment and the Lincoln militia provided guards and patrols along the riverbank and close to the shore. The conclusion of the armistice between Prevost and Dearborn, while it assisted the Americans, making it possible for them to build up the strength of Van Rensselaer's Army of the Center, also enabled Brock to grant his militiamen leave to work on their farms, and for Brock himself to rush with a few reinforcements to Amherstburg and achieve his dramatic success at Detroit. Meanwhile, the watch on the Niagara was never relaxed. One American soldier, looking across at the Canadian side of the river, wrote, "Niagara on the British side, or as it is sometimes called, Newark, looks wicked everywhere. It is a charming, fertile village, but all a camp fortified at every point."[10]

Returning to York after the capture of Detroit, Brock found both the general populace and the Indians filled with satisfaction. The formerly reluctant militia and Six Nations Indians now decided that it would be worth their while to throw in their lot with the winning side and drop the attitude of neutrality they had adopted earlier. The pro-American element remained silent for the moment, or took advantage of the opportunity to flee the country in open boats, "logs, rails, slabs, and even by many without any buoy whatever".[11] From York, Brock went to Kingston to review the militia and then back to Fort George, where he was happy to greet six companies of his own regiment, the 49th Foot. "Although the regiment has been ten years in this country, drinking rum without bounds," he wrote to his brother, "it is still respectable and apparently ardent for

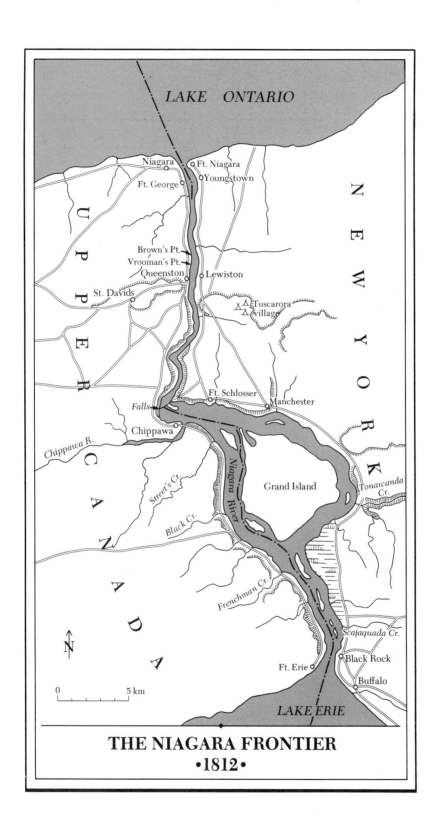

THE NIAGARA FRONTIER
•1812•

an opportunity to acquire distinction." In the same letter, which was dated 18 September, he added:

> You will hear of some decided action in the course of a fortnight, or in all probability we shall return to a state of tranquillity. I say decisive, because if I should be beaten the Province is inevitably gone, and should I be victorious, I do not imagine the gentry from the other side will be anxious to return to the charge.[12]

Brock was aware of the buildup of the American forces. Although the Americans may have succeeded in masking some of their batteries, he suspected throughout September that an enemy attack was in the offing. The objective, he believed, would be Fort George, which might have its flank turned "during a calm night" or might be faced with a frontal assault covered by artillery fire.[13] Oddly enough, Van Rensselaer was equally convinced that Brock was preparing to attack him. The loss of the two vessels, *Detroit* and *Caledonia*, was a blow to Brock. In a moment of pessimism, he wrote to the Governor General:

> This event is peculiarly unfortunate and may reduce us to incalculable distress. The enemy is making every effort to gain a naval superiority on both lakes, which, if they accomplish, I do not see how we can retain the country.[14]

The night of 12 October, Brock sat up late at Fort George, preparing his letters and dispatches. It was there that he wrote his last words to Sir George Prevost:

> The vast number of troops which have been added this day to the strong force previously collected on the opposite side convinces me, with other indications, that an attack is not far distant. I have in consequence directed every exertion to be made to complete the militia to two thousand men, but I fear I shall not be able to effect my object with willing, well-disposed characters. Were it not for the number of Americans in our ranks we might defy all their efforts against this part of the Province.[15]

Before dawn, towards 0400 hrs, Brock was awakened by the sound of heavy guns. Dressing quickly and followed by his aide, Lieutenant Colonel John Macdonell, he set off on horseback towards Queenston, 11 km distant. As he was leaving Fort George he ordered the regulars and the militia to be roused and marched to Queenston. On the way he passed the batteries erected to guard likely crossing points from the American side. At Brown's Point, about 3 km from Queenston, he waved to

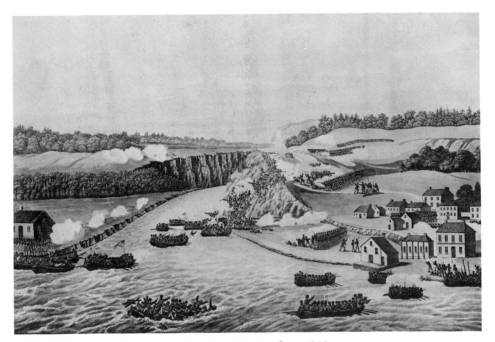

33. *The Battle of Queenston Heights, 13 October 1812.*
The engraving is based on a sketch by Major James Dennis,
49th Regiment, who took part in the battle.

the garrison, calling on them to hurry along towards the escarpment. At Vrooman's Point, where a long 24-pounder was blaz-
ing away at the American troops crossing the river, he paused
briefly. At Queenston he took a quick look at the situation. It
was worse than he had expected; he had wondered if it was
just a feint, but clearly the Americans meant business.

Up to this time the defenders had done well, and as Brock
approached Queenston he could see for himself the groups of
prisoners—"miserable wretches suffering under wounds of all
descriptions, and crawling to our houses for protection and comfort" was the way one militia officer saw them.[16] With the approach of another wave of landing craft, Brock wondered if
the light company defending the redan battery halfway up the
escarpment would not be more useful if it were to descend to
the village. Still mounted on his horse, he climbed to the battery to see for himself. At that moment Captain John Wool,
of the 13th United States Infantry Regiment, and his men
debouched from the cliff along a pathway just above the battery. It was a perilously exposed position for a commanding officer to find himself in. All Brock could do was to order the gun

34. *Uniform worn by Major General Isaac Brock at Queenston Heights*

to be spiked and the gunners to scramble down the mountain. He himself followed, finding cover in the village. It was now daylight and becoming obvious to the Americans as well as to Brock that his Queenston force was too small to hold out much longer. The Americans held the Heights and the bulk of the British troops were still on the march from Fort George to Queenston. Perhaps he should have waited, but boldness in action was the very nature of the man. Any delay would serve the purposes of the Americans more than his own. He was not ready to allow the enemy to seize the initiative, not if he could keep it for himself.

Two months before, at Detroit, Brock had said that he would never ask men to go "where I do not lead them".[17] Wholly disregarding the danger of such a course of action, he led his men on foot up the hill, on the double. The first charge was shattered by the intensity of Wool's fire; one participant called it "a most galling fire".[18] Even the grenadiers began to falter. Brock rallied them with the shout, "This is the first time I have ever seen the 49th turn their backs."[19] The men picked up the challenge, and with Brock in his red tunic well ahead of them, brandishing his sword, slipping and stumbling in the wet grass, the charge went on. At about 50 m Brock cried to his men to hold their fire and use the bayonet. A short distance away, from behind a clump of bushes, an American scout raised his long rifle and, taking careful aim, sent a musket ball tearing into Brock's chest, just above the heart. According to Major Glegg, Brock only had time to utter in a feeble voice, "My fall must not be noticed or impede my brave companions from advancing to victory."[20] The charge lost its impetus, however, as the men of the 49th, carrying their general's body with them, withdrew down the slope to Queenston village.

Brock's aide, John Macdonell, tried to retrieve the situation. He collected about fifty men, including some of the 49th and a few York militia, and attempted another dash towards the battery. But the determination of the original charge was lacking. The Americans were ready and waiting at 30 m range. According to one of the survivors,

> Lieutenant Colonel Macdonell, who was on the left of our party calling up on us to advance, received a shot in his body and fell. His horse was at the same instant killed. Captain Williams, who was at the other extremity of our little band, fell the next moment, apparently dead.[21]

Macdonell, mortally wounded, was carried back to the village by another militia officer who had been at Brown's Point. There was little more the British could do. Wool's undetected clamber up the cliff and the single shot of a sniper had turned the battle from probable defeat to possible victory for the Americans. And Isaac Brock died a soldier's death, just three days after his elevation to the rank of Knight of the Bath by George III. It was his reward for the victory at Detroit, an honour he never knew he had received.

But the battle was not yet over. Following the deaths of Brock and Macdonell, the British defenders—the survivors of the two companies of the 49th Foot and the militia, commanded by Cap-

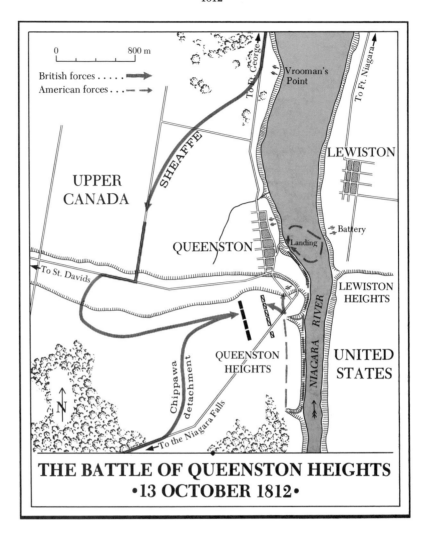

THE BATTLE OF QUEENSTON HEIGHTS
•13 OCTOBER 1812•

tain James Dennis—sensibly withdrew from Queenston to Vrooman's Point. There they awaited the arrival of the main body of the British, now under the command of Major General Roger Sheaffe. All along the river the word spread that Brock had been killed and that the Americans were in Queenston. The result was anger rather than discouragement. The batteries redoubled their fire, and soon the guns of Fort Niagara were silenced. Early in the afternoon, Sheaffe's forces reached Queenston. Sheaffe had not the panache of Brock, nor his successful way of dealing with men, but he was deliberate and methodical, perhaps just the kind of officer needed at this moment. He saw no purpose in any dramatic charge up the slope behind the village in the face of the enemy's advantageous position. Instead, he led his men along a lengthy detour inland, running parallel to the escarpment, hoping thereby to gain the Heights without having to battle for the position. His force, too, was growing, and to the garrison of Fort George he added a number of Mohawks from the Grand River Reserve, a troop of militia cavalry, some regulars and militia from Chippawa, and a company of negroes. Then, once on the high ground, he moved eastwards again towards the American position on the Heights.

At this point began the second phase of the battle of Queenston Heights. It was now mid-afternoon. To all intents and purposes the Americans had won the day. They held the redan battery and had established a deceptively strong position on the heights on the Canadian side of the river. But they badly needed to consolidate and to add to their numerical strength, their supplies of ammunition were low, and their senior officer, a militia brigadier from Buffalo, despite exhortations and profanity, seemed to have remarkably little success in disciplining and ordering his men. Thus, when Sheaffe's force came within shooting distance of the American position, the enemy troops on the Heights did not show the same degree of interest in the battle that they had displayed earlier. The Indians were the first to open fire, yelling and shouting, and as they moved through the trees they distracted the attention of the Americans from the British main body. In the smoke and confusion of battle the Americans found it difficult to orient themselves and to find the proper direction from which to meet the fierce onslaught of the advancing red- and green-coated troops. Under threat of the scalping knife, the tomahawk and the fire of Sheaffe's men, the Americans began to withdraw; but where could they go? There was no room for manoeuvre. The redan battery position was now in British hands; behind were the cliffs, the whirlpool and the deep, rushing waters of the Niagara River; on their flanks were the Indians; and in front was a determined mass of infantry moving steadily forward through the clouds of gun smoke. Winfield Scott, standing on a log, tried to rally them with a dramatic harangue, but his call to redeem the honour forfeited by General Hull's surrender had little appeal. Some of the terrified Americans tried to run down the hill, some sought concealment in crevices and gullies, some leaped from the cliffs to die on the rocks or drown in the swirling waters below. "The river", wrote one officer who was there, "presented a horrid spectacle, filled with poor wretches who plunged into the stream from the impulse of fear, with scarcely the prospect of being saved."[22]

35. John Brant, son of Joseph Brant. He led the Six Nations Indians at the Battle of Queenston Heights.

Most of the American troops accepted the inevitability of defeat and gave themselves up. After two messengers bearing white flags had been shot, the young American officer, Winfield Scott, seized a white cravat and held it high on his sword. The signal was seen and the British ceased fire, rushing forward to fend off the Indians from their prey. They then marched their prisoners away. When counted they were found to number 958, "the most savage looking fellows I ever saw", wrote Lieutenant George Ridout to his brother at York. "To strike a greater terror in their enemies they had allowed their beards on their upper lips to grow."[23] The number of enemy killed and wounded was never ascertained. The British losses, if we except the irreparable loss of Brock, were comparatively light: 14 killed and 77 wounded among the regulars and militia, and 14 casualties among the Indians. Most of the British casualties had been suffered in the first phase of the battle, those of the Indians in the second.

The wounded, American and British alike, were brought to Niagara in boats and wagons and placed in improvised hospitals in St. Mark's Church, Government House and the Indian Council House. The bodies of the dead soldiers lay on the field of battle during the night of the thirteenth. On the morning of the fourteenth, when they were picked up by the burial parties, they were covered with a white blanket; snow, the first of the season, had fallen during the night.

Brock's body was placed in Government House, and on 16 October he and Macdonell received a formal but simple funeral. Their bodies were buried in the cavalier bastion at Fort George, called the York Battery, which had been constructed under Brock's watchful eye. During the funeral procession, cannon salutes from both the British and American batteries greeted the cortège.

On 14 October, Stephen Van Rensselaer sat down to explain his disastrous defeat to the Secretary of War. He had no difficulty finding scapegoats; one, for instance, was Brigadier General Alexander Smyth, who had failed to give him the help that he, as commander, had every reason to expect. Above all, there were those timid, barrack-room lawyers, the members of the New York State militia. They had shown remarkably little stomach for crossing the river. After all, they argued, it was not one of their obligations as militiamen to leave the confines of their state. Crossing into Canada was not a measure essential for the defence of the State of New York. Even when it looked as if the Americans were going to carry the day, they were prepared to argue their constitutional rights, and as soon as they caught a glimpse of the long line of redcoats marching to Queenston from Fort George, no exhortations, no appeals to patriotism, pride or duty, no threats from the military or civil authorities could persuade them to cross the Niagara River. They would not move. They would provide no succour to the beleaguered wretches on the heights above Queenston. They did not even maintain that there were no boats to convey them, which was true, for the boats were dispersed and the boatmen had fled, "panic-struck", Van Rensselaer said. "I can only add", he wrote despondently, "that the victory was really won, but lost for the want of a small reinforcement; one-third part of the idle men might have saved all."[24]

THE BRITISH VICTORY at Queenston Heights meant the end of Van Rensselaer's military career. The unfortunate general submitted his resignation to Dearborn, who cheerfully accepted it and then turned to the flamboyant Smyth, sending him copies of his previous instructions to Van Rensselaer and urging him to collect landing craft to make another effort at crossing the Niagara River. Smyth, while happy to have his own command, did not wish to remain under Dearborn's direction. He hoped to be free of supervision and to enjoy independence of action. He therefore wrote to Eustis:

> I wish to have one hundred boats that will carry across at once four thousand men, and twenty or thirty scows or flats to take over artillery or cavalry; and if you will increase my force to eight thousand men, with twenty pieces of light or field artillery and some troops of cavalry, I will enter Canada and leave the rest to Heaven.[25]

After warning Eustis to "place no confidence in detached militia" and not to rely on local contractors, who have no salt meat and "only damaged flour", he asked Eustis for funds, without which "we cannot get transportation by land, build boats, procure forage or anything else wanted by the army. . . . Give me here a clear stage, men and money, and I will retrieve your affairs or perish." The Secretary of War's reply was chilly. He simply reminded Smyth that there were proper channels of communication and that he should observe them. He should submit his ideas to Dearborn.

Familiar as Eustis must have been with Smyth's gasconading, he was unlikely to have been prepared for the Brigadier General's next effusion. It took the form of a proclamation, dated 10 November 1812, and was addressed to the "Men of New York", the militiamen who had declined to follow Van Rensselaer at Queenston. After reminding them of the devotion of the United States to peace, and the valour American soldiers were "conspicuous" for, he laid the blame for the failure of 13 October on the incompetence of their military leaders, "popular men, 'destitute alike of theory and experience' in the art of war". Van Rensselaer was obviously the main object of this attack, but Smyth's words cut a pretty broad swath. He went on to assure them that "in a few days" the troops under his command "will plant the American standard in Canada". Then would the men "accustomed to obedience, silence and steadiness" conquer the enemy "or they will die". As the proclamation went on, it became even more grandiloquent:

> Will you stand with your arms folded and look on this interesting struggle? Are you not related to the men who fought at Burlington and Saratoga? Has the race degenerated? Or have you, under the baneful influence of contending factions, forgotten your country?. . .
> The present is the hour of renown. Have you not a wish for fame? . . . Then seize the present moment; if you do not, you will regret it and say: "The valiant have bled in vain, the friends of my country fell and I was not there."
> Advance, then, to our aid. I will wait for you a few days. I cannot give you the day of my departure, but come on. Come in companies, half companies, pairs or singly. I will organize you for a short tour.[26]

It had been Dearborn's plan that Smyth should effect the river crossing with as little delay as possible and should put himself in touch with Harrison, who, Dearborn presumed, "is now at Detroit with a very respectable force".[27] Dearborn was not living in a world of reality, for in a subsequent letter to Smyth he promised American progress on the Montreal front, where Brigadier General Bloomfield will "beat up the several posts between his camp and the River St. Lawrence", and draw British troops away from the Niagara.[28] Smyth was advised to take counsel with his officers, however, before undertaking offensive operations; according to Dearborn, it was Van Rensselaer's failure to do this that led to his defeat. In any event, the crossing would be made, not, as previously, below the Falls, but in the upper part of the river. This was what Smyth wanted. "If I can beat the enemy on the plains of Erie and take that place," he assured Dearborn, "I will find means to get to Fort George."[29] The fundamental problem was to find men in sufficient numbers to do it. The reverse at Queenston Heights had been followed by a wholesale desertion on the part of the New York militia, and a report dated 3 November to the *New-York Evening Post* noted that Smyth's militia corps were "mere skeletons" and that some of the companies contained a "less number of privates than of officers".[30] Smyth's efforts to breathe fire into his militia were thwarted by the mutiny of two regular regiments because they had not been paid and the refusal by several hundred militia to obey orders until their barrack conditions were improved. That something was radically wrong was obvious from the high incidence of dysentery and pulmonary complaints, the lack of meat rations, the absence of winter clothing, and the general atmosphere of insubordination in the American army, which was apparent to everybody, newspaperman or officer, who saw the various corps at Buffalo; apparent, too, from the reply of the Men of New York to Smyth's appeal: "Go, General, if you will", they said. "Should you ever reach the walls of Quebec, the shade of Montgomery will reproach you for not having profited by his example, and when you fall, the men of New York will lament that folly has found new victims."[31] Scarcely an encouraging climate for launching an invasion. The War Hawk, Peter B. Porter, who had obtained a commission as a brigadier general, tried his hand at doing at Buffalo what Henry Clay had done in Kentucky—except that New York was not, like Kentucky, one of the war-minded states, and Porter never had the popular appeal that Clay enjoyed. All that followed was a small-scale riot led by the former editor of the *Baltimore Whig* and encouraged by the militiamen who had taken part in the Baltimore riot against "all Federalists and damned Tories". Abel Grosvenor, who received a bayonet thrust from one of the rioters, told the story to his brother Thomas, a Federalist congressman from New York, reassuring him that he had "providentially succeeded in rescuing myself from the bloody miscreants":

> We are all yet in confusion, tho' the mob is put down; we have a guard of three hundred regulars posted at the village, but they all cross to Canada to-morrow morning, and what our fate will be God only knows.[32]

Meanwhile Smyth continued his rodomontades. On 17 November he drafted another proclamation, this one addressed to the Army of the Center. After instructing his men that they were about to enter "a country that is to be one of the United States", he urged them to avoid plundering, and to respect private property insofar as "our imperious necessities will allow"—which, incidentally, included "whatever is booty by the usage of war". Forty dollars would be paid for the "arms and spoils of each savage warrior who shall be killed". Then came the hyperbole:

> Soldiers, you are amply provided for war. You are superior in number to the enemy. Your personal strength and activity are

greater. Your weapons are longer. The regular soldiers of the enemy are generally old men, whose best years have been spent in the sickly climate of the West Indies. They will not be able to stand before you when you charge with the bayonet. . . . Come on my heroes! And when you attack the enemy's batteries, let your rallying word be: "The cannon lost at Detroit or Death."[33]

Ten days later Smyth issued the order for the invasion. He could not, of course, let the occasion pass without a little boast. In his general order he stated:

> At reveille to-morrow [that is, 28 November] every soldier will put on his knapsack, shoulder his musket, and prepare for battle with flints and cartridges, will march to the navy yard on his way to Canada. . . .
> Friends of your country! Ye who have "the will to do, the heart to dare", the moment you have wished for has arrived. Think of your country's honor lost, her rights trampled on, her sons enslaved, her infants perishing by the hatchet. Be strong! Be brave! And let the ruffian power of the British king cease on this continent.[34]

This kind of thing was absent in the note he wrote to Porter. He did not want to be bothered with the troublesome militia:

> Be pleased to attend to those volunteers and give them arms and necessaries, and if you can manage without sending such parties to me, I will be glad, as I am excessively engaged.[35]

About 0300 hrs, 200 American sailors climbed into their boats and took the oars in their hands; the soldiers piled in and together they set out quietly across the Niagara River, on their way to Canada at last.

THE BRITISH VICTORY at Queenston Heights had been followed by a short armistice, arranged by Sheaffe and Van Rensselaer, to permit the return of the wounded and the burial of the dead. By mutual agreement the truce was extended indefinitely, until such time as one side or the other might give thirty hours' notice of abrogation. Both sides felt that they could profit from a cessation of hostilities to rebuild their stocks and strengthen their forces along the river frontier. As far as the British were concerned, there was an immediate relaxation of alertness and a substantial increase in drunkenness among the soldiery; at least, that is the inference to be drawn from the strict orders imposed on the troops at Fort George, refusing the men the privilege of leaving their quarters without permission and prohibiting the sale without licence of spirituous liquors "on the line of defence". An increase in pickets was ordered, and a night-ly patrol of dragoons was instructed to visit the outlying posts.[36] At the same time additional militia units from Norfolk, Oxford and Middlesex counties were called out to maintain firm lines of communication between Fort George and Long Point, and to man observation posts along the north shore of Lake Erie between Fort Erie and Long Point. Sheaffe believed that the Americans, having tried to cross the Niagara River and failed, would most likely try to outflank the extremities of the river defence line, either at Fort George or at Fort Erie. He therefore disposed his men in detachments at Fort George, Chippawa and Fort Erie, and along the road from Fort George to the western part of the province. Below Fort Erie, just opposite Black Rock, New York, two companies of militia watched the ferry landing. To supplement the regulars, militiamen were called in from the Niagara peninsula and the York and Long Point regions, and arrangements were made for some of the men from the militia flank companies to serve the guns. To ensure the efficiency of the militia levies, Lieutenant Colonel Cecil Bisshopp periodically inspected militia posts along the Niagara frontier and ascertained the needs and requirements of the men. As a result, new issues of clothing and blankets were made, along with the reminder that blankets and greatcoats were "public property and intended for general use, and no man is to carry from his company either of those articles unless he be employed on duty and be authorized to take them."[37]

As soon as the Americans gave notice on 19 November of the termination of the truce the following day, Sheaffe made ready for the expected invasion. By this time he was convinced that the attack would come at the Lake Erie end of the Niagara River, and to distract the attention of the Americans he authorized a heavy bombardment of Fort Niagara on the twenty-first. The forts exchanged a steady fire all day, and both sustained a certain amount of damage; the town of Niagara also suffered from the enemy's use of hot shot. Finally, in the early hours of the twenty-eighth, two assault columns of Smyth's invasion force embarked at Black Rock, under the command of Colonel William H. Winder and Lieutenant Colonel Charles G. Boerstler. Winder's object was to capture the British batteries immediately opposite the point of embarkation, Boerstler's to destroy the bridge at Frenchman Creek and thus sever all communications with the British camp at Chippawa. Once the bridgehead was firmly established, the main body of Smyth's force would cross to exploit it.

Winder's men succeeded in landing, and one group came up in the rear of the British guns, which the gunners hastily abandoned after spiking them. The other group then moved in to attack the defended posts along the river. They were met and opposed by two weak companies of militia and a detachment of the 49th Foot, under Lieutenant Thomas Lamont, who were forced to retreat, abandoning their guns and leaving behind 30 of their number, including the wounded Lamont, to become prisoners of war. At this point some of the Americans returned to Black Rock with their prisoners; others, under Captain William King, continued downriver, where they encountered a British detachment from Fort Erie and were compelled to lay down their arms. The second column, under Boerstler, rowed towards Frenchman Creek, where it encountered a stronger British force, which included not only the detachment from Fort Erie but also a contingent of militia and regulars from Chippawa, under Lieutenant Colonel Bisshopp. The American attacking force was greeted with cannon fire and, after losing two boats and suffering damage to others, turned about and went back to the American shore. For the remainder of the day the British and Canadian forces assembled in strength, 1100 in all, including the Indians under Major James Givins of the Indian Department. They recaptured the lost guns, removed the spikes and aimed at the east bank of the river. At that point, under a flag of truce, Smyth sent Bisshopp a demand that Fort Erie be surrendered at once "to spare further effusion of blood". Bisshopp could see no reason to comply since the Americans had made no effort to launch an attack upon the fort and had failed to secure more than a temporary bridgehead on the Canadian shore. Smyth's demand was therefore just another empty gesture, even though the American general went through the motions of embarking his main body in full sight of the Canadian defenders. He did not, however, send any of them across the river, contenting himself with the thought that it was late in the day and they ought, instead of fighting, to disembark and partake of dinner. The whole episode, which involved losses to both sides—in the case of the British and Canadians, nearly a hundred men killed, wounded or taken prisoner—, thus ended in an anticlimax.

Smyth had not yet abandoned the idea of an invasion. He spent the next day in preparations, and ordered his troops back to the point of embarkation for a night attack on the thirtieth. But his men dragged their heels, and by the time he had 1500 of them in the boats—some of his militia, incidentally, refused to leave American territory—it was broad daylight. The American general therefore summoned a council of war and, supported by the unanimous decision of his officers, decided to call off the invasion, at least for 1812. In explaining his reasons for abandoning any further attempt to invade Canada, Smyth wrote, rather bitterly:

> The affair at Queenston is a caution against relying on crowds who go to the bank of the Niagara to look on a battle as on a theatrical exhibition, who, if they are disappointed of the sight, break their muskets, or if they are without rations for a day, desert.[38]

Poor ludicrous caw-handed Smyth. His militia deserted and went home, his officers broke their swords, and his men beat their muskets over stumps in their rage. Brigadier General Porter harangued the volunteers and called Smyth a scoundrel and a coward. The miserable Smyth took lodgings in Buffalo, but, the mob becoming dangerous, the landlord required him to depart. As he fled to his own camp for safety, a soldier snapped a pistol at him. To defend his honour, Smyth challenged Porter to a duel. Cyrenius Chapin gave the following account of the episode to Lieutenant Colonel Solomon Van Rensselaer, who had led the volunteers across the river at Queenston and who must have derived considerable satisfaction from Smyth's discomfiture:

> You will hardly believe me when I tell you that our two doughty generals, Smyth and Porter, got into a boat yesterday with something like 20 men, and with flying colors went over to Grand Island, burnt a charge of powder at each other, shook hands, and came back again without staining the ground with even one drop of their precious blood.[39]

AMERICANS HAD little cause to celebrate the beginning of 1813. In June 1812, they had entered a war that they had been assured would be of short duration, a war that was to bring them new and expanded boundaries and the elimination of any threat from the north. Six months later they found that they had gained nothing; in fact, they had lost Michigan and all lands as far south as the Maumee. Even their generals, the heroes of the Revolution, had been reduced to figures of shame, butts of lampoons, objects of abuse. Their militia had emerged as cowardly, ill-disciplined, poorly motivated and lacking in soldierly qualities. What the war demonstrated, if it demonstrated anything at all, was that the people of the United States were involved in an armed conflict they did not understand and on whose virtues and necessity they were divided. Why, with a vast West, extending beyond the Mississippi, did the United States want Canada? "What is this invasion for?" asked Josiah Quincy. "Is it for land? We have enough. Plunder? There is none. New states? We have more than is good for us. Territory? If territory, there must be a standing army to keep it; and there must be another army to watch that." The only explanation Quincy could see for the war was the little Anglophobe Madison reciting his nursery rhyme:

Fee, fi, fo, fum,
I smell the blood of an Englishman,
Be he alive, or be he dead,
I will have some.[40]

Even so, Madison got himself re-elected in the autumn of 1812 with the support of the western and southern states, the same states that had voted for him and for the war. But if the president did not change, the secretary of war did. Dr. Eustis capitulated to congressional criticism of his failure to achieve military success and for having appointed "too many Federalists to office".[41] Madison first turned to Monroe, then to Dearborn and finally to Senator William Harris Crawford. None of them wanted the responsibilities Eustis had resigned. Finally, although Madison did not like him, he appointed the indolent and bad-tempered John Armstrong secretary of war.

Canadians had reason to be satisfied with the course the war had taken. They had not wanted the war, they had not declared it, and few believed that they would emerge successfully from it. To their surprise and delight, they had not only survived the American invasion but had beaten it back, and had expanded their country to the west and northwest. Admittedly, this was largely the work of Brock, and now Brock was gone. But even Prevost came in for praise from those who remembered the factious tenure of Sir James Craig. Comparing Craig and Prevost, a Canadian newspaper editor remarked: "During the administration of the first, we had perpetual war in peace; during that of the last, we had perpetual peace in war."[42] Canadians, generally, would have been happy to see the beginnings of peace talks at the outset of 1813. But there were still two years of war ahead of them, and the problems that had emerged during the first six months were still there: how to combat the sinister influence of the pro-American element in Upper Canada, how to retain naval control of the Great Lakes, how to find and transport food in sufficient quantities to meet the needs of soldiers and civilians alike, how to contain rising prices, and where to find somebody who could replace Isaac Brock as an inspiration and a leader? And, looming over all, was the enormous disparity in men and resources between British North America and the United States.

1813

6

The Erie Frontier

THE FIRST FIGHTING in 1813 took place on the Erie frontier. Late in 1812, after Dr. William Eustis had retired and before John Armstrong took over as secretary of war, James Monroe filled the appointment on a temporary basis. On 26 December he wrote Brigadier General William Harrison, who was stalled on the Maumee waiting for new regiments from Ohio and Kentucky, to express his dissatisfaction with Harrison's inactivity; the General should be up and moving, at least taking some action to annoy the British naval base on Lake Erie. Harrison did not have to contend with Monroe, however, as before the letter arrived John Armstrong had, on 13 January, taken over the War Department in Washington. Armstrong's views were different from Monroe's. He instructed Harrison to remain on the defensive until the Americans had built a fleet on Lake Erie. Optimistically, he informed the General that "our first object is to get a command of the lakes . . . and we have the fullest assurance that, by the first day of June, it will be accomplished."[1] He also promised Harrison 7000 regular soldiers to build up his army as well as adequate numbers of militia to defend supply depots and make good any wastage among the regulars.

Whatever Armstrong in Washington might think about the conduct of the war, Brigadier General James Winchester, Harrison's subordinate on the lower Maumee, wanted to see action. He was out of humour at having been superseded in command of the North Western Army as a result of Harrison's political

143

36. Major General William Henry Harrison, who commanded the American forces on the Lake Erie frontier in 1813

manoeuvring and was eager to prove the superiority of the regular military man over the amateur soldier. His informants had told him that Frenchtown, the British post on the River Raisin, was occupied by no more than 50 Canadians belonging to the Essex militia and about 100 Indians, and that an American force, moving quickly and decisively, could seize the post; this would give the Americans a chance to take possession of the provisions stored there before the British could remove them to Amherstburg. Here, then, was an opportunity to acquire much-needed supplies and, at the same time, remove some of the tarnish from the record of the North Western Army. Acting on his own responsibility, Winchester sent Lieutenant Colonel William Lewis of the Kentucky militia with 550 men towards the River Raisin. A few hours later he sent another detachment of 110 men under Lieutenant Colonel John Allen to join the first. Both groups encamped for the night on the north side of Maumee Bay, and continued the next day along the shore of Lake Erie towards the mouth of the River Raisin. There they ran into the Canadians and the Indians, and after an exchange of shots lasting several hours, the Canadians withdrew with their fieldpieces, conceding the encounter to the Americans. Meanwhile, Winchester ordered Colonel Samuel Wells and his regulars to move to the River Raisin, and he himself set off for the same destination in his cariole. By the time Winchester and Wells arrived, on 20 January, there were some 1000 men milling about the village of Frenchtown, a small settlement on the north side of the river. Little seems to have been done to set up a proper encampment. The troops had no artillery and no protection except a rail fence. Some of the officers were quartered at a distance from their men. Winchester chose as his headquarters a pleasant little house on the opposite side of the river; he could not bring himself to believe that there might still be Canadians and Indians in the vicinity. That is why he did not bother to send a patrol to keep an eye on the detachment that Lewis and Allen had driven away but that had pulled back only as far as Brownstown, some 30 km distant. Nor did Winchester pay any attention to reports circulating in the village that the British were planning a counterattack. Colonel Wells, the regular, was shocked at such negligence and asked for Winchester's permission to absent himself—ostensibly to hurry along the heavy baggage, but in reality to get word back to Harrison about the dangerous situation Winchester's men might very well find themselves in.

Wells's apprehensions were justified. Unknown to him or Winchester, Colonel Henry Procter of Amherstburg was on the move. News of the loss of his outpost on the River Raisin travelled quickly, Procter having learned of it during the night of 18 January. Without delay he summoned the Kent militia to take over the defences of Detroit and Amherstburg, and with all the troops available to him at both posts, including two companies of Newfoundlanders serving with the Provincial Marine, he travelled over the ice to Brownstown. With the troops that had retired from Frenchtown he assembled an armed force that, with the Indians commanded by the Wyandot chief, Round-head, approximated the American force in numerical strength. John Richardson, who, with his fourteen-year-old brother, accompanied Procter, described the move across the ice from Amherstburg to Brownstown:

> No sight could be more beautiful. . . . It was the depth of winter; and the river at the point we crossed being four miles in breadth, the deep rumbling noise of the guns prolonging their reverberations like the roar of distant thunder, as they moved along the ice, mingled with the wild cries of the Indians, seemed to threaten some convulsion of nature; while the appearance of the troops winding along the road, now lost behind some cliff of rugged ice, now emerging into view, their polished arms glittering in the sunbeams, gave an air of romantic grandeur to the scene.[2]

From Brownstown Procter went on to Stony Creek, about 6 km short of the River Raisin, and made ready to attack the enemy. Although his force was no larger than Winchester's, Procter had the advantage of initiative, and should have had the advantage of surprise. A prompt and sudden attack, while the Americans were still under their blankets, would probably have brought victory before the battle was fairly begun; at least it would have given the British possession of the rail fence that afforded the American regulars some protection, however meagre. But Procter chose to fight a set-piece battle. He drew his men up in three divisions, with the artillery in the centre, and while inspecting his guns was spotted by an American sentinel, who gave the alarm. The gunners, despite a galling fire from the centre of the American position, concentrated their bombardment on the American right, which finally gave way and was virtually cut to pieces by the Indians as it struggled in disorder through the snow to get across the river. Lewis and Allen, with two companies from the village, rushed to support the retreating soldiers, but were caught up in the rout. General Winchester hurried forward from his remote headquarters, only to be taken prisoner along with Lewis. Allen was tomahawked. The prisoners' coats and arms were taken from them while Roundhead escorted them to Colonel Procter. Elsewhere the American line held its position, but Winchester, in order to avoid further loss of life and a possible massacre of American soldiers by the Indians, gave the order to surrender. "So complete was the surprise of the enemy", wrote Richardson, "that General

Winchester, when brought in, had no other covering than the dress in which he slept."[3]

It had been a short but savage battle. The losses were heavy. Over 500 Americans became prisoners of war, and of the remainder of Winchester's force most had been killed, including a brother-in-law of Henry Clay; there were only about 100 stragglers left to make their way back to the Maumee Rapids. Procter, whose casualties, excluding those of his Indians, totalled over 180, did not remain on the battlefield, but promptly pulled back to Brownstown. He had neither enough men to go ahead to the Maumee nor enough soldiers to guard his large contingent of prisoners. Some of the wounded were therefore to be left behind at the River Raisin under an Indian guard, but many of the Indians, filled with looted whisky, returned to the battlefield, plundered the houses of local inhabitants and scalped any wounded Americans too weak to walk. Those who were not murdered were taken to various Indian villages and kept as prisoners until they were ransomed or released.

The fight at Frenchtown on the River Raisin was a British victory, sufficient to justify Procter's promotion to the rank of brigadier general at the age of twenty-six; it was, by the same token, a crushing defeat for Winchester,[4] but was not a decisive encounter in the larger picture of the war. It delayed, but did not prevent, Harrison's subsequent advance on Amherstburg. To the pro-war American press, the events on the River Raisin were a godsend, if only because they provided numerous writers with a propaganda weapon of tremendous strength to be used against the British, and in particular against Procter. The so-called "Indian massacre" was the kind of story that could be exploited to stimulate recruiting and stir up public feelings against the British and against the Indians who had allied themselves to the British cause. Of course there were brutalities and atrocities—that is the very nature of war—but brutalities and atrocities were by no means the monopoly of one side, and some of the stories told were palpably untrue. Even Harrison, who should have known better, was a victim of anti-Indian propaganda. "I have seen one man", he wrote, "who asserts that he saw General Winchester killed, scalped, and his bowels taken out."[5] This was written at the very time when Winchester, imprisoned in Fort Malden, was composing his account of what had happened at the River Raisin. "However unfortunate may seem the affair of yesterday", he wrote to the Secretary of War, "I am flattered by a belief that no material error is chargeable upon myself, and that still less censure is deserved by the troops I had the honor of commanding."[6] After reading these words, John Armstrong must have wondered who, then, was to blame for the defeat at the River Raisin. Was it Harrison?

Winchester, it should be recalled, had acted contrary to Harrison's orders. By his own rash action he had placed himself at the River Raisin beyond the range of ready help. Nevertheless, Harrison, who was at that time at Upper Sandusky, made every effort to help his subordinate. But by the time he reached the Maumee Rapids it was too late; the battle had been lost and Winchester was in the hands of the British. If Harrison had erred at all, it was in allowing Winchester too free a hand.

HARRISON LEARNED a lesson from the American defeat at the River Raisin. That was to use more caution when dealing with the British and the Indians. Winchester had acted rashly, without adequate thought and preparation. Harrison therefore determined to find himself a firm base to operate from, one closer to Amherstburg than Fort Wayne, yet with defences and armament sufficient to resist any British attempt to penetrate the Maumee River line, a place more permanent than the one Winchester had chosen. He therefore selected a location near the old battlefield of Fallen Timbers; it was elevated, near the river, and yet guarded on two sides by a ravine and a stream. Here, just below the Maumee Rapids, he built a strong fort to which he gave the name Fort Meigs. It became his headquarters for future operations. While employing most of his men in constructing the new fort, Harrison decided to try a probing attack on the naval base at Amherstburg, where, he was told, the British had laid down the keel of a new warship. Intended as a hit-and-run raid, devastating but not costly, this little effort did not get beyond the shore of the lake. The plan was for the American raiders to cross on the ice, but when the raiding party reached the lake, the ice was breaking up and they could see, far out from the shore, the ripple of moving water. There would be no attack on Amherstburg at that time, but, by the same token, no raid from Amherstburg on the new fort on the Maumee. Harrison therefore set off for Cincinnati. He would drum up a few recruits and, incidentally, visit his family, leaving Fort Meigs to be completed before his return.

Back at Amherstburg, Procter's thoughts were running along the same lines as Harrison's. He had carried out one successful operation against Winchester; why should he not try the same

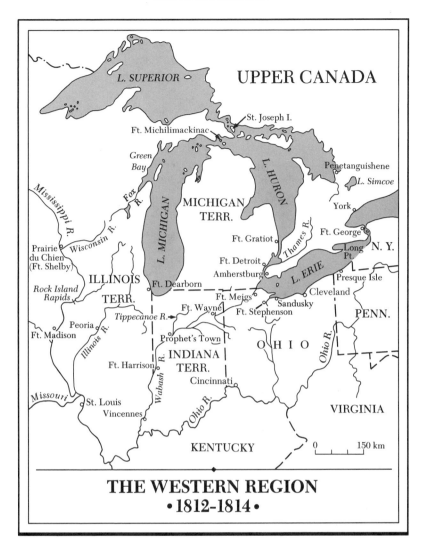

THE WESTERN REGION
• 1812-1814 •

thing against Harrison? Why not make a show of force against Fort Meigs? Success there would probably ensure peace on the Erie frontier for the greater part of the summer, and enable Procter to build up his stocks of provisions until the harvest was reaped in the autumn. The militia call-out in the fall of 1812 had reduced the food resources in the area, and a critical shortage would threaten later in the year if additional supplies were not obtained. Moreover, Michigan was a territory worth holding, and Brock's offence-is-the-best-defence strategy was the best means of securing the British position. Procter, with the backing of prominent Canadian civilians, sent an urgent appeal to Prevost for more soldiers; meanwhile Tecumseh sent instructions to the various Indian nations to forgather as soon as possible at Amherstburg. Time was the important thing. Any attack upon Harrison's new position on the Maumee ought to be carried out before Fort Meigs was completed and before reinforcements were available from Ohio and Kentucky. But the spring weather was unusually wet that year and it was late in April before Procter, with a force of over 520 regulars (largely men of the overused 41st Regiment), 450 militia and some 1500 Indians, along with artillery and a couple of gunboats, left Amherstburg for the mouth of the Maumee River. There the troops disembarked, and while the gunboats moved slowly up the Maumee, oxen began the difficult task of dragging wagons and cannon, several of them guns captured at Detroit, through mud frequently up to the axles, along what passed for a road, towards Harrison's fort below the rapids. On 28 April they reached their destination, and set about preparing a camp on the flat ground just below the old fort, Miami. For several days, while the Indians were rounding up cattle in the neighbourhood, the troops worked on building gun emplacements close to Fort Meigs. From time to time the two gunboats, each carrying a 9-pounder gun, would advance upstream to lob a few shells at the walls and divert the attention of the American defenders from the British work parties on the north bank of the Maumee.

By 1 May, Procter was ready to begin the siege. According to John Richardson, a steady bombardment went on for four days without intermission, while the Indians, on the south bank of the river, kept up a smart small-arms fire at the fort. However, Harrison refused to either surrender or come out from behind the walls of his fort. His position was still a strong one, and he was well aware that a relief force, some 1200 Kentuckians under Brigadier General Green Clay, was no more than a few hours distant. On the evening of 2 May, Harrison dispatched a messenger to tell Clay to send one of his brigades downriver on flatboats to the north bank, where they could land and carry the British cannon by a surprise attack, spike the guns and break their carriages, and then hurry into the fort. The other brigade would land on the south bank and fight its way through the Indians to the fort. Then Harrison himself, with his superior force, would sally forth to engage the whole of Procter's besieging army.

On the morning of 5 May, the first of Clay's brigades, Colonel William Dudley's, appeared. It encountered no opposition and, in conformity with his instructions, Dudley landed and

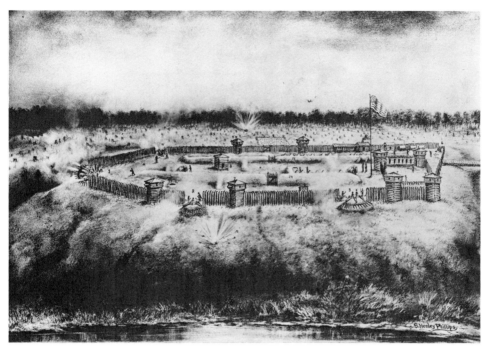

37. Fort Meigs, 1813

spiked the British siege cannon. Finding some of his men engaged with the Indians, and elated with his initial success,
Dudley disregarded his orders and began chasing a group of
Indians towards the British camp. It was the kind of thing no
Kentuckian could resist. Thinking that Dudley's force constituted the main American attack, Procter pulled Tecumseh's
Indians away from the south bank and sent Brevet Majors Muir
and Chambers of the 41st Regiment to regain the guns and
engage Dudley. Throwing aside his sword and grasping the
musket of a soldier who had been shot just a moment before,
Chambers, followed by Lieutenant John Le Breton of the Newfoundland Regiment, led a mixed group of infantry and gunners
to recapture the cannon. Meanwhile, Muir and Tecumseh became involved with the main part of Dudley's force, now moving through the woods without any direction or cohesion. It
became a bloody field day; large numbers of Americans were
killed, including Dudley himself, and others were taken prisoner. John Richardson reported that no fewer than 450 American troops fell into British hands. Only 150 of the 800 men who
landed on the north bank succeeded in making their escape to
the boats. On the south bank the story was different. There the

THE SIEGE OF FORT MEIGS
•1-5 MAY 1813•

second brigade overran the battery that Procter had established to provide crossfire with the guns from the opposite side of the river, and drove the Indians who had remained on the south side of the river into the woods. Some 40 men of the 41st were taken prisoner. This ended the fighting for the day. A white flag was hoisted from the fort, ostensibly for the sake of a parley to negotiate the exchange of prisoners, but possibly to gain time for some of Clay's supply boats to make their way to Fort Meigs. However, the remaining craft, which contained baggage and private stores, fell into the hands of the Indians who were still pursuing the fugitives of Dudley's brigade. General Harrison, having obtained what he required most, a reinforcement of men and foodstuffs, withdrew behind the walls of his fort and waited to see what Procter would do. There was no fighting for the next two days, during which negotiations went on for an exchange of prisoners. By 7 May, Procter was ready to resume the siege.

The impetus that had carried Procter's men from Amherstburg to the Maumee and sustained them during the siege and the victory over Clay had, by now, evaporated. The killing of a number of American prisoners by those whom Richardson, who took part in the siege of Fort Meigs, called "a few cowardly and treacherous Indians who had borne no share in the action" sickened many of the British soldiers and Canadian militia, just as it sickened Richardson and Tecumseh, who, when he learned what was going on, rushed to the scene, threatening to kill any Indian who murdered a prisoner. But there were still more pressing reasons than an excess of bloodshed for Procter to give up the siege. His Indians were now tired and were anxious to go home to display their plunder; his militia were pressing to go home to attend to their crops. This last was a powerful argument. Only a small amount of seeding had been done prior to the call-out in April, and if the farmers among the militia could not get home to plant their corn the whole Detroit River region would be faced with a serious food shortage. Without the Indians and the militia, Procter did not have enough men to carry Fort Meigs; neither did he have enough heavy guns to batter the fort to pieces. These considerations left Procter little choice but to break off the battle and return to Amherstburg. It was not a happy journey for it was accompanied by a sense of failure, despite the victory over Clay. It also had an aspect of the ludicrous, particularly among the Indians sporting the loot they had taken from Clay's boats. Richardson described them:

> . . . decked out in the uniforms of the officers; and although embarrassed to the last degree in their movements, and dragging with difficulty the heavy military boots with which their legs were for the first time covered, strutted forth much to the admiration of their less fortunate comrades. Some were habited in plain clothes; others had their bodies clad in clean white shirts, contrasting in no ordinary manner with the swarthiness of their skins; all wore some article of decoration, and their tents were ornamented with saddles, bridles, rifles, daggers, swords, and pistols, many of which were handsomely mounted and of curious workmanship.[7]

There were also less amusing "revolting" sights, the "scalps of the slain, drying in the sun, stained on the fleshy side with vermilion dyes and dangling in the air, as they hung suspended from poles to which they were attached". These, too, were the accompaniments of warfare in the wilderness; and they were the trophies of not only the Indians.

The siege of Fort Meigs was a curious affair. Procter won a tactical victory on 5 May with the defeat of Clay, but the strategic laurels rested with Harrison, who still held his fort. Procter's military capability had been seriously damaged, and in a sense his campaign was a failure. Yet he did achieve one thing. He further delayed the inevitable offensive that Harrison was planning to undertake against Upper Canada. Procter realized this and pointed it out in the dispatch he wrote to Prevost from Sandwich on 14 May: "If the enemy had been permitted to receive his reinforcements and supplies undisturbed, I should have had, at this critical juncture, to contend with him for Detroit, or perhaps on this shore."[8] But there were even more critical days ahead for Upper Canada, not only because Procter never could muster sufficient men to give adequate protection to the Erie frontier, but also because he faced the almost insurmountable problem of feeding the men he did have, regulars, militia and Indians alike; problems that were not of Procter's own making and that he could not solve; problems stemming from the limited resources of the area; problems affecting the transport of provisions and supplies from other parts of the province. In fact, Procter had to undertake spoiling expeditions against the Americans, such as the operations against the River Raisin and Fort Meigs, to forestall any major enemy offensive and, if possible, to make good the deficiencies in British supplies by capturing stores from the Americans.

A cursory reading of Procter's correspondence in 1813 would suggest that the officer commanding the Right Division of the British forces in Upper Canada was a chronic complainer. Complain he did, but he had much to complain about. His position was one that would have tried the temper of older and more experienced officers. Procter realized that he commanded a region likely to be abandoned in the event of a major American offensive against Upper Canada at either the Niagara area or Kingston, and that he commanded the army that would be withdrawn or sacrificed as a forlorn hope to meet the needs of other regions and other armies. For strategic reasons, the British military and political authorities were unlikely to detach too large a percentage of their armed strength to the Erie and Detroit frontier lest it be cut off by American penetration farther east. Should this happen, without communications with the seaport regions of British North America, severed from the rest of the province, the western regions of Upper Canada must fall automatically into the grasping hands of the enemy. That is why Procter was left to operate with only the overworked 41st Regiment, the Essex and Kent militias and the western Indians. When Procter asked for reinforcements of British regular troops, he was told they were unavailable. Writing to his friend Robert McDouall, in the adjutant general's office, Procter said:

> If His Excellency does not interfere, I shall be kept so weak as to tempt the enemy forward. If Sir George's intentions had been fulfilled, I could venture to ensure the safety of this flank for some months at least.[9]

A month later he wrote, "I stand very little chance here at this end of the line, if I am to receive only reinforcements that can be spared."[10]

And there were distinct limitations on the uses to which Procter could put his Indians and militia. Neither possessed the quality of readiness or stability. In a letter to Sir George Prevost after the withdrawal from Fort Meigs, Procter put his finger on the weakness of his auxiliaries. The Indian force, he wrote, "is not a disposable one, or permanent, tho' occasionally a most powerful aid".[11] In a letter to McDouall, he pointed out that the principal officer of the Indian Department, Matthew Elliott, was "past seventy, I have understood near eighty".[12] Elliott was, in fact, a vigorous seventy-four, who took an active part in the engagements at the River Raisin and Fort Meigs, but who had become inured to cruelty and had lost his will or desire to exercise a tight control over the Indians. In any event, the responsibility was Procter's, and he could not escape it by trying to lay the blame for any Indian excesses on Elliott or by urging the military authorities to retire the old man from the service because of "his age and long service".[13] The evidence suggests that Procter was exaggerating the significance of Elliott's age, if only because of his strong dislike of the Indian Department at Amherstburg.

Neither did Procter feel that he should place too much reliance on his militia. Admittedly there were some militiamen of dubious loyalty but, broadly speaking, the response from the Essex and Kent contingents had been good. The weakness of the militia lay in the sporadic nature of its service and the need to give the members leave to work their farms. It was this uncertainty, whether militiamen would be available at any given time, and how many, that prompted the suggestion that a special corps of Canadian rangers should be formed to take the place of the militia, to be employed on a full-time basis with the Indians. Procter put the suggestion up to Sheaffe and advanced the name of William Caldwell, a militiaman and a captain in the Butler's Rangers of Revolutionary War days, as commander of the corps.[14]

But it was not only men that Procter needed. His posts at Amherstburg and Detroit—for he was responsible for the civil administration of Michigan[15] as well as for the command of the Right Division of the British army in Upper Canada—were short of just about everything: barrack furniture, bedding, cooking utensils (kettles in particular), camp equipage, clothing, stationery, money and, above all, meat. Provisions were always a problem at Amherstburg. In June 1813, Procter wrote:

> "The want of meat does operate much against us. As does the want of Indian arms and goods. In short, our wants are so serious that the enemy must derive great advantage from them alone."[16]

THE SIEGE OF Fort Meigs was followed by a breathing space for both the American and the British forces. Harrison spent his time recruiting and training new regiments and carrying out mounted reconnaissances with Colonel Richard M. Johnson's newly organized cavalry. Ninian Edwards, the governor of the Illinois Territory, formed patrols and built defended positions at Peoria, Prairie du Chien and Fort Madison, and on the Rock River. Meanwhile, all western Americans were awaiting the completion of the fleet then building at Presque Isle (Erie, Penn.), which Armstrong had confidently predicted would be ready by 1 June.

Procter, in addition to writing reports and requisitions, found time to worry about his supply lines, about the bad news of American victories at York and Fort George, and about the growing restlessness of his Indians. He believed that if only he had more regular soldiers he could satisfy the Indian demand for action, capture much-needed provisions from the enemy, and, most important of all, by a successful land–water attack on Presque Isle, nullify any advantage the Americans might gain in the Niagara peninsula; this by itself would ensure the survival of the British Army's Right Division in Upper Canada. It all seemed so very obvious that he could not understand why his ideas were not acceptable in high places. It hardly improved Procter's state of mind to receive a gloomy directive from Major General Francis de Rottenburg, who had succeeded Major General Roger Sheaffe as commander in Upper Canada, telling him that, in the event of the British losing naval control of Lake Ontario, all British troops would be withdrawn at once to Kingston; and that Procter and his men would probably have to retreat to Lake Superior, whence, by obtaining transportation in the North West Company's canoes, they would proceed to Montreal via the Company's old canoe route. In haste, as well as in a state of annoyance, Procter wrote Prevost to point out that, were Rottenburg's proposals to become generally known, the British could say farewell to any further Indian support. He argued that the whole scenario proposed by Rottenburg could be altered by determined action on Lake Erie to capture the American fleet before it became waterborne. As matters stood, however, Procter did not have a sufficient number of men to capture Presque Isle, although he would be willing to make an attempt on Sandusky.[17] That letter was dated 11 July. Two days later he wrote again to Prevost, this time to make the point that the Indians were reluctant to attack Sandusky, but that they were prepared to make another attempt to take Fort Meigs. It was not what Procter wanted—he could not transport the kind of siege weapons such an operation would require—yet he had no choice but to go along with the Indians since they were supplying the bulk of the attacking force.

The second siege of Fort Meigs was Tecumseh's idea. It was also conducted according to his plan. With a force comprising about 400 regulars, including some of the men who had served at Queenston Heights and had recéntly been sent to Amherstburg, a few militia and about 1000 Indians, Procter and Tecumseh set out for the Maumee. Since the British still controlled Lake Erie, Procter was able to move his troops quickly and easily. The boats made straight for the Maumee and deposited the assault force not far from the position they had occupied during the previous siege. On this occasion, Procter's force was a weaker one than he had used in May, and it lacked strength in artillery. Only the Indians were out in greater numbers. Unfortunately for Procter, the fort itself was in better condition to withstand a siege, and the commander, Clay, having seen how Dudley's impetuosity had ended, was inclined towards caution. Tecumseh knew that he could not expect to take Fort Meigs by assault. He therefore planned to entice the garrison out from behind the walls by staging a sham battle among the trees to convince the Americans that another American force, *en route* to the fort, had been caught in an ambush. He expected the garrison to open the gates and hasten out to help their comrades. The Indians would then attack the garrison, rush into the fort and put it to the torch. Here is how John Richardson, who took part in every operation conducted by the Right Division during 1812 and 1813, described what followed:

> We were all instantly, although noiselessly, upon the alert, but in vain did we look for any movement in the fort. Many of the garri-

157

son lined the ramparts in the rear, and seemed to look out anxiously in the direction of the firing, but they gave not the slightest indication of a design to leave the fort, even when the musketry had become so animated and heavy that we were half in doubt ourselves whether the battle was a sham one or real. Either they had obtained information of our presence, or they suspected the nature and object of the ruse, and we had the mortification to find ourselves utterly foiled in the grand design of the expedition.[18]

Under normal circumstances the Indian strategy would probably have succeeded, but on the morning of the proposed attack a messenger had reached Clay with information indicating that no American troops would be moving towards the fort. The American commander suspected a trap and therefore did not spring it. Tecumseh was disappointed, but he was prepared to admit that the little 6-pounders the British had brought with them would have no effect on the walls of the fort, and on 28 July he agreed with Procter that the siege, if such it could be called, should be raised.

At this point many of the Indians went home. Some remained with Tecumseh in the forest and swampland between the Maumee and Sandusky rivers to stage raids and intercept travellers. The others went with Procter, who, hoping to salvage something from the expedition, was intent upon taking the fort on the Sandusky. This had been his original intention until he was over-ruled by the Indians.

Procter and his force, very much reduced in numbers, reached the Sandusky early in the morning of 1 August. He landed and set his men to erecting gun emplacements along the edge of a wooded area from which he proposed to bombard Fort Stephenson. The object of the attack was a small wooden structure, constructed in 1812, which stood on the western bank of the river. The defence works were elementary—a ditch, a stockade and a single 6-pounder cannon. The garrison consisted of 160 American regulars under the command of an obscure officer of the regular army, Major George Croghan, who had taken part in the battle of Tippecanoe. Croghan had actually been instructed by Harrison (who had been warned by Clay that Procter was in the vicinity) not to attempt to defend the fort but to withdraw as soon as the British were sighted, but Procter had appeared so suddenly that Croghan was unable to carry out his orders.

The siege began with an ineffective bombardment by Procter's guns, but the 6-pounders were too light to make any impression on the stockade. Procter then decided that he would have

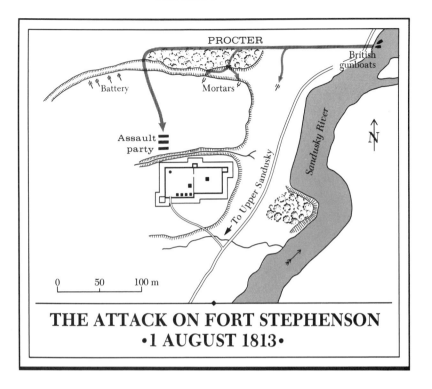

PROCTER

British gunboats

Battery

Mortars

Assault party

Sandusky River

N

To Upper Sandusky

0   50   100 m

THE ATTACK ON FORT STEPHENSON
•1 AUGUST 1813•

to take the place by assault. Accordingly, in the late afternoon, between 1600 and 1700 hrs, his infantry formed up in three assault columns, and on the word of command went forward, as Richardson said, "in double-quick time",[19] covered to some extent by the lingering smoke of the cannon. The sky was threatening, but the ground was dry and the troops had no difficulty in reaching the ditch surrounding the stockade. Croghan had ordered his men to withhold their fire, and it was not until the assault troops were about 50 m away that he gave the order to fire, not only with muskets but with the fort's one cannon, which to this time had been kept hidden. The effect of the grapeshot was devastating. Procter's Indians had no stomach for this kind of fighting and withdrew at once to whatever cover was within reach. "Our men, generally," wrote a private soldier of the 41st, Shadrach Byfield, "were determined. I saw one of them turn around, his comrade observed it and said, if he did not face the fire, he would run his bayonet through him."[20] Such was the effect of discipline, and it was discipline that compelled the soldiers to keep on trying. Some actually reached the walls of the fort, but, without fascines or ladders, and with axes that were dull from constant use, they could neither climb over

159

the walls into the fort nor hack their way into it. Repeated attempts were made, but to no purpose. To continue would be suicidal. Byfield and several others managed to hide under a bank and to crawl back when darkness fell. Catching sight of them, Procter asked, "Where are the rest of the men?" Byfield replied, "I don't think there are any more to come; they are all killed or wounded."[21] During the night the Indians brought back the wounded and the dead, and by morning there were no British troops or Indians in the vicinity of Fort Stephenson. The soldiers were in the boats on their way back to Amherstburg; the Indians were travelling overland on foot.

It is difficult to determine just what Procter hoped to achieve with this expedition to Fort Meigs and Fort Stephenson, other than to keep his Indians employed. He knew from the outset that he was not strong enough to take the former, and the latter had no strategic value; that was evident from Harrison's willingness to give up Fort Stephenson without a struggle. If it had no value to Harrison, what use would it have been to Procter? The British commander was inclined to blame the Indians for both the futile journey to the Maumee and the lack of success on the Sandusky. Perhaps the true explanation is to be found in the sentence in Procter's report that said, "The neighbourhood of Sanduksy, and the settlement on the Huron River, eight miles below it, could have afforded cattle sufficient to have fed my whole Indian force for some time, had they been induced to accompany us."[22] And perhaps there is an element of truth in his remark that "the Gentlemen of the Indian Department, who have the direction of it, declared formally their decided opinion that unless the fort was stormed we should never be able to bring an Indian warrior into the field with us." It is easy enough to shrug off this kind of explanation for what was clearly a tactical as well as a strategic misjudgement on Procter's part, but it is not easy to shrug off his prophetic remarks to the Commander-in-Chief:

> The enemy's vessels are out of Presqu'isle Harbour, and so decidedly stronger than ours that Captain Barclay has been necessitated to return to Amherstburg, and with all haste to get the new vessel ready for sea, which she will be in eight or ten days at farthest, and then only want hands. Whatever may happen to be regreted may be fairly attributed to the delays in sending here the force Your Excellency directed should be sent. Had it been sent at once, it could have been used to the greatest advantage, but it arrived in such small portions and with such delays that the opportunities have been lost. . . . You will probably hear of the enemy's landing shortly at

38. The British repulsed at Fort Stephenson, 1 August 1813

Long Point, whence they may gain the rear of the Centre Division, and also affect my supplies. An hundred & fifty sailors would
have effectually obviated this Evil.[23]

Such sad words, "What might have been"! Procter's experience
on the Erie frontier in the midsummer months of 1813 was just
a foretaste of what was to befall him in autumn of the same year.

ONCE THE STRUGGLE over the future of British North America began in the eastern and central parts of the continent, it was inevitable that it should expand westwards across the continent to the Pacific. The bourgeois of the North West Company were particularly concerned about the war. They felt that their interests had suffered from what they regarded as a territorial sell-out when Great Britain signed the peace agreement at the conclusion of the American Revolutionary War, and especially when John Jay persuaded the British authorities to sign the treaty that bears his name. With Great Britain and the United States once more at war, the Company saw an opportunity to regain its former position and to consolidate its commercial ambitions in the western regions of North America. Hence its offers to extend help to the British military authorities in Upper and Lower Canada, and its requests to the British government to send adequate troops to the Northwest to protect British interests.

American penetration of the more westerly regions of the continent had lagged behind that of the French and later the Canadian and the British fur traders. Not until 1805 did the United States government send Lewis and Clark and their companions on an overland journey through the mountains to the mouth of the Columbia River. This journey was followed, a few years later, by the formation of the Pacific Fur Company by John Jacob Astor and the opening, in 1811, of the trading post, Fort Astoria, on the south bank of the Columbia, about 7 km from where the river empties into the Pacific Ocean. The post was staffed largely by Canadians, formerly in the employ of the North West Company.

News of Madison's declaration of war against Great Britain did not reach the American post on the Pacific until seven months after its publication in Washington. Even then it travelled in a roundabout manner. Donald McKenzie, one of Astor's employees, saw the printed declaration in the hands of a Canadian fur trader when he visited Spokane, and revealed its contents to the astonished occupants of Astoria on his arrival there on 15 January 1813. What were they to do? Gabriel Franchère, a fur trader, wrote:

> When we learned this news all of us at Astoria who were British subjects and Canadians wished ourselves in Canada; but we could not entertain even the thought of transporting ourselves thither, at least immediately; we were separated from our country by an immense space, and the difficulties of the journey at this season were insuperable.[24]

39. Fort Astoria in 1813. The British renamed it Fort George.

They reasoned that a British naval blockade would be established and that it was unlikely any American ships would reach the port bearing Company goods; meanwhile they might as well carry on with their usual activities.

Then, on 11 April, two birch canoes bearing the British flag arrived at Astoria. They were commanded by John George McTavish and Joseph Larocque and manned by nineteen Canadian voyageurs. Employees of the North West Company, these men had called at Astoria to await the arrival of a Company vessel, *Isaac Todd*, which was expected in the summer. Meanwhile, they arranged to purchase needed articles from the Astorians and repay them in furs or bills of exchange on the North West Company in Montreal. There were no further developments until September, when McKenzie, McTavish and Angus Bethune arrived at Astoria followed by a flotilla of canoes bearing furs. This time McTavish carried a letter from one of the North West Company partners addressed to Duncan McDougall, in charge of Astoria, telling him that the *Isaac Todd* had sailed from London in March, equipped with letters of marque and accompanied by the frigate *Phoebe* carrying instructions to seize Astoria as "an important colony founded by

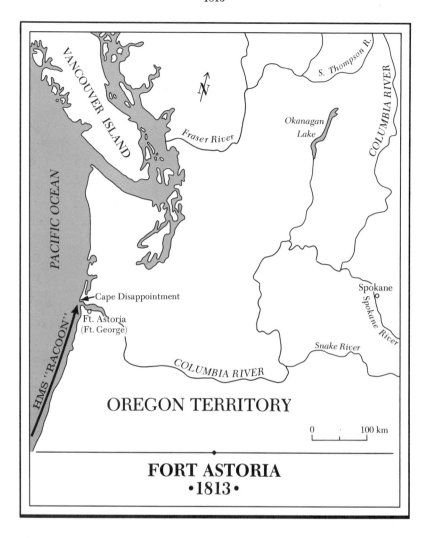

N

VANCOUVER ISLAND

PACIFIC OCEAN

S. Thompson R.

COLUMBIA RIVER

Fraser River

Okanagan Lake

Cape Disappointment

Ft. Astoria (Ft. George)

HMS "RACOON"

Spokane

Spokane River

Snake River

COLUMBIA RIVER

OREGON TERRITORY

0   100 km

FORT ASTORIA
•1813•

the American government".[25] Although in a strong position, armed as they were with cannon, and the Nor'Westers not only short of food but without siege weapons, the Astorians wondered what action they should take. It was the threat of the arrival of the warship that frightened them, and when the Nor'Westers proposed that the post be sold to the North West Company rather than seized by a group of British sailors, Duncan McDougall agreed. The Nor'Westers then took possession of Astoria, agreeing to pay the servants of the Pacific Fur Company the arrears of their wages, supply them with provisions, and give free passage to those who wished to return to Canada overland. The American colours were hauled down and the British flag was hoisted "to the no small chagrin and mortification of those who were American citizens", according to Franchère.[26] The greater number of Astor's employees decided to enter the service of the North West Company, the remainder to go home.

The deal between the Astorians and the Nor'Westers was concluded on 16 October.[27] Several weeks later, Alexander Stewart and Alexander Henry the younger arrived in Astoria. They were four months out of Fort William and they brought with them Canadian newspapers, the first that the people of Astoria had seen since the war began. The news of British successes in Canada was gratifying, as was the news that the British frigate could be expected any day. But when, on 30 November, a strange vessel was seen standing in under Cape Disappointment, both McDougall and McTavish were nervous: was she American or British, and what might happen should she prove to be an American warship? However, the vessel was HM Sloop of War *Racoon*, with 26 guns, and one of the men she carried was John McDonald ("Le Bras croche"), a partner of the North West Company. Several days later, on 13 December 1813, when the *Racoon* had made her way up the river, her captain, Commander W. Black, RN, came ashore, accompanied by a lieutenant of marines, four soldiers and four sailors. There was a formal dinner, and Black hoisted the Union Jack on a specially erected flagpole in the square. Then, breaking a bottle of Madeira on the flagstaff, he declared in a loud voice that he took possession of the establishment and the country in the name of His Britannic Majesty. The old name of Astoria was dropped and the post was renamed Fort George in honour of the King. Three rounds of artillery and musketry were fired, and the King's health was drunk to mark the occasion. Standing by were a few puzzled Indians wondering what it was all about. The one jarring note on the occasion was Commander Black's all-too-obvious disappointment that the fort had already passed into British hands through the agency of the fur traders and that there were no American vessels in the river laden with furs. Neither he nor his crew would receive the expected prize money. "What!" cried Black, after he had inspected the fort for the first time, "Is this the fort that was represented to me as so formidable! Good God! I could batter it down in two hours with a four-pounder!"[28]

7

The Niagara Frontier

JOHN ARMSTRONG, the secretary of war, placed a restraining hand on Harrison in the early months of 1813, preferring to keep the Erie frontier quiet until the United States had achieved naval superiority on Lake Erie; but as far as Lake Ontario and the Niagara frontier were concerned, he was all for immediate action. Thus, in 1813, the main American thrust shifted from the west to the central theatre of operations. During 1812 the Canadian naval base at Kingston had attracted a certain amount of talk but little action. No menacing move had been made in that direction other than an exchange of shots on 10 November between the American fleet from Sackets Harbor and the corvette *Royal George* and the Kingston shore batteries.[1] However, in January 1813, at his first cabinet meeting, the new secretary of war suggested an early strike at Kingston and York, for the purpose of eliminating the vessels of the Provincial Marine prior to commencing a land-based offensive against Upper Canada by way of the Niagara River. Lake Ontario would be free of ice by 1 April; any American assault forces should therefore be ready before then. Once the British vessels were disposed of, the American fleet, with an assault force of 4000 men, would return to the United States to join forces with another army of 3000. Together they would carry the British defence fortifications on the west bank of the Niagara River and take possession of the Upper-Canadian military headquarters at Fort George. Several weeks later this plan was altered when Armstrong learned that the spring thaw might be later than expected.

167

He therefore ordered Dearborn to send Zebulon Pike's brigades to Sackets Harbor in time to carry out an over-the-ice assault upon Kingston. Such a manoeuvre would be wholly unexpected, and the British vessels, frozen in the harbour, would be helpless.

In addition to this new strategic approach for 1813, Armstrong tried to give the United States army a new image. Six new major generals were appointed and several brigadiers. Most of the major generals bore familiar names, however, and were of ancient vintage; excluding Harrison, they averaged fifty-seven years of age. The brigadiers were mainly younger men and brought somewhat more vigour to a notably sluggish high command. Among them were officers like Zebulon Pike and George Izard, probably the best-militarily-educated officer in the United States; and McArthur, Cass and Winder, all of whom had displayed vitality, if not very much skill, during the operations of 1812. There were also a few reassignments of postings. Dearborn and Harrison retained their areas of offensive action in northern New York and on the Erie frontier. The surprise move was the shifting of Major General James Wilkinson from his comfortable post at New Orleans to the more demanding and significant one at Sackets Harbor. Wilkinson took his time about moving, however, and could claim no credit or responsibility for what happened in the early part of the year.

Whether the over-the-ice scheme that Armstrong favoured was really a practical military operation is open to question. Ultimately, Armstrong conceded that it might be too dangerous and in March he rescinded his order. The Americans were to wait until the ice was gone and the troops could be ferried in boats. The American naval commander, Isaac Chauncey, favoured this approach. He also had his own ideas about priorities and urged that York, rather than Kingston, should be the first objective, partly because he had heard that Kingston had been reinforced, but principally because the British had a fine new ship in the stocks at York that Chauncey was anxious to capture or destroy before she was launched. The possibility that this might alter the plan for a combined attack on the Niagara frontier would have to be accepted; York and then Kingston should be the sequence of the operations. The commander-in-chief, Dearborn, who never liked making decisions, accepted Chauncey's line of reasoning and persuaded Armstrong to do the same. That is why, when Chauncey and Dearborn, with 1700 soldiers and an undetermined number of marines, set sail in fourteen vessels on 25 April, their destination was York, not Kingston. The next day they were within 40 km of the capital

40. The blockhouse at York

of Upper Canada. People standing on the cliffs at Scarborough could see them and hear the warning guns fired in the town.

York, although not as large as Kingston, was the seat of the provincial government. P. Finan, who was with the Royal Newfoundland Regiment stationed there, referred to it as a

> pleasant little town, the houses generally of wood, and containing some good shops. Being the seat of government of the upper province, it has a house of assembly, court house, etc. It is situated at the lower end of a long bay formed by a narrow peninsula stretching up the lake, parallel with the shore, about two miles. On the extremity of this, called Gibraltar Point, stands a light-house, and exactly opposite to it, on the mainland, the garrison is situated, where we resided.[2]

York was not a strongly defended location. General Brock had planned to build a fort there, but he had had to content himself with a temporary magazine, a blockhouse, and a ditch enclosing Government House and various barrack buildings. In addition, there were several batteries along the shore to the west and a battery within the confines of the so-called fort. On the stocks a new ship was under construction for the Provincial Marine, and in the dockyard the *Duke of Gloucester*, an old Provincial Marine vessel, was undergoing repairs. As far as the garrison was concerned, it consisted of the flank companies of the York militia, the dockyard workers, a few gunners of the Royal Artillery, a company of the Glengarry Light Infantry, two weak companies of the Royal Newfoundland Regiment, two

41. Private of the 8th Regiment of Foot, 1814–15

companies of the 8th, or King's, Regiment of Foot and a few
Indians. A mixed bag of, in all, about 700 men.

In the early hours of the morning of 27 April, Chauncey's
invasion fleet sailed round Gibraltar Point towards the west of
the town. The weather was good, the waters of the lake were
calm, and the sailing vessels, gliding slowly over the surface in
a gentle breeze, each towing several boats for landing the troops,
displayed what the Newfoundlander P. Finan described as "an
elegant and imposing appearance".[3]

As soon as it became evident where the Americans proposed
to land their troops, the grenadier company of the 8th moved
off. Theirs was the task of stopping the enemy on the beaches.
They were, as Finan put it, "as fine men as the British army

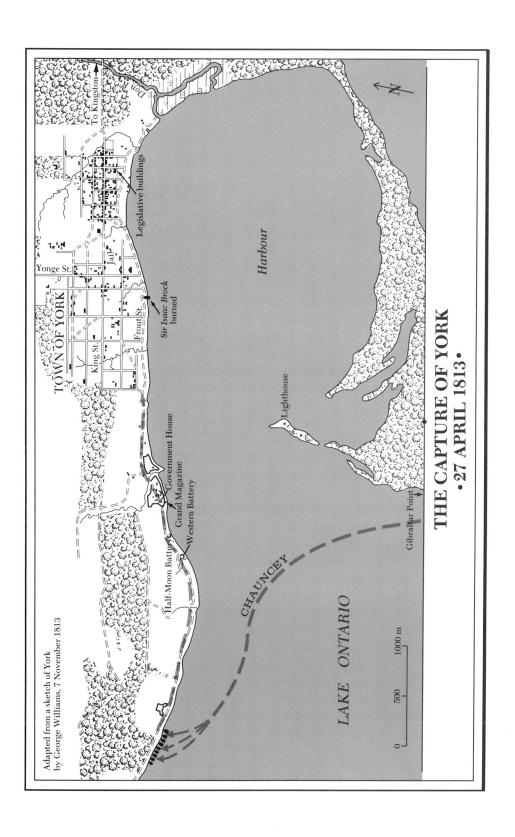

Adapted from a sketch of York
by George Williams, 7 November 1813

TOWN OF YORK

To Kingston

Don

Legislative buildings

Yonge St.

Jail

King St.

Front St.

Sir Isaac Brock
burned

Government House

Grand Magazine

Western Battery

Half-Moon Battery

Harbour

Lighthouse

Gibraltar Point

CHAUNCEY

LAKE ONTARIO

0   500   1000 m

THE CAPTURE OF YORK
•27 APRIL 1813•

could produce", and their sergeant-major was "a remarkably fine-looking man".[4] The initial American landing party was composed of Major Benjamin Forsyth's riflemen, the fellows who had previously been engaged in twisting the lion's tail by raiding the Canadian shore along the St. Lawrence. Their approach in flat-bottomed "Schenectady" boats was covered by gunfire from the American warships. What the British needed now was the brass cannon resting in the "fort"—it would have been deadly against the overloaded boats—but all the defenders could produce was musket fire from the Indians near the shore. The sniping by the Indians was apparently very accurate, at least sufficiently so to cause Forsyth's men to abandon their oars and take up their own weapons. Meanwhile, Zebulon Pike's infantry began to approach in other boats, outflanking the Indians, who then pulled back into the woods. At this point the grenadiers arrived and, disdaining to use their muskets, charged with the bayonet. It was a matter of one company against three. Captain Neal McNeale was killed; so was a volunteer with him, Donald McLean, clerk of the Upper Canada House of Assembly. When the grenadiers were compelled to withdraw, about half of their number were left behind on the beach and along the shore. The Newfoundlanders who came upon the scene also fought hard, suffering no fewer than 36 casualties. It was, throughout the battle, always a matter of too little too late.

Everything seemed to go wrong. The Glengarrians, who had been ordered to support the grenadiers, lost their way, and the 8th and the militia, as Sheaffe reported later, could not, despite all efforts, maintain the contest "against the greatly superior and increasing numbers of the enemy".[5] The British therefore retired under cover of the batteries. An attempt was made to rally the defenders at the Western Battery. Unfortunately, the gunner accidentally dropped his match into the travelling magazine, a large wooden chest containing cartridges for the gun. "Every man in the battery", wrote Finan afterwards, "was blown into the air, and the *dissection* of the great part of their bodies was inconceivably shocking!"[6] The cannon was hurled from the gun carriage and the battery rendered useless. This unfortunate mishap was probably the turning point of the day as far as the defenders were concerned. Had Sheaffe been present, he might have restored the morale of the men by a show of coolness or by some dramatic Brock-like gesture, but, lacking leadership at a critical moment, the defenders

began now visibly to melt away; there was no person to animate
them nor to tell them when they were to make a stand, their officers knew nothing of what was to be done, each was asking of
another, enquiring after the General and running after his aides
and messengers in order to ascertain what they should do. In the
meantime the General walked backwards and forwards on the road
. . . more than half a mile from the troops.[7]

It was now after twelve o'clock.

Meanwhile, Pike moved towards the Half-Moon Battery, just
to the east of the Western Battery. But there was no opposition
there; the defence work was nothing more than a bank of sod
without any guns. All that remained was the so-called fort itself,
where the only weapons left were those constituting the Government House Battery and the magazine. Was there any point
in the British putting up a fight for it? This was the question
facing Sheaffe. Pike was now moving his guns into position,
and the guns of Chauncey's vessels would soon be able to
batter the British position to pieces. The Government House
Battery did lob a few shells at the Americans but, predictably,
it was soon put out of action. And, if the story told later by
some of the citizens of York is true—that the British batteries
had only round shot, the kind of projectile to be used against
vessels, and had no supplies of grape or cannister for anti-
personnel work[8]—then clearly not much more in the way of effective resistance was possible. Sheaffe himself had already come
to that conclusion. He would give the fort to the Americans,
get out of York and retire to Kingston with whatever troops he
could salvage. But there was no point in leaving the enemy with
anything that would be of use to them if it could be demolished
first. Sheaffe therefore withdrew his troops from the fort area
(leaving the British flag flying) and gave instructions that the
Grand Magazine on the shore of the lake should be destroyed.
A hundred metres or so away, Brigadier General Zebulon Pike
was interrogating a captured British soldier when, suddenly,
there was a terrific detonation. Finan felt the earth shake and
watched fascinated as "an immense cloud" ascended into the
air. "A great confused mass of smoke, timber, earth," he wrote,
"but as it rose, in a most majestic manner, it assumed the shape
of a vast balloon."[9] As the force that impelled it was spent, the
debris came raining to the ground, killing and injuring men in
both armies. Pike was crushed; an officer was killed beside him;
so was the British prisoner. Sheaffe's mounted aide-de-camp was
injured and his horse killed.

42. Detonation of the Grand Magazine at York, 27 April 1813

At this moment a sudden attack by the British might well have turned the battle in their favour. But there was no commander to give such an order. Sheaffe was already on his way out of York with the remnants of his army. At the edge of the town he halted and told the Anglican clergyman, the Reverend John Strachan, Lieutenant Colonel William Chewett and Major William Allan that he was taking the regulars with him; as the senior militia officers, Chewett and Allan would have to get in touch with the American commander and surrender the town, extracting the best terms they could from the enemy. Some of the Canadians were happy to see Sheaffe leave. He had never won the popularity Brock enjoyed among the militia or the public, perhaps because he was New England–born, and perhaps because rumours were circulating that Sheaffe had been too ready to run away from the braggart Smyth, and that he had declined to provide the popular Lieutenant Colonel Cecil Bisshopp with the help he applied for at the time of the American attack at Frenchman Creek.[10] As he marched away, Sheaffe must have seen the smoke rising from the partially completed warship on the stocks, which had been set on fire at his order. She was to have been called *Sir Isaac Brock*.

During the next twenty-four hours Chewett and Allan, assisted by the Reverend John Strachan and Captain John Beverley Robinson, carried on negotiations with two American commissioners for the surrender of York. The Americans were indignant. Sheaffe had escaped with the surviving regulars they had expected to take as prisoners; the ship they had come to get was on fire; the Provincial Marine vessel *Prince Regent* had slipped out of York before they arrived; and the destruction of the magazine had been as unfair as it was unexpected. Finally, however, the negotiators agreed that all regulars and militia remaining in York should give themselves up as prisoners of war and all military and naval stores should be turned over to the United States. In return, the people of York were promised security of their private property. It was also agreed that all public documents would remain untouched in the possession of the civil authorities. These terms were not immediately ratified, however, and Strachan, in high dudgeon—he was a formidable man at any time, and particularly so when angry—accused Dearborn and Chauncey of holding up the ratification deliberately to give the American troops the opportunity to loot private property. That being the case, he was going to do something about it. It might have been Strachan's threats, or perhaps his importunities, that did it, but Dearborn suddenly relented on 28 April and signed the terms of capitulation. Strachan emerged triumphant. He had shown the kind of courage and determination that was to mark his whole career, ecclesiastical and political. He would have made a good military officer.

Ratification or not, the looting went on. The Americans remained in York until the embarkation was ordered on 1-2 May, and their ships were detained in the harbour until 8 May by adverse winds. But in the days between the battle and the embarkation, the people of York watched the looting of empty houses, silly vandalism, theft and senseless destruction by armed men without self- or outer-imposed discipline. The claims for compensation that were presented later to the provincial government included such items as furniture, linen, silverware, carpenter's tools, surgical instruments, soap, tobacco, liquor, a 400-kg hogshead of sugar and one piece of Russian shirting.[11] But there were more significant depredations, such as the damage to Elmsley House, the public subscription library, the courthouse and the legislative building. Joseph Hendrick saw his schooner go up in flames; but at least he received £300 from Dearborn to ease his loss, the money being paid by Dearborn out of public funds seized from the provincial treasury! Un-

175

43. *The Reverend John Strachan*

doubtedly some of the thieving and vandalism was the work of criminal elements—for the Americans opened the jails—or perhaps of some of the disloyal pro-American element in the town who had surreptitiously passed information to the enemy;[12] but the evidence clearly shows that the soldiers and sailors of Dearborn's military force and Chauncey's fleet were responsible for most of what went on. It was a long time before the people of little York forgot Major General Roger Sheaffe or the American occupation of 27 April–2 May 1813.

44. *Major General Sir Roger Sheaffe, who succeeded Brock as administrator of Upper Canada and commander of the forces, 1812–13*

Scarcely had Sheaffe left York when he encountered the light company of the 8th, which had hurried west from Kingston, arriving too late to take part in the defence of York, and being obliged, suggested Finan, "to their *great satisfaction*, no doubt, to turn and march the self-same track again".[13] The journey to Kingston was some 270 km, at an inclement time of year, over a rutted road on which the snow was melting and that was becoming almost impassable. The troops were ill-equipped for such a march, lacking greatcoats and other clothing and constantly looking over their shoulders to see if they were being overtaken by the Americans. The women and children sat huddled together in clumsy wagons drawn by plodding, slow-moving oxen, while men and officers alike proceeded on foot. From time to time they encountered civilians who displayed open hostili-

45. The Royal Standard captured by the Americans during the occupation of York

ty towards the retreating army, for this was one of the regions inhabited by immigrants from the United States, who had seen fit to keep their politics to themselves in 1812 but, the American troops having shown their prowess, were now prepared to demonstrate publicly their pro-American sympathies. According to Finan:

> The majority of the inhabitants of this part of the country evinced great disloyalty as we proceeded, being much gratified with the success of the Americans; and, considering they had nothing to fear from us, did not hesitate to avow it. In many instances they concealed their horses, waggons, etc., in the woods, to avoid accommodating us with them, and told us they had none.[14]

Finally, after fourteen days, during which the rain never ceased falling, Sheaffe's Falstaffian array reached Kingston. Because the town was filled with soldiers, the bedraggled troops were forced to find dry quarters in the merchants' stores and in the Catholic church, which also served as a hospital. The remarkable feature of the march was not so much the speed with which it was accomplished under terrible difficulties, but the fact that those who made it suffered no ill effects.

46. Royal Artillery drivers

Late on 8 May, Chauncey's fleet arrived at the mouth of the Niagara River after an uneventful journey across Lake Ontario from York. The troops disembarked near Fort Niagara under cover of darkness. They were in a "very sickly and depressed state" and Dearborn proposed to give them an opportunity to "recruit their health and their spirits", while authorizing Chauncey to go to Sackets Harbor to pick up additional soldiers. Notices were also sent to Utica, Rome and Oswego that any troops at those places should be sent at once to Fort Niagara; other troops were moved forward from the Lake Champlain area to replace those from Sackets. "My intention", Dearborn wrote to Armstrong, "is to collect the main body of the troops at this place and, as soon as Commodore Chauncey returns and the forces from Oswego arrive, to commence operations in as spirited and effectual a manner as practicable."[15]

THERE WAS LITTLE ACTIVITY along the Niagara frontier during the winter of 1812–13. Steps were taken to form a troop of provincial Royal Artillery drivers to improve the mobility of the gunners and make them less dependent on civilian assistance; at the same time the provincial legislature gave authority to Sir Roger Sheaffe to form a battalion of incorporated militia to serve on a full-time basis for the remainder of the war. There was always talk of the Americans mounting another attack over the river, but nothing occurred except a sharp bombardment of Fort Erie by the guns at Black Rock on 17 March, which did little damage but inflicted several casualties on the detachment of the Royal Newfoundland Regiment. Whether this was a prelude to invasion or a St. Patrick's Day frolic was not clear. Probably the latter, as the Americans had not yet assembled in strength at Fort Niagara.

Brigadier General John Vincent, who was commanding on the Niagara frontier, could count on 1222 regulars, including 392 men of the 41st, 394 of the 49th, and 170 Glengarrians and Newfoundlanders. And arrangements had been put in hand by Sir George Prevost to move reinforcements of regulars to Upper Canada, including the 8th and the 104th (which had marched overland during the winter from New Brunswick), a company of the Royal Scots, and a troop of Provincial Light Dragoons that had recently been organized by William Hamilton Merritt.

The great weakness in the Upper-Canadian defences was the militia, whose desertion rate was high despite severe sentences imposed by general courts martial. On 19 May, Brigadier General Vincent reported:

> It is with regret that I can neither report favorably of their numbers nor their willing co-operation. Every exertion has been made, and every expedient used, to bring them forward and unite their efforts with those of His Majesty's forces, with but little effect.[16]

Prevost said much the same thing in his dispatch to the British secretary for war, Lord Bathurst, on 26 May, adding that, as a result of "growing discontent and undissembled dissatisfaction of the mass of the people of Upper Canada, in consequence of the effects of the militia laws", many of the inhabitants of the province had returned to the United States, from which most of them had originally come.[17] The main problem with the militia still came from the pro-American element in the population. According to Colonel Thomas Talbot at Dover Mills, most of the militia were prepared to respond when required, the exception being a "violent and systematic band" that had caused trouble before. He wrote:

> Should Sir George reach the lines with a strong force, I will recommend that all the aliens should be sent out of the Province with

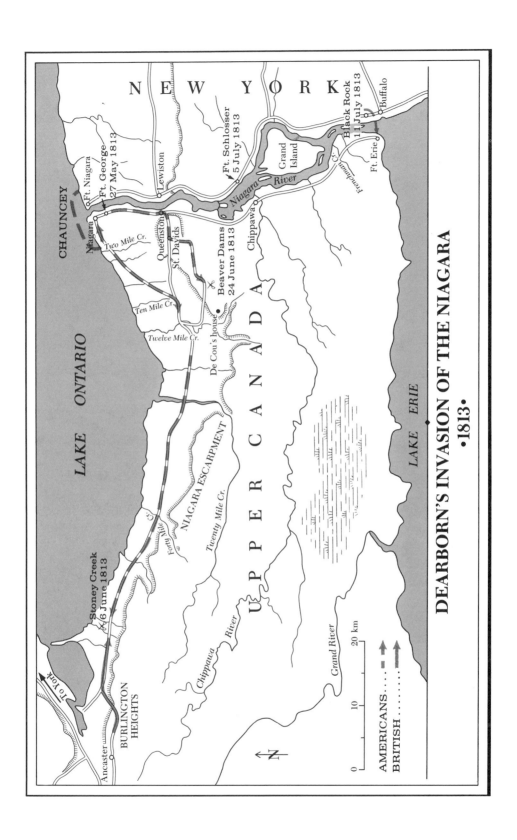

DEARBORN'S INVASION OF THE NIAGARA
•1813•

NEW YORK

LAKE ONTARIO

U P P E R   C A N A D A

LAKE ERIE

CHAUNCEY

Ft. Niagara
Ft. George
27 May 1813

Lewiston

Ft. Schlosser
5 July 1813

Grand Island

Niagara River

Black Rock
11 July 1813

Buffalo

Cr.

Frenchman's

Ft. Erie

Niagara
Two Mile Cr.

Queenston

St. Davids

Ten Mile Cr.

Chippawa

Beaver Dams
24 June 1813

Twelve Mile Cr.

De Cou's house

NIAGARA ESCARPMENT

Forty Mile

Twenty Mile Cr.

Chippawa River

Grand River

Stoney Creek
6 June 1813

BURLINGTON
HEIGHTS

Ancaster

To York

N

AMERICANS . . . . . .
BRITISH . . . .

0   10   20 km

*47. American water-borne assault on Niagara and Fort George,
27 May 1813*

as little delay as possible. They are indefatigable in spreading discord
amongst the inhabitants, and it would be a most salutary measure
did circumstances admit to send 100 or even 50 regulars to be stationed at Turkey Point under an active and *steady* officer, as the
presence of such a force would create the necessary confidence in
the well disposed and traitors would be *intimidated into* subordination.[18]

On the morning of 25 May, the American batteries along the
Niagara River opened fire. They were using hot shot, and almost
immediately fires broke out within the walls of Fort George,
damaging or destroying every log barrack. It was the prelude
to the expected invasion. Then, on the twenty-sixth, American
troops began to embark on Chauncey's vessels, each of which
had assault craft in tow. The initial landing was to be attempted
by the light troops led by Winfield Scott and Benjamin Forsyth; they were to be followed by the brigades led by Generals
John Boyd, William Winder and John Chandler, in that order.
Dearborn, wracked by illness and doubts about the capabilities
of his commanders, was in supreme command. Early the next
morning, taking advantage of heavy fog, the ships set out, relying upon sweeps rather than sail because there was no breeze.
Then, as they stood in towards the lake shore on the Canadian
side of the Niagara River, the fog lifted and the British could
see Chauncey's fleet, forming a vast arc on their flank.

48. *The American landing at Fort George as it was depicted in American newspapers*

The Americans did not achieve a strategic surprise, but they did achieve a tactical one. Vincent knew that they were coming, but he did not know where they were going to land. The batteries of Fort Niagara had once again opened fire on Fort George, and Vincent drew many of his guards and pickets away from the lake shore to keep an eye on the riverbank. As soon as he saw Chauncey's ships to the left and the assault boats moving towards shore, he hurriedly dispatched his light troops to his flank, sending the Glengarrians to the lake shore near Two Mile Creek. Thus, it was the men from Glengarry who took on Scott and the first wave of the assault troops as they emerged from their boats and began to clamber up the bank; Scott himself narrowly missed a bayonet thrust, falling unceremoniously into the water. Spilling out of their boats, the Americans steadily forced the defending troops—the Glengarrians, Newfoundlanders and militia—to fall back upon the regulars of the 8th Regiment commanded by Major James Ogilvie. The whole defence in this region was under the direction of Lieutenant Colonel Christopher Myers. When Myers was wounded, the command devolved upon Lieutenant Colonel John Harvey, who brought up the 49th and another detachment of militia in a futile effort to halt the American advance. Seeing what was happening, Vincent decided that there was no point in sacrificing his outnumbered troops for the sake of glory, and gave orders that

Fort George be evacuated. The guns of the fort had been of no use against the invaders; they had all been sited to repel attack from the river rather than the lake side. Nothing could have been gained by swinging them around to the flank, if only because the village of Niagara lay between the fort and the lake. Vincent therefore spiked his guns, destroyed his ammunition dump and withdrew with his men.

The fighting had lasted three hours and Vincent had already suffered 358 casualties. As the British commander moved away from Fort George towards Queenston and then cut inland, he sent word to Bisshopp, commanding at Chippawa, to abandon that position and join him at the supply depot previously established at Beaver Dams (Thorold), about 25 km by road from Fort George. By noon the Americans were in possession of Brock's former headquarters at Fort George. Captain Merritt expected that, once his forces were concentrated at Beaver Dams, Vincent would give battle to the Americans to stop them from penetrating farther into the province, but to his surprise Vincent issued instructions for the impressment of all wagons, authorized the militia to return home, and then continued with his withdrawal to Forty Mile Creek (at what is now Grimsby). Merritt was disturbed. He began to suspect that Vincent had in mind the abandonment of the whole of the upper part of the province, a suspicion that appeared to be confirmed when he learned later in the evening that the army had been instructed to retire to Burlington Heights. According to Merritt, the militia was given no encouragement to follow the regulars. Accordingly, most of them went home, believing that the British would eventually pull back all their regular troops to Kingston. Dearborn apparently suspected as much, for he wrote a short note to the Governor of New York:

> We are now in quiet possession of both shores from Lake Erie to Lake Ontario, but the enemy has, I fear, escaped by pursuing the ridge of the mountain from Queenston towards the head of the lake, but if the winds favor us we may intercept him at York.[19]

The Americans were now in a position to do exactly that. They had captured Fort George with a loss of only 150 men, and, at the upper end of the Niagara River, Lieutenant Colonel James P. Preston had crossed from Black Rock to take possession of what remained of Fort Erie. The British were on their way, as quickly as they could move, to Burlington Heights. There was nothing to prevent Chauncey and Dearborn from taking advantage of their mobility on Lake Ontario to intercept

49. Sir James Yeo, who commanded the British fleet on Lake Ontario

the retiring British at any point along the shoreline. Nothing, that is, except the weather, which provided plenty of rain but no wind for the American vessels, and the possibility that the new British naval commander on Lake Ontario, Sir James Yeo, might bring his vessels from Kingston to the western end of Lake Ontario. And he did.

The arrival of the thirty-one-year-old James Yeo at Kingston with several experienced officers from the Royal Navy, and his attempt to capture Sackets Harbor on 28 May, the day after Dearborn had taken Fort George, and to destroy Chauncey's new ship, *General Pike*, sent Chauncey scudding back to Sackets Harbor to look after his own interests. He wrote to the Secretary of the Navy on 11 June, "I prepared to proceed in quest of the enemy, but upon mature reflection, I determined to remain in this place and preserve the new ship at all hazards."[20] This was typical of Chauncey. His ships came first. And so, until nearly the end of July, Yeo had Lake Ontario pretty much to himself. There would be no American ventures to York during that period.

There was another factor to consider. Vincent may have been in a hurry to get beyond the Niagara peninsula to avoid being trapped in that area, but he could not afford to go any farther than Burlington Heights. With Forts George and Erie in American hands, the British had lost one of the main supply routes for their Lake Erie fleet. Henceforth they would have to rely on Burlington Heights as the principal depot and road centre for communications between Kingston and York, and Amherstburg and the Detroit frontier; from Burlington Heights the route was by road to Turkey Point and thence by boat along Lake Erie, or by another road to the Thames and Detroit rivers. To abandon Burlington Heights would be tantamount to abandoning Procter and the whole right wing of the British army south of Lake Huron. That Vincent was fully aware of the problem is obvious from his remark to Colonel Baynes: "If I am reduced to the necessity of retreating to Kingston I am afraid it will be adding to Brigadier-General Procter's misery. . . . I am too much afraid he is at this present moment in great distress for provisions."[21] And yet, if Vincent were to remain on Burlington Heights, might he find himself cut off from Kingston by Dearborn's reoccupation of York? The question was just how long he and Procter could afford to remain where they were before making a run for safety at Kingston. Clearly the timing and the implementation of Vincent's decision would critically affect the whole future of Upper Canada. So too would any decision Dearborn might adopt as his next step.

DESPITE THE CAPTURE of Fort George and Fort Erie, Dearborn's victory on 27 May 1813 had not been as decisive as the Secretary of War had hoped for and the President greatly desired; the British had been beaten but not annihilated. Vincent's army was still intact and had moved quickly away from the threatened area. The Americans had moved slowly. Dearborn, feeble and sickly, would not delegate his command, and his subordinates dawdled so long before taking up the pursuit of the British force that Vincent had got away unscathed. Instead of moving with speed and purpose, Winder and Chandler, who were in charge of the pursuit, moved gingerly along the shore road, not reach-

50. Officer of the United States line infantry, 1813

ing Stoney Creek until 5 June. Their object was to prevent any
junction between Procter and Vincent, and under their command they had a well-balanced combat force, including infantry, artillery and dragoons. That day they encountered some
of Vincent's pickets near Stoney Creek and then formed camp.

The idea of attacking the American camp at night may have
originated with a local scout, Billy Green, or with Lieutenant
Colonel John Harvey. In any event, it was Harvey who reconnoitred the American camp and passed the suggestion of a night
attack on to Brigadier General Vincent. Everything seemed to
favour such a course of action. The night was unusually dark

for that time of year and, although guards and pickets were posted, the rest of the camp seems to have been strewn about in a careless fashion, each commanding officer choosing such ground and place as he thought proper, some on a hill, others in a hollow, all in a haphazard fashion, with no watchword and no order of battle. About half an hour before midnight, Harvey led some 700 men of the 8th and 49th regiments towards the American lines. They began quickly and quietly, bayonetting the sentries without any noise. The surprise, which should have been complete, was, as Harvey himself admitted, only "tolerably complete".[22] As the troops charged across a line of campfires, shouting and firing, they became visible to the Americans, who recovered "in some degree" from their initial panic and began to direct a destructive musketry fire on the advancing troops. The British broke up, and charged and stabbed any men and horses they could discern in the uncertain, flickering light. Lieutenant James FitzGibbon of the 49th, who took part, wrote two days later, "The business was, I think, very ill executed by us, and the great error was shouting before the line was formed for the attack."[23] A night attack, even when well planned and rehearsed, frequently ends in confusion, and the night attack at Stoney Creek was confused and noisy. "Noise and confusion," wrote FitzGibbon, "which confusion was chiefly occasioned by the noise. . . ." An American account of the battle emphasized the utter disorder:

> The horses of the cavalry and infantry bursting in amongst us at every direction. General Chandler running about crying, "Where is the line? Where is the line?" General Winder in the same manner exclaiming, "Come on!" And both in among the British soldiers. No orders passing from or to any corps or any officer. May my eyes never witness such a scene again.[24]

Not surprisingly, Winder and Chandler were both taken prisoner. Winder was in the act of presenting his pistol to Sergeant Alexander Fraser of the 49th when Fraser raised his musket and said, "If you stir, Sir, you die." Winder then threw down his pistol and sword and said, "I am your prisoner."[25] He must have realized that Fraser meant what he said, for Fraser had bayonetted seven Americans that night, and his young brother four. Chandler, who was wounded, stumbled into a group of soldiers, whom he endeavoured to rally until he found them to be men of the 49th. Fraser was a member of Major Charles Plenderleath's twenty-man party that, during the fighting at Stoney Creek, took as prisoners, not only the two generals,

51. *Lieutenant Colonel John Harvey, who led the night attack at Stoney Creek in 1813. Harvey later became governor of Newfoundland and lieutenant governor of New Brunswick and of Nova Scotia*

but also five field officers and captains and about a hundred other ranks.

Vincent himself might well have been captured. He got lost in the woods in the dark, finally turning up at his headquarters the next morning without hat or horse and almost famished. Thus, it was Harvey who, fearing to reveal to the Americans the small size of his attacking force, gave the order to withdraw before daybreak.

In his account of the Battle of Stoney Creek, FitzGibbon attributed the success of the night to Plenderleath's company, sug-

52. *The night attack at Stoney Creek, 6 June 1813*

gesting that the Americans might have held their ground but for the capture of their two general officers. This might have been the case, for Vincent's gamble cost him 214 men while the Americans lost only 168, including prisoners. But luck was on the British side, and that luck held. With the return of daylight, Colonel James Burn of the 2nd Light Dragoons found that the command of the American forces devolved on him; not knowing what to do "in the unpleasant dilemma occasioned by the capture of our Generals" and finding that his men had expended most of their ammunition, Burn called a council of field officers, "of whom a majority coincided in opinion with me that we ought to retire to our former position at the Forty Mile Creek, where we could be supplied with ammunition and provisions and either advance or remain until further orders."[26] The Americans wasted no time in pulling back. They did not stop at Forty Mile Creek but continued to within easy reach of Fort George. Major Thomas Evans wrote on 8 June from Forty Mile Creek:

So precipitate has been their flight that their . . . stores, arms, ammunition and provisions have been secured. The naval part of our force has captured fourteen or sixteen boats laden with supplies. Many prisoners have been made.[27]

Evans put his finger on the decisive factor. That was the appearance of Yeo's vessels, which had left Kingston on 3 June to bring reinforcements and supplies to Vincent's army. When he saw the American encampment at Forty Mile Creek, Yeo sent in two of his ships of war to bombard it, after he had first issued the routine demand for surrender. Believing that the British vessels were carrying a large number of troops and that he would be caught between the water-borne and the land-based troops, Burn fled, with Canadian militia and Indians snapping at his heels almost the whole distance to Fort George. One of the reinforcements who landed at Forty Mile Creek was Sergeant James Commins of the 8th Foot, who wrote to a friend, "It being the King's birthday we gave them a Royal Salute in honour of our old King, but the Yankees did not participate with us as they did not seem to relish our anniversary mirth."[28]

The effects upon American morale of the events of 6 June were widespread. Not only did the Americans abandon practically every position along the Lake Ontario front as far as Fort George, they also abandoned those along the Niagara River they had occupied without fighting. On the evening of 9 June they set fire to and abandoned Fort Erie and withdrew their troops from Chippawa and Queenston. They threw up new earthworks about Fort George and gathered boats on the British side of the Niagara to hold in readiness for a crossing of the river to Fort Niagara. In addition to the surrender of territory, the Americans abandoned vast quantities of camp equipage, provisions, arms, ammunition and ordnance. In submitting his report, the quartermaster general of the militia, Robert Nichol, recorded the capture of 200 tents by the troops, 180 by the Indians and another 120 by the local population, to which could be added boats, wagons, horses, barrels of flour, barrels of pork and even a medicine chest. Major Thomas Evans also recorded, as one of the good features of the British recovery of their position in the Niagara peninsula, the revival of "the spirit of the loyal part of the country".[29]

The disloyal part of the country was also aroused by the events that had occurred in the Niagara peninsula. The American capture of Fort George in May 1813 and the advance to Stoney Creek had, like Dearborn's capture of York in April, given great satisfaction to the pro-American group along the Niagara frontier. Obviously the United States was now winning the war, and they felt that there could be no harm in revealing their sympathies publicly. On 8 June, General Dearborn, writing from Fort George, informed the Secretary of War that,

> on taking possession of this place, the inhabitants came in numbers and gave their paroles. I have promised them protection. A large majority are friendly to the United States and fixed in their hatred against the Government of Great Britain.[30]

Another American officer wrote from Fort George, "Our friends hereabouts are greatly relieved by our presence. They have been terribly persecuted by the Scotch myrmidons of England. Their present joy is equal to their past misery."[31] Imagine their alarm after the news of Stoney Creek. Some of them, for example Joseph Willcocks and Benajah Mallory, had so far committed themselves that they knew there could be no drawing back. Accordingly, they went to Dearborn and offered him their services as scouts. Dearborn, pleased to be able to improve his intelligence service with the aid of men with knowledge of the local area, was ready to accept them. On 10 July he authorized Joseph Willcocks, a resident of Niagara and a former member of the Upper-Canadian House of Assembly, where he had been a thorn in the flesh of Brock and Sheaffe, to form a corps of volunteers. One week later Willcocks was able to bring on parade a corps known as the "Canadian Volunteers", numbering 8 officers and 44 other ranks. They paraded on 17 July, "well supplied with arms and accoutrements", and passed their first inspection.[32] The Volunteers carried out patrol duties during the summer of 1813 for the American army. They were hated by loyal Canadians, largely because they were given various police duties, reporting on and arresting prominent anti-Americans in the Niagara region. Brigadier General John Boyd, who succeeded Dearborn in command of the Niagara army, expressed a hope that Willcocks's force would be able to recruit up to 600 or 800 men. By September they numbered 130, and wore the distinguishing feature of a white cockade with a green ribbon on their hats.

MEANWHILE VINCENT BEGAN to tighten the net around Fort George. He had received reinforcements with the forwarding of the 104th Regiment from Kingston, and was well supplied with provisions—not only those captured from Winder and Chandler and the British stores recovered at Fort Erie and Chippawa, but also the flour, corn, pork and salt captured by Yeo's men when they descended on the American depot at the mouth of the Genesee River on 15 June. Vincent pushed his outposts towards Fort George. His own headquarters were located at Forty Mile Creek, with an advanced base at Twenty Mile Creek under Bisshopp and other posts along the two principal roads leading to the Niagara River. One was located at Twelve Mile Creek on the main shore-road leading to Niagara and Fort George, under Major P.V. DeHaren, and the other on the inland road leading from St. Davids to Queenston, under the command of Lieutenant James FitzGibbon.

Estimating the American force at Force George to be in the vicinity of 6000 men, Vincent was unwilling to venture an assault upon the old British headquarters. Instead, as he put it himself, his purpose was to "feel the pulse of the enemy".[33] To do this he had available two companies of the 104th from New Brunswick, the light company of the 8th, a few Six Nations Indians, and about 350 Iroquois Indians from Lower Canada under the general direction of Captain Dominique Ducharme of the Indian Department.[34] From time to time there were minor encounters between Merritt's dragoons and an irregular force of mounted guerrillas recruited by the notorious Buffalo partisan leader, Cyrenius Chapin, and between the Indians and American foraging parties.

These troublesome encounters encouraged the American commander at Fort George, Brigadier General John Boyd, who had taken over from the ailing Dearborn on an acting basis, to strike a blow at Vincent's outposts. In the past Boyd had openly expressed his criticism of the weakness of American generalship, and here was an opportunity for him to not only prove his own superior military capacity but also to redeem the honour of the senior American command. On 23 June, he ordered Lieutenant Colonel Charles Boerstler of the 14th United States Infantry, who had taken a leading part in Smyth's attack on the batteries near Fort Erie, to dislodge FitzGibbon from his outpost and to overawe the surrounding countryside. Boerstler's command was to include, in addition to a troop of light dragoons and a company of light artillery, his own regiment and several additional companies of infantry from other regiments—in all about 700 men, in Boyd's opinion an ample number to deal with the situation at Beaver Dams. Along with Boerstler went Chapin and his volunteers, known to the regular soldiers as the "Forty Thieves". Chapin had claimed, although, as it turned out, untruthfully, that he and his men had already reconnoitred some miles beyond De Cou's (DeCew's) and knew the country. Chapin's role was therefore to act as guide for the expedition. Accompanying the troops were two large supply wagons, each drawn by a four-horse team. Every precaution was to be taken to preserve secrecy; surprise was essential to success. There would be pickets at side roads, and Queenston would be cordoned off to prevent anyone from learning about the expedition and its destination. There were certain problems attending the operation. One was Boerstler's distrust and dislike of Chapin, whom he called that "vain, boasting liar"; another was the rain, the most prolonged in twenty-five years, which turned the roads into seas of mud and slowed down the movement of men, horses and wagons alike over what was no more than a 27-km march.

When Boerstler's combat force reached Queenston at midnight, they had covered about 12 km the first day and had 15 more to go. Starting early in the morning of 24 June, they struggled along the St. Davids road towards Beaver Dams. From time to time they caught glimpses of Indians, but no one interfered with their progress. As they approached within a few miles of De Cou's house, they entered a well-wooded tract where the road degenerated into a mere set of slippery wagon ruts "intersected in many places by deep gullies and closely bounded on either side by an almost continuous wall of trees and underbrush".[35] Just the place for an Indian ambush, as Boerstler discovered to his discomfort. As the troops began to descend a small declivity, with the "Forty Thieves" in the vanguard, they saw Indians crossing the road behind them, and shortly afterwards firing broke out in front. A running battle continued for some time, until the American troops found themselves in a kind of hollow, where they tried to reverse their march. They had already suffered casualties and had lost several horses; their wagons were immobilized, and their cannon had proved useless in the thick underbrush.

Subsequently, some of the survivors claimed that they could have made it back to Fort George, and were only stopped when Boerstler agreed to consider FitzGibbon's demand for surrender. Of course, FitzGibbon had not the men to either halt the Americans or force them to abandon the fight; all he had was one company of infantry, carefully concealed so that its weakness would not become apparent. But by a mixture of blarney and bluff he was able to persuade Boerstler that further fighting would be as dangerous as it would be futile. He claimed to be acting in the name of his superior officer, Major DeHaren, who was at the time hurrying with all possible speed from Twelve

53. *Lieutenant James FitzGibbon, who accepted the American surrender at Beaver Dams, 24 June 1813*

Mile Creek with two companies of the 104th and the light company of the 8th. Suspecting that FitzGibbon might be deceiving them, the Americans demanded to see the size of his force before admitting defeat. FitzGibbon agreed; later he produced a statement, allegedly from his superior officer, that such a demand was highly irregular. By such stratagems he was able to fill in time until DeHaren actually appeared and signed the terms of capitulation. Boerstler and his officers and men became prisoners of war, 462 in all; the American militiamen had been allowed to return to the United States on parole. Two field-pieces, two wagons and a stand of colours of the 14th United States Infantry were turned over to the British military authorities.[36] Boerstler, who had taken little part in the actual fighting, preferring to remain with the wagons, managed to escape and find safe refuge in American territory. In defence of his surrender, he told Dearborn that because of "the exhausted state the men were in", he was convinced that "the far greater part could never reach Fort George."[37] He wrote the same thing to his father. The court of inquiry that was held in 1815 to consider Boerstler's conduct accepted his defence and concluded that his surrender at Beaver Dams "was justified by existing circumstances".[38]

Beaver Dams was essentially an Indian victory. Dominique Ducharme chose the site, placing the Caughnawaga warriors on the right and, on the left, the Six Nations Indians under Captain William Johnson Kerr of the Indian Department and John Brant, son of the Mohawk chief, Joseph Brant. During the battle most of the Six Nations seem to have slipped away, leaving the Caughnawagas to bear the brunt of the fighting. By the time FitzGibbon appeared, Boerstler had had enough. He was wounded and unnerved by loss of blood and by the stories that circulated among the American troops about the horrible events at the River Raisin and Fort Meigs. "For God's sake, keep the Indians from us", he begged FitzGibbon.[39] When writing his report of the battle, Colonel Bisshopp gave all the credit to the Indians. So did Dominique Ducharme. John Norton, the Cherokee-Scotch Métis who associated himself with the Six Nations, remarked with more than a little truth that at Beaver Dams "the Cognawaga Indians fought the battle, the Mohawks or Six Nations got the plunder, and FitzGibbon got the credit."[40] FitzGibbon virtually admitted as much when he wrote several years later:

> With respect to the affair with Captain Boerstler, not a shot was fired on our side by any but the Indians. They beat the American detachment into a state of terror, and the only share I claim is taking advantage of a favorable moment to offer them protection from the tomahawk and scalping knife. The Indian Department did all the rest.[41]

Because they received nothing more than formal thanks, many of the Caughnawaga Indians went home, which Captain Merritt felt "was a very great loss".[42] According to Ducharme, the Indian casualties during the battle were 15 killed and 25 wounded.

Some years later the story circulated that FitzGibbon had been warned in advance of the American plans by Laura Secord, the wife of a Loyalist militia officer, who lived at Queenston. She claimed to have overheard American officers talking about the plan and, by slipping through the American cordon and walking by a roundabout route, she had reached the Indian camp near Beaver Dams. Convincing the Indians that her information was true, she was taken before FitzGibbon, who then made the dispositions that brought about the American defeat.[43] FitzGibbon made no mention of her name in his initial report, but subsequently he publicly certified that Laura Secord, "a person of slight and delicate frame", did, in fact, make the journey she claimed to have made in 1813.[44] Laura Secord thus emerges as one of Canada's heroic figures and her achievement as one of the great stories of the war. Throughout the nineteenth century she remained a living reminder of our past. She lived to see Confederation, dying in 1868 at the age of ninety-three. That other figure of the Beaver Dams drama, James FitzGibbon, the Irish-born boy who joined the Tarbert Fencibles, an Irish home-service regiment, at the age of eighteen, became a military knight at Windsor Castle and died in 1863. He was eighty-three years of age.

FOLLOWING THEIR SUCCESS against the Americans at Beaver Dams, the British forces kept up a steady pressure on the enemy, pushing closer and closer to Fort George. Major General the Baron Francis de Rottenburg, who took over Sheaffe's responsibilities, secured the position at Burlington Heights against a possible *coup de main* and then moved his headquarters up to Twenty Mile Creek. On 19 July, Charles Askin, who had been with FitzGibbon at Beaver Dams, informed his father that there were no fewer than 1000 British troops within a mile of the Niagara River. In actual fact, British and Canadian raiding parties periodically crossed the river, without any interference, to destroy enemy property on the east bank. On 5 July, Lieutenant Colonel Thomas Clark, with a party of Lincoln militia and a handful of regulars, landed at Fort Schlosser in New York State, surprised the guard and took possession of various stores, including barrels of salt—a necessity for the preservation of pork—, tobacco and whisky, as well as a brass 6-pounder and various stands of arms and ammunition. Several days later, on 11 July, a more ambitious effort was made by a force numbering about 250 regulars and militia under Lieutenant Colonel Cecil Bisshopp. Crossing the river during the night, the British landed at Black Rock, destroyed the blockhouses, naval-yard

54. *Laura Ingersoll Secord, the heroine of Beaver Dams*

barracks and a cargo schooner, and loaded artillery and stores
on board several captured enemy boats. The Americans, recovering from their surprise, counterattacked strongly. Even
so, the raiders were able to bring back with them 123 barrels
of salt, 46 barrels of whisky and 11 barrels of flour, together
with bales of blankets and 7 large bateaux. But they paid heavily
for their plunder. Thirteen men were killed and twenty-five
wounded. Among the latter was Lieutenant Colonel Bisshopp,
whose wound proved fatal. This was a serious loss, for Bisshopp
was one of the few regular officers equally at home with regulars
and militia and able to ensure that they cooperated with one
another. One American taken prisoner at Black Rock described
Bisshopp as "a mild humane-looking man and about 36 years

of age, rather tall and well made and a man of exceeding few words". When the prisoner protested against being taken to Canada when he was ill, Bisshopp merely replied, "Young man, you must go to Canada." The American made the best of it, writing later:

> As my capture was unavoidable, I was pleased with the idea of seeing the country and the British army. Being an expert swimmer, I knew I could recross the Niagara River by lashing two or three rails together with strips of bark, if nothing better offered.[45]

Obviously a young man of parts, as well as of a philosophical turn of mind.

Meanwhile, on 8 July, Norton's Indians engaged a party of Americans at Ball's farm near Fort George. The purpose of the fight was to provide cover for an attempt to recover medical supplies the British had buried when they withdrew from Fort George in May. Among the few white troops present was a young lad, John Lawe, thirteen years of age, whose father had been wounded and taken prisoner and his elder brother killed at Fort George. Apparently he was determined to revenge the loss his family had sustained. According to Captain Merritt, "He would not be persuaded to leave the field till his mother, after it was nearly over, came out and took him away in her arms by force."[46]

By the end of July, it appeared to be only a matter of time before the British would recover Fort George and thereby nullify whatever gains Dearborn might have made by his victories at York and Fort George earlier in the year. The War Hawk, Peter B. Porter, was disgusted. Writing to the Governor of New York from Black Rock on 27 July, he said:

> The truth is (and it is known to every man of common sense in this part of the country) that we have had an army at Fort George for two months past, which at any moment of this period might by a vigorous and well-directed exertion of three or four days have prostrated the whole of the enemy's force in this division of the country, and yet this army lies panic-struck, shut up and whipped in by a few hundred miserable savages, leaving the whole of this frontier, except the mile in extent which they occupy, exposed to the inroads and depredations of the enemy.[47]

THERE WAS CONSTERNATION in the House of Representatives when the news of Beaver Dams reached Washington. Speaker Henry Clay promptly sent Representative Charles J. Ingersoll to President Madison with the demand that Dearborn be dismissed at once. Armstrong had been thinking along these lines for some time and Madison agreed with his secretary of war. Armstrong therefore addressed a short note to Dearborn:

> I have the President's orders to express to you his decision that you retire from the command of District No. 9 and of the troops within the same, until your health be re-established, and until further orders.[48]

Dearborn could not believe his eyes. He was certain that Madison had never approved this order, and so he sent it to the President, protesting that he had fully recovered his health and was ready to resume command on the Niagara frontier. But Madison stood behind Armstrong, who was not going to change his mind. The new commander-in-chief in the field had already been chosen. He was Major General James Wilkinson, a Revolutionary War veteran who had served in the Canadian campaign of 1776. He had, earlier in the year, been asked to leave his posting in New Orleans to take up a new one in the North, but after four months he had got no farther than Georgia. It would take another four weeks before he would eat his way through the banquet circuit to report to Armstrong.

When Wilkinson finally did reach Washington, he learned that drastic changes were contemplated in the general strategy of the war. There would be no further emphasis upon the central or western theatres of operation. Henceforth, the bulk of the American forces would be concentrated at Sackets Harbor, and thus be available for either an attack on Kingston or a move down the St. Lawrence to join the Lake Champlain army for a decisive assault on Montreal. The Lake Erie and Niagara River frontiers would remain quiescent. The plan, marked "Approved and Adopted, July 23, 1813", was given to Wilkinson on 5 August, but Wilkinson did not like it. He was thinking instead of pressing forward on all three fronts in order to force the British to either spread their resources thinly from Montreal to eastern Upper Canada or concentrate in one area to the disadvantage of the other two. But Armstrong had abandoned these ideas— they had been tried and found wanting in 1812—and were the kind of thing that, as he put it, only "wounds the tail of the lion".[49] No, Kingston or Montreal or both of them were the logical objectives of any further American offensive operations. Wilkinson would be allowed to choose, but just to make sure that the new American commander would carry out his orders, Armstrong would go to Sackets Harbor and personally give the new offensive its initial movement.

8

Moraviantown

THE SUMMER OF 1813, hot and dry, was a period of worry and concern for Brigadier General Henry Procter. The Americans had occupied Fort Erie, and were threatening the Niagara frontier as a result of their victory at Fort George and the retirement of the main body of British troops to Burlington Heights; but the more immediate threat lay in the construction of a new American fleet on Lake Erie at Presque Isle.

Procter knew what the loss of control over the lake would mean to the British position in western Upper Canada. True, Robert Heriot Barclay, commander of the British naval forces on Lake Erie, was building a ship of his own at Amherstburg and was still sailing freely about the lake, but that would not last forever. An attempt should be made to destroy Presque Isle and to burn the American ships before they were launched. For that, Procter would need regular troops, not just Indians and militia, and it was always difficult to persuade the high command in Upper Canada to weaken the Centre Division by sending regulars to Amherstburg. Brigadier General John Vincent did not offer Procter any help until after Stoney Creek, when he proposed sending him 100 men of the 41st, who were being held in reserve at army headquarters on Burlington Heights. Sir George Prevost was sympathetic towards Procter, but the new commander in Upper Canada, Major General Francis de Rottenburg, was not. All he had to suggest by way of helping Procter was to arrange with the North West Company for canoes to bring Procter's force back to central Upper Canada should

the British lose control of Lake Ontario and should Procter succeed in getting his troops as far north as Lake Superior in the
event of a forced withdrawal from Amherstburg. Nor was Commodore Yeo very helpful in aiding Commander Barclay.

The result was that neither Procter nor Barclay was ever in
a position during the summer of 1813 to take offensive action
against the American ships, even while they were still on the
stocks at Presque Isle. Thus, Procter and Barclay stood impo-
tently by when they should have been engaged in a pre-emptive
strike at the American naval base on Lake Erie. Procter was
not being unfair when he wrote to his friend Robert McDouall
in July:

> I have only to say that the detention of the force ordered here by
> the Commander of the Forces has prevented this district being in
> a state of security, which the destruction of the enemy's vessels at
> Presque Isle would have effected—a service that might very easily
> have been completely effected a very short time since, but which,
> I apprehend, may now be attended with much difficulty. I should
> also have had it in my power to have supplied myself, at the enemy's
> expense, with provisions, of which we have not an adequate supply
> at present.[1]

Procter had reason to complain. Not only did he not get his
promised reinforcements, he did not even get the gunners, clerks
or artificers he needed, nor the powder, the specie, the flour,
the meat.

The lack of provisions on the Lake Erie front was perhaps
the most serious problem Procter had to cope with. As early
as 7 June, John McGillivray had told Simon McTavish of the
North West Company that the British position in Michigan was
"doomed to become the prey of an overwhelming force, or be
forced to surrender for want of supplies of provisions and
ammunition".[2] It was a prophetic statement. From time to time
Procter was able to ease the situation by capturing enemy supplies during his spring and summer operations on the Lake Erie
front, but he was never able to acquire the reserve he needed
for the upper part of the country. Under normal conditions he
might have managed to obtain provisions locally, but he would
have had to impose martial law to do so. The poor harvest of
1812 had induced Sheaffe, in the early months of 1813, to ask
the legislature for controls over the quantity of grain to be
used for distillation, and he had considered imposing martial
law to collect provisions for the troops, both in the Niagara area
and at Amherstburg. Martial law was a drastic and politically

unpopular measure, but the situation at Amherstburg was such that in the end it had to be applied briefly in the most westerly regions of the province. Another way of acquiring grain was that followed by Rottenburg, who in July seized the grain fields and stocks of the American defectors who had joined the enemy after the fall of Fort George.

The dryness of the season compounded the problem. The absence of rain caused water supplies to be low, too low to operate the local gristmills; and the lack of wind stilled the windmills, including the two provincial mills on the Thames: McGregor's and Arnold's. Robert Gilmor, the commissariat officer at Amherstburg, wrote on 6 August to inform the deputy commissary general, Edward Couche, that the wheat on hand and that being harvested in the district "will be of little immediate service . . . for want of mills to grind it".[3] Gilmor also pointed out that, owing to the large number of Indians and their dependents hanging around Amherstburg and subsisting on government rations, he was issuing thousands of rations every day. "I can only say", he wrote, "that for 2000 men I could easily supply provisions for six months", but in fact he was trying to feed 15 000! "I pay $10.00 per bbl. of 196 lbs for flour and 7s 6d per bushel for corn", he added.

A little over a week later Gilmor reported to Procter that he had flour in store for only fourteen more days, "according to the quantities now issued daily". Flour shipped from Long Point by the schooner *Mary* would help, but "as this is all that I have to depend on we shall very soon be in absolute want."[4] It would depend on what could be brought in by water, since land carriage would be most difficult "in the present state of the roads". Agents were out in the countryside trying to buy supplies, not only in the valley of the Thames but also in Michigan. The food problem was never solved at Amherstburg, and for a period when flour was not available the troops were obliged to resort to potatoes as a substitute for bread. Moreover, poor Couche was threatened by the western Indians that if he did not feed them more bountifully, they would take him to their camp and starve him. The remarkable thing is not that the commissariat system failed but that, throughout the whole of the war, it failed on only this one occasion.

THE DETAILS OF THE BATTLE that took place at Put-in-Bay on 10 September between the American fleet under Master Commandant Oliver H. Perry and the Provincial Marine under Commander Robert H. Barclay are not essential to a history of land operations. It is sufficient to note that, while Barclay had a slight advantage in the number of guns, Perry had the advantage in the number of vessels and the weight of shot. Early in August the very eventuality that Procter had feared had come about. The American vessels had emerged from their protective harbour of Presque Isle and taken control of Lake Erie. They were able to blockade the Canadian shoreline and prevent the movement of bateaux from the British supply depot on Long Point to Amherstburg. The British were going to have to fight the Americans or starve. When the sun set on the scene of battle on 10 September, the British squadron of two ships, two brigs, one schooner and one sloop had struck their colours to the commander of the American fleet.

Under the disheartening circumstances, Procter's position was critical. He had sent five bateaux to Long Point the day before the naval engagement and, although they managed to get back to Amherstburg with 171 barrels of flour, they were unlikely to be able to do the same again. At least this flour made it possible for Procter's cooks to bake bread and biscuits for the troops before they began their withdrawal up the Thames River. Procter must have found it ironic that the reinforcements he had asked for earlier should have trickled into Amherstburg throughout the summer and that, by September, when they were no longer of any use to him, he should have the largest number of regulars he had yet commanded in the Amherstburg region! All were members of the 41st Regiment. Procter did not need them because at no time had he intended to stay and try to defend the position at Amherstburg. It was already autumn, and that meant a return of the rain and added difficulties in moving troops either to or from the British front on the Detroit River. Was there any chance that Rottenburg, who had been so reluctant to let him have reinforcements, would be willing to send a relief force of the size necessary to get Procter out of his hole at the end of the line? How could Procter continue to victual his troops; where could he find supplies for them? Retreat, too, involved problems. What was to be done about the women and children at Amherstburg? How could the retreating army convey its guns and the military impedimenta? What about the provisions needed for a retreat? And yet, what were the alternatives to a retreat? He could fight or surrender. The first seemed to Procter impractical, the second dishonourable. So retreat it would have to be, despite Indian charges of cowardice.

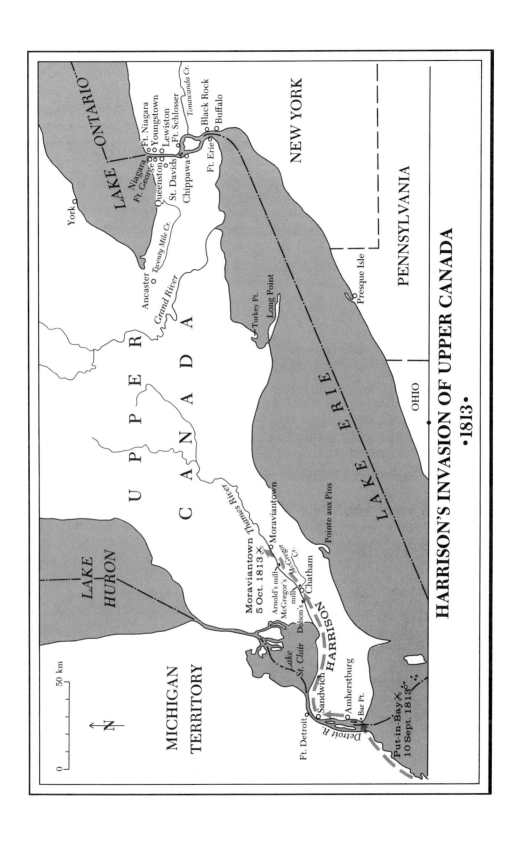

LAKE ONTARIO

York

Niagara
Ft. Niagara
Ft. George
Queenston
Youngstown
St. Davids
Lewiston
Ft. Schlosser
Chippawa
Tonawanda Cr.
Ft. Erie
Black Rock
Buffalo

Ancaster
Grand River
Twenty Mile Cr.

NEW YORK

U P P E R

C A N A D A

Turkey Pt.
Long Point

PENNSYLVANIA

Presque Isle

L A K E   E R I E

OHIO

LAKE HURON

Thames River
Moraviantown
5 Oct. 1813
Moraviantown
Pointe aux Pins

Arnold's mill
McGregor's
mill
McGregor's Cr.
Dolson's
Chatham

MICHIGAN TERRITORY

HARRISON

Lake St. Clair
Sandwich
Amherstburg
Bar Pt.
Ft. Detroit
Detroit R.
Put-in-Bay
10 Sept. 1813

N

0   50 km

HARRISON'S INVASION OF UPPER CANADA

·1813·

On 12 September, Procter sent a letter to Rottenburg stating that he could no longer occupy Amherstburg "to advantage"; it was a position "so easily turned by means of the entire command of the waters here" that he had no choice but to retire on the Thames River "without delay".[5] Procter also wrote to Colonel Thomas Talbot, asking him to send provisions to the Thames and to have the road "as far as possible repaired thro' the wilderness".[6] He then proclaimed martial law to enable the commissary to impress supplies and to remove any disaffected person from dangerous points along the route of retirement. Gilmor collected cattle (oxen and milk cows) from loyal farmers, who were fleeing the Americans with the troops, and arranged for ovens to be built at Dolson's for the baking of bread and biscuits during the retreat.

Rottenburg was none too pleased with Procter's decision, as he did not consider him to be in a particularly perilous position. Neither did the Indians. When Procter met them in council on 18 September, Tecumseh was not sparing of his censure. He recalled Procter's earlier assurance that the British would never abandon the Indians; why then was he proposing to retreat without even having seen an American soldier or suffered a single defeat on British soil? To Tecumseh, Procter was a coward, nothing more or less. Such charges did not bother Procter. After his experiences in the spring he had lost confidence in the Indians; and now they had lost confidence in him. However, they agreed to go along with him and to fight at some defensible point along the Thames. Procter therefore collected his personal baggage, his heavy baggage (there was too much of it for speedy travelling), his reserve supplies, his women and children and his cattle, and sent them off in advance. They were to take the road leading to the mouth of the Thames, and then follow the winding river past the location where Simcoe had proposed building the capital of Upper Canada (London) and on towards the Grand River. Every step on this long passage through the heart of western Upper Canada would bring Procter's force nearer Vincent's base at Burlington Heights; just as every step along that same route would take the pursuers, General Harrison and his American troops, farther from their own source of supplies.

On 27 September, Procter abandoned Detroit, then Sandwich. He moved on to Dolson's, about 4 km below Chatham and an oasis in the wilderness, and then to McGregor's mill. Contrary to orders, the long column of wagons moved slowly, in easy stages, keeping pace with the bateaux delayed by low water and tortuous streams, the rearguard neglecting even the elementary precaution of burning all the bridges behind them. It was left to the Indians to tear up the bridge at McGregor's. Daily it became more obvious that Procter's command was going to pieces. The commander seemed unable to make up his mind. He thought of making a stand at Dolson's, at a spot that reminded Tecumseh of his homeland. "When I look on these two streams, I shall think of the Wabash and the Tippecanoe", he said.[7] But there was no battle at Dolson's, nor at McGregor Creek, only a rearguard skirmish between the Indians and the Americans. Spending much of his time with his wife and child, who were travelling in the advance party with the heavy baggage, Procter left the conduct of the retreat largely to his second-in-command, Lieutenant Colonel Augustus Warburton, but gave him little direction. And so the retreat dragged on. Crossing the Thames at Arnold's mill, the British continued towards Fairfield, a mission to the Delaware Indians that the Moravians founded in 1792, across the river from the present site of Moraviantown. Procter sent his family on to the mission village, and in the early hours of 5 October retraced his steps westwards, finding his struggling army encamped about 5 km from Moraviantown. Here he would stand and fight. Dawn was breaking when he ordered his men to halt and face the enemy. Weary as they were, the troops seemed almost glad of a chance to engage their relentless pursuers.[8]

MEANWHILE, Major General William Harrison had been busy building up his army to the authorized strength of 7000. By the end of July he had 3000 regulars, but he wanted more and appealed to Governor Isaac Shelby of Kentucky for volunteers. The appeal met with a hearty response, for the Kentuckians were always foremost among the supporters of the war against Canada, and they were fearsome fighters. One British soldier, Sergeant James Commins of the 8th Foot, who fought against them, did not like them. He described them in a private letter as

> wretches suborned by the Government and capable of the greatest villainies. They are served out with blanket clothing like the Indians, with a long scalloping [scalping] knife and other barbarous articles and with red paint with which they daub themselves all over and in summer nearly went naked. In this manner they would surprise our piquets, and after engagements they scallop [scalp] the killed and wounded that could not get out of their way.[9]

This reaction of a regular soldier to the Kentucky militia explains why the British, when accused of using Indians in the War of 1812, invariably came back with the counter-accusation that the Americans used the Kentuckians.

After Perry's naval victory at Put-in-Bay on Lake Erie, Harrison began to bring together the various components of his army, including the corps of mounted volunteers raised by the Kentucky congressman, Colonel Richard M. Johnson. To join Harrison's force came Governor Shelby of Kentucky and Hull's old antagonists, Brigadier Generals McArthur and Cass. Finally, with his army totalling about 5000 men, Harrison began to move from the Sandusky area towards Detroit. A scouting party he sent ahead to reconnoitre found the blockhouse on Bar Point at the entrance of the Detroit River destroyed, and could see no signs of British troops anywhere in the neighbourhood. Harrison therefore felt it safe to land on the British side of the river. He divided his army into two columns: the left column, made up of three militia brigades, was allotted the task of clearing the Indians away from the British right flank; the second column, the assault troops proper, was to deal with Procter's regulars and militia. To Harrison's surprise and satisfaction, the Americans encountered no opposition during the landing, which was carried out under cover of the guns of Perry's ships. Then, with all his men ashore, Harrison wheeled towards the left and headed for Amherstburg. It was empty. The American troops settled down for a peaceful night's rest, and early next morning began moving northwards. Because all the bridges between Amherstburg and Sandwich had to be repaired, it was not until 29 September that Harrison reached the scene of Hull's initial landing fourteen months before.

Halting at Sandwich, Harrison sent McArthur to occupy Detroit, and opened talks with some of the disaffected Indians who had deserted Procter as soon as the fortunes of war had turned in favour of the Americans. At the same time he made arrangements with Commodore Perry for the transportation, by water, of the supplies that he knew he would need while he pursued the retreating British commander. On 2 October, he was ready to set out again; he would take about 3500 men, including 1500 of Johnson's mounted Kentuckians, and leave the remainder of his force to occupy Amherstburg and Detroit. From this point the pursuit accelerated, owing to Procter's failure to destroy the bridges and to carry out rearguard delaying actions. At Dolson's, Harrison prevailed upon Matthew

Dolson, who had deserted from the Canadian militia the previous year, to join the American force as a guide. It was at this point that Harrison abandoned his boats, preferring to move overland rather than be delayed by the windings and current of the Thames River. At McGregor Creek a few Indians tried to delay Harrison but without success. It was obvious to the Americans that they were hot on Procter's heels, as they frequently encountered half-burned buildings, burned-out boats and discarded military equipment. Finally, on 5 October, they captured two of Procter's gunboats, both carrying supplies of ammunition, and also a British wagoner, who told his captors that the British were only a short distance ahead. Colonel Johnson relayed this information to Harrison, who with his officers planned the attack. The Americans would approach the British with their infantry in front to overcome the enemy by a vigorous charge. This would be the responsibility of Cass's brigade. The Kentucky infantry under Major General Joseph Desha would watch the left flank to prevent the Indians from outflanking the Americans. Johnson's horse was to be held behind to back up the American infantry when and where required. Then, at the last moment, the order of battle was changed. The Kentucky cavalry would attack first, followed by the American infantry.

More by accident than design the British chose a position that, at first glance, seemed to offer certain advantages as far as defence was concerned. It restricted the area of attack to a narrow frontage, and rested both flanks of the defending force on strong natural obstacles, the river on the left and a deep swamp on the right. The Indians were placed on the extreme right, at the edge of the great swamp, in a position from which they might be able to outflank the attacking force. Along the road, on the left, the British placed their one available cannon, loaded with canister.

Later, the weakness of the British position became apparent. Except for the small cleared area occupied by the troops, the countryside was heavily forested, and was dark and dreary and littered with fallen and rotting trees. The colour of the vegetation, as young John Richardson pointed out later, made it difficult for the British defenders to distinguish the rather sombre uniforms of the Americans, while the "glaring red" tunics of the British soldiers "formed a point of relief on which the eye could not fail to dwell".[10] Even more critical for the regular soldier of the day was the absence of any room for manoeuvre.

Dependent as he was upon cohesion and manoeuvre, the British infantryman was helpless when hemmed into a small space where retreat meant scattering among the trees of an unfamiliar and inhospitable forest. And the small swamp splitting the narrow front of scarcely more than 180 m compounded the problems of movement and control. Should the attacking force be successful in meeting the initial volleys of the infantry and maintaining heavy pressure on the defenders, there was no place for the latter to go. No drill movements would be of any use and there would be nothing the British troops could do but lay down their arms and surrender.

Of course, surrender was not inevitable, certainly not to a force with a strong *esprit de corps* and under strong leadership. But the soldiers of the 41st had neither at Moraviantown. They were dispirited by the retreat, without confidence in Procter, and lacking any will to fight, any direction from above and adequate supplies of ammunition. What ammunition each man had was in his pouch; the Americans had captured the reserve supply. Moreover, the one cannon, which was placed to guard the main road, did not fire a single shot. To cover his own inadequacies Procter blamed his men for the defeat. He wrote after the battle: "If the troops had acted as I had ever seen them, and as I confidently expected, I am still of opinion, notwithstanding their numerical superiority, the enemy would have been beaten."[11]

The same criticism could have been applied to Procter himself, for his role in the battle consisted largely of moving his men about in an irregular fashion, which caused one of them, Lieutenant Richard Bullock, to remark that "they were ready and willing to fight for their knapsacks; wished to meet the enemy, but did not like to be knocked about in that manner, doing neither one thing nor the other."[12] When the shooting started, Procter mounted his splendid charger and, accompanied by his personal staff, rode with all possible haste from the field of battle to escape Harrison's mounted infantry, who had entered the battle shouting, "Remember the River Raisin!"[13] Two volleys and the engagement was over; it had lasted scarcely ten minutes. Procter, of course, needed scapegoats. His account of the Battle of Moraviantown was not supported by the statements of his officers nor by the statements of others who took part. In fact, Procter tried to prevent unofficial accounts of the disaster from reaching the high command; and it was in defiance of his orders that Staff Adjutant John C. Reiffenstein—"a little

55. *Oshawana, second-in-command of the Indians at the Battle of Moraviantown, under Tecumseh*

red-faced yellow-haired obese German",[14] Richardson called him—proceeded forthwith to York, spreading stories about Procter's incompetence, which led to Procter's court-martial and his suspension from rank and pay for six months.

One man who emerges from the story of Moraviantown with credit is Tecumseh. The Shawnee chief had spent the evening before the battle in conversation with the old Butler Ranger, William Caldwell, and a group of Indians. Comparing Procter and Brock, Tecumseh told Caldwell, "Procter no Brock."[15] On the morning of the battle Tecumseh placed his Indians on the

211

British right, along the edge of the great swamp. The Sioux and Chippewa were under the command of Oshawana. According to Caldwell, Tecumseh had a premonition that he would not emerge alive from the forthcoming battle. The Indians continued fighting for some time after the British regulars had been compelled to surrender, their heavy fire from the swamp forcing the American horsemen to dismount and continue the battle on foot. Both Indians and Americans fought with an impetuosity and a spirit that would have surprised Hull and Procter alike. Tecumseh's voice could be heard between the bursts of gunfire, rallying the Indians, urging them to remain firm, seeking to nullify the effect of Procter's flight and Warburton's surrender. Wounded several times, Tecumseh refused to give up. When Caldwell saw him using his rifle as a crutch and questioned him, Tecumseh showed Caldwell a gaping chest wound. But still he fought on. The Indians by this time had used all their ammunition and were relying on their slashing tomahawks. Gradually, however, they yielded to the Americans and withdrew deep into the swamp. With them they carried the body of their chief, Tecumseh. What actually happened, who killed him, or where he was buried remain mysteries to this day. Richard Johnson claimed that he had killed Tecumseh, and ghoulish Kentuckians cut pieces of skin from the body Johnson believed to be Tecumseh's; these souvenirs were to be fashioned into razor strops.[16] Other Indian bodies suffered similar indignities from American souvenir hunters, but there is no proof that any of the mutilated bodies was that of the Shawnee chief. Today Tecumseh's bones rest in an unknown grave somewhere in Ontario, perhaps near the site of the battlefield where he gave his life for his people and for the cause to which he had committed himself.

On 9 October, Colonel Robert Young wrote to Major General John Vincent from Burlington Heights, telling him that Procter's army had been "completely annihilated" on the Thames.[17] This was no exaggeration. Scarcely 259 men of the Right Division managed to reach Ancaster within a fortnight of the battle, 28 officers and 606 men having been killed or taken prisoner. The bodies of about 33 Indians were found on the battlefield, and no more than 400 of the 1000 Indians who had been with Procter continued eastwards to join the British forces at Burlington Heights. The remainder, dispirited and dismayed, retired to the hunting grounds remaining to them. In addition, Procter lost his artillery, which, save the one gun that was to

56. The Battle of Moraviantown, 5 October 1813, portrayed by an American primitive artist. Colonel Richard M. Johnson is shown on horseback, about to cut down an Indian chief, widely believed to be Tecumseh. On the right is an Indian scalping an American drummer. Serried ranks of Indians and Americans are drawn up in medieval style on the right and left flanks.

have guarded the road, had all been moved to Moraviantown and were not used in the battle. Some of these weapons were British guns lost during the American Revolutionary War and recovered by Brock when he took possession of Detroit. Procter also lost his wagons, his camp and other equipment, and his private papers.

Complete as Harrison's victory was, it did not lead to strategic success. On 5 October, Harrison's army on the Thames was like a dagger pointed at the heart of Upper Canada. The Americans needed only to continue the threat to advance on Burlington Heights, at the head of Lake Ontario, to sever the land communications of Vincent's army in the Niagara peninsula with the rest of the province. That might well have led to the loss of a second British army or, at the very least, its retirement to Kingston, the contingency that had haunted Rottenburg earlier in the year, after Dearborn's initial successes. Should Burlington Heights and York fall to the Americans, communications with Fort Michilimackinac and the upper Great Lakes would be limited to the North West Company's old canoe route along the Ottawa River and the French River to Georgian Bay. Michilimackinac would be exposed to attack from Detroit, with no prospect of help from the British forces in Upper Canada. Clearly Harrison's victory at Moraviantown had the potential for being one of the decisive battles of the war.

But Harrison did not, indeed could not, take full advantage of his success on the Thames; thus, for the Americans, Moraviantown remained a tactical rather than a strategic success. Harrison had already outmarched his tenuous supply line, and further advance to Burlington Heights was impossible. The Americans were stalled by bad roads, which the autumn rains were turning into a thick yellow quagmire, and by the lack of provisions. Logistical problems, which had already forced Harrison to reduce his force from its original 5000, now forced him to withdraw it speedily from Moraviantown instead of continuing the pursuit of Procter's stragglers. By 9 October, Harrison and the mounted troops were back in Detroit, and the remainder of his army arrived the next day. By the fifteenth, the Kentucky militia (with the exception of Johnson's mounted riflemen) were on their way home. Harrison signed a provisional armistice with the Potawatomi, Wyandot, Miami and Chippewa Indians on the fourteenth, and began issuing them rations, just as Procter had done in Amherstburg. And, finally, on the seventeenth, Harrison turned the civil administration of Michigan Territory and western Upper Canada over to Brigadier General Lewis Cass, after confirming in their appointments such Canadian officials as were willing to take the oath of fidelity to the United States during the period of the American occupation.

Then the victorious general set out on a triumphal progress to Washington via Buffalo, Sackets Harbor, New York and Philadelphia. Everywhere crowds of people turned out to greet the only American officer yet to win a significant victory on land. But the Secretary of War was no friend, and Harrison's reward was a minor command at Cincinnati, a quiet sector where fighting was unlikely. When Harrison responded by resigning, Armstrong promptly accepted his resignation. Madison, who was not yet ready to overrule his secretary of war, concurred.

WITHOUT FIGHTING, the Americans almost gained the strategic success implicit in their victory at Moraviantown. When the first news of the battle reached the British commander-in-chief, Sir George Prevost, he ordered the abandonment of all of Upper Canada west of Kingston. Perhaps, in so doing, he was influenced by Rottenburg, to whom this had long appeared a logical military move. However, Major General Vincent, who resumed command in Upper Canada when Rottenburg returned to Kingston with Prevost, appreciated the strategic threat but considered that a withdrawal from the Niagara peninsula would be sufficient. He therefore pulled into Burlington Heights all the Niagara outposts as far as St. Davids and Fort Erie. If Harrison should advance beyond Moraviantown, he would find Vincent ready and waiting for him at Burlington Heights. Prevost, once he had an opportunity to examine the situation more carefully, confirmed Vincent's action and instructed him to stand firm on Burlington Heights. There were, indeed, any number of arguments for staying there. Many soldiers were sick, at both Burlington Heights and York, and could not, without endangering their well-being, be removed to Kingston, where the hospital facilities were inadequate. And with the roads at their worst at this time of year, it would be as difficult to travel by wagon as it would be to move by boat on Lake Ontario, exposed to Chauncey's ships of war. Moreover, could the British forces afford to abandon all their ordnance, provisions and baggage? To transport everything to Kingston would not be practical in terms of logistics. Besides, was a full-scale American attack by land likely at this time of year? Would not the Americans, too, face the same logistical problems that affected the British? And why move when Burlington Heights was considered a position of real defensive strength? For all these reasons Vincent stayed put with a strong force, awaiting an attack that never materialized.

Nevertheless, when the British moved out of the Niagara peninsula, the Americans were prompt in filling the vacuum, though not aggressively nor in any great numbers. The authorities in Washington had their eyes on another theatre of war and had already shifted the bulk of their military resources to Sackets Harbor, with a view to carrying out a two-pronged attack on Montreal. All American regular troops were withdrawn from Fort Niagara, and the task of looking after American interests in that theatre of operations was left to the New York militia, under Brigadier General George McClure, and to the band of Canadian irregulars led by Joseph Willcocks, now reinforced by Benajah Mallory and Abraham Markle, both former members of the Upper Canada legislature who had once joined Willcocks in opposing Brock's attempt to impose an oath of allegiance and suspend *habeas corpus*. Thus, the fighting that took place in the Niagara peninsula in November 1813 took the form of pillaging farms and burning barns in the regions ostensibly under the control of American troops.

The news of McClure's exactions and Willcocks's arrests having reached the British headquarters on Burlington Heights, Colonel John Murray suggested to Vincent that, as a full-scale American offensive now seemed unlikely, he be permitted to take a small force of regulars and move back into the Niagara area to protect the inhabitants. Vincent agreed and Murray, with a force comprising 378 regulars of the 8th Regiment of Foot and a few volunteers and Indians, established himself at Forty Mile Creek (Grimsby). His orders were to avoid pressing the Americans too hard, and not to advance beyond that point. At that moment neither Vincent nor Murray realized just how weak McClure's position really was.

In a manner reminiscent of his predecessor, Brigadier General Alexander Smyth, McClure had already had recourse to his pen, calling upon the people of New York in October to accompany him across the Niagara River and to "enter upon that part of the enemy's country already conquered by your arms" and to ignore "the false, absurd and ridiculous scruples of the injunctions of the constitution". He made it clear that he wanted no "faint-hearted effeminate poltroons, who cannot bring their courage to the sticking point" to go with him.[18] Advertisements in a similar vein, but in less florid language, appeared in the press. But the response had not been what McClure had hoped for, and when he learned through Willcocks's scouts that Murray was at Forty Mile, he fell back to Twenty Mile Creek, and then back to occupy General Brock's old headquarters at Fort George itself. McClure's position became daily more sensitive. Murray had become more aggressive, advancing beyond Forty Mile, to Twenty Mile and on to Twelve Mile Creek (St. Catharines), just at the time when the short-term enlistments of the American volunteers were beginning to expire. McClure's force, despite his appeals, was simply melting away. According to a letter in the *Buffalo Gazette*, McClure "offered a bounty, but neither the love of country nor the shame of abandoning him when the enemy were advancing" could prevail upon the draftees to remain under arms.[19]

December of 1813 was a very cold month in the Niagara peninsula, unusually cold for that time of year. To McClure, it was not the weather in which to confront Murray's regulars, despite their small numbers. He was discouraged, too, by the reports from Willcocks's Canadian Volunteers as to the attitude of the public in the Niagara area. Early in December, Willcocks's men had come off second-best in a brief encounter with one of Murray's outposts.[20] McClure therefore resolved to withdraw from

To The
PATRIOTS
OF THE
Western District.

THE period being at hand which is to decide the fate of the province of Upper Canada, and the command of the Niagara frontier having devolved on me; I think proper to invite

The Old and Young PATRIOTS of the Western District, to join my Brigade in defence of their Country and rights—Any number not exceeding one thousand will be accepted and organized immediately on their arrival at Lewiston, and officered by the choice of their men. As the movements of an army require secresy, objects in view cannot be particularly developed; but those who feel disposed to distinguish themselves and render services to their country, may be assured that something ef... two months, if not sooner discharged And every thing shall be done to render their situation as comfortable as possible. I wish none to volunteer who may have any constitutional objections to cross the Niagara river. One thousand four hundred of my brigade, have already volunteered to cross the river, and go wherever they may be required; and six hundred of them are now doing duty at Fort George. I flatter myself that no other consideration need be urged, than a love of country, to excite the patriotism of the hardy yeomanry of the Western District.

Given at Head Quarters, Lewiston, Oct. 2d, 1813.

GEO. M'CLURE, *Brig. Gen'l,*
Commanding Niagara Frontier.

BUFFALO GAZETTE OFFICE, Saturday Evening, Oct. 2, 1813.

57. *McClure's appeal of 2 October 1813*

Fort George to Fort Niagara. As early as October he had received from John Armstrong in Washington instructions to destroy the town of Niagara, if necessary, but to first notify the inhabitants of his intentions, giving them the opportunity to salvage what they could of their personal property and retire to a place of safety. Acting on this authority, McClure informed the people of Niagara shortly before dusk on 10 December that he was issuing orders that the town be put to the torch. The news came as a great surprise. The people felt that they were guilty of no treachery. Those suspected of being "malignants" had been arrested and taken to prisons in the United States. The town had never interfered with military operations; Dearborn and Chauncey could bear testimony to that. Why then should it be destroyed? McClure had no answer except to lay the blame on the Secretary of State for War, who, he claimed, authorized him to burn the town if necessary.[21] The dirty work of setting the fires was left to Willcocks, the man who had represented Niagara in the legislature before the war. While the town was in flames, the Canadian Volunteers acted as a rear guard to protect the Americans while they fled from Fort George. Murray's men arrived just too late to prevent the burning or the escape of the Americans, although the rear guard lost two killed and several taken prisoner to the rapidly advancing British.

The burning of Niagara was an act much resented by the British and the Canadians, especially after the burning of various public buildings in York earlier in the year. But if the actions at York could be justified on military grounds, those at Niagara could have no such excuse. Niagara was a pleasant little town, with upwards of 300 buildings of various kinds. It was an active commercial centre and had formerly served as the seat of government for Upper Canada, losing that distinction to York because of its exposed position in relation to the United States. It contained a good public library, two churches and the provincial registry office. It was larger, and in many ways a more significant town, than the provincial capital at York. The story of the destruction is told by the *Ontario Repository* of Canandaigua, New York, for 21 December 1813:

> In the village, at least 130 buildings were consumed; and the miserable tenants of them, to the number of nearly four hundred, consisting mostly of women and children, were exposed to all the severities of deep snow and a frosty sky, almost in a state of nakedness. How many perished by the inclemency of the weather, it is, at present, impossible to ascertain.[22]

A special indignity was suffered by Mrs. William Dickson, whose husband was a prisoner of war in the hands of the Americans and who was seriously ill at the time. She was removed from her bed and left lying in the snow to watch the burning of her home and of her husband's law library.[23] McClure sought to justify his actions on the grounds of military necessity, but there were few who accepted his excuses as valid. One of his officers even resigned his commission in protest against what he regarded as a "most abhorrent" act. To argue, as McClure did, that the burning of Niagara was necessary to deprive the British of the means of housing their troops during the winter became palpably absurd when it was discovered that Butler's Barracks, one of the buildings that contained tents and military stores, was untouched by the flames. Under the circumstances, McClure's remark that "the enemy is much exasperated" remains one of the few wholly accurate statements made by the American commander.

Retribution followed swiftly. On 13 December, Sir Gordon Drummond was appointed president of the Council and administrator of Upper Canada as well as commander of the troops. He was Canadian-born, his father having served as an officer in the British garrison at Quebec. He had entered the 1st Regiment of Foot at the age of eighteen and had served in Holland, Egypt and the West Indies. After arriving in Upper Canada, he lost no time in proceeding to Vincent's headquarters at St. Davids, just a few days after McClure had abandoned Fort George. On 17 December he told Murray that he wanted an attack to be made as soon as possible on Fort Niagara. For taking Fort Niagara by a fast, sudden descent at night, the militia brought boats 68 km overland from Burlington Heights, notwithstanding the bad roads, and Murray was given a group of regulars of the 100th Regiment of Foot and the Royal Scots—both of which had arrived in the province during the summer to reinforce the Upper-Canadian forces—along with the flank companies of the 41st and some militia and Indians, about 500 in all. Silence and surprise were essential.

> The troops must preserve the profoundest silence and the strictest discipline. They must on no account be suffered to load without the orders of their officers. It should be impressed on the mind of every man that the bayonet is the weapon on which the success of the attack must depend.[24]

So ran the instructions given to Murray on 17 December.

Late on the night of the eighteenth the troops embarked in bateaux several kilometres above Fort George, and slipped quietly across the river, landing about 5 km beyond Fort Niagara. They surprised the guard at Youngstown and obtained the countersign. One of the guards succeeded in firing a warning rocket, but the Americans did not see it, and the British column moved off, with a party of grenadiers of the 100th leading. Their task was to assault the main gate and climb over the adjacent works. Other companies would storm the east demi-bastion, the Royals would occupy the salient angle of the fort, and the flank companies of the 41st would back up the main attack. Each party was provided with scaling ladders and axes. Shadrach Byfield, who had survived the misfortunes of the 41st under Procter, took part in the attack. He described it in a few words:

> We advanced quietly, and a party under the command of a sergeant went in front. When he came near the outer sentry, at the entrance to the fort, he was challenged; he advanced and gave the countersign, seized the sentinel, and threatened him with immediate death if he made any noise. He then proceeded to the gate, and was challenged by the sentry inside; he gave the countersign and gained admittance but the sentry cried out, "The British—turn out the guard." Our force was fully prepared and in a very short time we had possession of the fort, with very little loss.[25]

What Byfield did not mention was that the fort was carried by the bayonet and that only 20 men escaped to carry the news to McClure at Buffalo that Fort Niagara had fallen.

Murray paid tribute to the officers and men who took Fort Niagara by storm on 19 December 1813. What is more, he gave credit to Lieutenant Frederic de Gaugreben, of the Royal Engineers, whose knowledge of Fort Niagara and the best way of gaining entrance to the fort contributed significantly to Murray's success, achieved at the trifling cost of 6 killed and 5 wounded. In killed, wounded and captured, the Americans gave up 422 officers and men. Among the prisoners was the fort commander, Captain Nathaniel Leonard, who, according to another prisoner, Robert Lee, was at his farm "about two miles distant" when the fort was taken.[26] McClure later stated that Leonard was in fact "much intoxicated".[27] In terms of equipment and provisions, the Americans gave up a great deal, 27 cannon, 3000 stands of arms, and large quantities of provisions, clothing and camp equipage.[28] Most significantly, the cells of the fort yielded

8 Canadians, all of them civilians, who had been arrested by the Americans during the few months of the American occupation; among them was one Peter McMicking, a man eighty years of age.

Immediately following Murray's seizure of Fort Niagara, Major General Phineas Riall, who had come to Canada with Sir Gordon Drummond, crossed the Niagara River with another 500 soldiers and 500 Indians, with the object of seizing Lewiston.[29] The Indians had a short encounter with the enemy, but when the British troops arrived the Americans decamped. Riall was able to report that a few more pieces of ordnance would be available to fill British needs and that another 200 barrels of flour could be added to the British stocks for the winter months. The result of the Lewiston attack was to free the village of Queenston of any immediate threat. At Lewiston, it might be noted, the troops involved included not only the Royal Scots but also the remnants of Procter's 41st Regiment under Major Richard Frend. Lieutenant Richard Bullock, another officer who had escaped from the disaster of Moraviantown, was among those who took part in the assault on Fort Niagara. The small community of Youngstown and the Indian village of Tuscarora, deserted by their inhabitants, were turned into heaps of burning rubbish by the British troops. Riall went on past Fort Schlosser and Manchester, both of which he burned, as far as Tonawanda Creek, a small river emptying into the Niagara above the Falls, opposite Grand Island. Here he was within 16 km of Buffalo, hard on the heels of the Canadian Volunteers. He had not planned on an attack on Buffalo, and since Benajah Mallory had destroyed the bridge over Tonawanda Creek, Riall returned to Lewiston and thence over to Queenston. Buffalo could wait a few days more.

It had been to Buffalo that General McClure had hurried after his flight from Fort George, but if he hoped to arouse any enthusiasm for fighting in the people of Buffalo, he must have been sadly disappointed. Not only could he raise no men, but he could not get the support of the local commander, Brigadier General Timothy Hopkins, who, on 20 December, informed the Governor of New York that

> I have to represent that the men of my brigade are unwilling to come under the command of General McClure, who is near Buffalo and assumes the command. His conduct since he has been out of the lines has disgusted the greater part of the men under his command and they have no confidence in him.

Then Hopkins got down to the real point of his letter:

We have reason to fear that the destruction of Newark [Niagara] and the retreat of General McClure from Canada have incensed the people of Canada and inspired them with courage to such a degree that nothing will save any part of this frontier but a respectable force.[30]

McClure was having trouble with more officers than just Hopkins. In his letter to Governor Tompkins, McClure pointed out that he had been compelled to arrest Lieutenant Colonel Cyrenius Chapin on charges of treason and mutiny. "There is not a greater rascal exists than Chapin, and he is supported by a pack of *Tories* and enemies to our government. Such as the men of Buffalo. They don't deserve protection."[31] In the end, the command at Buffalo fell to the lot of Major General Amos Hall. McClure's military career was at an end. Armstrong resented McClure's attempts to lay the blame for the destruction of Niagara at his door, and writing, as others had done, to Governor Tompkins, Armstrong simply said of McClure, "Relieve this man." Then, holding up the example of other states to Tompkins, he made it clear that the Niagara frontier was no longer a priority for the federal government. "The invaders must be expelled by the militia of the west, and if it be not done shame light upon them! Why should Virginia, Georgia, Tennessee and Kentucky men so far out-act and outshine us?"[32]

Meanwhile, Drummond set in motion plans to end any possible annoyance to the British settlements west of the Niagara River for the remainder of the winter. He was aware of the efforts of McClure, Hopkins and Hall, in the vicinity of Buffalo, to assemble a force of militia to either attempt a recovery of Fort Niagara or cross the Niagara River to the Canadian side, and on 28 December issued a general order for another raid into the United States. It was characteristic of the new commander in Upper Canada that he should enjoin the strictest discipline and reliance upon the bayonet. Looting would be punished by death, and "intoxication in the presence of an enemy" would be considered as "the most dangerous crime which a soldier can commit".[33] There was no nonsense about Drummond. The object of the assault would be to put both Buffalo and Black Rock to the torch to deprive the enemy of the cover these places provided and to destroy three of the enemy's armed schooners. The expedition was to come under the command of Sir Phineas Riall.

On the night of 30 December, Riall, with a force of about 1400 men, 400 of them Indians, crossed the Niagara River. The first wave, led by Lieutenant Colonel James Ogilvie of the 8th Regiment and Major Richard Frend of the 41st and comprising the 8th, the Light Company of the 89th and a party of militia and Indians, landed unopposed about 3 km below Black Rock. Moving quickly, the Light Infantry surprised and captured an American picket and secured the bridge over the Scajaquada Creek to the north of Black Rock; its boards had been loosened so that they could be readily carried off. Crossing the stream, the British troops took up a position in advance of the bridge. The second large contingent of troops, including the Royal Scots with more militia and Indians, under the command of Lieutenant Colonel John Gordon, began to move in at daylight. They were to land above Black Rock for the purpose of turning the American position, while the first group carried through the main assault. Several of Gordon's boats grounded and the troops, having suffered heavy losses from the fire of the defending forces, were unable to accomplish their purpose in the manner planned. The 8th and 89th succeeded in reaching the outskirts of Buffalo and began a spirited attack on the American position. According to Riall, the Americans under General Hall fought "with very considerable obstinacy for some time", but eventually gave way and retired through their batteries into and beyond the town of Buffalo. A large body of American infantry and cavalry made another effort to halt the British advance but, finding this ineffectual, took to the woods.

Riall then turned to executing "the ulterior objects of the expedition", namely the destruction of two schooners and a sloop, together with their stores; they were part of the American Lake Erie squadron, drawn up on shore a little below Buffalo. After the vessels were burned, the soldiers returned to the town and the stores that it contained. The population had abandoned their houses, and the whole of the public stores, including "considerable quantities" of clothing, spirits and flour, "which I had not the means of conveying away", were set on fire "and totally consumed". The Americans had evacuated Black Rock, which was also burned, and a party of the 19th Light Dragoons and infantry was sent along the river towards Fort Niagara to "destroy the remaining cover of the enemy upon his frontier".[34]

In this expedition the British lost, in killed, wounded and missing, 112 men. One of the casualties was Shadrach Byfield, who was wounded in the left arm. When told by the surgeon that his arm would have to be amputated, Byfield asked one of his comrades who had had a similar operation what it felt like. The man replied, "Thee woo't know, when it's done." According to Byfield:

> They prepared to bind me, and had men to hold me; but I told them there was no need of that. The operation was tedious and painful, but I was enabled to bear it pretty well. I had it dressed, and went to bed. They brought me some mulled wine, and I drank it. I was then informed that the orderly had thrown my hand to the dung-heap. I arose, went to him, and felt a disposition to strike him. My hand was taken up and a few boards nailed together for a coffin, my hand was put into it and buried on the ramparts. The stump of my arm soon healed, and three days after I was able to play a game of fives, for a quart of rum.[35]

The American commander, Major General Amos Hall, writing to Governor Tompkins, placed the American losses at 30 killed and 40 wounded, with 69 American prisoners in British hands. He attributed his defeat to the shrinkage of his command of some 2000 men on the morning of the alarm "to less than 1200", because of the defection of the Indians the Americans had sedulously cultivated during the last few months, desertions among the militia, and "the loss of the services of the cavalry and mounted men, by reason of the nature of the ground" on which they had to act.[36]

From the British standpoint, the expedition to Buffalo was in every way a success. Riall had achieved what he had set out to do. He had destroyed several American vessels and rendered the whole Niagara frontier a scene of desolation. To all intents and purposes, the American frontier was now defenceless. There were no American regulars on the frontier and the militia was demoralized. All that remained was Benajah Mallory's corps of so-called Canadian Volunteers, whose numbers were diminishing as a result of casualties. The situation had now become stabilized, and the Canadian settlers could hope to sleep at night without fear of sudden raids or major military operations emanating from Buffalo, Black Rock, Lewiston or Fort Niagara throughout the winter months. But the war had taken an ugly turn with the more extensive use of the scalping knife and the torch, and it would continue in this fashion in Upper Canada throughout 1814.

9

Montreal

MONTREAL HAD LONG BEEN the strategic centre of Canada. It covered the approach to Quebec by way of the upper St. Lawrence and dominated the water routes leading to the Great Lakes. Whoever controlled Montreal controlled the Northwest. But Montreal possessed few natural defences. It was accessible by water to any force moving eastwards down the St. Lawrence from Lake Ontario and also to any force moving northwards along the water route provided by Lake Champlain and the Richelieu River. In years past the two water highways, the St. Lawrence and the Richelieu, had provided ready access to invading armies. The Iroquois Indians had followed them during the seventeenth century, the Anglo-Americans during the eighteenth. The Canadian French had understood the geomilitary importance of these water routes and had erected fortifications along both. In 1760 Jeffrey Amherst and William Haviland had combined forces to use both routes to capture Montreal and bring about the capitulation of New France. Fifteen years later Richard Montgomery and his army of American rebels followed the Richelieu River, overcame British resistance at Saint-Jean and Chambly, and occupied Montreal as the first step towards the conquest of Quebec. It is surprising that a rereading of history did not prompt the United States to put forth another major effort in this sector.

There is evidence to support the view that John Armstrong, at least, was aware of the strategic importance of Montreal even before the outbreak of war in 1812. In January of that year he wrote to his predecessor as secretary of war, Dr. William Eustis, emphasizing how much Upper Canada depended on Montreal for the continued westward flow of supplies, military and commercial. But the Niagara and Detroit regions seemed to exert a hypnotic fascination on the war planners in Washington, and even after Armstrong took over the War Department in 1813 he could not immediately dispel the strategic concepts with which the United States had entered the war. Not until they were well into the second year of hostilities did the Americans make any serious effort to return to historical strategic patterns by directing a major offensive towards Montreal.

If the Americans were peculiarly insensitive to the military importance of Montreal, the Canadians were, perhaps, oversensitive to any show of force in this direction. Underlying all Prevost's planning was the possibility of abandoning Upper Canada to concentrate the whole of his military resources in the Montreal area. In order to keep informed of the movements and strengths of the American forces within striking distance of Lower Canada, particularly those in New York, he established an intelligence system that served him well. It was directed principally by Léon Lalanne of Montreal and Edward Doyle of Prescott. These men sought out Americans who were willing to aid the British in return for the privilege of importing goods from the Canadas into the United States. To provide a cover for the Americans' activities, the British agreed to furnish them with snippets of unimportant information, "fictitious or real", that could be passed on to the officers commanding various American military establishments.[1]

Confident that Lower Canada was in no danger of invasion during the winter months of 1812–13, Prevost left Montreal to return to the seat of government at Quebec, where he had to meet his legislature on 29 December. Much to his satisfaction, the members of the Assembly proved to be less bellicose than those of Upper Canada, although Prevost did experience some trouble with James Stuart, a recalcitrant Scotsman who had been removed from the appointment of solicitor general by the previous governor general, Sir James Craig, and had assumed the role of leader of the opposition. The most rancorous issue was over the use of martial law, which Stuart argued could be imposed only to enforce the obedience of men in the services and could not be made to apply to the civilian population. The session lasted rather longer than Prevost had hoped, but by 15 February 1813 the legislature had been prorogued and the

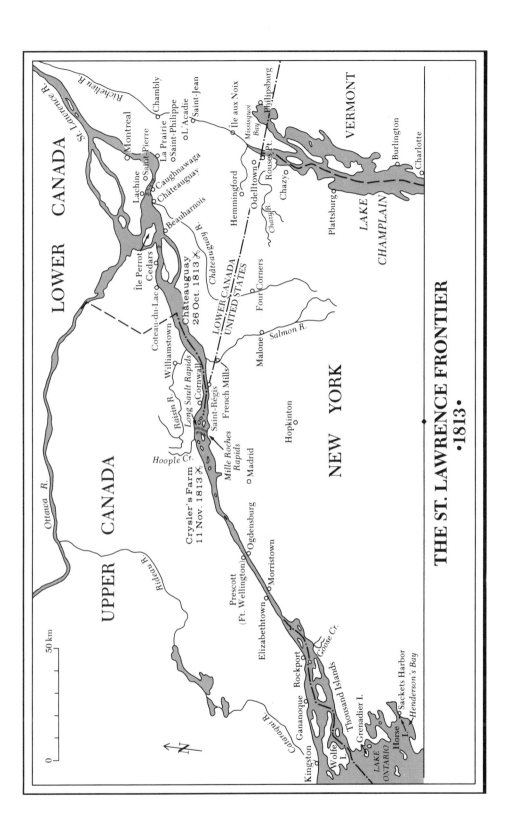

THE ST. LAWRENCE FRONTIER
·1813·

58. *Lieutenant Colonel "Red George" Macdonell, who led the Canadian attack on Ogdensburg on 22 February 1813*

Governor General was on his way to Kingston to look at the military situation in the upper province. On 20 February he reached Fort Wellington, at Prescott, the most important military station between Lachine and Kingston. Here, to his annoyance, he found himself importuned by the local commander, Lieutenant Colonel Thomas Pearson, and Lieutenant Colonel "Red George" Macdonell, commanding the Glengarry Light Infantry

Fencibles, to authorize an attack over the ice against the American base at Ogdensburg, opposite Prescott.

The officers wanted to retaliate against Major Benjamin Forsyth, commander of the American troops at Ogdensburg, who had raided Gananoque in the autumn of 1812 and had later carried off another successful cross-river raid, this time against Elizabethtown. On 7 February he had led his riflemen and some militia, about 200 in all, from Ogdensburg to Morristown. After crossing the river on the ice, a perilous undertaking since the ice was still rather thin, he had moved into Elizabethtown, undetected in the darkness. Setting pickets to guard the various streets, Forsyth occupied the courthouse square and liberated the prisoners in the town jail, except for a man charged with murder who begged piteously that he too be allowed to escape to the United States. There was minimal resistance and neither side suffered any casualties other than a wounded sentry. Forsyth took some 50 prisoners in triumph to Ogdensburg, although he paroled one prisoner, the local physician, and allowed him to return to Elizabethtown. Forsyth also took muskets, rifles and various public stores to Ogdensburg.

The American officer's success was both a stimulant and an irritation to Macdonell. It prompted him to suggest a retaliatory raid on Ogdensburg, directed particularly against Forsyth. Prevost, however, did not want to stir up action; better to leave well enough alone. After all, Forsyth's prisoners had all been paroled, except the officer in charge of the guard. What useful object would be promoted by an exchange of hostilities? Macdonell argued that the Americans had probably spent enough time on "fruitless and unfortunate attacks on the remote extremities", and might now be prepared to try something more significant, such as an attack on Prescott, which was vitally important to them. Occupation by the Americans, as Major General James Wilkinson was still arguing a year later, would "cut off all communication between Montreal and Kingston".[2] But Prevost was adamant, yielding to Macdonell only to the extent of authorizing him to make a military "demonstration" on the ice in front of Ogdensburg. No more. As Prevost climbed into his carriage, Macdonell warned him that the Americans might well attempt to waylay him at Elizabethtown. The Governor General, having thought over Macdonell's warning and balanced it against the Glengarrian's rashness, decided, when he broke his journey to breakfast, to send a written order back to Prescott. It read:

You will not undertake any offensive operations against Ogdensburg without previous communication with Major-General de Rottenburg, unless the imbecile conduct of your enemy should offer you an opportunity for his destruction and that of the shipping, batteries and public stores, which does not admit of delay in availing yourself of it, as I would not have the essential service of the transport of stores to Upper Canada interrupted on any consideration; nor do I think it proper to beget irritation in the mind of the people of the United States by any act that does not bear on the face of it a just retaliation on the military force of that country for wanton and unprovoked injuries.[3]

Macdonell was a stubborn Scot. He sent his men out on the river in two columns and began his demonstration, but, having convinced himself of the strength of the ice and the virtue of his cause, he disobeyed Prevost's command and ordered the "advance" to be sounded. The Americans were slow to realize that the demonstration was, in fact, an attack. When they did, they opened fire on the right column, led by Captain John Jenkins of the Glengarry Light Infantry, compelling him to give way, but Macdonell, leading the left column, continued over the undulating and cracking ice into the deep snow on the American bank of the river. Inspired by Macdonell, Jenkins rallied his own column in a charge, despite having received a blast of canister in his arm. The impetuosity of the troops, the examples of Macdonell and Jenkins and the admonitions of the chaplain, Father Alexander Macdonell, carried the day. The Americans were hesitant about surrendering, and in the end took refuge in flight, the militia into the countryside and Forsyth, with the regulars, to Sackets Harbor. The British troops then dismantled the American fort, burned the barracks and transferred all the military stores and provisions to Fort Wellington. The whole action lasted about one and a half hours and cost Macdonell 6 men killed and 34 wounded.

Macdonell's victory had an even more favourable result than he had expected: never again during the war was Ogdensburg occupied by an American garrison; in fact, the inhabitants expressly asked the American authorities not to send Forsyth back again as he would only provoke further retaliation.[4] The victory also opened the way for negotiations between the British military authorities and the principal merchants of the town— men like John Ross and David Parish, both of whom were Federalists and opposed to the war—for a constant supply of provisions. "It is incredible", Ross wrote to Parish, "what quantities of cattle and sheep are driven into Canada. . . . The day

59. Officer in the Glengarry Light Infantry Fencibles, 1812–16

before yesterday upwards of 100 oxen went through Prescott, yesterday about 200."[5]

In these circumstances Prevost decided to change his tune, and wrote to Macdonell: "Although you have *rather exceeded*

60. *David Parish, the American merchant who supplied provisions to the British troops at Fort Wellington during the war*

my orders, I am well pleased with what you have done, and so I have just told you in a General Order, which is to announce to the troops in British America your achievement."[6] The Order to which Prevost referred stated: "His Excellency feels much pleasure in publicly expressing his entire approbation of the gallantry and judgment with which it appears to have been conducted. A salute to be fired immediately."[7] Despite a reference to Macdonell's "splendid victory", the Canadian did not receive a medal or a promotion or a pension, although brevets and medals were showered on aides and staff officers who had served in the Spanish Peninsula and had never commanded even a company under fire. But Macdonell was neither the first nor the last to voice this familiar complaint.

AFTER MACDONELL'S successful action against Ogdensburg, the Americans gave little trouble to Canadian towns along the St. Lawrence during the remainder of the war. Instead, they took to the river itself, keeping a close watch on the movement of British supplies up the river from the newly expanded depot at Lachine. Not having the naval vessels necessary to intercept the convoys, the Americans authorized the arming of private boats and allowed them to operate out of Sackets Harbor under letters of marque. Commodore James Yeo replied by stationing gunboats at Prescott, Gananoque and Kingston. Encounters occurred from time to time, the most serious on 18 July, when two American privateers surprised a British convoy near Rockport in the Thousand Islands section of the St. Lawrence. The Americans seized both the escorting gunboat and fifteen bateaux, and then hurried across the river to Goose Creek, where they landed their prisoners and sent them overland to Sacket's Harbor. Learning of this mishap, Yeo dispatched four gunboats and detachments of the 100th and 41st regiments to recover the bateaux and the supplies they carried. But the British gunboats could not navigate Goose Creek, the channel, blocked with trees, being too narrow for manoeuvre. This little sideshow might have been disastrous for the British had not the soldiers leapt from the boats and, carrying their muskets over their heads, made for the shore, where they charged the Americans, causing them to withdraw. The gunboats were then put to rights, but the hoped-for recapture of the British bateaux was abandoned. Little engagements such as this, short and sharp, frequently produced heroics on the small scale, but not much more than that. They had little effect on the progress or the outcome of the war. Nevertheless, they bulked large on the local scene and often served as the inspiration for local pride and local legends.[8]

As the spring approached, Dearborn and Chauncey talked vaguely about a possible combined naval–military attack on Kingston; and then, instead, they went off to take York and Fort George. Meanwhile Prevost and Sir James Yeo, the British naval officer who had recently arrived to take over command of the old Provincial Marine and make it into a freshwater branch of the Royal Navy, were talking about a combined naval–military operation against Sackets Harbor. Such a stroke, if successful, would greatly embarrass Chauncey and cripple

61. Adjutant General Colonel Edward Baynes, who was in charge of the unsuccessful attack on Sackets Harbor, 28–29 May 1813

the naval arm of the United States on Lake Ontario. The American fleet would have no place to go, no place to refit, no place to find adequate shelter. Moreover, any British movement in the direction of Sackets Harbor was bound to bring Chauncey back posthaste, thus providing relief for Vincent in the Niagara peninsula. That is why, on 27 May, the very day that Dearborn and Chauncey were engaged at Fort George at the western end of the lake, Prevost and Yeo were sailing out of Kingston bound for Sackets Harbor at the eastern extremity.

On board Yeo's vessels were detachments of the 100th, the Royal Scots, the 8th, the 104th, the Voltigeurs and the Glengarry

Light Infantry, in all about 750 men. Sir George Prevost accompanied the expedition, although the immediate command was in the hands of Colonel Edward Baynes, Prevost's adjutant general. There was little or no wind and the waters of the lake were as "still as a pan of milk"; even though the British ships had all their canvas spread, the sails hung "as loosely as a lady's apron".[9] The slowness of their progress allowed Yeo's vessels to be clearly seen from Sackets Harbor long before they arrived, and Brigadier General Jacob Brown, the one-time smuggler now in charge of defending the town, had ample time to prepare his defences. He correctly appreciated that the British landing would probably take place on Horse Island and that the British troops would advance over the natural causeway to the mainland and then swing around to attack the American position at Fort Tompkins. He therefore arranged three lines of defence, the first and second consisting of American militia strung out along the shoreline and just behind in the woods; the final defence line was made up of regulars based on Fort Tompkins and the fort's heavy guns. On the other side of the harbour was another military work, Fort Pike.

Owing to the lack of wind, the British ships could not reach Sackets Harbor on the same day that they left Kingston. About sunset, however, the troops were transferred from the vessels to bateaux that had been towed across the lake. With a change of wind the ships of war might be able to get close enough to furnish covering fire. When it began to appear as if there would be no wind and that Yeo's vessels were unlikely to be able to approach close enough to carry out their proper role, the operation was called off, and the troops, or at least as many as could be accommodated, were ordered aboard HMS *Wolfe*. At this point two events took place that prompted another change of orders. First an onshore breeze sprang up, and then several bateaux bearing American soldiers with a flag of truce approached the British flagship. The British officers were just sitting down to dinner when the American officer who accompanied the flag came aboard and offered to surrender his whole party as prisoners of war. They numbered about 115. Describing the event, Lieutenant Colonel Edward Brenton, one of the provincial aides-de-camp, wrote to Noah Freer of the Nova Scotia Fencibles, then on Prevost's staff:

> This very singular event, depriving the enemy of part of the intended reinforcements and marking so clearly the description of people we had to contend with, together with a state of wind so favourable for reaching the harbour, led to further consultation,

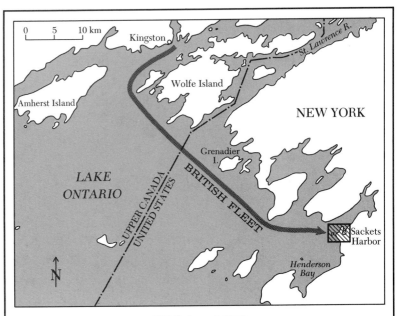

27 May 1813

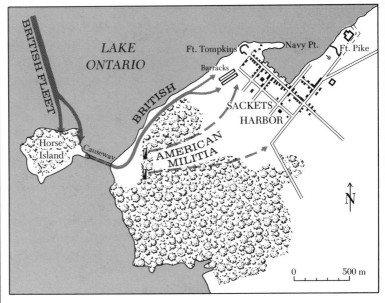

28-29 May 1813

THE ATTACK ON SACKETS HARBOR

when Colonel Baynes, who was in command of the expedition, with Colonel Young, Gray and others, were decidedly of the opinion that the attempt should be made.[10]

Accordingly, the boats were ordered to reassemble about the *Wolfe*. The troops re-embarked and were given orders to move towards the shore, about 3 km distant, so as to arrive at first light. They were to land under the cover of fire from the gunboats and HMS *Beresford*, should she succeed in reaching the landing place in time. The other vessels were to weigh anchor about an hour before daylight and act "as circumstances might point out". Prevost, "who could not rest satisfied on board and yet who could not consistently command the expedition", put out in a canoe with several of his staff officers, including Lieutenant Colonel Brenton. In the dark the boats tended to drift with the currents, and when dawn broke there was a certain amount of scrambling about to find their proper stations. Finally, all pulled towards Horse Island. The grenadiers of the 100th were the first ashore, followed by the Royal Scots and the remainder of the attacking troops. They encountered a sharp volley from the American militia, but as the British regulars continued to push forward along the narrow 1.2-m-wide causeway, over the "four hundred paces" of its length, the defenders broke and ran, some, according to one American historian, not stopping "until they reached their homes".[11] Even Brown's most urgent appeals failed to halt them. Thus, with comparatively few casualties, the British troops reached the mainland and, marching in two columns, swung towards Fort Tompkins.

It was there, against the American regulars, that the stiffest fighting took place during the next two hours. Despite repeated efforts, the British were unable to take the American defence works, including the blockhouse and stockaded battery; neither could they reduce the defences with the small-calibre fieldpieces they had brought ashore with them. Yeo's ships found it impossible to draw into the harbour to bring their heavy ordnance to bear, and the gunboats, armed with carronades, proved ineffective for the purpose. According to Brenton, who watched the whole operation at Sir George Prevost's side, Baynes came to Sir George and told him that "the enemy was so strongly posted and so sheltered by blockhouses and other works that our men could not approach them, weakened as they were by the losses of the morning, with any prospect of success."[12]

One last assault was made, and it almost came off. Troops of the 8th, 100th and 104th, on the left, penetrated to one of

62. Sackets Harbor on Lake Ontario, 1813. Fort Tompkins is in the right foreground, and Fort Pike is on the left.

the barracks, captured a piece of ordnance and, sheltering in the barracks, prepared for a further advance. The other wing of the assault force, on the right, was among the logs and stumps where Prevost and the staff were located. Here the fire was "tremendous". "I do not exaggerate", wrote Brenton, "when I tell you that shot, both grape and musket, flew like hail." Prevost, while trying to fix his glass on a stump for better viewing, was almost hit by falling shrapnel. At this moment the British troops on the right made one last dash towards the enemy, but the American fire was so destructive that the British broke and began to retreat. Sir George, "disdaining to run, or to suffer his men to run, called out repeatedly to them to retire in order". Not that anybody was really prepared to dawdle—that would suggest foolhardiness. As Brenton put it, the British staff officers, including Prevost, "retired with the hindmost, nor was it, I assure you, with a quickstep, though showers of grape were falling about us."[13] It was indeed fortunate that the Americans made no effort to pursue them. A charge might have upset Sir George's deliberation.

Halting before re-embarking, the staff held a short discussion as to whether any further attempts should be made against the American position. But the answer was no, partly because of the heavy casualties already suffered and partly because of the inability of the ships, for want of suitable wind, to get into a position to offer close support. Yet, another attack might have turned a defeat into victory. The Americans, impressed by the steadiness and discipline of the British troops in the face of a most stubborn resistance, were setting fire to their naval stores, preparatory to destroying their new ship on the stocks, and were otherwise making ready to withdraw. But neither Baynes nor Prevost was aware of this, and so they re-embarked.

By 0900 hrs all were aboard. Prevost and some of his staff departed by canoe at 1000 hrs, and arrived at Kingston in the early evening. The ships, held up by adverse winds, did not reach the mouth of the Cataraqui River until 30 May. The British casualties, officers and men, totalled 48 killed and 211 wounded, and 16 of the latter were taken prisoner by the Americans. Subsequently, Brigadier General Brown made arrangements for the care of the British dead and wounded left in his hands. Reporting to Governor Tompkins, Brown said that he "made them satisfied on that subject. Americans will be distinguished for humanity and bravery."[14]

One of the objects of the attack on Sackets Harbor had been to direct American attention away from the British troops in the Niagara peninsula. In that sense the battle, although a tactical failure, did achieve a temporary strategical success. Commodore Isaac Chauncey did come rushing back to his base at Sackets Harbor to reconstruct the defences and ensure the safety of his new vessel on the stocks, leaving Yeo free to cooperate with Vincent after the Battle of Stoney Creek and to accelerate the American retreat towards Fort George. But, generally speaking, the reaction in Canada was that Prevost's encounter at Sackets Harbor had been a failure. The Canadians were well aware of Sackets' importance to the American lake fleet; they believed that its elimination was the key to the safety of Upper Canada. There were those who felt that the destruction of Sackets Harbor was of such vital importance that Prevost should have provided himself with a larger assault force, and should have pressed forward with the attack regardless of the risk and sacrifice involved. It was pointless to reply that Baynes, not Prevost, was the real commander. Rightly or wrongly, Canadians were coming to regard Prevost as just another fumbling, indecisive commander, lacking in leadership and firm resolution. It would be unfair to come to such conclusions on the basis of Sackets Harbor alone, but when a year later, in 1814, Prevost was presented with an opportunity to retrieve his military reputation by leading a British force in another battle of strategic importance, he failed even more miserably than he had at Sackets Harbor. Originality and strong leadership were not the mark of Prevost's command in Canada during the War of 1812.

SOUTH OF MONTREAL, the British military authorities under Major General Francis de Rottenburg kept a close watch on the movements of American troops. They did not plan any offensive actions in that quarter, for it was in the British interest to avoid hostilities and to keep the cattle, grain and provisions purchased from American contractors moving steadily along the Lake Champlain route into Lower Canada. Evidence of the importance of this source of supplies is afforded by Prevost's remark in 1814 in a letter to Lord Bathurst, secretary for war and the colonies, to the effect that "two-thirds of the army in Canada are at this moment eating beef provided by American contractors, drawn principally from the States of Vermont and New York." Prevost continued, "This circumstance, as well as the introduction of large sums of specie into this Province, being notorious in the United States, it is to be expected that Congress will take steps to deprive us of those resources."[15]

It was very much in the American interest to halt this illicit trade. To this end, American vessels on Lake Champlain moved north to Plattsburg on 1 May 1813 and established a blockade at the north end of the lake. On 2 June, two sloops, *Eagle* and *Growler*, anchored at Rouses Point. Early the next morning, while the mist was still thick upon the ground, *Eagle* and *Growler* moved into the entrance of the Richelieu River and began to make their way slowly downriver towards the British post on Île aux Noix.

The British garrison at the old French post on Île aux Noix (later known as Fort Lennox) consisted of a detachment of the Royal Artillery and several companies of the 100th Regiment of Foot under the command of Major George Taylor. Through spies Taylor had kept himself well informed of the movement and concentration of American forces on Lake Champlain, and was not surprised when a sentry reported seeing a sail about 1.5 km distant, rising above the level of the ground fog and moving downstream. He therefore manned three gunboats with troops trained especially for the purpose, each boat armed with a 6-pounder, and sent them to investigate the strange sail. Detecting a second sail, he sent infantry in several bateaux and rowboats to assist the men in the gunboats. Caught by surprise,

63. The British garrison on Île aux Noix in the Richelieu River

since the mist concealed the small British boats, the Americans endeavoured to turn around, but the river was only 185 m wide and the navigating channel was even narrower. Forced to beat back against the wind, with the crews exposed to a peppering from the troops, and the sloops to a battering from the gun-boats, the Americans were compelled to surrender. Few of the Americans were killed or wounded, but over 90 were taken prisoner. Their vessels, damaged by gunfire, were captured by the British and renamed *Broke* and *Shannon*.[16]

Taylor's success in the unexpected encounter was a source of considerable satisfaction in Montreal. It was something that could be built upon: perhaps a waterborne expedition could be sent against Plattsburg. Thus a request was sent to the senior naval officer at Quebec, asking to borrow some seamen to man the captured vessels. Secrecy was to be observed. The seamen were to travel in civilian clothes and be told that they were go-ing to Lake Ontario. Major General Roger Sheaffe, who had been transferred to Montreal after the débâcle at York, named Major General Richard Stovin to the overall command, and issued instructions that the captured vessels be used to attack both Plattsburg and Burlington, with the object of dispersing the troops occupying those towns and burning public buildings and stores. However, the naval officer at Quebec was hesitant about participating in such a scheme. The Governor General then got into the act, arguing that the main objects of the pro-

64. Although entitled Action on Lake Champlain, June 3, 1813, *this painting depicts the American sloops* Growler *and* Eagle *caught by surprise by the British near Île aux Noix on the Richelieu River.*

posed operation were to delay the movement of American forces from the eastern area to reinforce the army on the Niagara frontier, and to take advantage of the fact that so many American troops were out looking for smugglers that places like Plattsburg were almost defenceless. Still the senior naval officer refused to take part; he was under orders to sail from Quebec on 1 August and could not, in any event, act without the approval of the British Admiralty. Fortunately the sloop of war *Wasp*, under Commander Thomas Everard, arrived at Quebec, and the Governor General's request was presented to him.

Everard was enthusiastic. Even though he could remain at Quebec for only a fortnight, he was ready to undertake any operation that could be carried out within that time. Arriving in Montreal on 24 July, Everard was joined by Lieutenant Daniel Pring, who had been named to command the Provincial Marine on Lake Champlain, and when the two officers arrived at Fort Île aux Noix they were joined by Lieutenant Colonel John Murray and a force of regulars comprising Royal Artillery, the 13th, 100th and 103rd regiments, and detachments from the Canadian Fencibles and the 1st Battalion Embodied Militia—in all,

946 officers and men. The British were well supplied with reliable information by Joel Ackley and other secret agents. They knew, for instance, that the Americans had made good the loss of the two sloops of war and that a new general, Wade Hampton, had been appointed to command the military forces on the Lake Champlain frontier. They also knew that the American vessels were short of sailors and were moored at Burlington, where Hampton's 4000 men, mostly regulars, were also stationed. That meant that Plattsburg was virtually empty of both ships and men. Everything looked favourable for a successful foray into the United States.

On the morning of 29 July the British flotilla set out. Murray landed a strong force at Chazy, where he destroyed considerable public property and distributed a proclamation telling the people that if they remained peaceably at home their property would not be touched. At Plattsburg, the local commander had difficulty assembling even a small force of militia and had to abandon the town, allowing Murray and Everard to occupy it unmolested for ten or twelve hours. The British destroyed a blockhouse, barracks and commissary's store at their leisure, and carried off arms and equipment. They did the same thing at Cumberland Head. Then Everard crossed the lake to reconnoitre Burlington, where he tried, but failed, to entice the Americans to send ships out to engage him. He contented himself with long-range shelling and then sailed off for Shelburne Bay and Charlotte, where he captured several American vessels and provisions belonging to the American army.

Apparently Everard captured or destroyed virtually the whole of the American merchant fleet on Lake Champlain, except for the vessels that had taken refuge at Burlington. All this he achieved without any losses other than a few deserters from the ranks of the 103rd Foot, a regiment that had a poor reputation in the British army and in Canada owing to the number of petty criminals in it who had chosen enlistment as preferable to punishment. Everard returned to Île aux Noix, and then he and his men rejoined their ships at Quebec, leaving the naval component on Lake Champlain to be looked after by Pring and what seamen and soldiers he could muster.[17]

It was well into summer before the Americans got around to implementing the strategy that Armstrong had earlier declared to be basic to the success of the United States in the war, namely the mounting of major operations against Kingston and/or Montreal. It would be up to Major General James

65. Major General James Wilkinson, who commanded the American offensive against Montreal in 1813

Wilkinson, the new senior commander, who arrived at Sackets Harbor about 25 August, to make the choice. After examining several alternatives, Wilkinson decided to concentrate all available American forces, both military and naval, at Sackets Harbor; he would make a feint upon Kingston, followed by a dash down the St. Lawrence to join forces with Major General Wade Hampton's Lake Champlain army. Together they would launch a final assault on Montreal.[18]

The plan was in many ways similar to that followed by Jeffrey Amherst in 1760 during the Seven Years' War, but if Wilkinson knowingly adopted Amherst's strategy he missed the essential point: Amherst had had a secure Lake Ontario behind him, whereas Wilkinson would have to contend with Yeo's ships and with the constant threat to his rear posed by the substantial garrison at Kingston. Moreover, the relations between Amherst and his colleague, William Haviland, were friendly, and Amherst clearly outranked his junior on the Lake Champlain front. In 1813, Hampton held the same rank as Wilkinson, was personally hostile to him, and was not at all disposed to act with the cordiality and vigour required by a combined movement such as that envisaged by Wilkinson. In fact, the stiff-necked Virginian slave-owner, Hampton, loathed the unscrupulous adventurer, Wilkinson, and accepted his appointment on Lake Champlain only on the clear understanding that his would be a distinct and separate command. When he discovered that Wilkinson was to be his senior officer, Hampton tendered his resignation, and it took all of Armstrong's persuasion to keep him at his post. Although Hampton agreed to cooperate with Wilkinson throughout the remainder of the campaign, he made it clear that he would resubmit his resignation when the fighting was over. Scarcely a healthy relationship with which to begin an important and potentially decisive operation.

Wilkinson remained at Sackets Harbor until 30 August, making his plans, inspecting his troops, gathering bateaux and other water craft, collecting field and siege guns, and corresponding with Brigadier General John Boyd on the Niagara frontier. It was from Boyd's army that he proposed to draw the bulk of the Montreal invasion force, making up the balance from militia promised by Governor Tompkins of New York. Because of his concern about the situation along the Niagara River, Wilkinson decided to spend the month of September at Fort Niagara and to return to Sackets Harbor early in October. Meanwhile, the Secretary of War moved to Sackets Harbor and proceeded to run his War Department from there for the next two months.

The presence of the civilian and military heads of the American army in the same small town did not facilitate cooperation; instead it brought them into greater and more frequent conflict. They could not agree on the strategy to be employed; each opposed the other on what would appear to have been no grounds other than opposition for opposition's sake. To Armstrong's proposals for an attack on Kingston, Wilkinson countered with arguments favouring a direct attack on Montreal; and when Armstrong, in mid-October, opted for Montreal as "the safer and greater object",[19] Wilkinson did a turnabout in favour of an attack on Kingston. Each accused the

other—and not without justification—of trying to shirk responsibility for making a firm decision. It would appear that neither
man believed, in his heart, that either Kingston or Montreal
could be taken, and each wanted to be sure that the expected
failure would be blamed on the other. What other conclusion
can be drawn from the fact that, on 16 October, just before
embarking on the offensive down the St. Lawrence, Armstrong
issued orders for the preparation of winter quarters for Wilkinson's army about 100 km above Montreal, and did so without
informing Wilkinson? And that, on 19 October, Wilkinson wrote
to Armstrong:

> I speak conjecturally, but should we surmount every obstacle in
> descending the river, we shall advance upon Montreal ignorant of
> the force arrayed against us, and in case of misfortune, having no
> retreat, the army must surrender at discretion.[20]

This letter indicated a pessimistic state of mind that did not
augur well for success in the operation to which Wilkinson committed himself when he embarked his men on a stormy 17 October at Henderson's Bay, just to the west of Sackets Harbor.
There were 7000 troops organized in two divisions, the first
under Major General Morgan Lewis, the other to be commanded by Wade Hampton after the planned union with his
Lake Champlain force. Lewis's brigadiers were John Boyd and
Leonard Covington, the others Jacob Brown and Robert Swartwout. The reserve was led by Colonel Alexander Macomb. For
several days the great fleet of bateaux, numbering about 300,
battled the wind, the snow and the waves; 15 were sunk and
others were heavily damaged. Not until 5 November did all the
survivors gather at Grenadier Island. "All our hopes have been
nearly blasted", wrote Wilkinson.[21]

HAMPTON, maintaining the fiction of his independent command, acknowledged Wilkinson's orders only when they were
forwarded to him through the Secretary of War. (This was one
reason for John Armstrong's continued stay at Sackets Harbor.)
Nevertheless, it was on Wilkinson's instructions that Hampton
moved his force back across Lake Champlain to Plattsburg from
Burlington, where he had spent the early summer trying to
restore the flagging morale of his soldiers by shooting and flog-
ging the delinquents among them. One poor sinner was sentenced "to receive twenty-five cobbs on his bare posteriors on
the parade in front of his regiment, be put to hard labor with

the ball and chain, for the remainder of the period for which he enlisted, and to have his liquor rations stopped for the same period."[22] In September, when Hampton believed his men ready for war, he marched them from their camp at Cumberland Head to Chazy and Champlain and then to the Canadian frontier. On the twentieth, his advanced guard crossed into Lower Canada, surprising a small picket at Odelltown.

There was a road from Odelltown to L'Acadie, and from there through flat, swampy, wooded country to the south shore of the St. Lawrence River. Numerous defensive works in the form of roadblocks and abatis had been erected along this route after the invasion of the year before. The region was defended by a few Indians and by members of the Frontier Light Infantry, a corps formed in 1813 from the light infantry companies of the six battalions of embodied militia and commanded by Captain Joseph Saint-Valier Mailloux. Mailloux's men managed to keep the Americans in check until reinforcements arrived in the form of Major Joseph-François Perrault's flank companies of the 4th Battalion of Embodied Militia and a detachment of Voltigeurs under Lieutenant Colonel Charles-Michel d'Irumberry de Salaberry. During the night of the twentieth, the Indians worried the Americans, and in the morning, after a personal reconnaissance, Hampton decided against proceeding any farther. He offered as explanation for his lethargy a shortage of water for his troops and cattle, owing to the extraordinary drought of the summer of 1813. Oddly enough, some 500 horses and between 1000 and 1200 head of cattle were smuggled into Lower Canada from Vermont that summer, apparently without suffering too much from the shortage of water.[23] Had Hampton pushed forward in force, he might well have established a firm footing in Lower Canada at or near Saint-Jean, and in doing so outflanked the British position on Île aux Noix.

Fortunately for the Canadians, the American commander did not appear to be aware of how thin the Canadian defence line was; hence his decision to evacuate Odelltown and try another route. He retraced his steps south to Chazy and then swung westwards towards Four Corners (Chateaugay, N.Y.), on the upper reaches of the Châteauguay River just south of the Canadian frontier. This place Hampton designated as his advanced headquarters. The change of route lengthened the line of advance to Montreal by 115 km, but there was plenty of water here and no danger of a flank attack such as there had been from Fort Île aux Noix along Hampton's earlier invasion route.

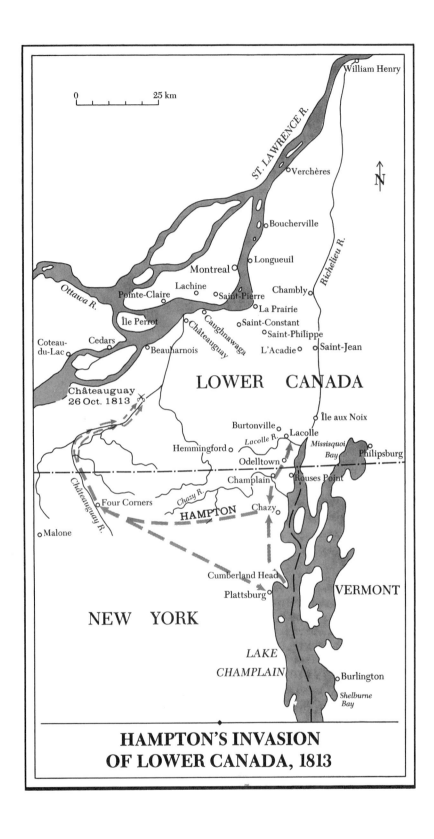

**HAMPTON'S INVASION
OF LOWER CANADA, 1813**

This danger, rather than the water shortage, probably provided the real explanation for Hampton's change of course. There was also a road north of the Châteauguay River that would lead the Americans directly to Caughnawaga, opposite Lachine.

The move to Four Corners was undertaken at a leisurely pace. Hampton was always disposed to move with deliberation, but on this occasion deliberation suited Wilkinson's purpose too, although Hampton did not realize it until 25 September, when, 21 km from Four Corners, he received a message from Armstrong telling him that there was no object in moving quickly since Wilkinson's force would be unable to join him for several weeks. Armstrong certainly had no objection to Hampton's change of route. Four Corners would be an admirable jumping-off point for an invasion of Lower Canada; "Hold it fast", he urged Hampton, "till we approach you."[24] It would not be advisable to try any separate attacks against the defending forces "when combined ones are practicable and sure".

Hampton therefore remained contentedly at Four Corners for the next twenty-six days. He could use the time to advantage: his men needed training, the road to Plattsburg needed improvement, and his artillery and supplies, sufficient for the next two months, needed to be brought forward. However, there was no harm in creating a diversion that would keep prying Canadian eyes away from Four Corners. Hampton ordered Colonel Isaac Clark, whom he had left in charge at Burlington, to make a demonstration in the direction of Missisquoi Bay, at the north end of Lake Champlain. This was done on 11 October. About 200 American militia seized a quantity of stores lately smuggled into Lower Canada from the United States. Encouraged by this success, Clark went on to Philipsburg, where he surprised a detachment of the 4th Battalion Embodied Militia, and took them prisoner. The reporter for the *Boston Messenger* wrote on 16 October: "I have just seen Colonel Clark's prisoners, who were paraded through this town. They are a motley crew of farmers, citizens, tavern-keepers, traders, etc.; not a regular soldier among them. They were surprised in their beds."[25]

Clark's raid was typical of much of the fighting along the Canadian–American boundary. The Frontier Light Infantry did much the same thing in an effort to facilitate the movement of smuggled goods into Canada. They raided American depots just south of the frontier and frequently clashed with the American dragoons trying to interfere with the illicit trade. There

66. Major General Louis de Watteville, who led his Swiss regiment at Châteauguay

was even a raid as far as Burlington to free men of the Lincoln Militia who had been taken prisoner at Fort George in May.

Meanwhile Sir George Prevost, in the face of the impending threat to Lower Canada, removed his headquarters from Kingston to Montreal, where he arrived on 25 September. At once he began to prepare for the expected assault. "Red George" Macdonell was ordered to Lower Canada with his militia flank companies; they would stiffen the 3000 militia from the south bank of the St. Lawrence whom Sheaffe had called out to man a new line of resistance along the Châteauguay River. Prevost, considering the situation serious, called out another 5000 and placed Major General Stovin in command of an advanced defence line running from the Châteauguay River, north of the frontier, to Hemmingford. The outer crust of Lower Canada's defences at this time consisted of artillery, four companies of light infantry from the Canadian Fencibles, four companies of Voltigeurs, two companies of the Frontier Light Infantry, the 1st and 2nd Battalions of Embodied Militia, sedentary militia from Beauharnois and Châteauguay, and the 1st and 4th Battalions of the Eastern Townships. Reinforcements of regulars were sent to bolster the garrisons of Saint-Jean and Île aux Noix, and a reserve was established under Sheaffe, comprising a car brigade of field artillery, a squadron of the 19th Light Dragoons, a company of guides, a provisional battalion formed of the flank companies of the regiments of the line, four companies of the Régiment de Meuron (a Swiss regiment recently arrived in Canada), eight companies of the 3rd Battalion of Embodied Militia, and the whole of the sedentary militia of Longueuil, Boucherville and Verchères. One flank of this force occupied La Prairie, with the line extending through Saint-Pierre, Saint-Philippe and L'Acadie to Saint-Jean. In the city of Montreal, the Montreal Volunteers and three battalions of Montreal militia were organized into a provisional battalion under the command of Colonel James McGill. Orders were issued that, in the event of invasion, church bells should ring the tocsin in every parish within 80 km to assemble men, even those who could only equip themselves with axes and spades. Meanwhile, civilian spies were watching Hampton's every move, for, from his position at Four Corners, he was free to move to almost any destination on the south shore of the St. Lawrence from Saint-Régis to Caughnawaga. These were all purely defensive measures, but to keep Hampton from feeling too secure, fighting patrols of militia and Indians were ordered to attack his pickets from time to time and to take a few prisoners when possible.

All of these preparations to meet the "great invasion", made possible by Wilkinson's and Armstrong's delays in getting the project under way, began to worry Hampton. Finally, on 12 October, he wrote to Armstrong:

My solicitude to know your progress and the real state of the *grand army* is extreme. . . . The point and moment of our junction is all-important, and that and not the moment of my departure from hence ought to be indicated, because I ought to be the best judge of the time necessary to surmount the obstacles in the way. Between

251

67. Lower Canada sedentary militiaman, ca. 1813

this and Caughnawaga much work on the road is necessary, and
I ought to advance upon it two or three days earlier than might
be judged necessary on a smooth and solid road. . . . You have said
"Hold fast", and it might be considered precipitate to advance
before I hear at least that the Rubicon is passed above.[26]

On the eighteenth a reply arrived from Armstrong dated the sixteenth, stating that there would be no feint against Kingston and that Wilkinson was about to set out down the St. Lawrence towards Île Perrot, "whence we shall immediately open a communication with you".[27] Meanwhile Hampton was to proceed to the mouth of the Châteauguay "or other point which shall favour our junction and hold the enemy in check". Because of this letter Hampton decided to resume his march. He knew now where he was to go and what he was to do, and he was thoroughly confident: reports from Canada indicated that the initial Canadian defensive positions in front of him along the Châteauguay River were lightly held, the first being manned by only 350 sedentary militia, commanded by a militia officer. The numbers reported were not far wrong, but the militia officer was Salaberry, an experienced French Canadian who held a commission in the 60th (Royal American) Regiment of Foot and had served in the British army throughout the Napoleonic wars. He had returned to Canada as aide-de-camp to Rottenburg and had been authorized in the spring of 1812 to raise the Provincial Corps of Light Infantry in Lower Canada, the corps that became known as the Canadian Voltigeurs.

It was on 21 October, a month after his reverse at Odelltown, that Hampton left his camp at Four Corners and began to move down the Châteauguay River. Always a better staff officer than a field commander, he had made his preparations with skill. He had hired or impressed a large number of wagons, sent expert axemen ahead to clear the road, and dispatched mounted relays to provide a line of communications direct to Ogdensburg. True, the New York militia were up to their old tricks of falling back on their constitutional rights not to cross the frontier, but their questionable services could easily be dispensed with. After all, Hampton had an effective force of regulars exceeding 4000, and he had a capable assistant in the person of Brigadier General George Izard. Hampton must have felt confident of himself and his men; even so, he was unlikely to have wholly approved the kind of thing that was appearing in the *National Intelligencer* in Washington:

> We may expect that General Prevost . . . intends to make war like Procter at Malden, and Kutusoff at Moscow, to give up everything to conflagration which he cannot rule. The ensuing week settles the fall of Upper Canada forever. The fall of Quebec in the ensuing spring will give our youth experience to ward against evils of thirty years' neglect of military knowledge. . . . Canada once ours,

we shall have no enemy but a few domestic traitors and foreign emissaries on our soil.[28]

Moving along the north bank of the Châteauguay, Hampton spent several days improving the roads, and then, on 25 October, knowing that he was close to the first of the British defence positions, as disclosed by British deserters, he matured his plans: one column would cross to the south bank of the river, outflank the British position and then recross the river in the British rear; meanwhile the main body would proceed along the north bank and push the militia defenders aside with a strong frontal attack. Since the column on the south bank was to provide the surprise, it would set out the night before the expected battle. In the morning, the main column would make its move under Brigadier General Izard.

Hampton was obviously well informed. Salaberry was even more so; his informants were the Perry brothers, who lived near Four Corners and watched and listened to conversations, and David Manning, who counted Hampton's every wagon and gun and passed the information to British officers. What Salaberry learned was that Hampton's forces were suffering from sickness and were short of winter clothing. From personal reconnaissance Salaberry knew the topography better than his opponent did and knew where to place his defences. He chose a site on the north bank where the road ran close and parallel to the river and where there was a marshy thicket on the opposite side. In front, at right angles to the road that Hampton was following, were a dip in the ground, a gully, and a tract of cleared land that would provide a good field of fire. Knowing that the enemy was approaching, Salaberry set his men to work felling trees and constructing barricades and abatis. Similar works were undertaken at successive intervals of 200 to 300 m. Within two days these rude barriers were in a fair state to withstand attack, and, with his mind on the possibility of a flanking action, Salaberry sent a working party to construct a lunette on the south side of the river to protect the ford across the Châteauguay in the rear of the British–Canadian position. He placed men behind the several barricades and others in a line facing the river to protect the defenders against any Americans seeking to strike him on the left flank. The Indians he placed in the swampy wood to the south.

Early in the afternoon of the twenty-fifth, a party of American light infantry reconnoitred the British position. They considered the wood swamp impenetrable, but believed that Sala-

68. Lieutenant Colonel Charles-Michel d'Irumberry de Salaberry, who raised the Voltigeurs in 1812

berry's position could be taken by a strong frontal assault combined with a stealthy flanking movement on the south side of the river. Hampton accordingly ordered Colonel Robert Purdy to take a select group of 1500 men across the river and through the woods during the night so as to be ready the next day to take the Canadians by surprise on the flank towards the rear. It was at this point that Hampton received his instructions from Armstrong to prepare winter quarters for the army. What did the message mean? Was the whole operation over, Hampton wondered. Was he to be sacrificed to no purpose? Such an order seemed to cast doubt on Wilkinson's determination to

255

proceed with the Montreal project; certainly there was no intimation that the grand invasion was to be pushed to a conclusion. However, Hampton had no choice but to go through with the battle. Unfortunately for the American commander, Purdy had been misled, perhaps deliberately, by civilians who were supposed to know the way through the swampy wood south of the Châteauguay. He strugged through the hemlock swamp, unable to locate either the ford or the place he had started from, and when he came into the open at last he was promptly engaged, not only by militia sent by Salaberry to the south side of the river, but also by the Canadians lining the north bank. The signal for the attack was to have come from Purdy, but Purdy's messengers never got back to the main body and Izard waited patiently as the forenoon wore away. Finally, at about 1400 hrs, he ordered the main body to move forward.

Salaberry was ready for him. With him at the first barricade were the light company of the Canadian Fencibles under Captain George R. Ferguson, two companies of Voltigeurs under Captains J.-B. and M.-L. Juchereau Duchesnay, a handful of Indians led by Captain J.-M. Lamothe, and Captain J.-M. Longtin's company of Beauharnois militia. Behind these men were two lines commanded by Lieutenant Colonel "Red George" Macdonell and Captains Dominique Debartzch and Benjamin L'Écuyer. Reserves from the 2nd Battalion Embodied Militia under Lieutenant Colonel J.-B. Hertel de Rouville, Lieutenant-Colonel Pierre Mailhot, Major Louis de Beaujeu and Major Pierre-René Boucher de La Bruère were drawn up in successive lines at right angles to the river. In the woods on the right flank were sedentary militia from Boucherville and Beauharnois under Lieutenant Colonel Louis-René Chaussegros de Léry and Major Hyacinthe Raymond. A small detachment of militia under Captain Philippe Panet guarded the ford over the river; on the left, or south, side, facing Purdy, were two companies of embodied militia, under Captains Charles Daly and Joseph-Bernard Bruyère, and a small militia *corps d'observation*.

It is difficult to ascertain how many troops were present on the ground at Châteauguay. According to Michael O'Sullivan, Salaberry's aide-de-camp, only 300 men took an active part in the battle, a figure repeated by Sir George Prevost.[29] However, this number did not include the reserves, nor the troops under Major General Louis de Watteville and Sir George Prevost, who were on their way to support Salaberry.

69. *Canadian Voltigeurs, night picket, 1812–13*

It was Salaberry, rather than Purdy, who started the battle, by himself bringing down a mounted American officer with a shot, much to the delight and enthusiasm of the Canadians. Shouts and cheers and bugle calls rang out through the woods, repeated from barricade to barricade, leaving an impression of multitudes of men. Standing on a large stump, exposed to enemy fire, Salaberry encouraged his men by word and example. For about two hours the contestants kept up a brisk fire, but Izard did not press ahead, and when Purdy's men, on the south bank of the river, were thrust back by chasseurs and militia under Captains Bruyère and Daly, Hampton lost any stomach he might have had for fighting and decided to withdraw, although he had lost only about 50 men. Salaberry's casualties were 16 wounded, including both Daly and Bruyère, and 2 killed, both militiamen; the 3 Fencibles feared killed were later discovered to have been taken prisoner. That same evening Salaberry wrote to his father, "I have won a victory mounted on a wooden horse."[30]

Some writers have tended to play down the fighting at Châteauguay as "a mere skirmish".[31] Nevertheless, the battle is

70. *The Battle of Châteauguay, 26 October 1813*

important in Canadian history, not only because of its strategic significance, but because of its impact on morale. A relatively small group of Canadian militia, some of them only partially trained, had successfully resisted and turned back an attack by American regulars.

Meanwhile Hampton had withdrawn, but Purdy had to undergo a night of sniping before he eventually managed to rejoin the main body of American troops across the river. Hampton then convened a meeting of his officers and put to them the question of what to do next. Unanimously they agreed that

> it is necessary for the preservation of this army and the fulfilment of the ostensible views of the Government that we immediately return by orderly marches to such a position [Four Corners]. . . as will secure our communications with the United States, either to retire into winter quarters or be ready to strike below.[32]

However, there was no question of a "strike below". The Indians, led by Lamothe, clung to Hampton's flanks and harassed his troops, who moved slowly and with their customary deliberation. After several days Hampton's force was back in American territory at Four Corners, but not to stay. Hampton received a request from Wilkinson to forward two or three months' supplies and join him at St. Regis, but Hampton had no supplies to send and he was on his way back to Plattsburg. His reply could not have come as a surprise to Wilkinson. If it served no other purpose, it would at least absolve Wilkinson of any responsibility for failing to continue the advance on Montreal. Hampton's action, he wrote later, "defeats the grand objects of the campaign".[33] At first Wilkinson toyed with the idea of ordering Hampton to be placed under arrest, but then decided it would be better to let Armstrong determine Hampton's punishment. The Secretary of War, however, was not prepared to do more than accept Hampton's resignation; this he did in March 1814.[34]

NOT THAT WILKINSON was any improvement on Hampton. His arguments with Armstrong and his indolence kept him in Sackets Harbor until 17 October. Then, having chosen the worst kind of weather in which to move his flotilla, he became storm-bound on Grenadier Island (just south of Wolfe Island). Many of the boats were so damaged they were rendered useless. Although the weather was unseasonably cold and remained so for the rest of the year, Wilkinson resumed his chilled initiative and continued his progress down the St. Lawrence. On the night of 6 November, his boats floated quietly past the British guns at Fort Wellington. Meanwhile his troops, having previously disembarked on the American side of the river, marched by land. The next day the army halted a few kilometres below Ogdensburg. There Wilkinson called a council of war. He was convinced that Armstrong did not really expect him to succeed and wanted to know what his subordinate officers thought about continuing the advance on Montreal. Personally he would happily have called the whole thing off: before him lay the St. Lawrence rapids, he was ill, Armstrong was no longer there to argue with, he did not yet know what had happened to Hampton, and, above all, he wanted someone else to assume responsibility for a decision that was bound to be controversial, whatever it might be.

Wilkinson was particularly worried about the small British force that seemed to hover like Nemesis at his heels. What should he do about it? Ignore it, or fight? The British force had been organized in Kingston, and consisted of 600 men of the 89th and 49th regiments under Lieutenant Colonel Joseph W. Morrison of the 89th Regiment. With Morrison was Lieutenant Colonel John Harvey, the hero of Stoney Creek, as well as a number of gunboats under Commander William Mulcaster, R.N. At Prescott, Morrison had picked up a few more men, including some Canadian Fencibles, Voltigeurs, Indians, and a group of militia gunners with a 6-pounder gun, bringing his total strength to over 800. Essentially a *corps d'observation*, the force was not large enough to challenge Wilkinson, but it was a constant threat and annoyance to the Americans. Each day Wilkinson felt that the whole Montreal expedition was becoming more hazardous. He debated with his officers the question of abandoning the expedition and then put it to a vote. Four of his six senior officers took the position that "we proceed from this place under great danger . . . but . . . we know of no other alternative."[35]

On 8 November, Wilkinson reached the Long Sault Rapids, 13 km long. It would be a tricky business getting all the boats safely down the river, and impossible to do so if the British were left free to occupy the north bank. The Americans therefore had to land on the Canadian side of the river and hold the British force at bay while Wilkinson's boats were moving through the swirling eddies of the rapids. On 10 November, Macomb's troops landed on the north bank, with Winfield Scott's men in the van; they accomplished this without interruption and pushed ahead rapidly towards Cornwall. At Hoople Creek they ran into a small force of regulars and Stormont militia, commanded by Scott's old adversary, Major James Dennis of the 49th Foot, who a little over a year before had borne the first shock of the American attack at Queenston Heights. After an exchange of shots, Scott used his advantage in numbers to outflank Dennis and force him to withdraw. Other American troops followed Scott, including Jacob Brown's brigade. The responsibility for protecting the American boats and Brown's men from annoyance by Morrison's *corps d'observation* as they made their way past the Long Sault and Mille Roches rapids in the direction of Cornwall was left to John Boyd and his brigade.

The rapids could not be run in a single day, and it was impossible for the pilots to navigate the river in the dark. Thus it was necessary for Wilkinson to moor his vessels just below Crysler Island, almost in front of John Crysler's farm. The next morning, on 11 November, after a night of rain and sleet, Wilkinson learned that Brown had reached a point 8 km above Cornwall and that the road was open at least as far as Cornwall. All that Wilkinson would have to do would be to fend off Morrison while the remaining boats and troops moved down the

71. *Fort Wellington at Prescott, Upper Canada*

river to join Brown. Time was of the utmost importance. There ought not to be further delays if only because, as Brown pointed out, the troops of the forward regiments were in a sorry state— cold, wet, without tents, and desperately weary. Wilkinson replied "from my bed", as he was unwell at this critical time. He instructed his flotilla to push on past the dangerous waters of the Long Sault. Meanwhile Boyd, with the rear guard, was to move parallel with the boats, at the same time keeping a sharp eye on Morrison.

It was just as the Americans began to move that the British began their attack. Mulcaster's gunboats opened fire on the American bateaux, and Morrison's troops advanced towards Boyd's rear guard. Morrison had chosen his position well, perhaps acting on the advice of Harvey; his right, resting on the river, was covered by Mulcaster's gunboats, and his left, anchored on a wood swamp, was covered by Voltigeurs and Indians. The centre, astride the King's Road to Montreal, was held by the 89th with one cannon, and a little to the right and to the front were the 49th with another gun manned by Canadian militia. The whole line covered about 650 m. In advance of the main line were skirmishers, consisting of a few Indians from Saint-Régis and Voltigeurs, their main task being to draw

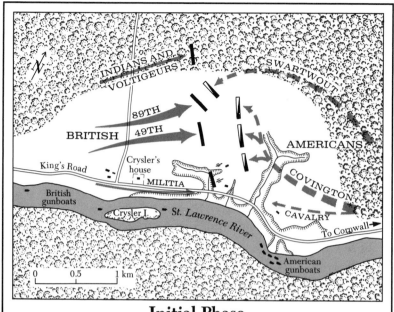

**Initial Phase
11 November 1813**

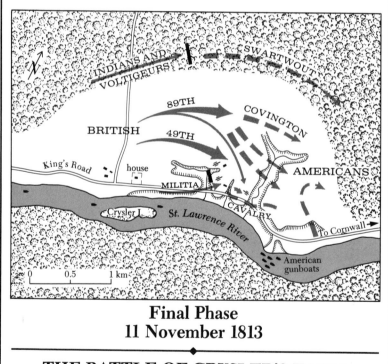

**Final Phase
11 November 1813**

THE BATTLE OF CRYSLER'S FARM

American troops towards the British main force. In many ways the actual position was similar to that chosen by Procter at Moraviantown, but on this occasion the morale of the British troops was high and that of the Americans questionable. Certainly the spirits of the American infantry must have steadily declined as they dragged their way through the mud across ploughed fields in the face of a "heavy shower of bullets and shrapnel shells".[36]

As soon as the shooting started the Americans turned about to face Morrison. Boyd ordered Swartwout's brigade to attack Morrison's skirmishers and then sent Covington to support them, in the hope of outflanking the British position. However, both Covington's and Swartwout's efforts proved abortive. Meanwhile a British charge to capture one of the American guns was thwarted by American cavalry. It was the steadiness of the British regulars that settled the outcome of the battle. Only momentarily shaken by the enemy's horse, the men of the 89th beat off a counterattack by American dragoons and went ahead to capture the disputed gun. By this time the fighting had gone on for several hours, and the Americans, their supply train already well on the way towards Cornwall, could not service the ammunition-hungry American troops. Covington's brigade began to slowly fall back, and Swartwout's men followed their example.

Morrison's troops had fought hard and well, and their commander had displayed more capacity for manoeuvre than had Boyd or his subordinates, with the possible exception of Colonel Edmund Pendleton Gaines, whose 25th Infantry had put up so stiff a fight that Morrison had sent him a note expressing the hope that the two might meet after the war as friends.[37] During the day the Americans had thrown 1800 brave and seasoned troops into the fray, including a regiment of dragoons, but had done so in dribbles; in fact, if we can believe Boyd, some of the American gunners did not manage to get away a single shot. Morrison, with his outnumbered army, remained in command of the field. Helping to look after the British wounded lying on the battlefield was a small boy who had watched the battle and, years later, told the story of his experiences to his grandson.[38]

At Williamstown, some 30 km beyond the battlefield, the Presbyterian minister, the Reverend John Bethune, found it hard to suppress his irritation at the activities of the American troops as they straggled eastwards. Some months later he sat down to

72. The Battle of Crysler's Farm, 11 November 1813

write his friend, the schoolmaster at Saint-Armand in Lower Canada, about the American invasion as he saw it:

> Those boasting invaders were shamefully defeated with considerable loss by a handful of men under Col. Morrison of the 89th Regiment. . . . Their movement across the river relieved us from the apprehensions natural to people who are exposed to an invading foe, and their retreat in winter was still more consolatory as it placed danger at a distance from this part of the frontier.[39]

Bethune was particularly indignant at the Americans for the way they behaved and the damage they did to private property:

> On his [the enemy's] march during the day, little mischief was done, but wherever he encamped there was great destruction of cattle, grain, fences and every species of property within their reach. . . . The weather was cold and as they were not well provided with camp equipage and still worse with clothes, they fell upon an easy expedient of keeping themselves warm at night, that of setting fire to the fences as they stood and lying down by them so that in the absence of the sun, the sky was so illuminated as if the whole country was in a blaze. . . . A few officers and stragglers came into town and, under pretense of searching for arms, rummaged houses, broke open trunks and committed considerable deprivations on clothing, dry goods and groceries. Ladies greatcoats and even children's flannels did not escape. Such as had plate, of course, hid it.

The engagement at John Crysler's farm, while only a rear-guard action, was a bloody one for all that. The Americans suffered 439 casualties in killed (102), wounded (237) and taken prisoner (100); among those mortally wounded was General Covington, the commander of one of Boyd's brigades. Morrison reported 179 casualties, or about 20 per cent of his total force. Clearly Morrison had the better of the day's fighting. He had won a tactical, even if not a decisive, victory. He had embarrassed the American advance though he did not effectively stop it. Wilkinson was still in a position to continue his move towards Montreal, and had he done so Morrison would no doubt have followed.

What gave Crysler's Farm the appearance of a decisive battle was Hampton's inability to brush Salaberry aside at Châteauguay and his refusal to join Wilkinson at St. Regis. Hampton's failure provided Wilkinson with a convenient excuse for abandoning an expedition in which, for some time, he had had little confidence. Thus, when Wilkinson learned that Hampton was not going to join forces with him, he summoned a council of war. It unanimously, and probably thankfully, decided that "the attack on Montreal should be abandoned for the present season",[40] and that the army, then near Cornwall, should move across the American frontier and take up winter quarters at French Mills (Fort Covington) on the Salmon River. This is what the Americans did, moving with greater alacrity and efficiency than they had displayed since leaving Sackets Harbor almost a month before. Of course there had to be an official justification for this abandonment of the expedition, and it was advanced in June 1836, when one of the officers who took part in the council of war stated that the decision had been taken because of "want of bread, want of meat, want of Hampton's division, and a belief that the enemy's force was equal [to], if not greater than, our own."[41] Perhaps he could have added: a want of determination and the willingness to fight.

Meanwhile, Montreal had been in a state of uproar. When news reached the city that Wilkinson's boats had successfully passed Prescott, there was an immediate mobilization and concentration of all troops in the Montreal district. Artillery and dragoons on the south shore were called into the city and to Caughnawaga. The Canadian Fencibles and companies of the 5th Battalion Embodied Militia were withdrawn from L'Acadie, Saint-Pierre and Saint-Philippe, and Colonel Pierre-René Boucher de Boucherville's battalion of Beauharnois militia, some

Yours truly

Dunlop

73. *Dr. William "Tiger" Dunlop*

of whose complement had been at Châteauguay, was sent to support Lieutenant Colonel Louis-Joseph Fleury Deschambault and the Caughnawaga Indians at Beauharnois. Word of the danger to Canada was conveyed to people throughout the area by the ringing of church bells and the lighting of beacons. Lieutenant Colonel Hercules Scott of the 103rd, at Coteau-du-Lac, and Lieutenant Colonel Deschambault, at Beauharnois, were given the responsibility of checking Wilkinson's advance along the river, and were instructed to retire, if necessary, on Montreal itself. Apparently the people were filled with the spirit of resistance, and the morale of the militia was high. William "Tiger" Dunlop, who saw them at this time, wrote:

Notice

all American Soldiers who may wish to quit the unnatural war in which they are at present engaged will receive the arrears due to them by the American Government to the extent of five months pay, on their arrival at the British out Posts. No man shall be required to serve against his own country—

74. *Handbill urging American soldiers to desert*

We came up with several regiments of militia on their line of march. They had all a serviceable, effective appearance—had been pretty well drilled, and their arms, being direct from the Tower, were in perfectly good order, nor had they the mobbish appearance that such a levy in any other country would have had. Their capots and trowsers of home-spun stuff, and their blue *tuques* were all of the same cut and colour, which gave them an air of uniformity that added much to their military look, for I have always remarked that a body of men's appearance in battalion depends much less on the fashion of their individual dress and appointments than on the whole being in strict uniformity.[42]

Just at this time of threat to Montreal, there arrived in Canada two British officers who were to play an important role in the defence of Upper Canada in 1814, Lieutenant General Sir Gordon Drummond and Major General Sir Phineas Riall. With them came a rocket company of Royal Marines and some 350 seamen from the Royal Navy. As the officer next in seniority to Sir George Prevost, Drummond took over command of all the troops on the south shore, with his headquarters at Châteauguay, and Riall was placed in charge of the troops on the north shore between Cornwall and the Cedars (Les Cèdres), with his headquarters at Lachine.

Obviously, then, the British were ready and waiting for the grand invasion. On 14 November, Prevost was told that Wilkinson had turned away. It was just a rumour, but when the news was confirmed by Prevost's spies, the militiamen were sent home and the other troops returned to their original stations or dispersed along the St. Lawrence and the Richelieu and among the parishes of the Eastern Townships. Active patrolling was ordered in the direction of Lake Champlain, Four Corners and French Mills in the United States. At Hercules Scott's suggestion, handbills were circulated, particularly at French Mills, to encourage discontented Americans to desert (see plate 74). These were not without some influence. One of the deserters, a Peter Eisenhower, who made his way to Cornwall, was, according to General Drummond, "extremely stupid and appears not to understand the English language sufficiently to be able to express what little he does know".[43] Not all deserters were as uncommunicative as Eisenhower. There was little that went on in the various American frontier posts that they did not tell the British authorities: the lack of adequate shelter, the absence of winter clothing, the shortage of hospital stores and provisions, the sickness and the daily deaths in military hospitals, particularly at French Mills and Malone. Finally, in mid-February 1814, the camps at French Mills and Four Corners were ordered evacuated. The moment this became known, Hercules Scott, with a number of picked troops—including regulars of the 89th and 103rd, Canadians from the Fencibles and 5th Embodied Militia, and militia from the counties of Stormont and Glengarry—, crossed the St. Lawrence, just as "Red George" Macdonell had done a year before when he attacked Ogdensburg. Moving quickly, the raiders reached French Mills in time to contact the American rear guard, then went to Malone, where they paroled a number of prisoners, many of them maimed, frostbitten, or too sick to be moved, and on to Madrid and Hopkinton to seize flour and salt-meat. Everywhere they went they burned barracks, blockhouses and boats and loaded their sleighs with supplies. One patrol even went to within a few miles of Plattsburg, where Wilkinson had established his winter quarters, and another went to Four Corners. It was the kind of warfare associated with Canadians in the heroic days of the French and Indian wars. It was the kind of warfare, too, that the Americans were to adopt in western Upper Canada in 1814.

1814

10

Western Upper Canada

1813 HAD BEEN A HARD YEAR in Upper Canada. The fighting had been bitterer, more intense and bloodier than in 1812, and had produced less satisfactory results. It is true that by the end of the year the Americans held only Sandwich and Amherstburg, while the British had captured Fort Niagara and scorched the east bank of the Niagara River; but the defeat at Moraviantown had not only destroyed an army, it had deprived the British of the whole of the Lake Erie frontier. The successes the British had achieved in the Niagara region occurred largely as a result of the American decision to concentrate their efforts on the "grand invasion" of Lower Canada. Moreover, the memories of York, Fort George and the burning of Niagara still rankled despite the victories at Stoney Creek and Beaver Dams. The most satisfactory development of the year had been the collapse of the Montreal offensive at Châteauguay and Crysler's Farm, but even that did not wholly atone for Moraviantown, for the withdrawal of all British troops west of Kingston had been a very near thing. As it was, Upper Canada west of Burlington Heights was left with very few regulars and had to rely on its own militia for protection from American raiders from Detroit and disloyal marauders from south of Lake Erie.

There were some bright spots in what might otherwise have been a cloudy future. Napoleon had been defeated at Leipzig in October and driven back into France; his ultimate overthrow would open the way for peace talks, which might also include the United States. Even if the Americans continued to be bel-

271

ligerent, the end of the Napoleonic wars would permit British troops to be transferred from Europe to reinforce the still scanty forces in North America. Perhaps the military command would then move from the defensive strategy that they had been following to an offensive policy designed to force peace on the Americans on British terms. An end to the war in Europe would also allow provisions and military supplies hitherto needed on the Continent to be sent to British North America to replenish the stocks in the two Canadas.

The 1813 grain crop had turned out to be a good one, particularly in Lower Canada, despite the cold, wet spring, and there was small likelihood of shortages in 1814 of the kind that had hamstrung poor Procter at Fort Malden. There were also good prospects for continued supplies of fresh and salt meat from the United States. Rottenburg told Noah Freer in January 1814 that "our beef contractor" in Albany was back in business and American cattle would soon be moving over the frontier again.[1] That Rottenburg's optimism was justified is borne out by the Commissary General's assurance in June 1814 that there was no cause for alarm as far as the food situation was concerned— "there is a sufficiency at this moment in the country for the summer"[2]—and that he had concluded a contract for fresh beef for all the troops between Quebec City and Coteau-du-Lac. Farther west, at the Salmon River, cattle were being gathered, ostensibly for the benefit of the American forces but in reality to drive them to Prescott to supply the British troops between Coteau-du-Lac and Kingston. The American contractor involved was, so Thomas Ridout told his father, a "Yankee magistrate".[3] Early in 1815, Commissary General William Henry Robinson told Lieutenant Colonel John Harvey in a letter that, thanks to the Yankees, the British troops were "supplied with all the necessaries of life in great abundance".[4]

From the strategic standpoint, the future looked none too hopeful. The two soft spots, as far as the Canadas were concerned, were western Upper Canada and the Niagara peninsula. Prevost hoped that the Americans would make another attempt against Montreal, for he had every confidence that, with the forces under his command, he would be able to defeat them. He had been vastly encouraged by the response of the province to the invasions of Hampton and Wilkinson. What he feared was another American attack in the Niagara region, where, he wrote to Drummond, "we have experienced so much difficulty in forwarding the necessary supplies and from the total want of accommodation for carrying on the service."[5] Drum-

75. Lieutenant General Sir Gordon Drummond succeeded Sheaffe as administrator and commander of the forces in Upper Canada, 1813–15

mond himself was convinced that the Niagara would see the main thrust of the United States forces in 1814. He knew that preparations were already being made for a new and well-trained army to cross the Niagara River, and he knew too that the events of 1813, if they had done nothing else for the Americans, had rid them of most of their incompetent general officers and opened the way for the promotion of such men as George Izard, Jacob Brown, Andrew Jackson, Edmund Gaines and Winfield Scott. Drummond therefore put in an early request for reinforcements to be sent as quickly as possible through Kingston to York, Burlington Heights and Long Point. He admitted that he did not like to see one of his most effective corps shut up in Fort Niagara, but the strategic situation demanded that the mouth of the Niagara River be kept free of enemy shipping. Also, to prevent any repetition of Dearborn's successful landing of May 1813, the British would have to maintain strong garrisons in Fort Niagara, Fort George and the recently constructed stone fort on Mississauga Point.

AS FAR AS Upper Canada was concerned, Drummond's hope was that he could reverse, or nullify, the effect of the American victory at Moraviantown. The best way to do this would be to recover Detroit, and what better way was there to recover Detroit than by a winter attack? It was not an impractical idea. With Buffalo eliminated for the time being as a jumping-off place, there was no likelihood of an American counterattack from that quarter to take the heat off Detroit. Moreover, the American army at Detroit was plagued with a long supply line extending all the way from Ohio. The small, mixed force of regulars and militia was estimated to number no more than 400, with another 200 troops occupying Fort Malden and Sandwich. In Drummond's opinion a British force of 1760 men (including the 100th and the light companies of the Royal Scots, the 41st and the 89th, as well as 250 militia, 400 Indians and a couple of hundred seamen) would be sufficient to carry the operation through to a successful conclusion. They could converge on Sandwich from separate directions—one column from the Talbot Settlement (in present-day Elgin County), another through Oxford (Woodstock), and the Indians from Pointe aux Pins (Rondeau Provincial Park). They would travel light, sleep out at night, carry axes and wear creepers. The supply train would move on the frozen Thames and the road south of the river with 300 sleighs.[6] On reaching the Detroit River, the main force would cross the ice at Sandwich, while another crossed at Bar Point below Amherstburg. The seamen would dash over the ice of western Lake Erie to Put-in-Bay and to any other place where American ships had been put up for the winter and were vulnerable to the torch. Once he had secured Prevost's permission for the expedition, Drummond sent his quartermaster general, Lieutenant Colonel Robert Nichol, to obtain intelligence of local resources, road conditions, availability of provisions and forage, and possible sites for supply depots. Nichol was also to report on arrangements for the relief of Michilimackinac, should that become necessary, by locating a suitable route by way of Lakes Simcoe and Huron; for the moment, Drummond was planning to build gunboats at Penetanguishene and establish a provisions depot on Matchedash Bay.

That the proposed expedition to Detroit never came off was owing, not to faulty planning, but to uncooperative weather. Everything depended on the continuation of the cold weather, which had set in fairly early. Only continued cold would keep the Thames River and the road south of it, which were the two principal highways for the expedition, in usable condition. It was essential, too, that the ice on the Detroit River and on the western end of Lake Erie be solid if men and sleighs and guns were to cross them to attack Detroit and to occupy the western shore. But no sooner had Drummond begun planning than a thaw set in. On 3 February, scarcely more than two weeks after he first sought Prevost's approval for the Detroit project, he was compelled to write once more to explain that, owing to the "peculiarly uncommon mildness of the season, which has been so unusually free from cold and frost", there was no hope of carrying the expedition through to a successful conclusion.[7] Drummond was disappointed, but he knew there was no use waiting in the hope of colder weather.

FOR THE REMAINDER of the war, western Upper Canada was a minor theatre of military operations for both the British and the Americans. Not that the region was ignored or that it enjoyed peace and stability, but neither the American nor the British high command saw it as strategically decisive. Regular troops were not made available in any number, and the fighting that took place consisted largely of hit-and-run raids, burnings, prisoner takings, and the working off of old scores on neighbours. In February, for instance, the traitor Andrew Westbrook led a party of Americans up the Thames on a cattle-stealing foray, which he abandoned on the arrival of the light infantry company of the Royals and Captain Thomas Coleman's Canadian dragoons. However, Westbrook did seize several prisoners at Delaware, including François Baby and two other "respectable inhabitants", whom he "shamefully and inhumanly tied with cords until it was found convenient to remove them to an unjust imprisonment".[8] When the British protested against Westbrook's action, the officer commanding the American troops at Detroit praised him as a patriot who had retained "the attachment for his native country which a citizen ought to feel", and claimed that the prisoners had served in the Canadian militia and that, in any event, the British had imprisoned one Blodgett, an American who had been sent into Upper Canada merely to make "purchases" in a region that had already submitted to Harrison's army.[9]

American raids were nothing new to the people of western Upper Canada, having been exposed to them in 1813, particularly after the defeat of Brigadier General Procter. Hardly had that battle ended when two bands of marauders, led by William Sutherland and Benajah Mallory, began scouring the countryside, one in the direction of Long Point and Port Dover, and the other along the Grand River, plundering and taking prisoners as they went. In the absence of any regular troops in the region, a group of militia officers led by Lieutenant Colonel Henry Bostwick raised a volunteer force that finally overtook the raiders at the mouth of Nanticoke Creek. The raiders were cornered and, although several escaped, some sixteen of them were taken prisoner and others were killed or wounded. Most of the plunder was recovered. Indeed, the quartermaster general, Robert Nichol, declared that Bostwick's action had saved some 7000 barrels of provisions that might otherwise have been destroyed, and had enabled Major General Vincent to maintain his position at Burlington Heights and, within a month, to recover the whole of the Niagara peninsula.

Early in December 1813 another American raiding party began operating along the Thames River. Lieutenant Henry Medcalf of the 2nd Norfolk Regiment, while on a routine patrol to the Rondeau district with a handful of militia and dragoons to collect supplies and cattle, learned of the presence of an American party near Chatham that was seizing supplies and extracting oaths of neutrality from harried inhabitants. Picking up a few Middlesex militia at Port Talbot and a handful of troopers and Kent militia along the Thames, he marched with all haste—covering 95 km in twenty-four hours through the unbroken wilderness and losing half of his men from sheer exhaustion—and discovered the Americans in a house belonging to one Thomas McCrae in Raleigh Township. Surrounding the house, Medcalf took the place by storm and then brought all his prisoners back to Long Point. He had covered, in all, 400 km. Remarkable as was Medcalf's achievement, one of his men showed even greater fortitude. Reuben Alwood followed Medcalf throughout the march and attack despite having been seriously wounded in November, when a boarding pike had been thrust into his left eye.

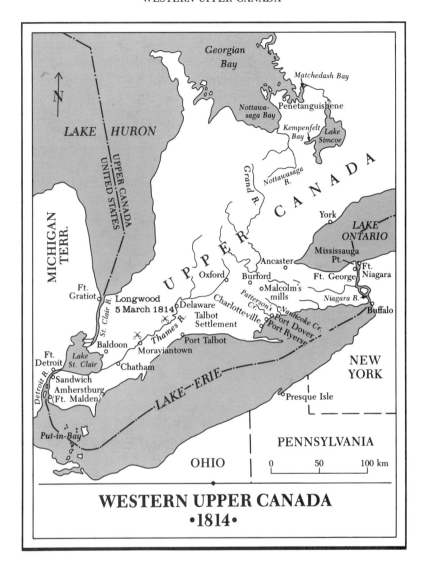

WESTERN UPPER CANADA
•1814•

At this point Lieutenant General Drummond issued instructions to Major General Riall to send the light infantry companies of the Royals and the 89th, along with militia from Kent and a few Indians, to Oxford and Delaware to collect supplies and "circumscribe the bounds of the enemy".[10] Several weeks later the Commanding General undertook to visit "that part of the district . . . as far as Delaware town on the River Thames and Long Point and vicinity on the shore of Lake Erie".[11] Drummond's purpose was to look over the country and ascertain just what its capabilities were. He found the Thames area "entire-

277

ly drained of its resources" and unable to support any force adequate for its protection without drawing for its supplies on Long Point, which he believed capable of furnishing a "tolerable quantity of flour and a few cattle". Since all the roads from the lake came together at one place, about 30 km from Turkey Point, Drummond proposed stationing a "considerable" garrison there, with detachments at Oxford ("to watch the road to the westward"), Charlotteville (now called Turkey Point) and Port Dover. The troops he thought of using were those from the 100th Regiment, who were "well disciplined", and not those of the light companies, who sometimes acted as if they were "banditti" rather than "British soldiers, employed for the protection of the country". He also suggested the use of a detachment of light dragoons from Kingston because the country was flat and only "thinly scattered with trees" almost to the mouth of the Grand River. The major problem Drummond encountered during his visit, apparently, was the terrible condition of the roads, which had been "so much neglected since the commencement of the war that during the wet weather in some parts they become wholly impassable". It was clear that whatever Rottenburg might have thought about abandoning western Upper Canada, this would not be the strategy employed by Sir Gordon Drummond.

Early in March 1814, Drummond's decision was put to the test. Late on the night of the third, word reached the British garrison at Delaware that some of William Caldwell's Rangers had come across an American foraging party moving up the Thames River at Longwood, about 25 km away. Early the next day a British force consisting of some 240 men—including the flank companies of the Royals and the 89th, and some Kent militia and Indians—under the command of Captain James Basden of the 89th Regiment, set out to back up Caldwell's Rangers. They came up with the Americans at about 1700 hrs on 5 March, finding them strongly entrenched and protected by a log breastwork on a commanding height. According to the official American report, their own force numbered about 165 men, including foot and mounted infantry, under the command of Captain A.H. Holmes of the 24th Infantry. Holmes had expected trouble after his initial encounter with Caldwell, and chose a strong position that was defended by a deep ravine on one side. To protect the other three sides he constructed a thick abatis. Also to his advantage was the 35 cm of snow on the ground, which would hamper an offensive force attacking his position.

With Basden were several men acquainted with the locality, who volunteered to guide the British force by a roundabout path to the rear of the American position. Although an indirect approach is usually considered the better tactical move, Basden chose to attempt a frontal attack. He therefore detached the militia and sent them to make a flanking movement to the right, while the Indians made a similar movement to the left; then, with his regulars, Basden dashed down into the ravine and ascended the hill on the other side, to come within firing distance of Holmes's men in their makeshift fort. Here the British troops were met with a series of sharp volleys at point-blank range. Captain David Johnston of the Royals was killed within ten paces of the American defence works. After a stubborn effort to dislodge the enemy, the British troops withdrew; or, as Captain Holmes put it, "The enemy at last became convinced that Providence had sealed the fortune of the day . . . and favoured by the shades of twilight, he commenced a general retreat."[12] "I regret", wrote Captain Alex Stewart of the Royal Scots, "that our loss is very considerable"[13]—14 killed and 52 wounded, including Captain Basden. The Americans reported only 7 killed or wounded. Holmes, having achieved all that he had hoped for, did not pursue the defeated British, but turned round and hurried back to Detroit. Stewart, as the senior British officer in the region, did not follow the Americans; he merely retired upon his base at Delaware.

The battle at Longwood did nothing for Upper Canada. It did not discourage the Americans from continuing their marauding attacks. In April, Andrew Westbrook led a raid on Oxford. In May, a substantial American force commanded by Colonel John B. Campbell landed at the mouth of Patterson's Creek (Lynn River). They burned mills, distilleries, public buildings and private houses. According to one source, only one house was left standing between Patterson's Creek and Turkey Point— the house occupied by the widow and family of Samuel Ryerse, at Port Ryerse. Alexander McMullen, one of the Americans who took part, wrote this vivid description of a raid on Port Dover:

> The situation of this village was pleasant, the houses generally frame, near a beautiful creek with a fine, large fulling-mill, grist-mill and saw-mill. . . . An order from Campbell to set fire to the houses was now executed by men detailed from all the companies. A scene of destruction and plunder now ensued, which beggars all description. In a short time the houses, mills and barns were all consumed, and a beautiful village, which the sun shone on in splen-

dour that morning, was before two o'clock a heap of smoking ruins. . . . A party of sailors appointed to man the artillery killed the hogs in the streets, and severing them in the middle carried off the hind parts, while the head and shoulders were left in the street. . . . A short distance from this house was a pasture lot, in which grazed a fine English cow. Some of us, who were farmers, had a curiosity to examine this fine animal more closely. This drew a small group together, when a private of Gordon's company fired his musket and broke both her forelegs. The farmer and his family said nothing, afraid, I suppose, that their own turn might come next, and the officers, taken up in examining some Canadian prisoners, paid little attention to it.[14]

At Charlotteville, the courthouse, blockhouse and public buildings were saved by the timely arrival of troopers of the 19th Light Dragoons and a body of militia. The raid was accompanied by considerable looting, probably because of the presence of several renegade Canadians. According to one Canadian officer, Lieutenant Charles Ingersoll of Merritt's troop of Provincial Light Dragoons, "the principal leaders" were Abraham Markle, a former member of the Legislative Assembly, and "young Green".[15] Apparently Markle acted as guide for the raiders. Among those who suffered heavy property damage as a result of the American action were Lieutenant Colonel Robert Nichol and other militiamen, including the Bostwicks, Abraham Rapelje, Samuel Ryerse, Henry Medcalf and Titus Finch. The traitorous element, indeed, made the most of the opportunity to vent their malice on former neighbours. Campbell offered as his excuse that Port Dover contained "a character who, during our Revolution, was a Tory" and that many of the townsmen were in the militia, "as was proved by the regimentals found in their houses".[16] Not only did some of Campbell's own men disapprove of his conduct—McMullen, in his account of the raid on Port Dover, stated that the American troops returned home "generally disgusted with the conduct of Campbell"—but it caused some uneasiness in Washington. Brigadier General Jacob Brown disclaimed any responsibility and the matter was investigated by a court of inquiry, which did no more than criticize Campbell for what it euphemistically termed an error of judgement. In any event, Campbell was killed shortly thereafter at Chippawa.

Less destructive, but equally malicious, were the raids Andrew Westbrook led on Port Talbot on 30 May, 20 July and 9 September 1814. The raiders damaged crops, took prisoners, burned gristmills, sawmills and houses, destroyed stocks of flour and killed cattle. On each occasion the real object of the raid,

76. Colonel Thomas Talbot, who commanded the flank companies of the London district and all the embodied militia in western Upper Canada

Colonel Thomas Talbot, was either absent or managed to escape. The reason the area could offer so little resistance to the raiders was that, during the spring and summer of 1814, loyal militiamen from Norfolk, Oxford and Middlesex counties were on duty with Talbot on the Niagara frontier when the Americans were making their final determined effort to break through the British defences on the central front.

The last, and most spectacular, raid in Upper Canada was
that conducted by Brigadier General Duncan McArthur in October and November 1814. It was well timed. The bulk of the
regular troops in Upper Canada were with Drummond on the
line of the Chippawa (Welland) River, and were not likely to
be available for dispatch to western Upper Canada as long as
there was any serious possibility of further American offensives
on the Niagara frontier. McArthur made his preparations well
and conducted the early part of his march with secrecy and dispatch despite having some 800 men with him. Just why he took
so many men is not clear. Was it to drive towards Lake Ontario and present a threat to Drummond's flank at Burlington
Heights? Was it to impress the Indians and draw them away
from their support of the British? Was it to forestall a British
winter offensive towards Detroit? Perhaps all of these thoughts
were in McArthur's mind, although Drummond looked upon
his action as no more than a plundering expedition. Whatever
his purpose, McArthur led his men north, along the American
side of Lake St. Clair, then across the St. Clair River through
Lord Selkirk's settlement at Baldoon, and up the Thames to
Moraviantown. By this time, the rumour was circulating that
McArthur's destination was Burlington Heights even though
Captain John Bostwick, when reporting the rumour to the officer commanding at Long Point, expressed his private opinion
that such was not the case. He suspected that McArthur's men
were mostly "undisciplined" Kentuckians and that they were
intent on "ravaging this district" rather than undertaking any
grand strategic exploit.[17] As McArthur moved into Oxford on
4 November, his men were becoming weary and hungry and not
a little edgy. They had heard that the Oxford militia was gathering to oppose them and warned the people of the village that
any man who dared send word to the militia would have his
property destroyed. Undismayed by the threat, two men,
George Nichol and Jacob Wood, slipped away and made in all
haste for Burford. Warned by a frightened or malicious neigh-
bour that the men had fled, McArthur carried out his threat
and burned their houses and all their buildings.

At Burford, Lieutenant Colonel Henry Bostwick, who was
in charge of the militia, was in no position to offer any real resistance to McArthur's much stronger force. He therefore retired
in front of McArthur, finally moving off to the flank to take
refuge in Malcolm's mills (on the road between Port Dover and
Burlington Heights), where he was joined by additional militia
levies, bringing his total strength to about 400 poorly armed,

77. Brigadier General Duncan McArthur, who served under Hull and led the raid into Upper Canada in 1813

hastily equipped and rather dispirited soldiers. At the same time, Major Adam Muir of the 41st, with a detachment of 50 men, withdrew to the line of the Grand River for the purpose of securing the ferry and rousing the Iroquois Indians. The Indians' response was less than enthusiastic, but a number of them did turn out, together with a troop of horse from Ancaster. Meanwhile, not far away were John Norton with a few Six Nations Indians who had been at Niagara and several companies of the 103rd Regiment of Foot. For the moment McArthur chose to push ahead to Burford and, ignoring Bostwick, made for the ferry over the Grand River, then in flood owing to the heavy autumn rains. He halted when he saw the Indians and troops

283

78. Lieutenant Colonel Henry Bostwick, 1st Regiment, Oxford Militia

on the opposite bank of the river, and after a sharp exchange of shots encamped for the night. At this critical moment he learned that the American troops at Fort Erie had abandoned their foothold in Canada and retired to the east side of the Niagara. To try to cross the Grand River in the face of opposition and to continue an advance towards Burlington Heights with no hope of assistance did not make military sense. So McArthur swung to the right and made for Malcolm's mills.

Bostwick had found a good defensive position on high ground, overlooking a deep ravine. His front was protected by an unfordable stream with only a single narrow bridge. On his left was a millpond, and across the road a strong barricade of logs.

But McArthur, after nearly three years of war, was too experienced a soldier to try a frontal attack, even if his enemy did have only 400 jittery men, depressed by rumours exaggerating the American strength to 2000 men armed with rifles, tomahawks and scalping knives! Leaving his Kentuckians to keep Bostwick occupied, McArthur led the remainder of his horsemen to a point where he was able to get them across the stream. Warned by his Indians of what was happening, Bostwick decided not to challenge McArthur but to pull out of his strong position, leaving McArthur to burn Malcolm's mills and other gristmills in the district.

As McArthur continued his march, uninterrupted, towards Port Dover, he was followed at a discreet distance by a *corps d'observation* from the Grand River, made up of dragoons, militia and Indians under Brevet Major Peter Chambers. At Malcolm's mills the pursuers found the bodies of a British sergeant and an Upper-Canadian militiaman, who had been killed during Bostwick's withdrawal. The bodies had been mutilated. According to Chambers:

> The enemy have plundered the country in the most shameful manner, stole the horses, clothing, etc., and burned all the mills as far as this.
>
> Sergeant Collins of the 41st Regiment and Private Barton of the militia were killed and mutilated in the most horrible manner. Barton was actually butchered (no symptoms of having been shot) both scalped and cut shockingly.[18]

As the American withdrawal continued, the pace accelerated. On the tenth, Chambers, now at Long Point, stated that McArthur was moving eastwards "with the greatest precipitancy", leaving some of his horses behind. Chambers was probably not far wide of the mark when he suggested that McArthur's object, whatever its earlier purpose may have been, was now simply

> to destroy all the mills in the country (so as to prevent our advancing this winter to Amherstburg), which I happily defeated by the rapidity of my advance. I did not give them time to complete the work of destruction, three mills being left. Had we not arrived in time the whole of this valuable settlement must have fallen a prey to famine this winter. At present not a single barrel of flour is to be purchased in the district. The enemy have plundered the inhabitants most disgracefully and stole every horse they could find.[19]

Seven days after Chambers wrote these words, McArthur was in Sandwich. His expedition, well organized and carried out with speed and decision, may not have achieved anything as far as the American army in the Niagara peninsula was concerned, but it did result in the destruction of most of the flour mills in western Upper Canada and, in this way, secured Detroit from any renewal of the project advanced by Drummond the previous February for recovering Michigan Territory by a winter expedition. There is no question that McArthur carried out one of the bold exploits of the Canadian War of 1812, and no question that he accomplished it with very little loss of life. But there is no denying that it added to the stock of bitter memories left by earlier raiding parties, particularly those led by the men whom Upper Canadians looked upon as traitors, and it further aggravated the anti-American feeling that was to play so great a part in Canadian political life for over a century.

NONE OF THE TRAITORS who had led or inspired the raids in Upper Canada ever returned to Canada. Some, like Willcocks, were killed in battle; others, like Markle, were outlawed by the courts. The largest group was that captured at Thomas McCrae's by Lieutenant Henry Medcalf. They were brought before the court at Ancaster on 23 May 1814. Close to the British army base at Burlington Heights, Ancaster was chosen in case there was an American attempt to free the prisoners. Bills for high treason were brought against nineteen men then in custody, and against fifty who had not yet been apprehended. On 7 June the trials began before Chief Justice Thomas Scott, Senior Puisne Justice William Dummer Powell, and Junior Puisne Justice William Campbell. The prosecution was conducted by John Beverley Robinson, a young man not yet twenty-three years of age, who was acting attorney general in place of D'Arcy Boulton, then a prisoner of war in France. Two weeks later the trials were over; fourteen of the prisoners were convicted on evidence, one pleaded guilty and four were acquitted. Since the law imposed only one penalty for treason—death—, respite was granted to allow each case to be reviewed to determine whether grounds could be found for leniency. Late in June the decision was announced: seven were to be granted reprieve.

The eight condemned men were executed on 20 July. According to an eyewitness, the victims were brought in two wagons to the gallows, the nooses were adjusted and the wagons driven off, leaving the victims to strangle. "Their contortion", he wrote years later, "loosened the gallows so that a heavy brace came loose, fell and struck one of the victims on the head, killing him instantly. Later their heads were chopped off, and exhibited as traitors."[20]

79. *John Beverley Robinson, who served under Brock at Detroit
and at Queenston Heights. As provincial attorney general, he
prosecuted the traitors at Ancaster in May 1814.*

Of the seven men who were reprieved, three died of the dread
"jail-fever", a type of typhus then believed to be caused by "filth
and overcrowding, bad diet and close foul air", but now attributed to a micro-organism transmitted by human lice; three
others were pardoned; and the last, Calvin Wood, managed
to escape from Kingston jail and make his way to the United
States. Thus ended the so-called Bloody Assize. Finally, in 1817,
judgements of outlawry were obtained against another thirty

287

alleged traitors, including Abraham Markle, and all who had lands in Upper Canada lost them by forfeiture to the Crown.[21]

THE BRITISH DEFEAT at Moraviantown in October 1813 not only affected the military situation in western Upper Canada, it also posed special threats to the British position on the Upper Lakes and to the continued British possession of Michilimackinac. Basic to British control of the Upper Lakes region was the fidelity of the Indians, whose economic interests were similar to those of the North West Company; but second in importance was the maintenance of a secure line of communications with York and Montreal. The North West Company's old canoe route via the Ottawa and French rivers to Georgian Bay remained open after Procter's defeat, but water communications between Michilimackinac and York via Fort Malden and Long Point were impossible after the battles of Put-in-Bay and Moraviantown; and the Americans, once again firmly ensconced in Detroit, were in a position to extend their naval supremacy of Lake Erie to the waters of Lake Huron. That they intended to do so became clear when McArthur took steps to construct Fort Gratiot at the foot of Lake Huron.

The new American post was to serve as a jumping-off place for any combined military–naval attack on Michilimackinac or St. Joseph Island. At the same time the Americans were anxious to undermine the hold that the British had over the western Indians. This could best be done, not by negotiations or promises, but by impressing the Indians with American determination and American military might. Hence the May 1814 expedition conducted by William Clark, Governor of the Missouri Territory, along the Mississippi towards Prairie du Chien, where the British had stationed a small outpost of Mississippi Volunteer Artillery under Captain Francis Michael Dease, a Nor'-Wester. Clark encountered only feeble resistance from the Sauk Indians at the Rock Island Rapids, and Dease, under no illusions about his ability to halt Clark's force of regulars and militia, pulled out of Prairie du Chien, leaving it wide open to the Americans. Clark promptly built a stockaded fort there, which he named Fort Shelby and garrisoned with a detachment of seventy men under Lieutenant Joseph Perkins.

For their part, the British had been taking steps to strengthen their position in the Upper Lakes region. Additional fortifications had been built at Michilimackinac, outposts pushed forward into the Wisconsin region at Green Bay and Prairie du Chien, and agents sent to keep in touch with the Indians of the upper Mississippi country. Although Dease had felt it advisable to yield to Clark, that was no reason for giving up the whole region. Prevost therefore sent Lieutenant Colonel Robert McDouall, an officer of the 8th and at one time his aide-de-camp, with some ninety men of the Royal Newfoundland Regiment and some seamen, to take over command at Michilimackinac from the ailing Captain Charles Roberts of the 10th Royal Veterans. At the same time, new routes were being surveyed from York via Lake Simcoe, one to Matchedash Bay, where a provisions depot was established during the winter of 1813–14, and another to Nottawasaga, at the mouth of the Nottawasaga, where the river could provide shelter for bateaux and where a blockhouse was built. Another site considered worth developing was that of Penetanguishene, to which a military road was completed from Kempenfelt Bay on Lake Simcoe in November 1814 and where a blockhouse was built in 1815.

When he arrived at Fort Michilimackinac, McDouall found himself faced with two problems, both of which demanded his immediate attention; the first was the presence of the Americans on the upper Mississippi and the second was the prospect of an attack on Michilimackinac by a military–naval force from Fort Gratiot. He first directed his attention to the upper Mississippi, perhaps because it posed an immediate threat to British influence over the Indians, whose help McDouall knew he would need in the event of an American attack on Michilimackinac. At the risk of weakening his own position at the entrance to Lake Michigan, McDouall organized, equipped and dispatched to Prairie du Chien a force of 75 Michigan Fencibles and 136 Indians under the command of retired fur trader Brevet Major William McKay, a member of the Beaver Club, who had held a commission in the Corps of Voyageurs and in the 5th Embodied Militia of Lower Canada. According to McDouall, McKay's task was "to dislodge the American Genl from his new conquest, and make him relinquish the immense tract of country he had seized upon in consequence and which brought him into the very heart of that occupied by our friendly Indians."[22] McDouall had grasped the essential aspects of the situation. In the same letter to Drummond he pointed out that if the enemy were not driven out of Prairie du Chien there would be

an end to our connexion with the Indians. . . . Tribe after tribe would be gained over or subdued, and thus would be destroyed the only barrier which protects the great trading establishments of the North West and the Hudson's Bay Companys. Nothing could then prevent the enemy from gaining the source of the Mississippi, gradually extending themselves by the Red River to Lake Winnipic, from whence the descent of Nelsons River to York Fort would in time be easy.

McKay was accompanied by Toussaint Pothier, Jacques Porlier, Thomas Gummersall Anderson and Joseph Rolette (brother of Frédéric, who had captured the *Cuyahoga* in 1812), all of them well-known personalities in the fur trade. They followed a course up the Fox River and down the Wisconsin, gathering recruits along the way until their force numbered about 650, by far the greatest number of whom were Indians.

The Americans were quite unaware of the approach of McKay's force. For that matter, neither was McKay aware that Clark was no longer at Prairie du Chien. It was not until the last moment that his scouts learned from Antoine Brisebois, a Canadian agent on the Mississippi, that Clark had returned to St. Louis and that the garrison at Fort Shelby was much smaller than McDouall had believed. Thus McKay sent off to Perkins a stern demand for the unconditional surrender of the post; "otherwise defend yourself to the last man."[23] The American commander had two blockhouses, several cannon, and the *Governor Clark*, a large gunboat mounting fourteen cannon, which McKay later described as "a floating blockhouse . . . so constructed that she can be rowed in any direction. . . . She goes remarkably fast, particularly down the current, being rowed by 32 oars."[24] Perkins chose to fight and for several hours the two sides exchanged gunfire. McKay directed his cannon fire against both the fort and the *Governor Clark*. In the end the leaking gunboat cut her cable and took refuge behind an island, later making her escape downriver. On 19 July, after two days of shooting, much of which was "perfectly useless", McKay marched to the forward breastwork, "from whence I intended to throw in the remaining six rounds [of] iron ball red-hot into the fort in order to set it on fire".[25] While the first shot was being put into the cannon a white flag was hoisted over the fort, and out of the gate came an officer carrying a note of surrender. By the terms of capitulation McKay took possession of the fort and all the arms and public property in it. The garrison of 66 officers and men, and one woman and her child, were permitted to withdraw unmolested.

Apparently every man in the Michigan Fencibles, Canadian volunteers and Indian Department "behaved as well as I could possibly wish", and no one was injured in the fighting except three Indians, who were wounded. The fort yielded 5 cannon, 61 stands of arms, 28 barrels of pork and 46 barrels of flour.

80. *Major Toussaint Pothier, who formed a corps of Voyageurs and took part in the capture of Fort Michilimackinac in 1812 and Prairie du Chien in 1814*

Reporting on his own troops, McKay remarked that the Sioux, Ojibwa and others, "though perfectly useless, obeyed my orders pretty well", but the Winnebagos "despise the idea of receiving orders from an officer that does not hold a blanket in one hand and a piece of pork in the other to pay them."[26] Most of the Winnebagos promptly departed after the battle and McKay was glad to see them go. By this time he was suffering from a swelling on the side of his face and a violent fever. "I believe it is what in Canada is generally called the *mumps*", he wrote.[27]

McKay had sent some of his Indians in pursuit of the *Governor Clark*. Using canoes and carrying several kegs of gunpowder,

291

they hurried to the Rock Island Rapids, hoping to intercept the American gunboat. Here they discovered additional American troops, who had been sent forward as reinforcements under Captain John Campbell for the relief of Fort Shelby. The Indians had assembled a force of about 400 Sauks, Foxes and Kickapoos. Fearing that the Americans would attack Indian villages once they had recaptured Fort Shelby, the Indians fought with desperation. Indian women even jumped on board the American river-craft "with their hoes, etc., some breaking heads, others breaking casks, some trying to cut holes in her bottom to sink her, and others setting fire to her decks."[28] The Americans admitted to 35 killed or wounded. When the *Governor Clark* managed to catch up with Campbell's force on its way down the Mississippi, the Americans were ready to make haste back to St. Louis. This battle at an obscure rapids on the Mississippi was, according to McKay, "one of the most brilliant actions fought by Indians only since the commencement of the war."[29] It ensured British superiority in the Wisconsin area and on the waters of the upper Mississippi until the peace treaty turned the region over to the United States.

When he recovered from his attack of mumps, McKay returned to Michilimackinac and subsequently went on to Montreal to report on the state of affairs in the Northwest to Sir George Prevost. His replacement at Fort McKay (the name he modestly bestowed on Fort Shelby to impress the Indians with the extent of the American defeat) was another fur trader, Thomas Gummersall Anderson, who strengthened the fort by constructing another blockhouse and accumulating a good stock of provisions. To keep his troops employed Anderson encouraged them to help the local farmers get their crops in during the autumn. The rest of the time they seem to have spent drinking rum and watching interracial lacrosse matches, in which the participants usually "got sore wounds from the ball and the hurl stick".[30]

WHILE MCDOUALL'S ATTENTION was focused on events at Prairie du Chien, the Americans made the expected effort to regain Michilimackinac. The expedition was conducted by Lieutenant Colonel George Croghan, who had successfully resisted Procter at Fort Stephenson. On 3 July he sailed from Detroit with five vessels and a military force of 700 men, including five companies of regulars and a number of Ohio militia. The first objective was the supply dump at Matchedash Bay, but since none of the Americans knew where that actually was, and a heavy fog had settled over the eastern part of Lake Huron, they gave up the search and sailed for St. Joseph Island, where they arrived on the twentieth, the day after William McKay took possession of Prairie du Chien. The British having abandoned St. Joseph Island in July 1812, when Roberts captured Michilimackinac, Croghan had to be content with burning empty buildings. Not far from the island he captured a North West Company vessel carrying a cargo of flour, and on 26 July his vessels finally anchored off Mackinac Island.

But Michilimackinac was a hard nut for Croghan to crack. Its defences were located on ground too high for the guns on Croghan's ships to reach, and there were few places where troops could land without fear of running into an Indian ambush. Roberts had had the advantage of surprise; but this was lacking to Croghan, who had no idea how many men, particularly how many Indians, were available to his opponent. Still, he could hardly sail away without making some show of force. He therefore landed at the same place Roberts had used, on the west side of the island. McDouall did not wait behind his walls to be attacked. Leaving 25 men in each blockhouse, he set his small force to erecting breastworks outside the fortifications, where his Indians could fight in their traditional manner, making use of the cover afforded by the trees. Croghan had not expected that particular tactic, which brought the Indians, especially the Menomini, on his flanks and left the British and their fieldpieces occupying the high ground. After suffering unexpectedly high losses Croghan withdrew to the beach and, re-embarking, sailed away, leaving two of his vessels, *Scorpion* and *Tigress*, to maintain a blockade of Michilimackinac. Before he left, Croghan learned of the surrender of Prairie du Chien and, to avoid having his expedition considered a total failure, landed at the mouth of the Nottawasaga River, where he burned the schooner *Nancy* and the new British blockhouse. But he considered this location too accessible from York and decided against establishing an American post there. When he arrived back at Detroit, Croghan was given extended leave. In the eyes of his superiors, his failure at Michilimackinac overshadowed his brief moment of glory at Fort Stephenson.

Having repelled the American assault force, McDouall was now anxious to get rid of the two American armed schooners. Not that they could take Fort Michilimackinac, but they were in a position to intercept vessels approaching the island and to rob the North West Company of furs on the way to Canada or his garrison of food supplies coming from Canada. McDouall

81. A view of Michilimackinac. The fort with two blockhouses dominates the heights, and the fur traders' houses face the waterfront.

found himself obliged to begin rationing provisions and to kill horses and salt their meat to keep his Indians well fed. On 1 September, to rid himself of this nuisance, he authorized a party under Lieutenant Andrew Bulger of the Royal Newfoundland Fencibles and Lieutenant Miller Worsley of the Royal Navy to capture the blockading schooners.

Worsley, in a canoe, had passed near the American schooners unobserved while *en route* from Nottawasaga to Michilimackinac on 31 August, and it was he who suggested to McDouall that the capture of the vessels might easily be effected by men approaching quietly in small boats. It would be a tricky operation because everything depended on being able to get close to the American ships without being discovered. Just about sunset, on 2 September, Worsley's four open boats, manned by seamen and Newfoundland Fencibles, discovered one of the American vessels near Drummond Island. Remaining concealed among the islands during the night and the greater part of the next day, they began to move slowly towards the enemy at about

1800 hrs. The distance was about 10 km and they had to row it in complete silence; the Indians who accompanied them travelled in canoes well to the rear. Worsley's boats arrived within hailing distance of *Tigress* at about 2100 hrs. An American sailor challenged them, and when Worsley failed to reply he shouted a warning and opened fire. But the British were on top of the Americans within minutes and, at a cost of two seamen killed and several soldiers wounded, they succeeded in boarding the schooner and forcing the Americans to surrender. The prisoners were sent to Michilimackinac.

Tigress, now under Worsley's command, prepared to engage her sister ship *Scorpion*, which was anchored some 25 km away. Keeping the American pennant flying and sending his men below decks so that they should not be seen, Worsley remained quietly where he was until *Scorpion* approached late on 5 September and anchored about 3 km away. Early the next morning, *Tigress* slipped her cable and bore down on *Scorpion*. Bulger wrote:

> Every thing was so well managed by Lieut. Worsley that we were within ten yards of the enemy before they discovered us; it was then too late, for in the course of five minutes her deck was covered with our men, and the British flag hoisted over the American.[31]

Once again the casualties were small; Lieutenant Bulger and seven other men were wounded. The results: the capture of two vessels and of American stores valued at $16 000, and an instant British fleet on Lake Huron. McDouall need no longer worry about his line of communications with Upper Canada.

BUT MCDOUALL had another worry, the threat of attack along the upper Mississippi, the Americans having made another attempt to recover Prairie du Chien. In August, Major Zachary Taylor had organized an expedition at St. Louis to regain control of the upper Mississippi. With a force of regulars and Illinois militia, about 350 men in all, he had set off upstream towards Prairie du Chien. He had hoped to maintain secrecy, but to do so in country where the Indians were generally in sympathy with the British was virtually impossible, and it was not long before word reached Captain Thomas Anderson at Fort McKay. Anderson decided that he would be no more successful at holding Prairie du Chien than Perkins had been if he adopted a defensive stance. What he did, therefore, was to send 30 men to the Rock Island Rapids under the command of Duncan Graham, who held a commission in the Indian Department, and James Keating, a Royal Artillery sergeant, whose command was the Mississippi Volunteer Artillery and whose weapons consisted of two swivel guns and a 3-pounder cannon.

Anderson's idea was that Graham should mobilize the local Indians—Winnebagos, Sioux and Sauks—under the Indian chief, Black Hawk, who was considered "a zealous partisan of the British cause",[32] and, with the guns covering the rapids, make a firm stand at the Rock Island Rapids. In the early morning of 5 September, as the Americans were slowly making their way upstream, they suddenly found themselves facing an Indian attack, supported by Keating's guns and Keating's gunnery, which was such as "to knock the splinters into the men's faces" in the gunboats.[33] Taylor quickly appreciated the hopelessness of his task and began to drop back to escape the devastating effect of the guns of the Mississippi Volunteer Artillery. Then, finding himself closely pursued by the Indians, Taylor ordered his boats to turn about and head quickly downstream. At the mouth of the Des Moines River he paused to build a small fort, but even this position was abandoned in October, and the whole American force on the upper Mississippi withdrew to St. Louis.

When he learned of the Taylor expedition, McDouall decided to send a regular officer to take command at Fort McKay pending the arrival of reinforcements; for McDouall suspected, even if he did not actually know, that the Americans intended to renew the offensive up the Mississippi in 1815. The officer he chose was Andrew Bulger, who had commanded the military component of the force that had captured the two American armed schooners. Although still suffering from the breast wound received during the capture of *Scorpion*, Bulger, accompanied by the fur trader Robert Dickson, set off for Prairie du Chien on 29 October 1814. Winter was beginning to set in and Bulger did not reach his new command until a month later.

It was not an enviable command. The men were discontented, undisciplined and hungry. There were a great many Indians, whose "good understanding" Bulger was expected to cultivate and whose loyalty he was to encourage. But Bulger was young, inexperienced and very much the military officer; he was a questionable choice for this particular appointment. Bulger was soon at odds with Dickson and with the officers of the Indian Department, and had trouble imposing regular army discipline on his Michigan Fencibles and Mississippi Volunteers, many of whom were either insubordinate or frankly refused to obey orders. To set an example he arrested two privates, La Serre Dupuis and

82. Black Hawk, a leader of the Sauk and Fox Indians

Hypolite Sénécal, tried them by court-martial and imposed a penalty of 300 lashes for each man, the sentence to be carried out in front of the assembled garrison, but he ordered the punishment stopped after 150 strokes of the lash.[34] Under the circumstances it was not surprising that Bulger, while reporting on 15 January that the imposition of iron discipline had had a salutary effect, considered it advisable to "sleep in the fort every night in a small room appropriated as an orderly room. . . . I know that most of them, being half Indian, possess the treacherous disposition of the Indian, who only wants for a good opportunity of taking revenge."[35]

During the winter McDouall impressed on Bulger the importance of holding Prairie du Chien. His orders were to fight "to the last extremity". To abandon Fort McKay would

297

83. "Captain W. Andrew Bulger Saying Farewell at Fort
MacKay, Prairie du Chien, Wisconsin, 1815"

be a measure in every point of view pregnant with the most emi-
nent danger, and not only occasion the loss of this Island
[Mackinac], but ultimately place the Canadas themselves in jeopar-
dy. For of this be assured, that the day that witnesses our departure from the Mississippi forever loses us the country, severs our
Indian connexion, [and] instead of their assistance as allies, we shall
find them ferocious enemies, indignant at being abandoned. . . .
No officer of your rank (and seldom even field officers) was ever
before invested with so important a command.[36]

McDouall was, of course, looking to the future, to the day
when the politicians would be negotiating the conditions of
peace. Actual possession of territory was always a difficult argument to counter. For the upper Mississippi to be in British hands
would give British negotiators the means of carrying out British
promises to the Indians and retaining them as allies. One could
never tell whether they might not be needed again in a future
contest with the United States. Therefore Bulger was concerned
during the next few months with how and when to defend Fort
McKay: should it be at Prairie du Chien? or at the Rock Island
Rapids? Or should the war be carried into American territory
to St. Louis? Robert Dickson favoured the last. So, too, did
Bulger, until the news of the Treaty of Ghent reached the Far
West in the spring of 1815.

11

Lundy's Lane

IT HAD NOT BEEN the intention of the United States War Department to stress the Niagara theatre of operations in 1814. When Jacob Brown marched his men from French Mills to Sackets Harbor in February, the Secretary of War wrote him a secret letter suggesting that he attack Kingston and direct a feint towards the Niagara peninsula. At the same time he wrote another letter to Brown, this one intended for British eyes and leaked to them discreetly, suggesting that Niagara should be the main objective of Brown's force. But this cunning was too much for Brown. Influenced by what the American historian Henry Adams called Chauncey's "invincible" repugnance[1] to risking his fleet in an attack on the British naval base in Upper Canada, and by "some extraordinary mental process", as Armstrong put it, Brown allowed himself to be persuaded that the main attack should be against the place indicated by the ruse, although it had been chosen "merely to mask" the true objective.[2] Brown thereupon marched his men to Buffalo. When Armstrong learned that he had outfoxed his own army commander he decided to go along with Brown's interpretation of his orders, and wrote to him on 20 March:

> You have mistaken my meaning. . . . If you hazard anything by this mistake, correct it promptly by returning to your post. If on the other hand you left the Harbor with a competent force for its defence, go on and prosper. Good consequences are sometimes the result of mistakes.[3]

In this way, Armstrong, whose concern about Kingston was strategically sound, accepted an alternative approach to the conquest of Canada that had failed on two previous occasions and had brought neither military credit nor strategic advantage to the United States.

At least the bewildered Brown was an improvement on the incompetent commanders who had previously operated on the central front in Upper Canada—Van Rensselaer, Dearborn and McClure. During the next several months, under the supervision of Winfield Scott, the American troops at Buffalo underwent a thorough course of training and morale-building. Like Steuben at Valley Forge, Scott began with the officers; they were exercised, like their men, in squad, company and battalion drill, and in handling their weapons—the flintlock musket and the bayonet. Emphasis was also placed on discipline, smart saluting and the importance of good field hygiene. It was all done according to the only textbook available to Scott, a tattered copy of French regulations issued by Napoleon Bonaparte. The result was that, not only did the military proficiency of the troops improve, so did their health and their morale. One of the military doctors remarked with surprise that "even the demon diarrhoea appeared to have been exorcised by the mystical power of strict discipline and rigid police!"[4] Ten hours a day, under Scott's eyes, the officers drilled their men until they could manoeuvre in the woods and on open ground with precision and confidence. An *esprit de corps* began to develop, and even the militia began to think of themselves as soldiers. Of course this was all Scott's work. Brown knew little of the technicalities of soldiering; his military virtues were those of aggressiveness and determination. But he supported Scott, even to the extent of approving the public execution of five deserters who had quit the camp in protest against the ten hours of drill each day. Only four were shot. The fifth, a boy in his teens, was put through a ceremonial execution, the firing squad having no balls in their muskets; he was spared because he was under military age.[5]

Painful as this kind of thing must have been to all concerned, it did have the desired effect: desertions came to an end and discipline improved. On 7 June, when Armstrong instructed Brown to move into Canada, the troops went willingly and confidently. Brown's orders were to cross the Niagara River above the Falls and, with the support of Chauncey's fleet, to move north; Burlington Heights and York were to be the ultimate

84. Major General Jacob "Smuggler" Brown, who commanded the American forces in the Niagara peninsula in 1814

objectives. Brown's force totalled slightly under 5000, exclusive of the Indians, but effectively numbered only 3500, allowing for the ill and the absent.

IN UPPER CANADA the legislature met on 15 February and continued in session until 14 March. When the roll of members was called, three were recorded as prisoners and two as deserters to the enemy. Acting as administrator of the province, Sir Gordon Drummond thanked Divine Providence for protecting it against the invaders, and spoke in particular of the defeat of Wilkinson at Crysler's Farm, the burning of Niagara and the occupation of Fort Niagara. He recommended confiscation of the property of traitors (the proceeds to be applied to the relief of suffering caused by the war), the embodiment of militia detachments of no more than one-third the strength of each corps, and restraints upon the distillation of grain. The members of the Assembly proved amenable. Among the Acts passed were those authorizing the suspension, when necessary, of *habeas corpus*, the forfeiture of inheritance upon attainder for treason, the declaring vacant of the seats of Joseph Willcocks and Abraham Markle, and the circulation of army bills. At the same time, Drummond applied to Lord Bathurst for authority to erect new legislative buildings at York to replace those burned by the Americans in April 1813. He also made arrangements for the purchase of a press from Ogdensburg for the sum of £84 7s 6d. However, Drummond could not persuade the Assembly to agree to impose martial law in special areas, particularly in the Midland and Newcastle districts, where he had encountered opposition to his measures to ensure adequate food and forage for the armed forces.[6] He did draft the necessary document, but decided to withhold it until "circumstances of necessity" should "imperiously" require its publication.[7]

Meanwhile, military plans were being matured in anticipation of an early renewal of hostilities. On 11 March, Drummond thanked Prevost for dispatching the 103rd Regiment to Upper Canada, but emphasized the need for further reinforcements. Without help from Lower Canada in both men and provisions, he doubted that he could hold the Niagara frontier, as he could, under no circumstances, draw upon the garrisons of Kingston and York, which were potential targets of hostile enemy action. Several days later he agreed with Riall that the enemy would likely make its major effort in the Niagara area, probably crossing the river and landing a subsidiary force at Long Point or Fort Erie. "An attack of such a general and combined nature," he wrote to Riall,

> if made, as it doubtless will be, in force, you can have no hope of successfully resisting by any other means than a concentration of your whole force at Burlington or Ancaster, leaving for the moment the garrisons of Fort Niagara and Fort George to themselves and those means of defence which it is expected that they possess and will most strenuously exert.[8]

That was not intended to mean that Riall should allow the Americans to march freely to Burlington Heights. Riall was to retire fighting. Should a small party of enemy threaten Burlington Heights by the back door from Detroit, a move Drummond considered possible but not likely, a *corps d'observation* of Indians and militia would be sufficient to occupy their attention. Meanwhile, all posts between Fort Erie and Fort George were to be occupied, especially Chippawa. One point on which Drummond was adamant was the maintenance of a strong garrison at Fort Niagara, with adequate support available from Fort George. Both forts would serve to tie down an American army in siege operations, and make it possible for British fighting patrols to operate against the American rear should the enemy contemplate bypassing the two forts for an attack on Burlington Heights.

DRUMMOND did not believe in maintaining a static defensive posture. Informed by an American deserter, Constant Bacon, of the extent of the American preparations at Buffalo and of the existence of supply depots along the south shore of Lake Ontario, Lieutenant Colonel Robert Nichol suggested to Drummond that a spoiling raid along the lake would provide the British with needed provisions and at the same time handicap the Americans, who were relying on these depots to supply their invasion force. Nichol's argument appealed to Drummond, for the assistant commissary general, Edward Dance, had told General Riall that, with the consumption of flour at the rate of 2000 barrels a month (excluding the militia and the garrison at York), "no effort of human exertions can supply this army many months longer, for the flour is not in the country."[9] Drummond had, in fact, been thinking along these lines earlier and had wondered about the possibility of another attack on Sackets Harbor. Such an attack, if successful, would cripple any operations the Americans might be planning against Upper Canada; it might even help bring the war to an end. But Prevost was wary of risking too much in a single operation. Moreover, the views of the British government respecting the conduct of the war did not encourage gambles of this kind. But when Drummond suggested an attack on Oswego as an alternative to Sackets Harbor, Prevost proved agreeable, and, on 4 May, Yeo's fleet sailed out of Kingston harbour with over 1000 soldiers drawn from Watteville's Swiss corps, the Glengarrians and the marines, and including a detachment of gunners and rocketeers armed with Congreve rockets. At 1500 hrs on the fifth, the ships lay to in front of Oswego.

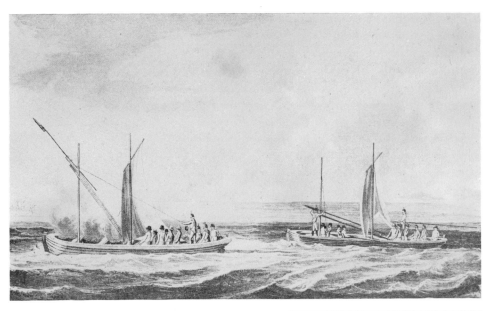

85. Top: *British armed boats with Congreve rockets on Lake Ontario in 1814.* Bottom: *The British also employed rocket gunners in the land battle at Plattsburg.*

Despite its important role during the Seven Years' War in North America, Oswego, the old Fort Chouaguen of the French period, was neglected during the War of 1812. Neither the Americans nor the British paid it much attention. The fort was not in good repair, even though large quantities of supplies were stored there awaiting transportation to Sackets Harbor. At an elevation of some 15 m above the lake the location was good, but the garrison numbered only 300 men. Thus, it was not a fortification calculated to offer much resistance to a determined attacker.

Given Drummond's temperament, one might have expected a speedy landing and a frontal assault on the American fort,

86. Storming Oswego, 6 May 1814

but it did not work out that way. Perhaps Drummond had absorbed some of Yeo's caution (Yeo had never displayed the aggressiveness of the officer under whom he had once served in the Royal Navy—Lord Nelson). In the early afternoon Yeo sent several gunboats in towards the fort to reconnoitre the extent of the harbour defences and to force the defenders to reveal the locations of their batteries. This accomplished, an attack was planned for 2000 hrs. Before then a wind blew up and, deciding that a landing should not be attempted during the squall, Yeo ordered the ships to move out into the lake. Meanwhile the American commander hurriedly set several hundred local militia to carrying the large quantities of war supplies housed in the fort to a hiding place in the woods some kilometres distant.

The next morning Yeo's ships were back again but, owing to the shallowness of the water near the shore, the two largest British vessels could not come in close enough to bring their cannon to bear on the fortifications. That task was turned over to smaller vessels, including *Montreal* (which was several times set on fire by red-hot shot) and *Niagara*. Weather conditions being favourable, the landing began. The Swiss were the first to disembark, under the command of Lieutenant Colonel Victor Fischer. Because the boats carrying the troops were facing the wind, they were slow getting ashore and were exposed to intense fire from the guns of the fort. Finally the landing was effected, and with a yell the Swiss and the Glengarrians stormed up the hill towards the defences, followed closely by the marines and sailors, armed with pikes. After that the fighting lasted only a matter of minutes. The American regulars retired in good order and the militia fled helter-skelter into the woods. Several of the attackers rushed towards the flagpole. One of them, Commander Mulcaster, was wounded and lost his leg as a result; another, Lieutenant John Hewett, "climbed the flagstaff under a heavy fire and, in the most gallant style, struck the American colours which were nailed to the mast".[10] That is how Yeo described it.

In the fighting, the British lost 15 soldiers killed and 62 wounded, and 3 sailors killed and 11 wounded. The American losses were largely in prisoners. Had the assault not been delayed by the wind and Yeo's caution, the gains in terms of stores would have been greater. As it was, the British were able to carry on board their vessels over a thousand barrels of flour, pork and salt, together with various naval supplies, including rope and tar. Nine guns were taken, and a quantity of shot and gunpowder was thrown into the Oswego River. The barracks and the works of the fort were burned. A schooner in the harbour that the Americans had scuttled was raised and taken to Kingston. Had the British pushed inland to the Oswego Falls, they would have found the big guns, cables and other equipment intended for the new ships Isaac Chauncey was building at Sackets Harbor. The capture or destruction of these items would have seriously handicapped the American fleet on Lake Ontario and perhaps kept it out of action for the rest of the summer.

To complete the task he had set himself, Yeo sailed for Sackets Harbor, and on 19 May set up a strict blockade to prevent the stores still at the Oswego Falls from reaching the American base. It was an action that stung Chauncey into writing:

> Five sail were now anchored between Point Peninsula and Stoney Island, about ten miles from the harbor, and two brigs between Stoney Island and Stoney Point, completely blocking both passes. . . . This is the first time I have ever experienced the mortification of being blockaded on the lakes.[11]

The only way for Chauncey to break the blockade and get the stores he needed would be to have troops sneak them along the

87. Carrying the cable from Sandy Creek to Sackets Harbor

coast in boats. This task he gave to Master Commandant Melancthon T. Woolsey, an old friend of James Fenimore Cooper. Woolsey loaded the cannon and heavy cables on bateaux and sent them downriver to Oswego; from there he attempted to run to Stony Creek under cover of darkness. But in the early dawn Woolsey's bateaux were sighted by Yeo's men, who captured one of them and chased the others up Sandy Creek. On 30 May, two British naval officers, Commanders Stephen Popham and Francis B. Spilsbury, with two gunboats and some smaller craft, moved into the creek in pursuit of the Americans, unaware that Woolsey had brought a number of riflemen and Indians with him. When the British landed they found themselves attacked in force. There was some fighting, short but desperate, during which Popham lost a master's mate, 18 men killed and nearly 70 wounded. When he discovered that he could not get his boats back along the winding creek, with Indians firing from each bank, he surrendered.

Not one of Popham's 200 men escaped to tell the tale, and Yeo learned of the extent of the disaster only when he received Popham's report, written from Sackets Harbor. It was the heaviest loss Yeo suffered during the whole war. If any advantage at all accrued to the British from this unfortunate episode, it was that the Americans did not again try to run the blockade; instead they constructed a wagon road from Rome to Sackets Harbor. The big ship's cable that had been stored at the Oswego Falls is said to have been carried from Sandy Creek through the woods on the shoulders of 200 farmer volunteers. True or not, the story of "carrying the cable" has become part of the folklore of northern New York State.[12]

MEANWHILE, Phineas Riall was still guarding the Niagara frontier with his long, thinly spread line of regulars, fencibles and militia. He did not have much longer to wait. Shortly after midnight on 3 July, the first units of the American invasion army embarked at Black Rock. It was raining, but despite poor visibility the first brigade, under the command of Winfield Scott, crossed the Niagara River and landed on the Canadian side exactly where planned and without casualties. Only Scott himself suffered a mishap. Anxious to be the first man ashore, he jumped too soon from his boat and, weighed down by a heavy cloak, high boots, pistol and sword, sank beneath the water, to be saved, indignant and spluttering with embarrassment and rage, by the boathooks of the oarsmen. The troops remained silent. Levity at Scott's expense could be dangerous. That much the American troops already knew. The lessons of Scott's discipline had been learned the hard way!

A mounted British patrol caught sight of the enemy, fired a few shots and then galloped off to inform Riall of the enemy landing. The American second brigade, under Eleazer Wheelock Ripley, followed Scott, landing at daybreak, and was followed in turn by Peter B. Porter's brigade. By noon all 3500 Americans were ashore. They encountered no resistance at Fort Erie. Its works were open and indefensible on the land side; the garrison numbered no more than 137, all ranks; and the commandant, Major Thomas Buck of the 8th, rather than sacri-

88. *Brigadier General Winfield Scott, who served throughout the war on the Niagara front*

fice his men, surrendered them and himself as prisoners of war after firing a few token shots from his cannon to save his honour. Drummond had hoped that Fort Erie would offer sufficient resistance to detain the Americans for several days while Riall could gather his troops, but Buck's surrender enabled the Americans to press forward at once for Chippawa. At the same time a force of American militia was sent from Buffalo to Lewiston to threaten Queenston and Fort Niagara and tie down the garrisons at those places.

It was 0800 hrs when Major General Riall, at his headquarters in Fort George, learned of the American landing. At once he ordered the Royal Scots to set out for Chippawa and, like Brock in October 1812, went on horseback to meet the enemy, gathering the garrisons in the various outposts as he went and dispatching them towards the enemy. The 8th Regiment of Foot, which had been ordered to Lower Canada for a period of rest and recuperation and had only reached York, was ordered to return at once to the Niagara peninsula. Captain William Merritt, who was just sitting down with his parents at Twelve Mile Creek to celebrate his twenty-first birthday, rushed off to Fort George, where he found "everything in activity, and all the troops which could be spared rapidly filing off on the road to Chippawa".[13] As the Americans pushed forward on the morning of 4 July, the clear sky gave promise of a warm and sunny day. Before them the British light troops from Colonel Thomas Pearson's command at Chippawa slowly withdrew, doing what damage they could to the bridges to hamper the American advance and buy time for the arrival of Riall and his reinforcements. Several times Scott was compelled to repair the planking over the bridges, and by sunset he had only reached the Chippawa River. North of the river, Pearson and the Marquis of Tweeddale, who had just arrived from Quebec to take over command of the 100th Regiment, joined hands with Riall's men when they arrived and threw up entrenchments for the guns. Winfield Scott, discovering that he had outdistanced the other two American brigades, fell back behind Street's Creek, about 1.5 km south of the Chippawa River. Here he encamped for the night, with Ripley's and Porter's brigades not far away.

On the following morning, Scott took breakfast in a Canadian farmhouse just north of Street's Creek, narrowly missing capture by some British Indians. Whether the lady of the house, Mrs. Samuel Street, had informed the Indians of Scott's presence is not known. Showing a fine burst of speed, Scott and his aides barely succeeded in getting safely back to their camp south of the creek. Behind the Indians came a few Lincoln militia, who skirmished in the woods with some American Indians until Porter's brigade of Pennsylvanians was ordered to chase them away. Neither Brown nor Scott was particularly disturbed by the presence of the Indians and the militia, as they doubted that Riall, with his smaller force north of the Chippawa River, would venture to attack; he would probably wait in his entrenchments until they took the initiative. For that reason, Scott arranged for a belated Fourth of July dinner to be served his men as a reward for their exertions on the previous day; it was to be followed by a dress parade.

89. Brigadier General Peter B. Porter, one of the War Hawks of 1812

In midafternoon Scott was taken by surprise to learn from scouts that British troops were crossing the bridge over the Chippawa and marching south in column, directly towards Street's Creek. He knew what this would mean: Riall would catch Porter's men on the flank. That is what did happen. Before long, Porter's Pennsylvanians, in complete confusion, came streaming back over Street's Creek on the double. At once Scott moved to Porter's aid. With his brigade already assembled for their parade, he crossed Street's Creek and drew up in line formation on the flat plain between the creek and the Chippawa River. From the north came the British. Riall was acting on advice from Sir Gordon Drummond, who had assured him that

311

90. "Those are regulars, by God!" Winfield Scott's brigade at Chippawa, 5 July 1814.

American troops lacked discipline and training, and that he could afford to take chances not normally acceptable in warfare in Europe; that was why Riall resolved to seize the initiative and attack the larger enemy formation opposing him. The tactical dispositions of the two armies were reminiscent of warfare in the Spanish peninsula, but not in the manner one might have expected. Scott relied upon the line formation favoured by Wellington, while Riall made use of the column approach characteristic of French infantry tactics. When he first saw Scott's men crossing Street's Creek, Riall, like several other British officers, believed that the grey uniforms worn by the Americans indicated militia; but as the regiments wheeled into line with precision and steadiness, Riall took another look at them. "Those are regulars, by God!" he cried.[14]

Then the battle began. Load and fire; advance a few paces; halt, load and fire again. Those were the standard field tactics of the day. Finally, when the two armies were close enough to one another, the exchange of musket fire would give way to a charge with the bayonet. As men fell to the ground, their places would be taken by others. As the British advanced, Winfield Scott held back his centre, pushing forward his wings, thus exposing the attacking force to both frontal and flank fire. Enfiladed from three directions, the British columns began to disintegrate. Their casualties had been severe, more severe than expected, too severe for the men to respond to the challenge of hand-to-hand combat. Almost all their officers had been wounded, including two of the battalion commanders, Lieutenant Colonel John Gordon of the Royal Scots and Lieutenant Colonel the Marquis of Tweeddale of the 100th. According to the latter, Gordon was shot in the mouth while urging his men to the attack; "he . . . became speechless", wrote Tweeddale in his recollections of the war![15] Riall did his utmost to rally his men. He had handled the tactical side of the battle with more impetuosity than skill, allowing his regiments to fight individually rather than as an army, and permitting gaps to develop between regiments, gaps that the enemy successfully exploited. Towards the end of the day, it almost seemed as if Riall deliberately sought death. When his army began to break, he did not, like Procter, mount his horse and dash away to safety. Instead, he drove his horse straight at the Americans as if intent upon suicide. His aide rode with him. But when his aide was wounded, Riall turned back to follow his men, one of the last to leave the field. History may consider him guilty of poor judgement, but never of personal cowardice.

The losses on both sides were heavy. The British reported 148 killed, 221 wounded and 46 missing or taken prisoner; 80 per cent of the casualties were among the officers and men of the Royal Scots and the 100th. Young Merritt, who arrived with a few militia dragoons after the battle was over, found "every house . . . filled with the wounded". In his journal he wrote, "I stopped at Street's, and spent a very unpleasant night; many of the officers were lying wounded, groaning with pain. Such was the result of the battle of Chippawa."[16] The American losses amounted to an aggregate of 327 killed, wounded or taken prisoner, practically all of them from Winfield Scott's brigade, which had borne the brunt of the fighting on the American side. In his confidential report to Prevost, Drummond spoke highly of the conduct of the British troops and the Canadian militia; but he spoke equally highly of the "steadiness" of the Americans.

Admitting that the enemy had won the Battle of Chippawa, Drummond was nevertheless not prepared to give up the Niagara peninsula. He ordered additional troops, including Morri-

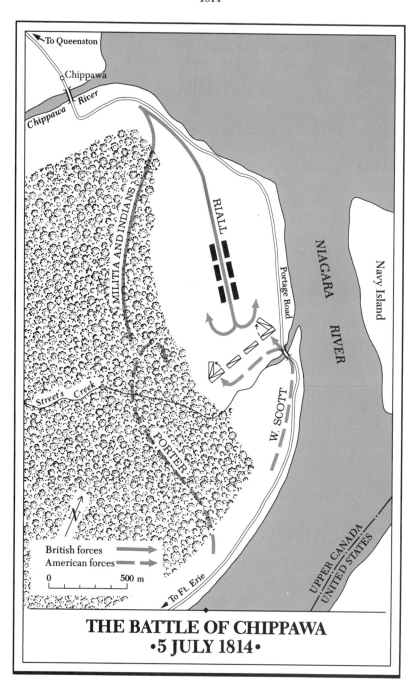

THE BATTLE OF CHIPPAWA
•5 JULY 1814•

son's 89th and the Battalion of Incorporated Militia, to be sent
at once to Fort George, and urged Prevost to hurry forward
the 6th and the 82nd to Kingston, where only Watteville's and
the 104th were in garrison. Meanwhile, Riall could not be ex-

pected to hold the line at Chippawa; he would have to pull back in the direction of Fort George.[17]

Two days after his victory, Brown started to move northwards. He turned Riall's position at Chippawa, and the British general promptly withdrew his forces. The Americans followed them along the Portage Road to Queenston. A small fortification had been erected on the Heights where Sheaffe had forced the surrender of Scott in 1812, and the Americans rather expected the British to attempt a stand there; but on their arrival they found that the British troops had abandoned the region and withdrawn to Fort George and Fort Mississauga. In the distance Brown could see the blue waters of Lake Ontario. He searched anxiously for the white sails of Chauncey's fleet from Sackets Harbor. Both Fort George and Fort Niagara were within his grasp—or so he believed—but he would need the big guns that Chauncey could bring, as well as Chauncey's cooperation on the lake to prevent any water-borne reinforcements from reaching the two forts. He also needed the supplies that were waiting in the several depots along the south shore of Lake Ontario. Without Chauncey's help, Brown would have to rely entirely on his lengthening supply line from Buffalo, which was exposed to interception by British Indians and Canadian militia. Not that he was afraid of either in a battle; but as raiders they could be a considerable nuisance, as Hull had found to his discomfort in 1812.

On 10 July, Porter arrived at Queenston, having mended the bridges along the supply line to Buffalo. Now where was Chauncey? For ten days Brown waited, growing daily more impatient and daily more annoyed by constant skirmishing with Riall's light troops and the Upper-Canadian militia.[18] And every day that passed meant Riall would be rebuilding his strength. Twice Brown approached Fort George, hoping to entice the garrisons into battle outside the defence works of Fort George or Fort Mississauga, but on neither occasion did they take the bait. Riall, though not in Fort George, hovered at Twenty Mile Creek, near enough to discourage Brown from undertaking a formal siege without the heavy guns he needed and the support of Chauncey's ships of war.

On 13 July, Brown sent an urgent appeal to Chauncey:

> I arrived at this place on the 10th, as I assured you that with the blessing of God I would. . . . Meet me on the lake shore north of Fort George with your fleet, and we will be able, I have no doubt, to settle a plan of operations that will break the power of the enemy

91. Commodore Isaac Chauncey, whose unwillingness to co-operate with Brown enabled the British to hold the Niagara peninsula in 1814

in Upper Canada, and that in the course of a short time. At all events let me hear from you. . . . I do not doubt my ability to meet the enemy in the field, and to march in any direction over his country—your fleet carrying for me the necessary supplies. We can threaten Forts George and Niagara, carry Burlington Heights and York, and proceed direct to Kingston and carry that place. For God's sake let me see you. . . .

If you conclude to meet me at the head of the lake and that immediately, have the goodness to bring the guns and troops that I have ordered from the harbor.[19]

But Chauncey did not come. He was laid up with a fever—a convenient malady, for he had no intention of allowing his fleet to be used to transport army supplies; that was too ignoble a task for the navy. Chauncey therefore ignored Brown's request. He ignored, too, instructions from Washington to give Brown his full cooperation. When word reached Sackets Harbor that Stephen Decatur might be sent to replace him, Chauncey quickly recovered and Decatur remained in New York.

On 15 July, Porter's brigade reconnoitred Fort George and Joseph Willcocks guided an American officer, an engineer, close to the walls of the fort to examine the defences in detail. Brown used Willcocks and Benajah Mallory extensively during the summer of 1814, and both narrowly escaped capture while leading foraging parties in the neighbourhood. Willcock's Canadian Volunteers and American militia made themselves thoroughly obnoxious to the people of the lower Niagara region during these weeks. According to William Merritt:

> The militia were daily skirmishing and driving in [United] States' parties, who were plundering every house they could get at; they even plundered women of everything they had [including "soft soap"]. . . . The bewildered families were obliged to leave their homes and place themselves under the protection of the army.[20]

Major Daniel McFarland of the 23rd U.S. Infantry wrote to his wife that the Canadian renegades and American militia had "plundered and burnt everything. The whole population is against us; not a foraging party but is fired on, and not unfrequently returns with missing numbers."[21] St. Davids, especially, suffered at the hands of the American marauders. McFarland mentioned that the American militia had burned thirty or forty houses on 19 July, and Major David Secord listed various buildings destroyed by a detachment that said that "it was their avowed intention to burn, plunder, and destroy that Tory village."[22] In fairness to Brown, it should be said that he highly disapproved of conduct of this nature. Lieutenant Colonel Isaac Stone, the New York militia officer who was responsible for the sacking of St. Davids, was promptly dismissed from military service.

Meanwhile, reinforcements had been steadily increasing the size of Riall's force. The militia came in good numbers, leaving their hay uncut; the Glengarrians arrived from York; the 89th arrived under command of the victor of Crysler's Farm, Joseph Morrison, and the 103rd under Hercules Scott; and two companies of the 104th under Lieutenant Colonel William

Drummond of Kelty came to Twelve Mile Creek from Burlington Heights. This buildup on his flanks worried Brown and he began to reconsider his plans. Perhaps the best course would be to retire to Chippawa, take stock of the situation, refit his army, bypass the two forts at the mouth of the Niagara, and go on to Burlington Heights. One thing was certain; he would have to get provisions from Fort Schlosser. He therefore pulled back from Fort George to Queenston, masking his withdrawal by a strong force of riflemen and dragoons.

Riall was kept well informed of what was happening in the American army by deserters as well as by his own militia and light troops, of whom one of the most active was Captain James FitzGibbon of Beaver Dams fame. But Riall was under orders not to act precipitately, since General Drummond was thinking of sending several companies from Fort Niagara along the east bank of the river to seize guns in the Youngstown area, as they would obviously be used by Brown for any siege of Fort George. All that Riall was supposed to do was march to St. Davids and "concentrate the whole of the regular force . . . at that place, throwing the militia and the Indians into the woods towards the enemy's position and the lake".[23] This move, Drummond believed, would deter Brown from sending reinforcements to Youngstown to counter any attempt to seize American guns on the east bank. However, should the enemy, "by pressing suddenly and boldly on you, make an action unavoidable", Riall was to,

> by means of the Glengarry Light Infantry and Incorporated Militia, endeavor to check his light troops until you reach an open space in which, keeping your guns in your centre and your force concentrated, your flanks secured by light troops, militia and Indians, you must depend upon the superior discipline of the troops under your command for success over an undisciplined though confident and numerous enemy.[24]

Sir Gordon would move to Fort George to check the accuracy of the intelligence Riall had received of the strength and intentions of the Americans. Should the situation look favourable, Drummond would be prepared to risk attacking with the whole of the British forces on the frontier, including the garrisons of Fort George and Fort Niagara. It would be an all-out battle. These were the instructions he sent to Riall from York on 23 July.

Meanwhile, Brown continued his slow retirement. He abandoned Queenston and moved south towards Chippawa. He rather hoped that Riall would be rash enough to attack at once and was disappointed when he found that only a few militia and light troops had followed him as far as Queenston. The "broken-wing" strategy that he had hoped would encourage Riall to rush into battle failed to produce the desired result, but even more disappointing was Chauncey's failure to bring him the heavy siege guns. On 25 July, Brown wrote to Armstrong, "You know how greatly I am disappointed, and therefore I will not dwell on that painful subject, and you can best perceive how much has been lost by delay."[25] When he wrote those words he did not know that within a few hours he would find himself engaged in what was to be the bloodiest battle of the War of 1812.

Brown was startled when he learned that British troops were moving south from Fort Niagara on the east bank of the Niagara River. What could this mean but a British attack upon Fort Schlosser, the advanced supply depot he had to rely on in the absence of help from Chauncey at Sackets Harbor? But to cross the river to assist Fort Schlosser would be difficult, and to get troops forward from Buffalo would take too long. His response would have to be to threaten Fort George. That is why he instructed Winfield Scott to turn about and move his brigade northwards along the west bank towards the mouth of the Niagara River. Perhaps this would induce the British to call a halt to the Schlosser operation. Scott moved with alacrity after receiving his orders at about 1600 hrs on the twenty-fifth. As he advanced he detected some mounted British officers in the vicinity of the Falls. They vanished after a few moments and, although he heard rumours that British troops were in the neighbourhood, Scott saw nothing suspicious and continued to push ahead. As he neared Lundy's Lane, a road running at right angles from the Portage Road up and over a gentle slope before angling off in the direction of De Cou (DeCew) Falls and the road to Burlington Heights, he suddenly caught sight of Riall's army. The ground near the Niagara was heavily wooded, but that along the lane had been cleared, and near the top of the sloping ground over which the lane ran stood a small church and a graveyard. Scott began at once to deploy his brigade for battle, at the same time sending a request to Brown to order the remainder of the American army forward as quickly as possible.

Aware that the Americans were preparing for battle but still under orders not to provoke attack, Riall began to withdraw. However, Sir Gordon Drummond, who had arrived with rein-

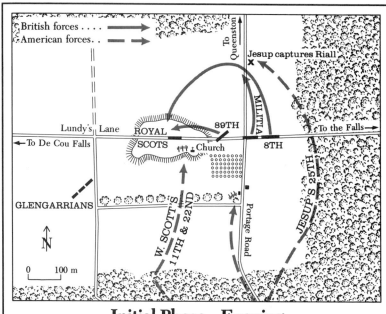

Initial Phase – Evening
25 July 1814

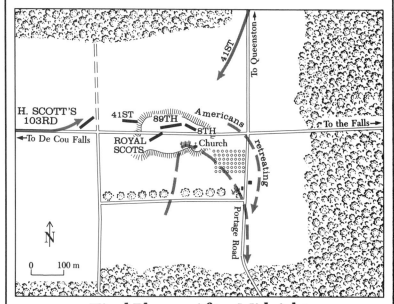

Final Phase – After Midnight
26 July 1814

THE BATTLE OF LUNDY'S LANE

forcements from York that morning, at once countermanded Riall's orders. He told the artillery gunners to hurry forward and place their cannons on the slope near the church; the 89th were to support them as quickly as possible. Thus, by the time Scott was out of the woods along the Portage Road and fully deployed, the British, stretched out along Lundy's Lane, were ready for him. The Glengarrians were on the right, with the 89th, some of the Royal Scots and a company of the 41st on the slope in the centre, behind the guns. The Incorporated Militia and a company of the 8th were on the left, covering the Portage Road. Not yet on the battlefield, but on their way to support Drummond, were Lieutenant Colonel Hercules Scott and the 103rd, ordered up from Twelve Mile Creek, as well as the force that Lieutenant Colonel J.G.P. Tucker of the 41st had led out of Fort Niagara towards Youngstown.

Drummond had scarcely completed these dispositions when the Americans began the action by sending their skirmishers forward to feel out the British position and, if possible, determine the British strength. At this point, Brigadier General Winfield Scott realized that he was in a tight spot. For the moment he was outnumbered and could not withdraw except by re-forming his line into a column and retiring along the Portage Road. To do this would be to invite attack while in a vulnerable position. His only choice then was to avoid disaster by attacking. As Drummond put it in his report, the British had scarcely taken up their positions "when the whole front was warmly and closely engaged".[26] Employing his full force, Scott thrust his men forward against the British left and centre. Despite their best efforts the Americans could make no impression on the centre, where the British gunners broke up charge after charge by two American regiments, the 11th and the 22nd Infantry. On the British left, however, Major Thomas Jesup's 25th Infantry succeeded in circling through the woods east of the Portage Road, thus outflanking the militia and the handful of Royal Scots present at that point. During this manoeuvre they came across a group of British officers, including General Riall, and in the ensuing skirmish Riall was wounded in the arm and taken prisoner. Shortly afterwards, the young Canadian dragoon, Captain William Merritt, was captured by "six fellows who were skulking from the fire which then raged with great fury".[27] These unexpected successes, however, gave the Americans no material advantage, as the British troops who had initially been forced back re-formed facing the road, thus securing their flank

92. *The British defence of the guns at Lundy's Lane, 25 July 1814*

and blocking any chance the Americans might have had of getting in behind the 89th. In the centre, supporting the artillery, the infantrymen of the 89th, Royal Scots, 8th and 41st, "with the most perfect steadiness and intrepid gallantry" resisted all the American attacks.[28] It was hand-to-hand, close-quarters fighting.

By this time it was 2100 hrs, the sun had set and it was beginning to grow dark. Yet no decisive success had been achieved by either side. Meanwhile, Ripley's and Porter's brigades had joined forces with the much-battered brigade commanded by Winfield Scott. At the same time the remainder of the British troops, including the 103rd Regiment under Hercules Scott, the headquarters company of the 8th, the flank companies of the 104th and some detachments of militia, had reached the battleground. After "a short intermission", the fighting resumed with vigour. To the Americans it was obvious that possession of the guns near the church was the key to success or failure, and Ripley made a determined effort to seize them. Masking the advance of the 21st Infantry in the dusk by a determined attack by the 23rd and 1st on the south face of the slope, Lieutenant Colonel James Miller succeeded in getting close to the British gunners, and in overwhelming them with a sudden bayonet charge. Once the 21st was in possession of the guns, the other American regiments advanced again and all of the high ground fell to Ripley's assaults. Sir Gordon Drummond described the action in this fashion:

> In so determined a manner were these attacks directed against our guns that our artillerymen were bayoneted by the enemy in the act of loading, and the muzzles of the enemy's guns were advanced within a few yards of ours. The darkness of the night during this extraordinary conflict occasioned several uncommon incidents. Our troops having for a moment been pushed back, some of our guns remained for a few minutes in the enemy's hands; they were, however, not only quickly recovered, but the two pieces, a six-pounder and a five-and-a-half-inch howitzer, which the enemy had brought up, were captured by us, together with several tumbrils, and in limbering up our guns at one period one of the enemy's six-pounders was put by mistake upon a limber of ours, and one of our six-pounders limbered on his, by which means the pieces were exchanged, and thus, though we captured two of his guns, yet as he obtained one of ours we have gained only one gun.[29]

In stating that the British guns had remained in American possession only "for a few minutes", Drummond was doing less than justice to both his own troops and those opposing him. The fighting actually continued for some hours after Ripley's successful assault, frequently at a distance of no more than twenty paces, during a night of crashing volleys, shouts, smoke, wild eyes, contorted faces.

Drummond had no choice but to do his utmost to recover his former strong position and to do so without the help of field-pieces. To fail was to fall. Three times his weary troops charged with the bayonet an equally weary enemy clinging desperately to the precious bit of ground they had gained. Had either army possessed fresh reserves the end would probably have come quickly, but both had already committed everything they had. Casualties on both sides were heavy even though, in the darkness, the troops could only aim at the flashes of their opponents' muskets. Jacob Brown and Winfield Scott were both wounded, the former by a Congreve rocket. Sir Gordon Drummond was also injured. Two bullets passed through Ripley's hat, but he remained unhurt.

It was the Americans who withdrew first. Brown realized that, unless the British were prepared to give up, he would have to do so, for his men were exhausted and so in need of ammunition and water that they could no longer continue to hold the high ground they had won. Brown, therefore, gave the order to Major Jacob Hindman to collect the American guns and retire immediately. "We will all go back to camp," he said, "we have done all that we can."[30] The American troops accordingly began to withdraw from the battlefield, but when Hindman returned with horses to draw off the British guns he found that the British had once again occupied the slope, had recovered their guns and even captured some of the American wagons and soldiers. In no position to contest the issue, Hindman slipped quietly away, leaving the weary British to lie down and rest on the field for which they had fought so hard. Drummond's own report had little to say about the second part of the battle, other than to attribute the British victory—after all, the British troops did remain in possession of the field—to "the superior steadiness and discipline of His Majesty's troops".[31] Perhaps he should have given credit to Brown's failure to keep a firm grip on the initiative that Miller and Ripley had won at considerable cost, and to the superiority of the British logistical arrangements over those of the enemy.

The British success was confirmed the next day. In the early morning Brown issued orders that Ripley should once more occupy Lundy's Lane; but when Ripley approached the battlefield he discovered that, not only had the British reoccupied the hill, but they had a few fresh troop reinforcements and had advanced to a position a little more than a kilometre in advance of the bloody lane. Ripley therefore turned about and went back to report to Brown. Drummond did not attack him, but watched him go. Because Brown had been injured seriously enough to require medical attention in Buffalo, Ripley found himself with command responsibility for the whole American force and decided to give up his position at Chippawa and retire to Fort Erie. This withdrawal was carried out with haste and disorder. Drummond's account stated that the enemy "abandoned his camp, threw the greatest part of his baggage, camp equipage and provisions in the rapids, and having set fire to Street's mill and destroyed the bridge at Chippawa, continued his retreat in great disorder towards Fort Erie."[32] Hardly the course of action that a victorious army would have followed.

Lundy's Lane was not only a hard-fought battle, it was a costly one. Drummond reported 5 officers and 76 other ranks killed, 30 officers and 532 other ranks wounded, and 14 officers and 219 men missing or taken prisoner. Brown gave his losses as 11 officers and 160 men killed, 53 officers and 520 men wounded, and 8 officers and 109 men missing or imprisoned. One of the British soldiers who took part was Sergeant James Commins of the 8th Foot; he described the battle at Lundy's Lane as "the most obstinate I ever was in, the Yankees was loth to quit their position, and being well fortified with whisky made them stand longer than ever they did. Some of them was so drunk as to stagger into our lines, but they suffered for their temerity."[33] Commins did not have a very high opinion of the Indians, who had remained clear of the fighting at Lundy's Lane but who, "as soon as they found the Yankees had retreated . . . assembled to the field to plunder the dead and dying." The scene the next morning was one that Commins never forgot:

> The morning light ushered to our view a shocking spectacle, men and horses lying promiscuously together, Americans and English, laid upon one another, occasioned by our advance and retreat. . . . It was found impossible to bury the whole so we collected a number of old trees together and burned them—which, although it may appear inhuman, was absolutely necessary and consequently justifiable.

It was an ugly and pathetic sight.

HOWEVER DISORGANIZED the American retreat from Chippawa may have been, there is no question but that Ripley promptly restored order and discipline on reaching Fort Erie. The fort had been too weak to withstand even two or three days' siege at the beginning of the campaign, but the Americans, anxious to maintain a bridgehead on the Canadian side of the Niagara River, had set to work at once to construct stone bastions to the rear and throw up earthworks by the water's edge. Batteries and breastworks had also been erected and the whole enclosed by an abatis. As soon as Ripley reached Fort Erie, he set his men to work adding to the strength of the fortifications to make them siege-worthy. Had Drummond moved with dispatch, he would have caught the Americans only partially prepared. But his men were exhausted; moreover, gaps in the ranks had to be filled, supplies obtained and heavy siege guns brought forward. Thus, it was 4 August before the British commander arrived at Fort Erie, with a force that included companies from Watteville's regiment and the 41st. The day before, he had sent a detachment of 600 men of the 41st and 104th regiments across the Niagara to Black Rock with the object of destroying the enemy's depots at Buffalo, but the men involved were overtaken by panic and an "unpardonable degree of unsteadiness, without possessing one solitary excuse".[34] Thus, an expedition that might have seriously handicapped the American garrison at Fort Erie had turned out to be a complete failure.

On 4 August the investment of Fort Erie began slowly and rather loosely. The next day a new American commander, Brigadier General Edmund Pendleton Gaines, arrived to replace Eleazer Ripley, who had been removed because of his retreat from Lundy's Lane. During the first week several armed American schooners moved freely between Fort Erie and Buffalo, occasionally sailing upriver to throw broadsides into the British camp opposite Black Rock. However, owing to the energy and initiative of Lieutenant Colonel Robert Nichol, several British boats were moved from below the Falls, and, on 12 August, Commander Alexander Dobbs of the *Charwell* and a handful of seamen and marines captured two of the three enemy vessels, *Somers* and *Ohio*, practically beneath the muzzles of the guns of Fort Erie. On 13 August the siege began in earnest, when Drummond's batteries fired the opening salvos at the fort. Hercules Scott, who was rather critical of the "innumerable delays" attending the opening of the siege—it had taken Drummond nine days to construct a four-gun battery—, believed that the siege guns were "not adequate to the reduction of the place",[35] a conclusion "Tiger" Dunlop agreed with. The fighting medical officer described them as being of George II vintage, "admirable guns in the field, though not quite the best that could be used for breaching the wall of a fort. . . . I very much doubt if one shot in ten reached the rampart at all, and the fortunate exceptions that struck the stone building . . . rebounded from its sides as innocuous as tennis balls."[36]

The date fixed for the assault of Fort Erie was 15 August. The operation, as planned, was one of the most difficult of all military manoeuvres, a night attack launched against different targets by three separate columns. The first, on the right, was to be led by Lieutenant Colonel Victor Fischer of Watteville's regiment; it comprised troops drawn from his own regiment and from the 8th, along with the light companies of the 89th and 100th, a dozen gunners and one rocketeer—in all about 1300 men. The second, or centre, column was commanded by Lieutenant Colonel William Drummond of Kelty, and included the flank companies of the 41st and the 104th and a number of seamen and marines. The third, or left, column consisted of the 103rd Regiment, under the command of Lieutenant Colonel Hercules Scott. A great believer in the intimidating effect

93. *The Regimental Colour of the Volunteer Incorporated Militia
Battalion, which was engaged at Fort Niagara on 19 December
1813, Lundy's Lane on 25 July 1814, and at the siege of Fort
Erie in August 1814.*

of the bayonet, Sir Gordon Drummond issued instructions that
his men were to remove the flints from the flintlocks, except
for "a reserve of select and steady men who may be permitted
to retain their flints".[37]

The first column to get under way was Fischer's, which began
to move towards its objective about 0200 hrs. Its task was to
capture a sandy mound called Snake Hill, which stood to the
right of the fort, between the fort and the lakeshore, and was
connected with the lakeshore by a line of palisades, ditches and
abatis. On top of Snake Hill stood an American battery under
the charge of Captain Nathan Towson, the American officer
who had commanded the American guns at Chippawa and Lundy's Lane. The initial assault troops, the "forlorn hope", led
by Major Charles de Villatte and Captain Thomas Powell,

managed to penetrate the American defence line, some of them by wading through the waters of the lake to bypass the palisade. Unfortunately, the noise made by the main body which followed alerted the defenders. Gaines put it this way:

> At half-past two o'clock, the right column of the enemy approached, and though enveloped in darkness black as his designs and principles, was distinctly heard . . . and promptly marked by our musketry and artillery.[38]

So galling was the fire of the American defenders that, not only did the main body of Watteville's regiment halt, it succumbed to panic. The men lost their discipline and, in their haste to get away, almost overwhelmed the men of the 89th, who tried to stand firm. The 8th, however, was carried away "like a torrent" by the terrified members of Watteville's corps.[39] Since this event took place in complete darkness, none of the three regiments were able to re-form until daylight, too late to renew the assault. The "forlorn hope", thus abandoned, gave themselves up as prisoners.

The centre and left columns, numbering about 250 and 650 men respectively, were supposed to advance as soon as Fischer's column became engaged and managed to secure a lodgement inside the American lines. When the sound of firing was heard on the right, Drummond of Kelty and Hercules Scott moved forward, the former towards the main fort and the latter towards a fortified battery referred to as the Douglass Battery. Unfortunately, Scott was killed early in the attack and his men, shaken by the intensity of the American fire, began to shift from their main axis of attack towards the centre, thus joining hands with the column led by Lieutenant Colonel Drummond. Three times this force tried to break into the fort; three times they were repulsed. The fourth attempt, however, proved successful. The British infantrymen overcame the American gunners and broke into one of the bastions. But they could get no farther; neither could the defenders dislodge them. There they remained, expecting support from the reserves. It does not stretch the imagination too far to suggest that, properly reinforced, they might in the end have captured Fort Erie. However, soon after daylight, during one of their repeated efforts to force a way into the main part of the fort, an ammunition chest caught fire and "a most tremendous explosion followed, by which almost all the troops which had entered the place were dreadfully mangled."[40] How Dunlop, who was with them, ever escaped alive he did not know. "I found myself scouring along the road at the top of my speed, with a running accompaniment of grape, canister and musketry whistling about my ears", he wrote in his war recollections.[41]

It was the battle of York all over again, except that on this occasion the British panicked, and none of the remaining troops could be persuaded to take advantage of the confusion. They were convinced that the explosion was deliberate, not accidental, and that other portions of the fort must be mined. The result was that the assault was abandoned and the Royal Scots, in reserve, were used, not as reinforcements, but to cover the retreat of the broken assault columns. The British losses were severe: 905 all ranks, of whom 366 were killed or wounded, the rest being classed as "missing", that is prisoners and deserters.

Both Hercules Scott and William Drummond were killed. Poor Scott had a premonition of death. Writing to his brother on 12 August, he gave instructions for the disposition of his estate, adding, "I expect we shall be ordered to storm tomorrow. I have little hope of success from this manoeuvre. I shall probably write you more, that is, if I get over this present business."[42] Oddly enough, William Drummond had felt a similar premonition and had given his sword to Dunlop. Another officer prepared for death, but with a happier outcome. James FitzGibbon asked for and received permission to leave the Fort Erie siege to go to Kingston to get married, promising to be back within three days. "I was desperate", he told Anna Jameson, "and the truth was, ma'am, there was a little girl that I loved, and I knew that if I could but marry her before I was killed, and I a captain, she would have the pension of a captain's widow."[43] He was married on 14 August, left his bride on the church steps and hurried back to Fort Erie, to survive the ill-fated siege.

The assault on Fort Erie was a disaster. Sir Gordon Drummond admitted as much when he wrote, in a private letter to Sir George Prevost:

> It signifies not to the public to whom the culpability of failure in military matters is attachable; the Commander, at all times, falls under censure, however high his character may have been. The agony of mind I suffer, from the present disgraceful and unfortunate conduct of the troops committed to my superintendence, wounds me to the soul![44]

While thus taking upon himself some of the responsibility for his defeat, Drummond was disposed to lay most of the blame for failure at the door of "the Foreign Corps".[45] Yet, the panic that overtook Watteville's regiment could just as easily have affected the British troops, and in actual fact did. Prevost, at least, saw it that way when he wrote, "Too much was required from De Watteville's regiment so situated and deprived, as I am told they were, of their flints."[46]

A more likely explanation of the British failure at Fort Erie than the unreliability of the foreign troops in British service was the inadequacy of the British artillery, the lack of surprise, and the adoption of a plan of operations requiring close timing and steadiness from troops neither experienced nor trained in night operations. It is not without significance that the only other night operation attempted during the War of 1812 was Murray's seizure of Fort Niagara in December 1813. In that instance, however, the surprise was complete and the numbers involved were small.

For the present, Sir Gordon stood his ground even though his situation at Fort Erie was grievous. Not only had his army been decimated by battle casualties—the 103rd, for example, had lost no fewer than 370 men—, it was also striken with sickness. Day after day the rain fell and the troops, living in makeshift huts, were constantly wet and their clothing and bedding damp and chill. The camp was becoming, as Drummond wrote, "a lake in the midst of a thick wood".[47] Provisions were in short supply and Chauncey was again sailing Lake Ontario without interference from Yeo, who was sticking close to Kingston while building his great ship *St. Lawrence*. Drummond had to give some relief to his men. He therefore sent his six companies of the 41st to Fort George and the remnants of the 103rd to Burlington Heights, replacing them with the 6th and the 82nd.

Changes in command and in the composition of the American garrison were also taking place. On 5 September the traitor Joseph Willcocks was killed when a detachment he was leading came under British fire. Ten days later Major General Jacob Brown, recovering from his wound, took charge at Fort Erie and brought to his command reinforcements of regulars and militia to strengthen the garrison. Anxious to redeem his reputation, Brown finally launched an attack on the British lines on 15 September. Taking advantage of a heavy rainstorm, the American assault troops managed to work their way through the woods to a position close to Drummond's batteries. Then, rushing the British position, they threw back the pickets and gained two of the batteries, which they proceeded to render useless, spiking the guns and blowing up the magazines. However, they could not capture the third battery, for the British recovered from their surprise and counterattacked the American assault force. The fighting was sharp and the casualties were severe on both sides. Drummond claimed a victory though it is hard to see why, since his position was now untenable. Three of his six ineffectual siege guns were disabled and his force had been so weakened by casualties and illness that to raise the siege was the only course he could, with reason, adopt. Immediately after the American sally, though reinforced by the arrival of the 97th Regiment, Drummond began making arrangements to withdraw. On 21 September he wrote to Prevost:

> The sickness of the troops has increased to such an alarming degree, and their situation has really become one of such extreme wretchedness from the torrents of rain which have continued to fall for the last 13 days, and from the circumstance of the division being entirely destitute of camp equipage, that I feel it to be my duty no longer to persevere in a vain attempt to maintain a blockade of so vastly a superior and increasing force of the enemy.[48]

The British withdrawal to Chippawa began that night.

Once again an opportunity seemed to present itself to the Americans to regain a firm hold on the Canadian side of the Niagara River. Major General George Izard, who replaced Brown as commander of the Northern Army, crossed the Niagara from Black Rock to a position several kilometres north of Fort Erie. With him came the first division of his army, 3500 strong, to be joined by Brown's second division, numbering 2800. At the Black Creek they halted for the night, while Drummond's rear parties were hurriedly destroying the bridges and burning all available forage. It must have all seemed very familiar to Brown, who had followed the same route only three months before. While at his camp on Street's Creek, Izard learned that Chauncey was no longer on the lake. The control of the waters had passed once more to Yeo, with his great ship of war the *St. Lawrence*, and Chauncey was back in Sackets Harbor, throwing up earthworks and batteries for the town's protection. Izard wrote to Armstrong:

> This defeats all the objects of the operations by land in this quarter. I may turn Chippawa, and, should General Drummond not retire, may succeed in giving him a great deal of trouble, but if he falls back on Fort George or Burlington Heights, every step I take in

pursuit exposes me to be cut off by the large reinforcements it is [now] in the power of the enemy to throw in twenty-four hours upon my flank or rear.[49]

Although he commanded not only the largest, but what was considered to be the most efficient, American army to march along the Portage Road during the Canadian War of 1812, Izard did no more with it than destroy several hundred bushels of wheat at Cooks Mills and retire to Fort Erie. He did not even remain there. He mined the fort and on 5 November blew it up, recrossing the river to Buffalo, where he sat down and wrote to the Secretary of War to inform him that he now proposed to devote attention to his health, "which has suffered considerably by the two last campaigns, and the restoration of which I can scarcely hope for if I remained the winter in this inclement climate".[50] Izard would spend the cold months in warmer and more pleasant regions; Drummond would spend them at Fort George and York.

12

The British Offensive

THE YEAR 1814 saw Major General James Wilkinson make a last feeble, limp-wristed gesture in the direction of Lower Canada before going to Washington to face the judgement of his peers. On 17 March he led an army of several thousand troops from Plattsburg to Chazy. From there he sent Colonel Alexander Macomb with a brigade of infantry to scour the country around Missisquoi Bay, and when Macomb returned the whole force crossed the frontier for the purpose of attacking the British position on the Lacolle River. The defences there consisted of a stone mill occupied by Major Richard B. Handcock of the 13th Regiment and a mixed bag of regulars, militia and marines, about 180 men in all. In the general vicinity were several other British posts, including Saint-Jean, Île aux Noix and Burtonville, that contained small garrisons. Probably there were about 1000 regulars and 400 militia available for the immediate protection of the frontier.

The snow was still on the ground when Wilkinson led his men into Lower Canada. Approaching Lacolle by way of Burtonville and Odelltown, he found his route along the Lacolle River blocked by Handcock's improvised fort. Wilkinson began his investment by closing off the line of retreat for Handcock's men, and then opened fire with his light artillery. A relief force from Île aux Noix tried to ease the pressure by charging the American gunners, but were driven off; a second attempt also failed. Two gunboats from Île aux Noix tried to help by throwing a few shells into the American position, with little apparent effect.

Meanwhile the men inside the stone mill were running perilously short of ammunition. Now was Wilkinson's chance, in fact his last chance. When he failed to take advantage of it and decided, instead, to withdraw his troops to the United States without assaulting the mill, he took the final step leading to military disgrace and historical obloquy. Wilkinson's failure at Lacolle was only one of the accusations brought against him during the investigation into his military command. It indicates the degree of mortification felt in high places in Washington over his miserable performance in Canada. But if Wilkinson lost a chance at Lacolle to apply a little polish to a tarnished reputation, so too did the governor general, Sir George Prevost, fail to halt the deterioration of his popularity. Had Prevost taken immediate advantage of the temporary collapse of American morale by moving aggressively into the area south of Burlington, where the Americans were busy building two ships of war, instead of waiting over a month to do so, he might well have altered the situation on Lake Champlain and spared himself the humiliation of defeat at Plattsburg later in the year.

DURING THE early months of 1814 Americans were reading with growing interest, not about the miserable meanderings of Wilkinson, but about the victorious progress of Allied arms in Europe. Napoleon had been pushed back across the Rhine. Despite his brilliant handling of his raw levies against the experienced troops of Blücher and Schwarzenberg in the valleys of the Marne and the Seine, it was obvious that the famous French commander was nearing his end. Finally forced back upon Fontainebleau, he abdicated at the demand of his war-weary marshals and the wishes of a war-weary France. Then, with Napoleon on his way to exile on Elba, stout old Louis XVIII, who had lived in exile for some twenty-three years, was invited to return to Paris to resume the throne from which his unfortunate brother had been expelled by the revolutionaries in 1791. In May 1814 a treaty was signed by the victorious Allies, and France and Britain resumed political and commercial relations. Once more in demand abroad, American goods, particularly cotton and tobacco, began to rise rapidly in price.

Everybody, military and civilian alike, knew that the events in Europe were certain to have a profound influence on the war in North America. The collapse of the French and British economic blockades and the disappearance of any need to impress sailors were bound to cut the ground from under the declared purposes for which the United States had gone to war. Even more significant, as far as continued hostilities in North America were concerned, peace in Europe would release for use against the United States both the ships and the soldiers Britain had previously employed against France. Thus, the British could adopt an offensive posture for the first time since Madison declared war in June 1812. Hitherto, British and Canadian actions in American territory had been limited to offensive–defensive actions, as the British forces in North America—regular, fencible and militia—had been too few and too poorly equipped to undertake any major offensives. But what would happen when Wellington's veterans, men proven in Spain and France, came up against the Hamptons and the Wilkinsons, or even the Scotts and the Browns, in North America? During 1813 the few reinforcements that Great Britain had been able to send to Canada, including such regiments as the 13th, the 89th and Watteville's Swiss mercenaries, had been able to hold their own against the best the Americans could hurl against them; but the dribble of 1813 would become the flood of 1814, with the 3rd (Buffs), 5th, 6th, 9th, 16th, 27th, 37th, 39th, 57th, 58th, 76th, 81st, 82nd, 88th, 90th and 97th arriving at Quebec in the spring, summer and autumn. It was inevitable that with these veterans would come instructions to Sir George Prevost to take the offensive against the Americans and attack their territory. As early as 6 January 1813, *The Times* of London had strongly criticized the War Office for failing to take positive action against the United States:

> Political cowardice alone, as we conceive, prevented Ministers from commencing the war against America in a style which the Americans themselves expected. It prevented them from having a plan matured and ready, for falling upon the sea-coasts of America, blocking up her ports, hindering her privateers from sailing and capturing and destroying every frigate she dared to send to sea. These would have been rigorous measures, but not more . . . than the Ministers had ample means at that time to effect. . . . The failure was not from want of means, but for want of a plan, and the plan, we have no doubt, would have been readily enough furnished by the proper Department, if the Cabinet had thought fit to call for it. . . . They bring out the impatient "dogs of war" muzzled and clogged.

The Times was perhaps less than fair in its criticisms, but peace negotiations could not be far off, and the British realized that if favourable terms were to be obtained they would need something to bargain with, and what better argument than actual possession when discussions turned to boundary adjustments? These adjustments were necessary to please the Indians and their friends the fur traders, and necessary, too, to improve communications between the Maritimes and the Canadas. A British offensive would not be designed to destroy the United States or reverse the Revolution, but rather to impose on the Americans a revision of the questionable boundary settlement of 1783.

THERE WERE three possible lines of invasion open to the British in 1814, the same three the Americans had used each year since the war broke out—Detroit, the Niagara and Lake Champlain. To these might be added a fourth, not yet attempted—the Atlantic coast. An operation down the Thames to the Detroit River would have recovered Forts Malden and Detroit, and possibly made inroads into southern Michigan and Indiana territories. But this was not a region of major strategic significance to the British any more than it should have been to the Americans; in any event, the British had neither regained supremacy on Lake Erie nor built up supplies in sufficient quantity at their depot at Burlington Heights to warrant such an operation. Sackets Harbor was a much more important military threat to Upper Canada than Detroit. To capture it would be to remove all fears of a serious attempt by the Americans against the Niagara peninsula. And control over Lake Ontario was even more important to the recovery of Detroit than supremacy on Lake Erie. Prevost would have liked to make another attempt against Sackets Harbor because of his failure in 1813. With 12 000 men standing idle in Montreal, he might have undertaken a twofold thrust against Sackets Harbor by land and by water, but was deterred by the lack of sufficient supplies and equipment at Kingston to meet the demands of the kind of force such a plan would require. As he pointed out to Lord Bathurst, transport on the St. Lawrence River had been stretched to the limit to meet the needs of the lake fleet and to build the *St. Lawrence*, and was simply not up to moving the necessary stocks in time for a major attack against Sackets Harbor.

Obviously, then, the offensive operation would have to take place along the Lake Champlain route. Montreal had the necessary provisions, military stores, men and boats, and the area had roads along which the stores could be moved as the army advanced. There were other arguments in favour of using the Lake Champlain route. Northwards, between French Mills and

Lake Memphremagog, through northern New York and Vermont, moved the herds of cattle and the fresh beef on which the British army in Lower Canada subsisted. The American army could not be permitted to interfere with this scarcely clandestine but wholly illicit trade that meant so much to the British. Actual occupation of the area would ensure the continuation of these supplies.

Some writers have suggested that there were political reasons for launching an attack along the Lake Champlain pass in that the northeastern part of the United States had been most outspoken in its opposition to the declaration of war and most lukewarm in its support of Madison and his War Hawks; perhaps the presence of a British army would encourage the opponents of the war to either rebel or make a separate peace with Great Britain. There is little documentary evidence to support this view, although it is known that a member of the House of Representatives for Massachusetts did consult Sir John Sherbrooke in Halifax about possible British help to New England should that region ever "stand in need of it".[1] A more significant political motive for the Lake Champlain invasion was that the British government had decided to do something about the huge Maine salient that the treaty of 1783 had thrust northwards between New Brunswick and Lower Canada and that irritated the people of the Maritimes as much as it handicapped the line of communications between Montreal and the Atlantic colonies. A short route from Montreal to an ice-free port was both a military and an economic necessity. An offensive along Lake Champlain would distract attention from Maine and would provide strategic cover to any British operation on the Atlantic coast.

DURING THE SUMMER of 1814, Major General Robert Ross was detached from Wellington's army for service in North America. His instructions were simply to "effect a diversion on the coasts of the United States of America in favor of the army employed in the defence of Upper and Lower Canada".[2] The troops allotted to him included three experienced British regiments, the 4th, 44th and 85th, all of which had served under Wellington. Together they numbered about 2800 men. In Bermuda they were joined by three more regiments, and the whole came under the strategic direction of the new commander of the North American Naval Station, Vice Admiral Sir Alexander Cochrane, whose predecessor, John Borlase Warren, had done little more than make "sportive thrusts"[3] against the United States coastline in the general direction of Washington and Baltimore. Cochrane's fleet set sail on 3 August, and twelve days later entered Chesapeake Bay. On the seventeenth, accompanied by a number of troop transports, Cochrane moved up the bay to the Patuxent and upriver as far as Benedict, Maryland, where he wrote a letter to the American secretary of state, James Monroe:

> Having been called upon by the Governor General of the Canadas to aid him in carrying into effect measures of retaliation against the inhabitants of the United States for the wanton destruction committed by their army in Upper Canada, it has become imperiously my duty, conformably with the nature of the Governor General's application, to issue to the naval force under my command an order to destroy and lay waste such towns and districts upon the coast as may be found assailable.[4]

The idea of attacking Washington, the capital of the United States, was not unreasonable, politically or militarily. Politically, such an operation, if successful, would demonstrate the power and mobility Great Britain possessed in her fleet and its capacity to strike at any point along the Atlantic coast; militarily, the operation would be simple because of the failure of the United States government to provide the capital with adequate defences. The American officer in charge at Washington was Brigadier General William H. Winder, whose achievements at the Battle of Stoney Creek were scarcely such as to inspire much confidence in the defenders. When word reached the city that British troops were on the way, the drowsiness characteristic of the people of Washington in the heat of mid-August gave way to excitement, action and confusion: civil servants rushing about, orders being issued to and by God-knows-who, women packing their belongings, crowds gathering, politicians talking, but little of anything being accomplished. Even Wilkinson got into the act, offering his services if his arrest were lifted. Meanwhile the militia gathered in great numbers, but few were adequately armed or uniformed, so they were dismissed and told to go home and find weapons. "Let no man allow his private opinions, his prejudices or caprices in favour of this or that particular arm or weapon of annoyance be pretended excuse for deserting his post", said Winder.[5]

After a gruelling march in the heat, from Benedict through Nottingham and Upper Marlboro, 3500 to 4000 British troops, commanded by Ross and supported by Rear Admiral Sir George Cockburn, reached the village of Bladensburg, a few kilometres

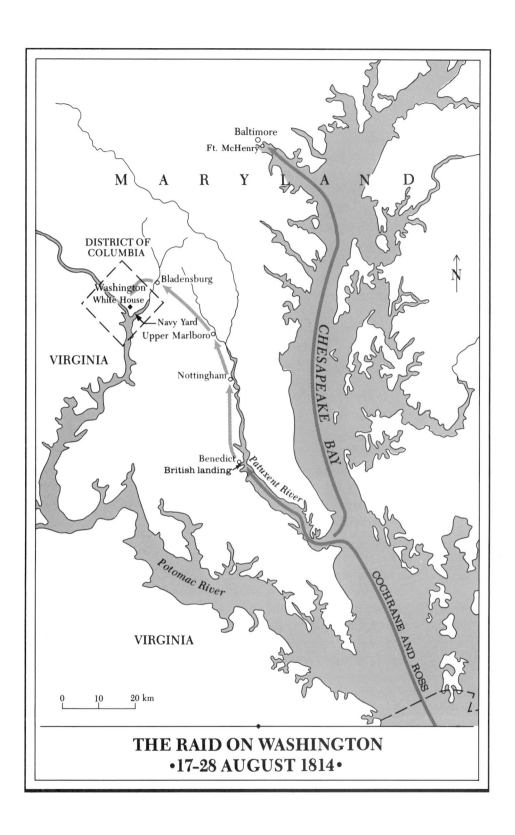

Baltimore

Ft. McHenry

M A R Y L A N D

DISTRICT OF
COLUMBIA

Bladensburg

Washington
White House

Navy Yard

Upper Marlboro

VIRGINIA

Nottingham

CHESAPEAKE BAY

Benedict
British landing

Patuxent River

Potomac River

VIRGINIA

COCHRANE AND ROSS

N

0   10   20 km

THE RAID ON WASHINGTON
•17–28 AUGUST 1814•

94. *The capture of Washington by the British, 24 August 1814*

northeast of Washington, where on 24 August they encountered the American defenders. The Americans outnumbered the British, and in Ross's opinion "were strongly posted".[6] The secretary of war, John Armstrong, did not take Ross's landing seriously and told his clerk he thought "we were under unnecessary alarm."[7] But Madison warned his wife to be ready to move on a moment's notice, before riding off to inspire the militia with his presence. Unfortunately for the Americans, their forces were dispersed and Winder was hopelessly indecisive. He was slow to get his troops assembled, and when he should have retired on Washington he delayed and then withdrew instead towards the Navy Yard, leaving the road to the capital open and undefended.

Bladensburg was not much of a battle. The British troops threw up a few sputtering rockets, and, when the light brigade attacked, most of the American militia turned and ran. "Never did men with arms in their hands make better use of their legs", wrote a young British officer, Lieutenant George R. Gleig.[8] One poor man ran himself to death; he was the sole casualty. To the British the battle became known as the "Bladensburg Races". Only Commodore Joshua Barney's seamen were prepared to stand and fight, and they inflicted the only casualties suffered by the British during the campaign. Perhaps Barney, rather than Winder, should have commanded the American troops, although the outcome is not likely to have been any different. Cockburn's report to London stated laconically that Ross had not followed up his victory more promptly because "the victors were too weary and the vanquished too swift."[9]

After a short rest, Ross's men resumed their march and reached the outskirts of Washington by nightfall. That night they burned the White House, the Capitol and other buildings; fires continued to burn the next day. But, the British soldiers apparently refrained from looting. Joseph Gales in the *National Intelligencer* said, "Greater respect was certainly paid to private property than has usually been exhibited by the enemy in his marauding parties. No houses were half as much plundered by the enemy as by the knavish wretches of the town who profited by the general distress."[10] Then, on 26 August, two days after the Bladensburg Races, Ross ordered his men back to the ships. Several months later, Sir George Prevost informed Canadians that, "as a just retribution, the proud capital at Washington has experienced a similar fate to that inflicted by an American force on the seat of government in Upper Canada."[11]

From Washington, Cochrane and Ross moved on to Baltimore. There the citizens were better prepared, having been warned in advance. The militia put up a stiffer resistance and retired fighting, and Fort McHenry withstood a strong naval attack. Major General Ross was among the casualties the British suffered. After two days' "demonstration", Cochrane and Ross's successor, Colonel Arthur Brooke, abandoned the attempt to take Baltimore and set sail for Halifax, where they rejoiced to learn that a British combined military and naval expedition under Sir John Sherbrooke had captured the American fort at Castine, at the mouth of the Penobscot River. Meanwhile, President Madison, who had spent almost four days on horseback despite his fragile health, also found cause to rejoice when news arrived from Lake Champlain that a small British fleet, urged by an impatient Sir George Prevost into a battle it was not ready for, had been pounded to pieces while thousands of British soldiers stood by watching in frustration.

ALTHOUGH THE Lake Champlain pass was clearly the most obvious route for any army based on Canada to carry war into the United States—a route that had been used at different periods by French, British and American troops alike—the War Department in Washington in 1814 did not seem to recognize it as such, perhaps because of Dearborn's and Wilkinson's failures in 1812, 1813 and the spring of 1814. In any event it was Lake Ontario, not Lake Champlain, that fascinated the makers of grand strategy in the United States in this, the last year of the Canadian war. Such, at least, seems to be the explanation for Armstrong's extraordinary order to Major General George Izard, who had taken over Wilkinson's army at Plattsburg, to march his army across northern New York State to Lake Ontario. If Armstrong believed, as he must have, that the Lake Champlain theatre of operations was going to remain quiet for the remainder of the year, then his intelligence service must have been deficient; or he simply did not read the London and Halifax dispatches that appeared regularly in the American newspapers. On 23 July, for instance, the *New-York Evening Post* printed news from both Great Britain and Nova Scotia dealing with the dispatch of Wellington's men to Canada to reinforce the British army in North America, and estimated their numbers to be between 10 000 and 15 000. Major General Izard was certainly aware of what was happening to the north. He was concerned about the buildup of British troops in Montreal, and he not only strengthened his own force to more than 6000 men, but also set about building new fortifications at Plattsburg. Nevertheless, on 27 July, Armstrong wrote to Izard asking him whether he would not be better employed in carrying out some spoiling actions along the St. Lawrence River between Lachine and Kingston than in remaining inactive at Plattsburg. Izard replied:

> I will make the movement you direct, if possible; but I shall do it with the apprehension of risking the force under my command, and with the certainty that everything in this vicinity but the lately erected works at Plattsburg and Cumberland Head will, in less than three days after my departure, be in the possession of the enemy. He is in force superior to mine in my front; he daily threatens an attack on my position at Champlain; we are in hourly expectation of a serious conflict.[12]

But Armstrong refused to give credence to Izard's fears. If anything, Izard's opposition only seemed to stiffen Armstrong's attitude, and he gave Izard a positive order to move to Sackets Harbor, and from there to carry out operations against Kingston or to go to Jacob Brown's assistance at Fort Erie. Izard obeyed, though with much reluctance. With about 4000 men he left Plattsburg for Sackets Harbor on 29 August. Behind him, under the command of Brigadier General Alexander Macomb, he left a miscellaneous collection of regulars and militia numbering about 3000. Admittedly, Macomb reported that his effective force totalled no more than 1500, but he counted only the effective regulars, omitting the convalescents, the raw recruits and the New York militia. Armstrong almost seemed to be inviting invasion, for within five days of Izard's departure for Sackets Harbor Sir George Prevost's army had crossed the American frontier and occupied the village of Chazy. Two days later, on 5 September, Sir George was within 13 km of Plattsburg.

Prevost's army was the largest yet assembled in British North America. It numbered 10 351 officers and men and was divided into three brigades, two of which were made up of Peninsular War veterans. The brigade commanders included Major Generals Thomas Brisbane, Manley Power and Frederick Robinson, all experienced officers who had served with distinction in Europe. Prevost's second-in-command was the solid but undistinguished Baron Francis de Rottenburg, whose command in Upper Canada had exhibited few signs of brilliance, originality or forceful determination. In view of the evident discontent of the British officers who, having occupied the centre of the European stage, found themselves committed to a colonial sideshow, it was particularly unfortunate that they should be berated by an unknown general for paying too little heed to such relatively unimportant matters as dress regulations. On 23 August, for instance, Prevost issued the following order:

> The Commander of the Forces has observed in the dress of several of the officers of corps and departments, lately added to this army from that of Field Marshal the Duke of Wellington, a fanciful vanity inconsistent with the rules of the service, and in some instances without comfort or convenience, and to the prejudice of the service, by removing essential distinctions of rank and description of service.
>
> His Excellency deems it expedient to direct that the general officers in charge of divisions and brigades do uphold His Majesty's commands in that respect, and only admit of such deviations from them as may be justified by particular causes of service and climate—and even then their uniformity is to be retained.
>
> Commanding officers are held responsible that the established uniform of their corps is strictly observed by the officers under their command.[13]

Sir George had made a poor start. To men to whom the Duke of Wellington had become a military genius greater than Napoleon, the untried, unproven Sir George Prevost would have to demonstrate that he deserved their respect and affection before he could get away with this kind of thing.

When Prevost crossed the frontier, Brigadier General Macomb withdrew his forward troops from Champlain, and the British continued to push forward. On the left was Brisbane's column using the road nearest the lake; on the right was Power's column taking the Beekmantown Road over higher and drier ground. Robinson's division marched in support of Power's. The American militia offered some opposition, but nowhere was their resistance such as to impede the British advance. However, there was some doubt in the minds of the troops as to what they were really doing. Robinson wrote some years later:

> It appears to me that the army moved against Plattsburg without any regularly digested plan by Sir George Prevost. There was neither guides, spies or plans. . . . A strange infatuation seems to have seized upon the mind of Sir George Prevost . . . that it was impossible to gain any intelligence that could be depended upon, and therefore it was throwing money away to attempt it.[14]

An odd stance for Sir George, who had many contacts in the United States with men who supplied him with information as well as beef. But if the British were puzzled, the Americans were frightened. According to Macomb, the American militia "fell back, most precipitately in the greatest disorder, notwithstanding the British troops did not deign to fire on them, except by their flankers and advanced patrols." So "undaunted" were the British regulars that they "never deployed . . . always pressing on in column".[15]

The British destination, Plattsburg, was a small place, located on both sides of the Saranac River. When the British entered the town on 6 September, Macomb pulled his men south of the river, removing the planking from the bridges and taking refuge in the fortifications erected by Izard prior to his departure for Sackets Harbor. These consisted of three redoubts and two blockhouses, the redoubts being known as Fort Brown, Fort Moreau and Fort Scott, the last on the lakeshore; the blockhouses were near the bay into which the Saranac River emptied. In the bay itself, under the protection of a protruding point called Cumberland Head, the American fleet was anchored, awaiting the arrival of the ships that Prevost had insisted should accompany the army on its advance. Other than their warships, the Americans did not have much to fight with; nevertheless, Macomb kept his militia busy annoying the British redcoats along the Saranac, hoping thereby to delay them from crossing the river. Meanwhile his regulars were set to work strengthening the fixed defences.

In all probability, had Prevost pushed his troops forward immediately upon entering Plattsburg, he would have destroyed Macomb's defending force. That, in fact, is what Prevost thought of doing; his first order to Robinson's brigade was to attack at once. However, when he found the passage over the Saranac blocked, Prevost countermanded the order. He would wait until the morning of 7 September, when the artillery, including a rocket battery, was to be brought up and placed in position on the bay shore. The battery was easily transportable and could be readily moved to threaten either ships or blockhouses. At this point Prevost admitted to Robinson that he did not know where the fords over the Saranac River were located or how far away the American fortifications actually were. By the time he acquired this information, Prevost had changed his mind again. Now he would await the arrival of Captain George Downie and the British ships on Lake Champlain; the battle for Plattsburg would be carried out simultaneously on water and on land.

On the ninth the weather changed for the worse, with more wind and rain. Taking advantage of these conditions, when men were inclined to stay under cover, a group of 50 Americans led by Captain George McGlassin, crossed the Saranac during the night and charged the British rocket battery. Rushing forward with fearful yells, the Americans were able to damage the battery sufficiently to put it out of commission. Prevost was mortified that his men should have been so easily put to flight. At the same time, towards midnight, he learned that Downie's fleet was ready and would round Cumberland Head at the entrance to the bay early the next morning.

Once again the attack was delayed. The troops were under arms, but when the ships did not appear they simply marched back to their quarters. Prevost wrote testily to his naval officer, stating that the land forces had been drawn up ready for battle and that he hoped the delay was the result of the unfavourable winds and nothing else. The taunt was obvious and it was not one that rested lightly on Downie. Another day thus passed without Prevost making any move. The weather began to improve, and the morning of the eleventh dawned bright and sunny, with a light wind. At first light the British ships began to make headway up the lake, heaving to at Cumberland Head to permit Captain Downie to make a reconnaissance in a small boat. After consulting his officers at 0800 hrs, Downie ordered his vessels to proceed to Plattsburg Bay. It had been understood that, as the British ships began to round Cumberland Head, Major General Robinson's division would press forward, cross the fords of the Saranac, covered by a feint by Brisbane at the two bridges, and, supported by artillery fire, would

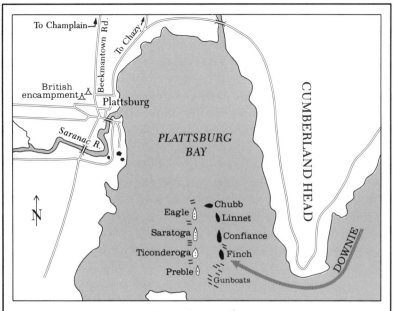

Naval Battle

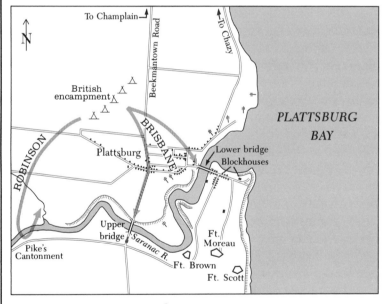

Land Operations

PLATTSBURG, 11 SEPTEMBER 1814

assault the flank of the American defence works on the south side of the river. On board the largest British vessel, Lieutenant James Robertson was encouraging the crew of HMS *Confiance* by telling them that the soldiers were about to commence their share in the battle.

The naval encounter lasted two hours and twenty minutes from the time the American brig *Eagle* fired the first broadside at about 0830 hrs. According to Prevost's own account, the land batteries began firing simultaneously with the guns of the ships of war, and the troops were given the order to proceed with their part of the plan. Unfortunately Robinson, whose assault force had been waiting since dawn, did not get his orders to start until 1000 hrs. When he did move, he took the wrong road and lost a whole hour retracing his steps to the ford at Pike's Cantonment. Meanwhile Sir George Prevost had kept his eyes glued to the battle in the bay, and when he saw both *Confiance* and *Linnet* strike their colours he decided to call off the land attack, "because", he wrote, "the most complete success would have been unavailing, and the possession of the enemy's works offered no advantage to compensate for the loss we must have sustained in acquiring possession of them."[16] Accordingly, Robinson was informed that, since it would "no longer be prudent to persevere in the service committed to your charge", he should "immediately return with the troops under your command".[17] The order came as a complete surprise to Robinson; true, Brisbane's men had been hotly resisted at the upper bridge, but his own veteran troops had already crossed the shallow waters of the stream, firing briskly by platoons as they advanced. Left to their own devices they would probably have continued with what both Robinson and Brisbane, who had faced the best that the French in Europe had been able to put into the field, considered to be a relatively simple attack. Brisbane protested. Given twenty minutes he would carry the American works; twenty minutes more was all he asked of Prevost.[18] But Sir George was adamant, his customary indecisiveness having hardened into obstinacy. He had convinced himself that his fortunes were linked with those of the fleet, and with Downie's defeat he had lost Lake Champlain, lost it without a fair chance of recovery. It carried no weight with him that the slight losses sustained by both sides in the land battle indicated that nothing like a serious encounter had taken place.

In fact, the greatest damage had been inflicted upon the civilian population, who subsequently returned to find most of the

95. *The Battle of Plattsburg, 11 September 1814. The British troops are on the right.*

buildings in Plattsburg scarred, indeed some were riddled, by gunfire, both British and American. Nine dwellings, thirteen stores and the courthouse and jail were burned, some obviously set afire by the hot shot the gunners used. With respect to manpower, the entire losses of the British army from 6 to 14 September were reported at no more than 35 killed, 47 wounded and 72 taken prisoner. The Americans had suffered little, with only 37 killed and 62 wounded. It is not surprising that one of the officers of the 33rd Regiment should have remarked contemptuously, after Plattsburg, that Sir George "had long been a candidate for a grannyship and now he ought to have a unanimous vote."[19]

While the Americans were celebrating their unexpected victory with toasts and bonfires and were striking a gold medal for their successful naval commander, Commodore Thomas Macdonough, and presenting him with extensive land grants and city lots, Sir George was dragging his disconsolate troops back to Canada. By 2100 hrs they were on the march, taking all the baggage they could transport, but leaving behind the sick and wounded, as well as stores and vast quantities of ammunition. A handful of American light troops started in pursuit but, after taking a few stragglers prisoner, they gave up owing to the torrential rain. Prevost halted at Champlain and then on 24 September quit the territory of the United States. But not with the same army that had entered three weeks before. It was no longer an army, but a mob of men devoid of discipline and spirit, and reduced in numbers as individuals deserted in disgust. Prevost had brushed aside Robinson's protest that a precipitate retreat from Plattsburg would probably cost more men than would a battle to cross the Saranac, but Robinson was right. The veterans of Spain and Portugal found it easy to cast aside the discipline instilled by the great Duke and to drop out of the trudging column to escape from a commander they had no respect for and from an army that had been defeated by an enemy made up, for the most part, of despised militia. Just how many men deserted is not clear, but 234 were officially acknowledged to have slipped into the woods and remained in the United States.

Prevost never lived down the disgrace that his dithering leadership at Plattsburg earned him. Forgotten were his political achievements in cooling the dangerous situation in Lower Canada aroused by the hot-headed Sir James Craig and in skilfully handling the Legislative Assembly. According to a London *Times* correspondent, Prevost, on passing some of his troops on the road, "was *hissed* by them".[20] The same correspondent wrote that General Macomb had informed the captain of the brig *Linnet* that "everything was prepared to surrender on the advance of the British Army" and that Lieutenant Colonel William Williams of the 13th had declared that he "would never draw his sword again while under the command of Sir George". Many considered Prevost a coward, and Sir James Yeo brought official charges of ineptitude and misconduct against the Governor General. He blamed him for pushing Captain Downie into premature action and then failing to support him. Perhaps there was some justification for Yeo's charges; his argument, thoroughly reasonable, was that, even if the fleet had been successful, "it could not in the least have assisted the troops in storming the batteries, whereas had our troops taken their batteries first, it would have obliged the enemy's squadron to quit the bay and give ours a fair chance."[21] This simply meant that Prevost's artillery could have forced the American ships from behind the protection of Cumberland Head and given Downie's long naval guns a distinct advantage over Macdonough's short-range carronades. The outcome might have been both land and naval victories for the British.

Sir George presented his side of the case in letters to Bathurst written on 22 September and 6 October. Both hint at the influence that earlier events obviously had on the writer's mind. His reference to the "disastrous results" that would have ensued had he pushed on, particularly when one recalled that "such operations . . . have been attempted before, and on the same ground",[22] suggests that Prevost was thinking of the fate of Burgoyne at Saratoga in 1777; and the reference to the possible impact that "the loss of the flotilla"[23] would have had upon subsequent land operations suggests the miserable fate of Procter after the naval defeat of Put-in-Bay in 1813. If it was not the ghost of Burgoyne that persuaded Prevost to pull back from Plattsburg, it might well have been the recollection of Procter's retreat along the Thames and his ignominious defeat at Moraviantown. Prevost, it should be remembered, was defensive-minded; that was the role he had been expected to carry out in North America. Better he had stayed in Montreal. If only the Duke of Wellington had come to lead the forces in North America; and, if not the Duke, then one of his brilliant subordinates!

Prevost was not without supporters. The Duke of Wellington was one of them. Writing about Prevost's retreat after Plattsburg, the Duke said, "I am inclined to think he was right. I have told the ministers repeatedly that a naval superiority on the Lakes is a *sine qua non* of success in war on the frontier of Canada, even if our object should be wholly defensive."[24] But Wellington also wrote to Lord Bathurst, "It is very obvious to me that you must remove Sir George Prevost. I see he has gone to war about trifles with the general officers I sent him, which are certainly the best of their rank in the army; and his subsequent failure and distresses will be aggravated by that circumstance."[25] The Duke was willing to accept almost any eccentricity in his officers provided they achieved the results he desired.

Whatever his contemporaries thought about Prevost—and they were not unanimous in criticizing him—he was recalled from Canada early in 1815, having been assured that his recall should not be interpreted as a mark of the Prince Regent's displeasure. But Prevost, suffering the inevitable misery of failure, knew what people were thinking and saying, and knew too that there was only one way to clear his name. He therefore requested a general court-martial. Unfortunately for Sir George, he was a sick man, and his journey from Quebec to Halifax, much of it on foot, made heavy demands on a constitution already weakened by dropsy. In the end he never found the opportunity to face his accusers or to answer them in public. One week before the court was due to convene, Sir George Prevost died. Years later, in conversation, the great Duke remarked that he had sent Prevost "some of his best troops from Bordeaux, but they did not turn out quite right; they wanted this iron fist to command them."[26] He was probably right.

THE BRITISH OFFENSIVE against Plattsburg not only misfired tactically, it also failed to achieve any strategic advantages. It did not draw American troops away from the Niagara; Major General Izard, instead of hurrying back from Sackets Harbor, stuck to his instructions and continued on his way to Fort Erie, where he took over comand from Jacob Brown. Neither did Prevost's invasion of northern New York hearten the New England "separatists", who were planning to hold a meeting at Hartford, Connecticut, of the representatives of the northeastern states that had provided the principal opposition to the war against Canada.

The idea of the separation of New England states from the United States was already familiar when Madison declared war in 1812. Eight years earlier, Timothy Pickering, the Massachusetts Federalist, had expressed in strong terms his opposition to the politics of Thomas Jefferson and his republican colleagues. In a letter to George Cabot, Pickering declared that he could no longer stomach the "rapid progress of innovation, of corruption, of oppression" and the violation of states' rights that marked Jefferson's administration:

> The principles of our Revolution point to the remedy—a separation. That this can be accomplished, and without spilling one drop of blood, I have little doubt. . . . The people of the East cannot reconcile their habits, views and interests with those of the South and West. The latter are beginning to rule with a rod of iron. . . . I do not believe in the practicability of a long-continued union.[27]

Pickering had in mind a northeastern confederacy that would "unite congenial characters and present a fairer prospect of public happiness". Connecticut and New Hampshire would, of course, form part of this new union. New York would have to be persuaded to enter, but New Jersey, Rhode Island and Vermont would follow suit. Pickering was not thinking and writing in isolation. William Plumer of New Hampshire shared Pickering's views; so too did Uriah Tracy and Roger Griswold of Connecticut, and Josiah Quincy of Massachusetts. George Cabot, though inclined to sympathize with the separatists, was too timid or too cautious to actively support a cause that some considered to be subversive.

Subversive or not, there was never anything secretive about the activities of the discontented Federalists. Both in Congress and in the press they advocated separation. When Louisiana was admitted to the Union as a state, all but two of the senators from New England believed that their response should be secession; Josiah Quincy even went so far as to declare that it would be "the right of all, as it would become the duty of some, to prepare definitely for separation—amicably if they might, violently if they must".[28] During the period of the Embargo Act, Pickering entered into correspondence with Great Britain and people talked openly of separation: John Quincy Adams stated in 1829 that he believed that a definite secessionist plot had existed in 1808.[29] Whether or not such a plot existed—and the evidence for it is slight—William Plumer was right when he expressed concern that in 1808 the United States was in greater danger from internal dissension than from a war with Great Britain. "Numbers who, a few months since, would have revolted with horror at the fatal idea of the dissolution of the Union now converse freely upon it, as an event rather to be desired than avoided", wrote Plumer.[30]

It was because they could see no advantage that war with Great Britain would bring to the northeastern states that Quincy and the Federalists were so forthrightly opposed to the policies of Madison and his southern and western War Hawks. In August 1812, the *Columbian Centinel* of Boston published a letter purporting to be "from a gentleman in a neighbouring state to his friend in Boston" that presented the case for separation:

> You ask my opinion on a subject which is so much talked of—a dissolution of the Union. On this subject I differ from my fellow-citizens generally, and therefore I ought to speak and write with diffidence. I have for many years considered the Union of the southern and northern states *as not essential to the safety and very much opposed to the interests of both sections*. The extent of territory is too large to be harmoniously governed by the same representative body.[31]

It was evidence of the strength of the separatist movement that, despite the obvious hostility of the several New England states, including Massachusetts, the central government at Washington made no attempt to coerce them into obedience; it did not even venture to interfere with press comment or individual utterances against the war. The British were aware of what was happening in the United States and, to encourage New England neutrality in a war to which the New Englanders were obviously opposed, exempted that part of the United States from the naval blockade. When the British issued proclamations prohibiting the importation of American products into the West Indies, New England ports were again exempted; and throughout the war New England and New York contractors supplied the British army with beef. In April 1814 there was a fight in which several men were wounded when American government officials tried to prevent American smugglers from taking a dozen sleigh-loads of goods to Canada. If not neutral in law, New England was to all intents and purposes neutral in fact between 1812 and 1814.

Major General Ross's easy victory at Bladensburg and the burning of the Capitol convinced many New Englanders that the national government, which had thrust the United States into an unpopular war, was incapable of defending the country when foreign troops landed on its shores. The successful action of Sir John Sherbrooke in Maine in September simply reinforced this impression. And had Downie and Prevost enjoyed the same success at Plattsburg, the early disruption of the American union might well have been the sequel. The political importance of Prevost's defeat at Plattsburg in 1814 cannot be overestimated. When, in October, the Governor of Massachusetts invited the other New England states to send delegates to a constitutional convention at Hartford in November, both New Hampshire and Vermont held aloof, at least officially. Perhaps the British were not as powerful as many Americans had at first believed. When the delegates to the convention were chosen, few of the old hard-line secessionists made it to Hartford. For the most part, the men who attended the convention were moderates. They were men such as George Cabot, Harrison Otis, Nathan Dane, and Theodore Dwight, who, nineteen years later, wrote a history of the Hartford Convention to prove that secession was not a pressing issue.[32] Federalist newspapers might advise Madison to get himself a swifter horse than he had used at Bladensburg if he was to escape the vengeance of New England, and Pickering might write to John Lowell that, should the British expedition against New Orleans prove successful—"and if they have tolerable leaders I see no reason to doubt of their success", he added—"I shall consider the Union as severed. This consequence I deem inevitable";[33] but Cabot saw his role as one of keeping the "hot-heads from getting into mischief".[34] Certainly there was no sense of urgency or inevitability in the convention's resolution:

It is a truth, not to be concealed, that a sentiment prevails to no inconsiderable extent . . . that the time for a change is at hand. . . . But as the evidence on which it rests is not yet conclusive, and as measures adopted upon the assumption of its certainty might be irrevocable, some general considerations are submitted, in the hope of reconciling all to a course of moderation and firmness, which may save them from the regret incident to sudden decisions, probably avert the evil, or at least insure consolation and success in the last resort. . . . If the Union be destined to dissolution, by reason of the multiplied abuses of bad administrations, it should, if possible, be the work of peaceable times and deliberate consent. Some new form of confederacy should be substituted among those states which shall intend to maintain a federal relation to each other. . . . A severance of the Union by one or more states, against the will of the rest, and especially in a time of war, can be justified only by absolute necessity.[35]

Having thus discouraged precipitate action, the convention suggested the Virginia Resolutions of 1798 as a possible basis for a new constitution, under which a state could interpose its authority to protect citizens against infractions of the constitution by the central government. The most immediate issue was the demand that Washington surrender to Massachusetts, Connecticut and Rhode Island "a reasonable portion" of the taxes collected within the individual states to enable them "to assume their own defence, by the militia or other troops".[36]

A British victory at New Orleans in January 1815 might very well have cancelled out the British defeat at Plattsburg. It might well have provided the stimulus for New England Federalists to break away from the Union. Secession was so near that a member of the House of Representatives of Massachusetts came to talk to Sir John Sherbrooke at Halifax in November 1814. This individual, whose name Sherbrooke did not reveal in his letter to Bathurst, expressed a fear that the Washington government would resist by force any attempt by New England to secede and asked "whether Great Britain would under these circumstances afford them military assistance to effect their purpose, should they stand in need of it".[37] Sherbrooke therefore requested Bathurst to send additional troops to Nova Scotia "to be in readiness either to oppose the levies now raising in New England, should they be inclined to act hostilely towards us, or to assist them if the contrary policy should be pursued in separating themselves from the Union and forming a government of their own." Castine would provide the British with the base from which "we can supply the Federalists with everything they can require should it be the policy of Britain to assist them in separating from the Union." As it happened, however, Major General Sir Edward Pakenham was no more successful than Major General Sir George Prevost. Plattsburg and New Orleans scuppered the plans for a New England confederacy and killed the Federalist party. Secession, when it did become an issue in the United States almost half a century later, emerged from separatist feeling in the South and not in the northeastern states.

13

The Castine Expedition

THE BRITISH OFFENSIVE against Washington was intended to impress the Americans with the superior strength and mobility of Great Britain and its ability to strike the United States wherever and whenever it chose. The offensive against Plattsburg had a more precise objective; it was designed, not only to draw troops away from the Atlantic coast, but also to provide flank protection for a planned British offensive against Maine. That operation, conducted by Sir John Sherbrooke in September 1814, was the only military action of the war whose deliberate intent was to occupy and hold American territory. Sherbrooke's political purpose was to revise, in favour of British North America, the 1783 boundary settlement that followed the American Revolutionary War, and to provide the Maritime Provinces with a shorter route to Montreal through the virtually uninhabited northern part of Maine. It was an operation to reclaim *Acadia irredenta* as far as the old boundary line along the Penobscot River. The Castine expedition was thus the most important, and incidentally the most successful, of the three British offensive operations of 1814.

The Maritime Provinces, like the two Canadas, had watched with alarm the steady deterioration of Anglo-American relations. When war with the United States appeared possible in 1806, Viscount Castlereagh suggested that, in the event of invasion, New Brunswick should be evacuated, all forces retiring upon Nova Scotia. Sir George Prevost, then lieutenant governor of Nova Scotia, had embodied three regiments of militia in 1808, and in 1809 he persuaded the legislature to distribute 2000 stands of arms. Haligonians did not resent the Jefferson embargo. Instead they looked on it with wry satisfaction as a stimulus to trade, illicit trade of course, between Nova Scotia and New England. John Howe, the king's printer in Nova Scotia, called it "a great blessing" and said that Jefferson's Act should be entitled "An Act for the Better Encouragement of the British Colonies".[1] Howe, incidentally, made two spying trips to New England, in 1808 and 1809, and sent information to Sir George Prevost that was at least as significant as that which John Henry sent to Sir James Craig. The difference between the two men was that, whereas Henry subsequently informed the Americans of what he had done, Howe discreetly kept his mouth shut. The substance of Howe's observations was to the effect that war between Great Britain and the United States was possible and that, if open hostilities should develop, then "a separation of the eastern states will ensue."[2]

When war did come there was unanimous support of the British cause in the Maritimes in both the newspapers and the legislatures. Everybody was pleased when the people of eastern Maine indicated that they wished to avoid acts of hostility, but the legislatures of New Brunswick and Nova Scotia nevertheless began to make preparations to counter violence if it should occur. To ensure the neutrality of the Micmac Indians, who had been pretty much ignored since the end of the American Revolutionary War, promises were made them of presents and provisions. The response was satisfactory. The Indians of Charlotte County and the valleys of the Miramichi, Richibucto and Tabusintac all pledged to remain faithful to King George III and to go peaceably about their ordinary business.

In Halifax, steps were taken to repair the crumbling bastions of the Citadel and to equip the Point Pleasant Martello tower. Blockhouses were constructed at Lunenburg, Parrsboro and Guysborough; a guard house was erected at Annapolis Royal; batteries were set up at Yarmouth, Pictou and Liverpool; and magazines for ordnance stores were built at Lunenburg, Shelburne, Yarmouth, Digby, Windsor, Parrsboro, Pictou, Guysborough and Chester.

Across the border, in New Brunswick, Fort Cumberland (Fort Beauséjour) was once again readied for military occupancy. In Saint John, a blockhouse known as Fort Drummond was erected in 1812, west of the Saint John River, to command the road along which an invading force might advance from the west.

96. Prince of Wales Tower, Halifax, one of several towers built before and during the War of 1812 in the Halifax area—at Fort Clarence, Georges Island, Maugher Beach, and York Redoubt

This fortification was linked with a blockhouse and battery on Carleton Point (Fort Frederick), also on the west side of the river, with Fort Howe, east of the river, and with Johnston's Point, Lower Cove, and Partridge Island at the mouth of the harbour.[3] Several blockhouses were also built at St. Andrews. During his inspection of the militia in 1811, Lieutenant Colonel Joseph Gubbins, the inspecting field officer, expressed the view that St. Andrews was a port "of the first importance" and "ought to be fortified".[4] Taking up his suggestion, the local citizenry undertook to build three new works in addition to refurbishing old Fort Tipperary on the hill behind St. Andrews. The new works consisted of blockhouses and batteries at the east and west ends of the town and at Joes Point, about 2 km farther along the shore. Two public-minded citizens, Robert Pagan and Christopher Scott, bore most of the expense, but when Scott sought to recover the sum of £143 0s 7d some years later, the authorities took the niggardly attitude that Scott had contributed the funds on his own initiative and had never been promised his money back.[5] Elsewhere in New Brunswick, military works were constructed at Evandale on the Saint John River,

97. *The blockhouse on Partridge Island, overlooking Parrsboro,*
which was erected in 1812 as one of a series for the defence of
the Nova Scotian coastline.

at Grand Falls and Fort Presque Isle, on the Eel River, and at
the fork of the Magaguadavic River and the Kedron Stream.

None of these positions were adequately manned with soldiers, particularly after the 104th Regiment had been dispatched
to Upper Canada. Militiamen were simply not up to the job;
Gubbins had reported them to be generally "bad" or "indifferent", those from Westmorland County being "the most efficient
corps I had to review in my district".[6] It was therefore necessary to rely upon regulars and fencibles. At the post on the Eel
River, which was considered a possible route for an American
invasion, the garrison consisted of a sergeant and eight privates
of the 104th Regiment, and even they were there only until the
104th was ordered to march overland to Upper Canada during
the winter of 1812–13. Regular gunners were also sent to the
Canadas, but they moved by boat rather than on foot. To
replace the 104th, which had originally been recruited in the
Maritime Provinces, Lieutenant General John Coffin attempted
to raise another regiment of fencibles; but with labourers
employed on the military works in Halifax and Saint John receiv-

98. *The Martello Tower, Saint John, New Brunswick*

ing 7s 6d per day, the single shilling provided daily by His Majesty was small inducement for a man to put on a uniform and risk his life. Coffin's Fencibles, therefore, never proved to be a popular corps. Even as late as 1814, Penelope Jenkins wrote to Edward Winslow, Jr.:

> Fredericton is shockingly dull this summer. No military here except Gen. Coffin's regiment—a great many of these are stupid married people, and a majority of the single not very brilliant, so that the rising generation of damsels have rather a gloomy prospect.[7]

In Nova Scotia the militia was called out for both the defence of the coast and the provision of escorts and guards for prisoners of war. In June 1813, Sherbrooke reported militia detachments at Fort Cumberland, Shelburne, Parrsboro, Guysborough and Yarmouth. Writing on 10 July 1813 about the situation at Fort Cumberland, Lieutenant Colonel Gubbins underlined some of the problems arising from the employment of volunteer soldiers:

> I found that much ill will existed between them and a young engineer officer lately from England whose duty it was to superintend their work. This gentleman took offence at their want of manners and gave it out in a written order that they were to take off their

99. *Lieutenant Colonel Joseph Gubbins, inspecting field officer of militia, New Brunswick, 1808–16. The 1814–15, he was military governor of Eastport, Maine.*

hats when they met him. This inconsiderate procedure was treated with contempt by some and ridicule by others. . . . The service was much impeded and the engineer could scarcely avoid personal injury but not insult.[8]

Sometimes militiamen were assigned to the armed sloops patrolling the coasts. More often they escorted prisoners of war during the period when Halifax served as the depot for American prisoners. In December 1813, Sherbrooke reported to Lord Bathurst that the people of Halifax were becoming alarmed at the number of prisoners in the city and suggested that they be sent elsewhere, if only because of the danger that information regarding licensed traders might be leaked to the Americans.

The British had devised a system of trading licences that allowed American ships to bring in, from any port in the United States, cargoes of flour, meal, corn, onions and provisions of all kinds, as well as pitch, tar and turpentine. The importation of food was essential, not only to feed the general population, but also to provision the troops and seamen. There is no doubt that American foodstuffs averted a potential shortage in New Brunswick in 1812, and provided the men of the 104th with the rations they carried on their famous march to Upper Canada. The licensed trade proved very popular with New Englanders. It appealed to their sense of adventure. Smuggling, after all, was much more exciting than fighting. Armed only with their licences, New Englanders could enter Halifax or Saint John with impunity, and in broad daylight. Sometimes Yankee merchants would arrange to have their vessels seized by the British and taken to Saint John or Halifax, where the owners, under the pretence of ransoming their vessels, would thereby collect the monies owing on their cargoes. Others would load for foreign ports and then, in some hidden cove in New Brunswick or Nova Scotia, transfer their cargoes to Nova Scotian bottoms. At other times British goods would be landed on Campobello Island and then be carried by "neutral" vessels—American or British but bearing a Swedish or Spanish registry—to Eastport, Maine, whence they were shipped to Portland or Boston. It was but the work of a moment "to transform Yankees or Bluenoses into natives of Stockholm or Uppsala."[9]

Sea, rather than land, operations provided the wartime excitement and drama for the people of the Maritime Provinces. In addition to the victory of HMS *Shannon* over USS *Chesapeake*, there were the activities of the privateers, *General Smyth, Liverpool Packet, Retaliation, Brunswicker*, and *Sir John Sherbrooke*. From 1812 to 1815, Maritime privateers brought in at least 200 prizes. This is a conservative estimate as it does not include recaptures or vessels not brought before the Court of Admiralty for adjudication; on the other hand the total is undoubtedly inflated by the many spurious seizures of American ships delivering pre-arranged shipments to Maritime importers.

THE INITIAL STEP TOWARDS mounting a military operation against Maine was taken by the New Brunswick legislature. In its March session, the members of the Council and the Assembly,

363

in a joint meeting, prepared an address, dated 3 March 1814, that advanced both military and economic arguments for adjusting the terms of the boundary settlement of 1783.[10] The joint address pointed out that the boundary line between Maine and New Brunswick ran close to the Saint John River, being only 20 km away at Meductic, north of Fredericton, and only 10 km distant at Fort Presque Isle, and that north of Grand Falls it crossed the river, cutting off the settlement of Madawaska (whose inhabitants held their letters patent from New Brunswick and "are faithful in their allegiance") and intersecting the line of communication between New Brunswick and the Canadas. The joint address also said that the boundary commission had made a mistake in identifying the headwaters of the St. Croix River, and had thus given the United States "a large tract of wilderness country, covered with extensive and immensely valuable forests of pine, which was clearly included within the ancient limits of the Province of Nova Scotia and upon which, as yet, very few American citizens have settled." The New Brunswick legislators therefore urged that "the advantages to be, at all times, derived from having His Majesty's North American Colonies connected by an open and uninterrupted communication, and especially in times of war," be brought to the King's attention. They hoped that any British delegates to a peace conference would be instructed to insist on an arrangement that might

> lead to the alteration of the western boundary of this province, by which the Madawaska Settlement will be re-annexed to New Brunswick, the line of communications with Canada secured, and the interests of the Empire advanced by the acquisition of a tract of country capable of affording inexhaustible supplies of masts and spars for the use of His Majesty's Navy.

This document was forwarded to Lord Bathurst by Sir Thomas Saumarez, the lieutenant governor of New Brunswick, on 22 March 1814. Bathurst replied on 1 June, promising to give the matter "due attention", but he soon experienced pressure from another quarter. Edward G. Lutwyche, the resident agent for New Brunswick in London, wrote to Lord Bathurst suggesting that the approach of peace in Europe would leave Great Britain "at leisure to prosecute the war in America, the result of which cannot be doubtful", and strongly urged that the Passamaquoddy islands, which the Americans had taken "surreptitiously" in 1791, be recovered since they afforded shelter for American privateers.[11] His main point, however, was that in any peace negotiations the eastern boundary of the United States must be moved farther west; the justification for this action was the "malignity" the United States had "manifested towards Great Britain in the course of hostilities, and their attempts to wrest Canada from her". According to Lutwyche, Great Britain should not lose an opportunity, "which may not perhaps occur again under such favorable circumstances", of fixing such a boundary "as may, at once, set at rest all disputes, and confirm to them security and those advantages which their local situation requires." Then, getting down to details, he concluded, "The river Penobscot presents a natural boundary and would obviate most of the inconveniences to which the British Colonies are now subjected." These arguments carried weight with the British government, and Lord Bathurst ordered Sir John Sherbrooke to occupy that part of Maine "which at present intercepts the communication between Halifax and Quebec".[12]

Unlike the methods used by the British government during the Revolutionary War, when Burgoyne's operations were determined in detail in London, the British were content to issue broad general directives during the War of 1812 and to leave to the local military authorities the details of how to put them into effect. Objectives in Maine were therefore left to Sir John Sherbrooke and his naval colleague, Rear Admiral Edward Griffith. Vice Admiral Cochrane was interested in conducting a raid on Rhode Island, but Sherbrooke and Griffith favoured Passamaquoddy Bay and the Maine coast as far west and south as the Penobscot River as the more acceptable area of operations. This region appealed to them, not only because it was contiguous to New Brunswick, but because its defences were weak, its population was small, and there was reason to believe that the sympathies of a fair number of the people living in the region lay with Great Britain. Sherbrooke was thoroughly familiar with the nature and extent of New England's opposition to "Mr. Madison's War" and of Governor Caleb Strong's unwillingness to cooperate in any aggressive move by the government in Washington. During the session of the General Court of Massachusetts in January 1814, petitions had been sent by more than fifty towns, many of them in the interior of the Commonwealth, outlining "the suffering condition of the people" and expressing "great dissatisfaction with the measures of the general government".[13] Sherbrooke, like the members of the New Brunswick legislature, had read the articles that had appeared in the

100. Lieutenant General Sir John Coape Sherbrooke

Boston Gazette—and, if not in the *Gazette*, at least in the *New-Brunswick Courier*, which regularly reprinted them—under the signature of "An Old Farmer", complaining that the New England states were the "greatest sufferers" of the war. He wrote, "I can see no benefit in the war; I can, in it, see loss and expense and disgrace. I can see no justice in it."[14]

To test the strength of American defences on the Maine coast and to determine the reactions of the people of Maine to a British threat, a small expedition under Captain Robert Barrie was sent on 21 June against Thomaston and St. George, just west of Penobscot Bay. It proved entirely successful. Most of the regular American troops had been sent off to support the American offensive operations against the Canadas, and the militia took no defensive action. Actually, the two forts in question had been built and manned not so much to keep the British out as to keep the Americans from going to sea to trade with the British colonies. Barrie's men blockaded the river, captured the forts, spiked the guns, and took possession of four vessels loaded with lime and lumber. According to a local inhabitant, they "came up within fifty rods of my store, which had 178 hogsheads of rum and the cargo of the brig *Conway*. . . . We are all ordered out, and I shall take my gun in about twenty minutes and be out all night."[15] Reporting on this episode, a Boston editor said:

> What a truly ludicrous figure the Americans cut at this present moment; they who were for disputing with England the dominion of the ocean cannot defend their own inlets; they who urged war for the avowed purpose of effecting a Free Trade, have now no trade at all; they who were for conquering Canada cannot protect their own territories.[16]

The sequel to the Thomaston–St. George raid was the mounting of a more formidable expedition, in July, against Eastport and the islands of Passamaquoddy Bay. The people of Eastport had taken the initiative in 1812 in proposing that the declaration of war ought not to be followed by any hostile demonstrations, British or American. Early in 1813, however, after the Maine militia had been disbanded, a few regulars of the United States army were sent to occupy Eastport and Moose Island. They constituted only a handful of men, but the presence of American regulars so close to their province alarmed New Brunswickers, who wondered if the American action should be interpreted as the prelude to invasion, so they asked Sherbrooke to send guns and stores to Saint John. *Diligence*, the vessel sent by Sherbrooke, was wrecked *en route* and only 400 stands of arms were salvaged. Subsequently, however, additional batteries were set up to guard the entrance to St. Andrews, and a sloop of war was stationed in Passamaquoddy Bay to reassure the residents of the area. In December there was further alarm when the American garrison on Moose Island seized a British commercial vessel. None of these actions indicated any strong inclination on the part of the Americans to act against the Maritime Provinces, but the British government in London had resolved to assert its claim to the islands in Passamaquoddy Bay, and early in July an expedition sailed secretly for Eastport.

The Passamaquoddy expedition was under the command of Sir Thomas Hardy, Horatio Nelson's old companion-in-arms. He commanded a naval squadron, including the 74-gun HMS *Ramillies* and several troop transports. With him were Lieutenant Colonel Andrew Pilkington, who had for some years been the deputy adjutant general at Halifax, and Lieutenant Colonel Gustavus Nicolls, R.E., who was familiar with Moose Island and was under orders to put the island into "a respectable state of defence as soon as it is in our possession" by constructing "such field works or other defences as he may think necessary for its security".[17] Hardy's orders were simply "to occupy and maintain possession of the islands in the Bay of Passamaquoddy". Reporting to London on the departure of the expedition, Sir John Sherbrooke wrote:

> As I conclude those islands in the Bay of Passamaquoddy that we are to take possession of will eventually belong to New Brunswick, I shall place them (when in our possession) under that government, until I can be acquainted with Your Lordship's pleasure upon this subject.[18]

Hardy achieved complete surprise and complete success, with no loss of life. On 11 July, at 1500 hrs, the British vessels anchored off Eastport. A demand was sent to Moose Island for the surrender of the fort and the garrison. There was the expected rejection for the sake of appearances, but when the British troops were seen getting into their landing boats the American commander, Major Perley Putnam of the 40th Regiment, agreed to capitulate. The American colours were hauled down, the defence works, known as Fort Sullivan, were turned over to the British, and Putnam and his 87 officers and men became British prisoners of war. The terms of the capitulation were signed by Hardy, Pilkington, Nicolls and Putnam. "I could have taken it with a gun, brig and my own militia", snorted Squire David Owen, the second principal proprietary of Campobello Island.[19] Following the seizure of Moose Island, Hardy issued a proclamation on 14 July, calling upon "all persons at present on the island" to appear before him "to declare their intentions".[20] Either they would take the oath of allegiance to King George III or they would leave the area within seven days. Two-thirds chose to become British subjects. The customs house was then re-opened under the direction of British officials, trade was resumed, Nicolls took steps to strengthen the defence works around Eastport, and Fort Sullivan was renamed Fort Sherbrooke. Moose Island and Eastport thus became part of New Brunswick, as Sherbrooke had promised they would. Finally, on 24 July, when Hardy left Eastport, he was presented with an address signed by Jonathan D. Weston, Jabez Mowry, Enoch Bartlett and Josiah Dana expressing the thanks of the people of Eastport for "the liberal and honorable conduct" Hardy and Pilkington had shown towards their town and for "the order and discipline of the Navy and Army", which had protected the people "from insult in what we hold most dear, our families and domestic firesides."[21]

The occupation of Eastport caused considerable alarm all along the coastline, not only at the ease with which it had been accomplished, but at the readiness of the people to change their allegiance. Every town to the southwest, even Portland and Boston, wondered if its turn would come next. This was particularly so after Hardy's vessels threw a few shells and rockets into Stonington on 11–12 August. But neither Portland nor Boston was the next British objective. That target was Penobscot Bay and the line of the Penobscot River, which was to mark the future boundary between New England and the Maritime Provinces.

IN HALIFAX, Sherbrooke had been proceeding with plans for the Penobscot Bay expedition. Additional troops had arrived from Gibraltar, under the command of Major General Gerard Gosselin, and Sherbrooke selected the 29th, 62nd and 98th regiments to undertake the task he had in mind. The 21st and 99th were to remain in Halifax for the defence of the Maritimes, along with Major General Duncan Darroch, who had been appointed administrator of Nova Scotia. Sherbrooke was also in communication with Sir George Prevost on the question of strategic priorities. The Governor General was inclined to view the Canadas as the first priority, but Sherbrooke had Bathurst's support and was determined to go through with the Penobscot plan. On 18 August he wrote Bathurst that "the most desirable plan" would be

> for us to occupy Penobscot with a respectable force, and to take that river (which was the old frontier of the State of Massachusetts) as our boundary, running a line from its source in a more westerly direction than that which at present divides us from the Americans.[22]

In this he had the full support of Rear Admiral Griffith, who was urging Sherbrooke to act without delay, particularly "if negotiations should be carrying on between His Majesty's Government and that of the United States at the time when this reaches you".[23]

On 26 August the fleet was ready. Sherbrooke had tried to ensure security, but the need for secrecy was something that the press, then as now, rarely appreciated, and on 13 August the *New-Brunswick Courier* reprinted the following news item from an unidentified Montreal paper:

> When a sufficient number of troops arrive on the coast, it is probable that a party of them will occupy that part of the district of Maine between Penobscot and St. John's rivers. . . . The district . . . is the most valuable in the United States for fishing establishments; has a coast of 50 leagues abounding in excellent harbours, from whence much lumber is sent to Europe and the West Indies.

This was published less than two weeks before the expedition set sail, but apparently it did not arouse alarm in New England or prompt Americans to take effective measures to counter Sherbrooke's plans.

Initially Sir John had planned to capture Machias, a town not far from Eastport that, during the early years of the American Revolution, had been a centre of anti-British activity and had assisted the rebels in New Brunswick. The Machias operation was not expected to delay the Penobscot expedition; on the contrary, it might frighten the Americans along the coast and hasten their surrender. However, when the British sloop of war *Rifleman* brought news that a damaged American frigate, USS *Adams*, had taken refuge in the mouth of the Penobscot River, Sherbrooke decided to waste no time on Machias but to proceed directly to Penobscot Bay. *En route* the convoy was joined by several other British vessels engaged in the blockade, and when Sherbrooke and Griffith arrived off Castine, at the mouth of the Penobscot, Griffith had under his command a formidable armada of ten or eleven ships of war and ten transports bearing some 2500 troops.

On the morning of 1 September, Sherbrooke's vessels approached Castine, the site of the principal defence works covering the entrance to the Penobscot River. The location was good, although the works themselves had been seriously neglected. The old fort and earthworks erected during the Revolutionary War were no longer in use and the only protection

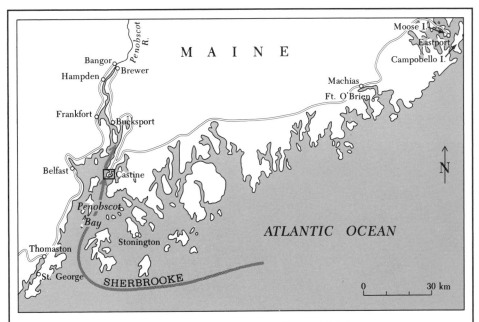

26 August–9 September 1814

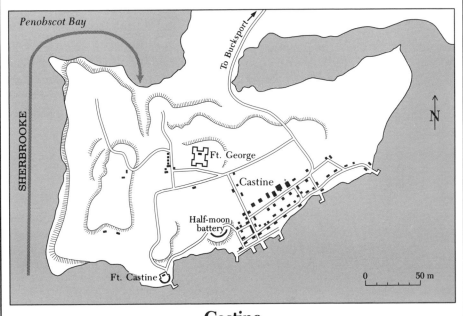

Castine
1 September 1814

THE PENOBSCOT BAY EXPEDITION

was afforded by a small redoubt and a half-moon battery facing the bay that were equipped with four 4-pounder cannon and were manned by some 40 regulars and 100 militiamen from Bucksport. Sherbrooke ordered Lieutenant Colonel Nicolls to proceed by schooner to reconnoitre the American position, and it was toward Nicoll's schooner that the Castine battery directed its first and only shots. Having let go a single volley, the American commander took to his heels to get over the narrow isthmus joining Castine to the mainland before the British should intercept him; the anxiety of the regulars to escape was rivalled, if not exceeded, by that of the Bucksport militia. Accordingly, when Lieutenant Colonel William Douglas landed with his infantrymen on the isthmus, he found the guns spiked and the town and peninsula empty of enemy troops. In this simple way the British secured possession of Castine and gained control over the entrance to the Penobscot River.[24]

The next step was to follow the *Adams* upstream; but first it was necessary to isolate the frigate and the American troops who had fled northwards along the river. Sherbrooke therefore sent Major General Gosselin and the 29th Regiment, with the frigate *Bacchante*, across the bay to the town of Belfast. This community, located on the high road leading from Bangor and Hampden to Portland and Boston, commanded the main route that would be used by any American relief force from the major centres of Massachusetts. Gosselin and his 600 troops encountered no opposition, and their presence acted as a deterrent to any action the Americans might undertake to annoy the British in their operations farther along the river. With Castine and Belfast secure, Sherbrooke and Griffith were free to continue their search for the *Adams* and to inflict a decisive defeat on the American forces in the vicinity.

The movement upriver was the work of a combined naval and military force commanded by Captain Robert Barrie and Lieutenant Colonel Henry John. The latter was in command of the military component that included a detachment of Royal Artillery and selected companies of the 29th, 60th, 62nd and 98th regiments, about 700 men all told, with two light field-guns. Barrie's naval component included several small vessels, the tender of one of the 74-gun ships of the line (HMS *Dragon*), and a number of barges. Together they set out late in the afternoon of 1 September and, travelling by water, were able to reach Marsh Bay near Bucksport before darkness set in. The following morning they were off again, but this time were greatly impeded by fog and by their ignorance of the river, its currents and its depths. Thus, Barrie's ships and John's men did not reach the village of Frankfort on the Belfast–Bangor road until about 1400 hrs. There they learned that the Americans had reached Hampden and that the damaged *Adams* was covered by the Americans' heavy guns and was anchored close to the riverbank. In no way discouraged, the British force, leaving *Dragon's* tender behind at Frankfort, moved slowly towards Hampden. A glimpse of some American militiamen near Frankfort led John to detach a few riflemen of the 60th and infantrymen of the 98th to intercept them. After this had been done and the Americans had been dispersed, the British force continued towards Hampden, landing the military contingent at Bald Head Cove, some 5 km from their objective.

As soon as the British had landed at Castine, Charles Morris, captain of USS *Adams*, had notified the militia commander of the area, Major General John Blake, of the serious developments at the entrance to the river, and had urged him to call out the militia. Blake, whose home was at Brewer, crossed over to Bangor, ordered out the 10th Massachusetts Militia Division, and then hurried on horseback to Hampden. There he found Morris removing the heavy guns from the *Adams* and mounting them on high ground close to the riverbank in a position that commanded the river. Morris had also taken a number of smaller guns and placed them on a wharf pointing downstream. As soon as Blake arrived, he conferred with Morris and his officers. The result was confusion. Each had his own ideas about what should be done to stop the British; stopping the British seemed to be the only thing they did agree on. *How* remained the question. Part of the problem was that Morris had no faith in Blake's untrained militia. By the evening of 2 September, nearly 600 militia had straggled into town, many of them without arms of any kind, looking to Blake or Morris to provide them with weapons and direction. Since neither of the commanding officers expected any fighting that night, the militiamen, inadequately clothed and insufficiently equipped, stood around talking aimlessly or taking shelter from the cold and the chilling rain wherever they could. As the hours passed, their enthusiasm for fighting ebbed like the tide of Penobscot Bay. Few of them had had any experience of war other than the annual muster parade, and they were as uncertain of what to do as they were of their inclination to do it. When dawn came, the whole valley of the Penobscot was enveloped in a dense fog that reduced visibility to a metre or two. Nevertheless, Blake managed to get his men drawn up in line of battle, their left anchored on the river and their right covered by a battery close by the church on the road between Belfast and Bangor. To their rear, along the river, the guns on the hill battery and those on Crosby's wharf would furnish protection against the advance of the British ships. Now it became a matter of waiting for the British to appear.

The British troops, who, like the Americans, had spent a damp, uncomfortable night, began to move at about 1500 hrs. The riflemen formed the advanced guard and the marines were on the flank. Barrie's vessels moved up the river on John's right; with them was a rocket apparatus, manned by a detachment of seamen. "The fog was so thick", John wrote later, "it was impossible to form a correct idea of the features of the country, or to reconnoitre the enemy, whose numbers were reported to be 1400."[25] Although he had enlisted the services of a local guide, John moved so slowly and cautiously that two hours elapsed before his skirmishers became "sharply" engaged. At that point John brought forward his light infantry. Relying more on what they could hear than on what they could see, the Americans began to fire into the fog. Generally their shots were too high, although they did cause some casualties, one of them being the unfortunate guide John was relying on for directions. More destructive of American morale, certainly much more than of life, were the British rockets, which even the naval gunner Barrie had to admit "threw the enemy into confusion". And simultaneously with the rocket salvo came John's order for the infantry to do a "double-quick" bayonet charge.

Given the nature of the troops engaged and the disparity in arms and commanders, only one conclusion was possible. The centre of the American line broke and the men fled, followed by their companions on both flanks. According to one of the American participants, "We gave them a fire by land and the battery of the wharf. They warmly returned it and pushed on— our militia gave way and fled in great disorder, it being impossible for the officers to collect them and make another stand."[26] Once the militia had gone, Morris's men had no choice but to set fire to the *Adams* and make for safety. The light company of the 29th was thus able to gain the hill battery, and Barrie's sailors, pushing upriver, found the *Adams* in flames and the guns on the wharf abandoned. In less than an hour from the time the first shot was fired, the battle was over. The British losses—killed, wounded and missing—numbered only 10, those of the Americans 94, of whom 81 were taken prisoner. Nor were the captured stores significant in quantity, as they included only a few guns, gun carriages, sponges, ladles and hand spikes, and forty barrels of powder. Barrie and Griffith would have taken greater joy in the capture of the *Adams* intact.

After the battle at Hampden, John and Barrie hurried forward to Bangor, one by water and the other on foot. A short distance outside the town limits, John was met by a flag of truce and a request for terms. There were no arguments, no discussions. The only terms offered were unconditional surrender; they were accepted. After an evening of jollification, drunken disorders and disgraceful looting by Barrie's sailors, the British bedded down in the local courthouse; the officers enjoyed the comforts afforded by Hatch's Tavern.[27] The next day Blake and a number of the militiamen came to Bangor and surrendered formally. Neither John nor Barrie remained there long, less than a day and a half, but during that time they burned several vessels and required the selectmen to put up a bond of $30 000 for the safe delivery to naval authorities at Castine of several unfinished vessels still in the stocks. Returning through Hampden, the British troops destroyed the town meetinghouse and confiscated all merchant vessels, including the privateer *Decatur*, as well as personal firearms and gunpowder. By 9 September the British were all back at Castine. They left behind an embittered public, most of whom were disposed to direct their indignation not so much towards the British as towards the unfortunate Blake, whose military incompetence they magnified into treason. He was burned and hanged in effigy, and went in fear of his life. A soldier's life is not a happy one, especially when he is a defeated general.

As soon as Barrie and John had returned to Castine, Lieutenant Colonel Andrew Pilkington and Captain Hyde Parker set out to occupy Machias, some 125 km to the east. Their landing place was Bucks Harbor, 16 km south of Machias. Although he could conceivably be ambushed along the small pathway that led through the woods to his destination, Pilkington decided to take advantage of such protection as might be afforded by the darkness. It was a tedious, harassing business, making a night march, but by daybreak Pilkington had got his men safely to Fort O'Brien, located on Sanborn Cove, about 8 km south of Machias. After fighting off a few pickets, the British troops approached the fort from the rear because its guns were sighted towards the water. They found to their surprise and delight that the garrison had decamped only moments before, leaving everything inside the fort intact. The retreat was so rapid, Pilkington reported, "that I was not enabled to take many prisoners".[28] Losing no time, the British continued their advance to Machias, which they occupied about an hour later, without encountering any resistance. Then, just as Pilkington was about to proceed farther in search of the enemy, he was handed a letter from the brigadier general commanding the district, promising that the American militia would neither bear arms nor take any hostile action against King George's men. When a similar proposal was made by the civil authorities of Machias and the principal citizens, Pilkington felt free to inform his senior officer that the British were now in complete control of "that intermediate tract of country which separates the province of New Brunswick from Lower Canada".[29]

Meanwhile, at Castine, Sherbrooke and Griffith had collaborated in making arrangements for the administration of the conquered area. They issued a joint proclamation announcing Britain's intention of retaining possession of the country lying between the Penobscot River and Passamaquoddy Bay and assuring the residents of protection for all who remained quiet as well as payment for all provisions furnished to the British military and naval forces. The proclamation also stated that the civil authorities were to continue executing the law as they had done prior to the occupation. Having discovered that the British practice of confiscating personal weapons greatly irritated the inhabitants of Castine, Sherbrooke accepted their protests that they needed arms to protect themselves against the ill-disposed elements of the population—who, "under the pretence of patriotism", would attack "the better part of the community", invade their property and plunder their homes—and decided that the seizure of muskets and pistols should cease. The Americans had put their argument to him in these words:

> New England may be conquered easily by kindness—permit it to be thought that she cannot be so easily by arms; and why should the people of New England, who have long viewed the English nation and government to be less hostile to them than the southern states, be less worthy of the generosity of the British Nation than those of France?[30]

It was a good argument, and Sherbrooke and Griffith agreed to accept a signed declaration that the arms would be used only "for the preservation of peace and tranquility". But Sherbrooke looked coolly upon American protestations of affection for England. While keeping a smiling countenance before the selectmen who came to see him at Castine, he was prepared to write privately to Bathurst that

> I have reason to believe that the people in the western part of the District of Maine, and particularly at Boston, are already much annoyed by our having taken possession of the Penobscot. It is from the extensive pine forests in the neighbourhood of this river that they have chiefly depended of late years both for their lumber and their fuel.[31]

On 18 September, Sherbrooke and Griffith returned to Halifax. They left behind, at Castine, about half the original complement of men and ships they had set out with a little over three weeks before. Major General Gosselin and Rear Admiral David Milne, captain of the *Bulwark*, were left in charge. Almost immediately Gosselin put his men to work reconstructing Fort George, the old British fort that had been started in 1779 and then allowed to fall into disrepair. The half-moon redoubt was rebuilt and new works were constructed, including a defensive canal through the isthmus, thus making Castine into an island. In his role as administrator of the region, Gosselin issued a proclamation directing all males over sixteen years of age living in the region between the Penobscot River and Passamaquoddy Bay to take the oath of allegiance and neutrality. In each of the several townships all the selectmen took the oath. Gosselin was apparently a popular figure at Castine. He maintained good discipline among his troops, and during the period of his administration relations between the Americans and the British were satisfactory in every way, not just because the British possessed military superiority or because Gosselin had agreeable manners, but also because of the inclination of many of the leaders of the American community to accept the political change implicit in the British occupation. Thus, there were no concerted attempts to dislodge the British and no efforts to make the lives of the troops miserable or to engage in individual acts of hostility. Trade went on as before, and a company of actors was brought from Halifax to provide entertainment for the troops and the people of Castine alike in Hooke's customs barn.

Nevertheless, from time to time rumours circulated throughout the Penobscot region that a seaborne counterattack was being planned against Castine. This suggestion had been put forward in the Massachusetts legislature, but had simply dissolved into talk. The anti-Federalist majority was not prepared to furnish the funds, and the Maine representatives were uncooperative because they believed that the funds voted for military purposes invariably went to strengthen the fortifications of Boston, with nothing left over for the district of Maine. Moreover, Caleb Strong still adamantly refused to accept the nationalization of the Massachusetts militia by the federal authorities. Finally the proposal evaporated when, on 16 October, the Massachusetts legislature decided to send delegates to the Hartford Convention. In Washington the secretary of war, James Monroe, still clung to the thought of trying to force the Massachusetts militia to serve in an expeditionary force against the British in Maine. He even selected Major General William King, a well-known shipowner in Maine who was strongly opposed to the Federalist position on the war, to command the proposed force. The question was, against whom should the troops be sent? Thomas Jesup, who had been wounded at Lundy's Lane, was advising the President to take prompt action against New England, and Madison directed Monroe to discuss with Generals Swartwout and Porter, both of whom were in Washington, the practicability of organizing a force of volunteers "to repel the enemy and put rebellion down".[32] But Madison had second thoughts, realizing that such an action might well push the New England states over the precipice of secession; to use force against Massachusetts would probably provoke more problems than it would solve. And so Madison quietly dropped a proposal that could have led to a civil war in which Great Britain might have intervened on the side of Massachusetts.

In any event, the British and the Americans were now engaged in negotiations at Ghent with a view to finding a peaceful settlement of the issues that had provoked the war. For Madison to resume hostilities at this late date would therefore serve little purpose. As far as Sherbrooke was concerned, he saw his task as one of holding the territory he had acquired, as he told Bathurst, "until I am honoured with orders from Your Lordship".[33] In New Brunswick the people read with satisfaction about Maine's peaceful acceptance of the British occupation. All that was needed now was endorsement of the occupation by the peace negotiators at Ghent. Eastern Maine was by all rights British territory, or so the New Brunswick press claimed, territory that had been shamefully filched by the United States in 1783:

> It would seem that we were merely taking possession of our own, for the Americans have only such a footing there as they had attained since the peace of 1783 by encroachment on their part and inattention on ours.[34]

The Restoration of Peace

14

The Treaty of Ghent

THE WAR OF 1812 had not been a popular war in either Great Britain or British North America. The Canadians had tried to avoid it because of military weakness and the vulnerability of their frontier; the British had not wanted it because they were heavily committed to fighting a war in Europe. Even the Americans had been divided in their views. Only the western and southern War Hawks had made war their political aim, and had forced it on the President and Congress. When the British finally realized that the War Hawks meant what they were saying and were not just indulging in empty rhetoric, they tried to stave off the war by repealing the obnoxious Orders in Council and instructing Admiral John Borlase Warren, commanding "His Majesty's Squadron on the Halifax and West India Stations and down the whole Coast of America", to arrange for an armistice pending further discussions. But the armistice, though agreed to by Dearborn and Prevost, was repudiated by President Madison and the war went ahead.

The failures of the American offensives in Lower Canada and the Niagara and Detroit regions during 1812 came as a shock to the American government and to the American public. Obviously the reduction of Canada was not going to be a mere matter of marching. Accordingly, when in March 1813 Tsar Alexander I proposed that Russia mediate the Anglo-American quarrel, Madison accepted his offer. Indicative, perhaps, of Madison's compliant mood, not one of the three men he named as the American delegates was a War Hawk, and one of them—

James A. Bayard, a Federalist from Delaware—had spoken in opposition to the war during the Senate debate in June. The other two delegates were John Quincy Adams, the American minister to Russia, resident in St. Petersburg, and Albert Gallatin, secretary of the Treasury.

But if the choice of delegates indicated a less belligerent attitude on Madison's part, the wording of their instructions left little room for diplomatic manoeuvre. The first set of instructions prepared by the secretary of state, James Monroe, demanded from Great Britain a formal renunciation of the practice of impressment and the elimination of all the trading concessions Canadian fur traders had received under Jay's Treaty; there was to be no more trading with the Indians in American territory. Any territorial settlement would be on the basis of the reciprocal restoration of conquests. Later, a second set of instructions was issued, obviously reflecting Dearborn's success at York and Fort George and Monroe's vision of the American occupation of the whole of Upper Canada. The American delegates were to impress upon the British "the advantages to both countries . . . promised by a transfer of the upper parts and even the whole of Canada to the U.S."[1] If this were done, then Great Britain would be free of the burden of supporting Canada, "which must be considerable in peace or war, especially in war". The cession of Canada would remove "a fruitful source of controversy" between the two nations, and in any event would merely anticipate the inevitable. Such was Monroe's argument. One might well imagine that he believed the war already won and the territory in question already occupied.

The Russian mediation scheme came to nothing. The British government was prepared to allow the Americans unmolested passage to Russia, but would have nothing to do with the Tsar's offer, proposing instead direct negotiation between Great Britain and the United States. Had Alexander been really anxious to assist the Americans he might have brought pressure to bear on his brother monarch, the Prince Regent, but the Tsar quickly lost interest in the United States, preferring to devote his efforts to overthrowing Napoleon. The Americans had never been very hopeful of getting help from Russia; what they did hope for was sympathetic support from Sweden, a country that had posed as the defender of the rights of neutral nations against Napoleon. But the Swedish government, with a French marshal, Jean-Baptiste Bernadotte, standing in the wings as heir to the throne, was much more interested in acquiring possession of Norway than in bringing pressure to bear on Great Britain on behalf

of the United States of America. Without friends or anybody
to talk to, the American peace commissioners sat cooling their
heels in St. Petersburg for a year, until early in July 1814, when
the United States government decided to accept the British proposal of direct negotiations.

Direct negotiation meant a new delegation, a new set of instructions and a new site for discussions. The members of the
original peace commission, since they were already in Europe,
were asked to continue, but two new delegates were added, the
War Hawk Henry Clay and Jonathan Russell, the minister-
designate to Sweden. The inclusion of Clay was intended to
stiffen the resolve of the commissioners who might be inclined
to bend too easily towards compromise. Despite the American
military failure on the Niagara frontier and the collapse of the
offensive against Montreal during 1813, Monroe saw no need
to soften any of his earlier demands. In the letter he wrote on
28 January 1814, Monroe said that the objects for which the
United States had gone to war remained unchanged and that
the reasons for maintaining them had "gained great additional
weight, by the vast amount of blood and treasure which had
been expended in their support".[2] After reiterating his arguments with regard to impressment and blockade, Monroe wrote
in a paragraph that was omitted from the printed version of
the instructions submitted to Congress:

> Experience has shown that the British Government cannot partici-
> pate in the dominion and navigation of the Lakes, without incur-
> ring the danger of an early renewal of the war. It was by means
> of the Lakes that the British Government interfered with and
> gained an ascendancy over the Indians, even within our limits. The
> effect produced by the massacre of our citizens after they were made
> prisoners, and of defenseless women and children along our fron-
> tier need not now be described. It will perhaps never be removed
> while Great Britain retains in her hands the government of those
> provinces.

Monroe went on to point out that American settlement had
reached the frontiers of Lower Canada, had extended along the
St. Lawrence to the southwestern extremity of Lake Erie, and
would soon reach the banks of Lake Michigan. Such proximity
of Americans and Canadians was bound to lead to conflict, with
the "inevitable consequence of another war". The solution? The
cession of Canada to the United States.

Several months later, at the instigation of John Jacob Astor,
Monroe issued another directive, this time condemning the British acquisition of Fort Astoria as an act of unjustified aggres-

sion (had he forgotten that Great Britain and the United States were at war?) and ordering the commissioners to insist on the return of Astoria to Astor's Pacific Fur Company. In availing themselves of assistance from Russia or Sweden, the commissioners were to remember that their object was to secure peace for the United States and *"not to combine with any Power, in any object of ambition*, or in claiming other conditions more favourable than that proposed which may tend to prolong the war."[3]

As for Great Britain, their aim was to secure those special interests of British North America that they considered had been sacrificed by the Treaty of Paris in 1783. The errors of the past would be corrected and assurances obtained for the future. That meant not only bringing all the islands of Passamaquoddy Bay under New Brunswick's jurisdiction, but also acquiring all of Maine north of the 45th parallel from the United States to provide a shorter route between the Canadas and Halifax. The boundary revisions should not stop there. They should extend westwards as well, perhaps along the south shore of the St. Lawrence, as some Canadians suggested, certainly along the Niagara, where a thin strip of land on the east side of the river should be ceded to Upper Canada to ensure Canadian control of the Niagara frontier.[4] In addition, Michilimackinac should remain in British hands as a site traditionally associated with the Indians and the Canadian fur trade. In the West, the boundary between the two countries was to extend from the Lake of the Woods to the source of the Mississippi; on the Pacific Coast, the British would remain firmly on the Columbia River. Since the Americans had forced the war on Great Britain, they should forfeit the fishing privileges along the Atlantic accorded them in 1783, and should confirm Jay's Treaty for the sake of the fur trade and the Indians. Above all, the British were convinced that they could not, a second time, risk losing the goodwill of the Indians, the most serious blunder the British negotiators had made in 1783. They would, therefore, press for the establishment of an Indian buffer state based on the Treaty of Greenville, which the United States had signed with the Indians in 1795. To press these terms on the Americans, the British government appointed James Gambier, Henry Goulburn and William Adams. Lord Gambier was an old naval officer who had earned his title by the bombardment of Copenhagen in 1807; Goulburn was a politician who served as under-secretary of state for war and the colonies; and Adams was a scholarly but indecisive specialist in maritime law. Not a group remarkable for diplomatic experience or expertise in carrying on high-level negotiations. In truth, Viscount Castlereagh, who had been appointed foreign secretary in 1812, regarded the British peace commissioners as little more than messenger boys. The Americans might talk and write to Gambier, Goulburn and Adams, but they were really dealing, in a roundabout way, with Castlereagh.

There was some initial argument about the site of the negotiations. London and Gothenburg were both considered, but Ghent was finally selected. It was the site of the ancient capital of Flanders, whose neutrality had been proclaimed when it was provisionally united with the kingdom of Holland in May 1814. Late in June the American representatives began to assemble, but it was early August before the British made their appearance. After some jockeying as to where, in Ghent, the peace talks should be held, they agreed on the Hôtel des Pays-Bas on the Place d'Armes.

GOULBURN OPENED THE NEGOTIATIONS on the afternoon of 8 August 1814 by suggesting three principal subjects for discussion—impressment, the establishment of a separate Indian state, and the revision of the 1783 boundary between the United States and the adjacent British provinces. With regard to the fishing privileges the Americans had enjoyed before the war, there would be no point in talking about that; the British would not renew them.

Of the three issues, the Americans would have liked most to discuss impressment, but they had received last-minute instructions to postpone the matter. As for the Indians and the boundary revisions, the Americans protested that they had no authority to discuss them, although they were prepared to listen to the British arguments, if only to learn the nature and extent of the British position. They pointed out that the American government had, in fact, already entered negotiations with the Indians, that the territory on which the Indians resided was American territory, and that treaties concluded in the past with Indian tribes could not be considered in the same light as treaties made between sovereign states. The Americans therefore regarded the British proposition as involving a cession of sovereign rights and territory to which the government and people of the United States would be unalterably opposed. With the British commissioners having taken the stand that Indian pacification and the establishment of a separate Indian state were a *sine qua non*, indispensable to any peace settlement, it began to look as if the conference might end in deadlock almost before it was fairly under way. At this point Lord Gambier called for an adjournment to obtain further instructions from London. This was the first of the intervals that punctuated the talks and gave both delegations an opportunity to reassess their positions.

The second round of negotiations began on 19 August. In the interval, Lord Castlereagh had visited Ghent while on his way to Vienna, where Metternich and other representatives of European monarchies had assembled to redraw the map of Europe after the collapse of Napoleon's empire. However, the British foreign secretary took no direct part in the Ghent discussions; his interest was not in the little diplomatic sideshow in Flanders but in the main performance in Vienna. When Gambier, Goulburn and Adams read their new instructions, they found them rather more positive than the earlier ones. The British government repeated its assertion that the pacification of the Indians and the fixing of a permanent boundary line between them and their white neighbours were essential; unless these issues were resolved, there could be no hope for a permanent peaceful settlement of Anglo-American differences. But, to soften the impact of these demands, the British commissioners disclaimed any desire or intention on the part of Great Britain to acquire for herself the lands belonging to the Indians; they suggested that both the United States and Great Britain should eschew the acquisition of any Indian territory.

When the British commissioners spoke of the boundary between the United States and the British provinces, they linked it with the idea of a lasting peace. If the Americans would accept a fair boundary settlement and agree to dispense with the armed naval forces on the Great Lakes, then peace would be assured. The existing situation in which both countries shared possession of the Great Lakes and patrolled them with armed vessels had proved to be no guarantee of peace; and since, in the future, the United States would always be the stronger power in North America, then the weaker British provinces should be afforded treaty protection against the possible aggressions of the larger and stronger power. At the request of the Americans these statements were put in writing, and Gallatin drafted the American reply. It was dignified and clearly stated. The British demands, it contended, were in no way related to the factors that had led to war; they were, instead, something wholly new, an unexpected challenge to the sovereignty of the United States and a

386

denial of the principle of reciprocal rights on the Great Lakes. They were, in fact, demands to which they, as delegates of the government of the United States, could not accede.

The trend of the negotiations was now becoming clear. The American delegates had dropped their demands for British concessions on impressment, the blockade, compensation for impressed American sailors, indemnity for the destruction of unfortified towns during the war, the return of, or payment in full for, every negro slave taken from the southern states, and the cession of the two Canadas, or at least Upper Canada, to the United States; all of them subjects that had exercised the Americans earlier and that Monroe had insisted on in his earlier instructions in January 1814. The Americans knew they would get nowhere by talking any longer about the alleged causes of the war; if they were to make progress towards a peace settlement acceptable to the United States, they would have to make sure that the United States, if it gained nothing, at least would lose nothing. They resolved, therefore, to dig in their heels, resist the British demands, and fight for a settlement on the basis of the situation that prevailed before the war *(status quo ante bellum)*. They were none too sure that even that was obtainable. In fact it looked as if the peace talks were pretty close to ending; at least, that was the substance of a dispatch the American commissioners sent to Washington. Henry Clay, the cardplayer and gambler, who hitherto had been inclined to believe that the British were bluffing, was now convinced that the negotiations only awaited their formal closing. He would at least have another short holiday in Paris before returning to the United States.

As Clay had earlier suspected, the British had indeed been bluffing. They did not want the peace talks to end. The British people were tired of war and wanted peace; and Lord Liverpool, the prime minister, was worried about the coming session of Parliament and what support the Opposition could muster should they challenge the government on the issue of the peace negotiations. Castlereagh, too, wanted the peace talks to continue. He was less concerned than Liverpool about the political implications of the hardline approach, but he knew that strong reinforcements had been sent to Canada and that offfensive operations were planned for both northern Maine and northern New York. After two years of indecisive defensive war, the British might be able to come up with worthwhile victories that would justify their arguing that a settlement must be based on the principle of retaining what has been acquired *(uti possi-*

detis). Thus, for different reasons, Liverpool and Castlereagh were prepared to make minor concessions just to keep the Americans at the conference table. The real opponents to concessions of any sort were Bathurst and Goulburn, the two officials from the Colonial Office; far better than their colleagues, they knew how strongly the Indians and the colonial legislatures felt about the issues being discussed at Ghent. Nevertheless, the views of Castlereagh and Liverpool prevailed, and the British returned a less argumentative and more conciliatory note to the United States delegation. No, the British had never contended that exclusive military command over the Great Lakes was indispensable; of course, the Indian question could be settled on the principles of moderation and justice. And so the negotiations were resumed with further exchanges of notes. But it was the British who were weakening, and not the Americans.

The British first capitulated on the Indian question. To Henry Clay, acceptance of the British proposals for an Indian state and for disarmament on the Lakes would deliver the whole of the western country, which he represented, over to the Indians. It therefore came as an agreeable surprise when the British proposed an alternative—that both countries agree to forego the employment of Indians in warfare and to restore "all the possessions, rights, and privileges" the native peoples had enjoyed before the start of the war.[5] This was a long retreat from the stand the British delegates had taken earlier, and did very little to meet the needs of the Indians. The American commissioners called the British demand an "ultimatum", but readily accepted it because it left the United States "free to effect its object in the mode convenient with the relations which they have constantly maintained with those tribes".[6] Diplomatically, the British were on the run despite their military victories at Bladensburg and Castine. The important aspect of their concession on the Indian question was that it was the first point on which the two delegations reached full agreement during ten weeks of negotiations.

Having taken the first step towards a final peace settlement, the commissioners moved on to the next issue, the boundary between the United States and British North America. The British had taken a stand on the principle of *uti possidetis*; the Americans were now adamant in demanding the *status quo ante bellum*. The British wanted to hold the American territory they actually occupied, which was considerable; the Americans wanted to return to the territorial situation that had existed

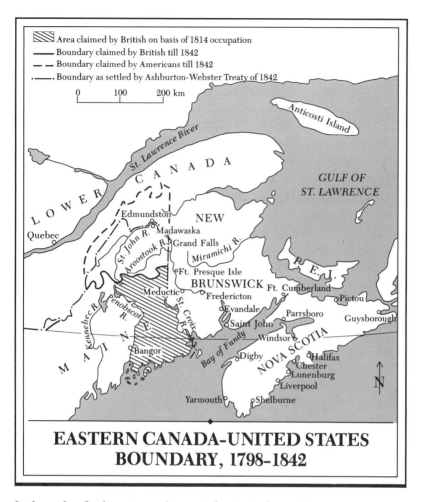

Legend:
- Area claimed by British on basis of 1814 occupation
- Boundary claimed by British till 1842
- Boundary claimed by Americans till 1842
- Boundary as settled by Ashburton-Webster Treaty of 1842

0   100   200 km

EASTERN CANADA-UNITED STATES BOUNDARY, 1798-1842

before the declaration of war. The British position was strong: at the time of the discussions in Ghent, British and Canadian forces were firmly established in Fort Astoria on the Pacific, Prairie du Chien on the Mississippi, Michilimackinac, Fort Niagara, and the territory of Maine east and north of the Penobscot River. The Americans held Fort Malden on the Detroit River and Fort Erie, but the balance favoured the British. In arguing *uti possidetis*, the British had in mind trading Castine and Machias for Fort Malden and Fort Erie; they would hold the western forts, the islands of Passamaquoddy Bay, and the territory north of a line drawn from the existing Maine–New Brunswick border on the coast to the height of land between the upper waters of the Aroostook, St. John, Penobscot and Kennebec rivers, and in a westerly direction to the boundary between Lower Canada and the United States. This meant the retention of the most northerly part of Maine, an area that even today, 167 years after the negotiations at Ghent, may still be reasonably described as a wilderness area. The proposal represented a retreat from the original idea of using the Penobscot as the boundary. Once more, negotiations headed for a deadlock. The American delegates refused categorically to agree to any concession that would involve the surrender of what they considered to be American territory. And when they learned of Prevost's defeat at Plattsburg, they dug their heels in even deeper.

What broke the deadlock was neither argument nor willingness to compromise, nor was it the news of victory or defeat in North America. It was Tsar Alexander I's idea of transforming Napoleon's Duchy of Warsaw into a kingdom of Poland and crowning himself king. To further this plan, Russia entered into an arrangement with Prussia whereby the latter would surrender a large slice of Polish territory in return for a free hand in annexing Saxony. Thus both nations would share the spoils of Napoleon's defeat. But England and Austria looked on the deal with extreme displeasure. Both Metternich and Castlereagh were suspicious of the Russians and were prepared to work together, the first because he wanted to strengthen Austria as against Prussia, and the second "because he was still sufficiently under the spell of the old idea of a balance of power" to feel unhappy about close Russian–Prussian collaboration.[7] Castlereagh carried his opposition to Russia as far as to bring about a realignment of European powers in an Anglo-Franco-Austrian alliance, signed on 3 January 1815.

With the old anti-Napoleon alliance breaking up, Castlereagh and Liverpool were disposed to move warily in their relations with the United States. Perhaps the best thing to do would be to consult the Duke of Wellington, who was the leading military figure in Europe at this time, and was serving officially as British ambassador to France and unofficially as a prop to the restored but none-too-solid government of Louis XVIII. Wellington's reply was clear and hardly unexpected. He may not have known, but he probably suspected, that Napoleon, from his exile on Elba, was watching the allied powers quarrelling among themselves and was wondering what his chances were to profit from the disputes and regain control of France. Wellington knew that the faint-hearted Bourbons would run away if Napoleon reappeared in France, and that in such an event he, Wellington, would again be called upon to lead the allied

101. The Duke of Wellington, by the English artist William Valentine, who emigrated to Halifax in 1818

forces against the man who had once threatened to invade England. He therefore told Lord Liverpool on 9 November:

> I am quite sure that all the American armies of which I have ever read would not beat out of a field of battle the troops that went from Bordeaux last summer, if common precautions and care were taken of them. That which appears to me to be wanting in America is not a General, or general officers and troops, but a naval superiority on the Lakes. Till that superiority is acquired, it is impossible, according to my notion, to maintain an army in such a situation as to keep the enemy out of the whole frontier, much less to make any conquest from the enemy. . . . The question is whether we can acquire this naval superiority on the Lakes. If we can't, I shall do you but little good in America; and I shall go there only

to prove the truth of Prevost's defence, and to sign a peace which might as well be signed now. . . .

Considering everything, it is my opinion that the war has been a most successful one, and highly honourable to the British arms; but from particular circumstances, such as the want of the naval superiority on the Lakes, you have not been able to carry it into the enemy's territory, notwithstanding your military success and now undoubted military superiority, and have not even cleared your own territory of the enemy on the point of attack. You cannot, then, on any principle of equality in negotiation, claim a cession of territory excepting in exchange for other advantages which you have in your power. . . .

Why stipulate for the *uti possidetis?* You can get no territory; indeed, the state of your military operations, however creditable, does not entitle you to demand any.[8]

In brief, Wellington's advice was to stop haggling and sign the peace, and the Duke's opinion, whether well-grounded or not, "had the character of a mandamus".[9] It was an opinion not displeasing to the British, to whom peace in North America was of more importance, in the event of a renewal of hostilities in Europe, than a few acres of forest land in northern Maine. Trade had declined and the Prime Minister was afraid of the political consequences of continuing to levy taxes on property merely "for the purpose of receiving a better frontier in Canada".[10] Colonial interests were rarely, if ever, given priority over what were deemed to be British interests, and so Great Britain proceeded to make peace as soon as practicable.

Evidence of the British change of heart appeared quite clearly in November, in an exchange of letters between the London banker, Alexander Baring, and Albert Gallatin.[11] This was followed on 27 November by a British note, appended to a draft treaty, stating that "the undersigned have forborne to insist upon the basis of *uti possidetis*, to the advantage of which they consider their country fully entitled."[12] The door to settlement was now open; all the Americans had to do was to keep it ajar. There were still a few spirited exchanges about the fisheries and free navigation of the Mississippi, the latter because of Clay's determination never to see a British ship on that river. But Gallatin won Clay over by suggesting a trade—American fishing privileges for British navigation of the Mississippi. Face-to-face meetings were resumed—they had been abandoned in favour of exchanging notes—and on the day before Christmas 1814, between 1600 and 1800 hrs, the British and American commissioners met, read the 2250-word draft treaty, compared all six copies and finally affixed their signatures. The next day, all the

102. The Signing of the Treaty of Ghent, Christmas Eve, 1814

commissioners sat down to a dinner of beef and plum pudding
brought from England specially for them. An orchestra played
"God Save the King" and "Yankee Doodle", and toasts were
drunk to George III and James Madison. Outside, the church
bells of Ghent were ringing in honour of the birthday of the
Prince of Peace.

IN BRIEF, the Treaty of Ghent—about which, for almost five
months, eight men had argued, threatened and swallowed their
pride—was essentially a negative document. It said no more
than that the situation that had prevailed before war was declared would continue unchanged when the shooting stopped.
The maritime grievances and the demands for sailors' rights and
free trade, while not forgotten, were not mentioned in the treaty
although Madison had cited them in June 1812 as the basic reasons for declaring war against Great Britain. Boundary issues,
which had been vigorously disputed during the peace talks, were
perfunctorily disposed of under the general principle of the *status
quo ante bellum*; all conquered territory would be reciprocally
restored "without delay, and without causing any destruction".[13] As for those regions where the location of the boundary

line had been in dispute before the war, they would be referred to special commissions to be appointed later. The Indians, whom the British had hoped to protect and to reward for their services, were left to the mercy of the Americans; the treaty only said that neither side was to employ them in any future war against the other. The fisheries issue was left open; it would be the subject of an agreement to be concluded later. Nothing at all was said about American disarmament on the Great Lakes. Perhaps the most that can be claimed for the treaty is that it enlisted the "best endeavours" of both countries against the traffic in slaves.[14] From the British standpoint, the Treaty of Ghent was an example of peace at any price; to the Americans it was, in Gallatin's words, "as favorable as could be expected under existing circumstances, as far as they were known to us".[15] Essentially, the peace was determined more by the threat of a potential war in Europe than by the realities of an existing war in North America.

The Treaty of Ghent—"The Treaty of Omissions", the French diplomat Jean-Baptiste Petry called it in a letter to Talleyrand[16]—was a triumph for American diplomacy. The five American commissioners had proved more skilful and more determined than their three British counterparts and had, in the end, received more than they were prepared to give. They did well by their country. Exactly how well was not known until 11 February 1815, when news of their achievements reached New York; several days later the treaty was presented to the United States Senate for ratification. Only a few days earlier, the British army, which had been beaten at New Orleans, had captured Fort Bowyer on Mobile Bay. It was the last operation of the war. Washington sent a messenger north bearing a copy of the treaty and its ratification, and on 1 March the news was proclaimed in Canada. The next day Sir George Prevost received word that he would have to return to London to explain his actions at Plattsburg.

In both the United States and Great Britain the end of the war was widely acclaimed, without regard to the terms of the peace settlement; but in British North America the response was less enthusiastic. Maritimers, particularly those living in Halifax, wondered if the unmatched prosperity the war had brought them would now evaporate; in the Canadas the fur traders felt that they and the Indians, upon whose continued loyalty to the British cause in North America the prosperity of their trade depended, had been, not just let down, but betrayed by an indifferent government in London. The victories achieved in the West by the old combination of British regulars, fur traders and Indians had been, as usual, sacrificed for the sake of appeasing a youthful and overly sensitive republic and securing its uncertain friendship.

SEVERAL YEARS elapsed before the arguments about frontiers died down. Bickering occurred sporadically throughout the whole of the nineteenth century, but none of the incidents involved the principals in another war. As far as Astoria was concerned, the Nor'Westers argued that their occupation of the post had resulted from a sale, not a conquest, and when the North West Company was amalgamated with the Hudson's Bay Company in 1821, the latter adopted that point of view. Finally, after more than thirty years of arguments and threats, the British gave up the battle to hold the Columbia Valley and withdrew to Vancouver Island. On the Mississippi, Captain Andrew Bulger burned the fort at Prairie du Chien—the buildings were largely of British construction and had not existed before 1812—and retired with his captured American cannon to Fort Michilimackinac. However, Michilimackinac was not given up as readily. The old Nor'Wester, William McGillivray, lobbied Sir George Prevost and, when Prevost returned to Great Britain, importuned his successor, Sir Gordon Drummond, pressing for British retention of the fort. He argued that the security of Upper Canada depended on retaining the friendship of the Indians; to give up Michilimackinac to the Americans would be a serious blow to British prestige, for the fort had long been something of a symbol to the Indians. As a result of McGillivray's intervention, Lieutenant Colonel Robert McDouall, commanding at Michilimackinac, was ordered not to move until another suitable post had been found for his garrison. The British stalled for time, McDouall replying to the American demand for the surrender of the fort by protesting his need to obtain direct instructions from England and, in any event, to construct new quarters on St. Joseph Island. However, two could play at that game, and the Americans responded by refusing to give up Fort Malden until they could be sure of getting possession of Michilimackinac. Again the British yielded and, by 18 July, Michilimackinac and Malden were in the hands of their original owners. As McDouall had feared, the loss of Michilimackinac did break the close British ties with the Indians. To make sure that they remained broken, Congress passed an Act in 1816 prohibiting the British, under severe penalties, from trafficking in furs with American Indians. The Americans followed this up with a programme to construct military posts in the Michigan Territory. Fort Dearborn was reoccupied, and a new fort, Crawford, was built at Prairie du Chien in 1816. The same year saw the construction of Fort Armstrong on Rock Island and of Fort Howard on Green Bay at the mouth of the Fox River. These were followed by Fort Snelling, built at the junction of the Minnesota and Mississippi rivers, thus blocking a water route used by Canadian fur traders since the days of the French regime.

On the East Coast, the return of British-occupied territory to the United States was achieved with little disturbance. All British troops were withdrawn from the Penobscot in 1814, despite the fact that many of the residents of the area had taken the oath of allegiance to George III. Major General Gerard Gosselin left Maine, taking with him some £11 000 that had been collected in customs duties at the port of Castine during the seven months of the British occupation. These moneys he turned over to the Nova Scotia treasury, and in 1820 they were put to use in paying for the construction of Dalhousie College in Halifax. The ownership of the islands in Passamaquoddy Bay remained controversial for several years. Until the matter was decided by the commission provided for in the fourth article of the Treaty of Ghent, British troops continued to garrison the islands, including Moose Island and Eastport. The commissioners having awarded Moose, Frederick (now Dudley) and Dudley (now Treat) islands to the Americans and confirmed Campobello and Grand Manan islands as British territory, the British troops pulled out of Eastport on 30 June 1818. The boundary of northern Maine was not settled until the so-called Aroostook War in 1838–39, when brawling American and New Brunswick lumberjacks forced Maine and New Brunswick to call out their militias, and British regular troops were moved from Halifax to the mouth of the St. Croix River. Brigadier General Winfield Scott and Sir John Harvey, who had faced each other in the Niagara peninsula, once more found themselves opposed, this time on the Maine–New Brunswick frontier. Fortunately, the British and American governments relied upon negotiators rather than soldiers, and the boundary question was settled in 1842 by Daniel Webster and Lord Ashburton.

On the Canadian frontier, relations between the two countries seemed to be constantly disturbed by unpleasant little incidents, all of them the legacy of the war. Among them: the efforts

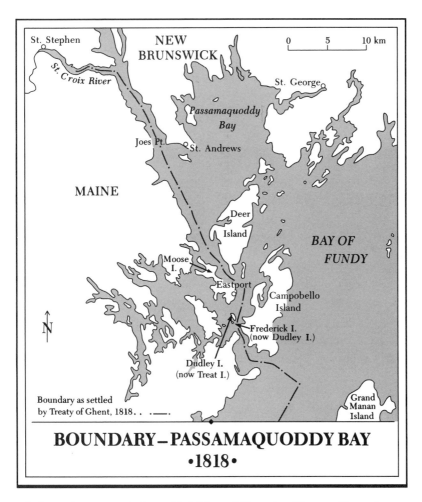

BOUNDARY – PASSAMAQUODDY BAY
·1818·

of Americans to induce British soldiers in Upper Canada to desert to the United States in return for money bribes or promises of military promotion; the seizure of the British schooner *Julia* in 1815; the determination of the United States to retain possession of Bois Blanc Island, opposite Fort Malden; the arrest of Lieutenant Alexander Vidal while he was searching for a stolen boat and deserting sailors on the shores of Lake St. Clair; the murder by Americans of a Kickapoo Indian shooting squirrels on Grosse Ile in the Detroit River; the threatening and posturing of the bellicose Cass, who saw in the protests of the British naval officer on the Lakes, Sir Edward Owen (who had been born on Campobello Island), and of Commander William Bourchier, evidence of British determination, "if not to make open war, at least to break the peace which has so happily been accomplished".[17]

These and other incidents brought up, once again, the question so conveniently shelved at Ghent, namely naval disarmament on the Lakes. The Americans were anxious for it. They wondered whether British plans to improve and augment their armed naval force on the Great Lakes—a consequence of Wellington's insistence that naval superiority on the Lakes was the key to the successful defence of Canada—were an indication of unfriendliness. To avoid a renewal of the naval-building race of the war years, they approached London about obtaining an agreement for the limitation of naval armaments. Castlereagh was suspicious when Americans came to London talking of mutual disarmament. He was apprehensive lest disarmament on the Great Lakes give the United States too much of an advantage in the event of war. Castlereagh believed in the maxim that the best way to ensure peace was to prepare for war, and others in Great Britain shared his opinion. The Marquis of Lansdowne, one of the Opposition leaders, took the same view, and, according to John Quincy Adams,

> one of the lords of the admiralty told the House of Commons last Monday that bumboat expeditions and pinchbeck administrations would do no longer for Canada; that Englishmen must lay their account for fighting battles in fleets of three-deckers on the North American lakes.[18]

Despite this kind of cutlass-rattling by British sailors, Castlereagh proved willing to talk with the Americans, and when he suggested transferring the talks to Washington, John Quincy Adams agreed. During the summer of 1816, the British minister in Washington, Sir Charles Bagot, and the American secretary of state, James Monroe, argued the disarmament question at a leisurely diplomatic pace, so that it was not until 28–29 April 1817 that the final exchange of notes constituting the disarmament agreement took place. Meanwhile, Monroe had succeeded James Madison as president, and the American signature that went on the document along with the British minister's was that of Richard Rush, the acting secretary of state. The agreement became effective at once.

In simple terms, the Rush–Bagot Agreement, which could be annulled by either party after a notice of six months, limited the Great Lakes naval force of each party to four vessels "not exceeding one hundred tons burthen", armed with no more than one 18-pounder gun. Each party would be allowed a single vessel on Lake Ontario, two on the upper Lakes and one on Lake Champlain. Ships of war still in the stocks at Kingston

103. View of Kingston from Fort Henry, overlooking the Dock Yard and the harbour. The war vessels are "in mothballs", that is, housed over.

and Sackets Harbor were to be disarmed at once, but not necessarily broken up. The ships in Kingston harbour were laid up in reserve. They were either housed over and tied up at the wharfs or set to ride at anchor in Navy Bay. In 1819–20 a large stone warehouse called the Stone Frigate, now a cadet dormitory at the Royal Military College of Canada, was built to house rigging, cordage, anchors, tallow, tar and tools, as well as guns and carronades. At Sackets Harbor all but a few of the small vessels were sold. Most of the larger ones were preserved in the manner of the day, by sinking them in deep water, where they could be kept for years and then raised and refitted as required. The unfinished ships-of-the-line were kept on the stocks and protected by ship-houses erected over and around them. The largest, *New Orleans*, was finally sold at auction in 1884. The pride of Yeo's fleet, the *St. Lawrence*, was sold to a Kingston contractor and sank during a summer storm in 1832.

In western Upper Canada, the naval establishment at Penetanguishene on Lake Huron was strengthened after the war. The previous bases at Kingston and on Île aux Noix and the trans-shipping depot at Lachine remained in existence. All were well maintained, judging from the purchase of twenty books of gold leaf and a quarter kilo of Prussian blue "for painting and ornamenting the King's Arms over the Dock Yard gate" at

104. The Commodore's house, Kingston Dock Yard, in 1815.
Note the unfinished ships of war on the stocks in the background.

Kingston in 1817.[19] Nevertheless, the Kingston Dock Yard had served its purpose and soon would no longer be needed. Commodore Robert Barrie might attempt to keep up the appearance of naval pomp and circumstance, but after three reductions in staff he was ordered in January 1834 to close the Yard for good on 1 July. Barrie then returned to England, a knighthood and the life of a country gentleman in Lancashire. Today all that remains of the old Dock Yard is the Commandant's House, the Stone Frigate, a small cottage and the Yard bell. The bell was recently given to the Royal Military College, which occupies the site of the old Kingston Naval Dock Yard on Point Frederick.

From time to time the Rush–Bagot Agreement of 1817 has been held up as an example of how well Canada and the United States solved the problems of frontier armament. Aside from the rather self-righteous aspect of this boast of an "undefended border", the fact is that the agreement was not between Canada and the United States, but between Great Britain and the United States. Moreover, it represented less a matter of high principle than a realistic appreciation of the advantage that the United States, with their men, materials and money close at hand, would have over Great Britain in any naval armaments race on the Great Lakes. In the absence of suitably large canals, the British could not take advantage of their superiority in ocean vessels by sailing them up the St. Lawrence and into Lake Ontario. Castlereagh did not go ahead with the expansion plans of the immediate postwar period, not because he believed them invalid, but because he considered them too costly and too dangerous and thought that the Americans could always outmatch them. The Rush–Bagot Agreement did not extend beyond naval defence. After 1817, the British spent enormous sums, not on ships, but on land fortifications and works along the Canadian–American frontier from Upper Canada to Nova Scotia—Fort Henry, the Rideau Canal, Fort Lennox, the citadels at Quebec and Halifax. In due course, when Canada inherited the problems of her own security and defence, as well as the former British forts, the great disparity between the two countries in men, money and arms made it a matter of common sense for Canada to take shelter under the naval disarmament agreement that had been concluded in 1817. A virtue was made of necessity.

15

Conclusion

IN A GENERAL HISTORY of warfare, the Canadian War of 1812 would bulk small. Perhaps it would merit a footnote, a few sentences, a short paragraph at most. Europeans, including the British, even if they have heard of it, know very little about it. After all, why should they be interested? The war produced no great historical figures, British, Canadian or American; no great field officers, theorists or strategists; no new or original tactical ideas. The military lessons to be learned from the extensive use of Indians, militia, rangers and light infantry had already been learned in the Seven Years' War in North America—the French and Indian wars of American history books. Moreover, the Canadian War was a small war, fought at a time when the people of Great Britain were focusing all their attention on what was happening in Spain, Russia, the Germanies, France and Flanders; the military men they were reading about were among the greatest commanders in history. And who were the leaders in North America? Isaac Brock was a brave man who took chances. He was a hero. But are heroics the role of the commanding officer, or are they the responsibility of those of more junior rank? Orderly logic and disciplined action are the qualities required of a good commander.

If "Tiger" Dunlop was not grossly unfair to his contemporaries, the British troops who served in Canada were "the rubbish of every department in the Army". "Any man," he wrote, "whom the Duke deemed unfit for the Peninsula was considered as quite good enough for the Canadian market."[1] Brock, Dunlop never knew. Prevost, he criticized:

403

> Timid at all times, despairing of his resources, he was afraid to venture anything: and when he did venture, like an unskilful hunter, he spurred his horse spiritedly at the fence, and while the animal rose, he suddenly checked him—baulked him in the leap he could easily have cleared, and landed himself in the ditch.[2]

Only Lieutenant Colonel William Drummond of Kelty, who commanded the 104th (New Brunswick) Regiment and was killed at Fort Erie in 1814, won Dunlop's praise as a man who was "everything that could be required in a soldier; brave, generous, open-hearted and good-natured, he added to all these the talents of a first-rate tactician." Sir Gordon Drummond considered his kinsman a bit eccentric, but agreed with Dunlop that "all these eccentricities would one day mellow down into sound common sense."[3]

If the Canadian War did not bring great distinction to any British or American officers, neither did it produce any Canadian-born officers of merit, with the possible exception of Sir Gordon Drummond. The one really outstanding figure was the Indian leader, Tecumseh.

Nor did the War of 1812 produce any literary figures to attract the attention of British readers. Some of those who wrote about the war were competent, but none were great. Among them were the participants who recorded the war as they saw it, men such as John Richardson, who served with the Right Division from the capture of Detroit to the disaster at Moraviantown, and Dr. William "Tiger" Dunlop, who spent his time as a medical officer in Montreal, on the St. Lawrence and in the Niagara peninsula. Both wrote lively, interesting accounts. Richardson's *War of 1812, Containing a Full and Detailed Narrative of the Operations of the Right Division of the Canadian Army* is an autobiographical and documented history of the war on the Detroit frontier written by a Canadian whose family background went deep into the early days of the fur trade. Richardson wrote with feeling for and understanding of the country and the people in it. Dunlop's *Recollections of the American War, 1812–14* is also autobiographical. It is critical, observant and forthright. Here is a sample of his prose:

> My patients gradually began to diminish—some died, and these I buried,—some recovered by the remedies employed, or in spite of them, and these I forwarded or carried with me to join the Regiment,—and others who, from loss of limbs or of the use of them, might be considered as permanently *hors de combat*, I sent by easy stages to Montreal General Hospital.[4]

105. Major John Richardson, who served with Brock and Procter and wrote an account of the operations of the Right Division during the war

The contemporary historians of the War of 1812, while producing useful works, were inspired largely by a desire to correct what they considered to be the bias of American accounts. William James, who had been a prisoner of war in the United States during the conflict, wrote *A Full and Correct Account of the Military Occurrences of the Late War between Great Britain and the United States of America*, published in 1818; David Thompson, who served with the Royal Scots and settled down as a schoolteacher in Niagara, published his *History of the Late War between Great Britain and the United States of America* in 1832. Another contemporary Canadian historian of the war was the Nova Scotia–born Robert Christie, who subsequently moved to Lower Canada and wrote several volumes dealing with the history of the administrations of Craig, Prevost, Drummond, Sherbrooke and others. Of all these writers, however, none had any literary pretensions except Richardson and Dunlop.

In view of the romantic bent of the age, it is surprising that the Canadian War did not inspire writers to take advantage of the dramatic material afforded by British redcoats and Indians fighting Americans along the Detroit River; Canadians and Kentuckians fighting on the banks of the Thames in Upper Canada; gunboats on the St. Lawrence, armed schooners on the Great Lakes and privateers on the Atlantic; stand-up battles and Indian scalpings; fur traders, voyageurs, militiamen; the figures of Isaac Brock, John Harvey, Drummond of Kelty, and even the boy, John Richardson. What tales Walter Scott or Fenimore Cooper could have related with heroic material like this! But Canada produced no Walter Scott, no Fenimore Cooper. Richardson, the best of the writers, produced good history but mediocre novels. His two fictional works, *The Canadian Brothers* and *Westbrook the Outlaw*, which made their appearance some years after the war, are not in the same class as his *War of 1812*.

At least Tecumseh attracted the attention of some contemporary writers. In the anonymous work, *The Lucubrations of Humphrey Ravelin, Esq., Late Major in the ** Regiment of Infantry* (a series of essays rather than a novel), there is an interesting study of Indian warfare and of the Shawnee chief. The author is believed to be one George Procter, who came to Canada with the 5th Regiment in 1814.[5] Another anonymous effort, attributed to George Longmore, believed to have been born in Canada, was *Tales of Chivalry and Romance*, which appeared in 1826. It included a long poem on Tecumseh, which may well have inspired the publication, though not the writing, two years later, of a metrical romance by John Richardson entitled *Tecumseh; or, The Warrior of the West*.

IN 1812 WAR WAS, as it still is, a political act. Without political objectives, war is a meaningless event involving irrational bloodshed. The great German theorist Karl von Clausewitz declared that war was but the waging of politics by violent methods; in his book *Vom Kriege (On War)*, he wrote, "State policy is the womb in which war is developed, in which the outlines lie hidden in a rudimentary state."[6] He judged the success or failure of any war by how completely the nation starting the war achieved the political purposes its leaders had in mind.

As for the events of 1812, the historical fact is that the United States declared war on Great Britain and sent its armies to invade Upper and Lower Canada; the Americans, with due deliberation, chose the time and place, forcing war on British North America when Great Britain was heavily involved in the struggle against Napoleon Bonaparte. The avowed objects of this act of political violence were to extract maritime concessions from the British, to put an end to the British–Indian alliance, and to conquer Canada. After three years of fighting, the government of the United States had failed to bend Great Britain to its will, and failed, too, to seize and hold effectively any part of British North America; instead, the Americans had been compelled to yield some of their territories in the West and on the Atlantic Coast to combined British and Canadian forces, assisted by Indian warriors. The United States had gambled on Britain being unable to provide its colonies with reinforcements and on the inhabitants of the Canadas being unwilling to fight. Unfortunately for the Americans, the British did put an effort into defending British North America. The outcome was a three-year war that the United States was unable to press to a decisive conclusion. By Clausewitz's standards, the war was a failure for the United States, which failed to attain its political ends.

At the peace table the United States was more successful. The American negotiators were able, by skilful negotiation and determination, to escape the penalty of military failure by obtaining Great Britain's adherence to the doctrine of the *status quo ante bellum*. This may have been because Great Britain's political aims were directed towards a satisfactory political decision in Europe rather than in North America. British North America was no more than a subsidiary concern of British foreign policy, and in November 1814 the British government concluded that territorial accessions to the Canadas and New Brunswick were not worth the price of continuing the war in North America, not with Napoleon waiting in the wings to return to the centre of the European stage.

The American government, though it never publicly admitted as much—it would have been political suicide to do so—, accepted the decision of the War of 1812 as a defeat for American policy. Despite the frontier episodes and war scares of the years following the Treaty of Ghent, at no time did the United States seriously consider the possibility of trying conclusions again with Great Britain. The American imperial drive was therefore diverted from the North to the West and South. Deprived by the Treaty of Ghent of the assistance of Great Britain, upon whom they had relied since the days of the Revolutionary War, the Indians were in no position to offer effective opposition to American pressure. The Upper Mississippi and Great Lakes region became a white man's, not a red man's, country. "Old America seems to be breaking up and moving westward", wrote Morris Birbeck in 1818 as he journeyed west. "We are seldom out of sight . . . of family groups behind and before us."[7] The last spark of resistance, the Black Hawk War of 1832, merely confirmed that the concept of an Indian state in the Northwest—the idea of Pontiac, the ideal of Tecumseh, and the proposal of Goulburn at Ghent—was never to be realized. It was dead, incapable of resuscitation in the North. Neither could it be realized in the South, where Creeks, Cherokees, Choctaws and Chickasaws all submitted to the government of the United States. In 1816, the only Indian holdouts, the Seminoles, were driven into East Florida by Andrew Jackson. But, in crushing the Seminoles, Jackson invaded land belonging to Spain. Spanish territory, rather than British, thus became the object of American expansionism, and in 1821 Spain was forced to cede East Florida to the United States. Texas, New Mexico and California all went the same way, as the United States pushed ever farther south and west. American continentalism did not involve another war with Canada and Great Britain, even though the threat continued to influence Canadian party politics and Canadian defence policy up to the twentieth century.

Although the war did not achieve the economic and territorial aims the United States government had in mind, it turned out to be an important step in the process of nation-building. American soldiers had stood up to the British regulars in Canada and acquitted themselves with distinction on more than one occasion, so it was not difficult for time to gloss over the errors, defeats and humiliations at Detroit, Queenston Heights, Châteauguay, Crysler's Farm and Bladensburg, and to inflate the victories of Fort George, Moraviantown, Chippawa, Plattsburg, and especially New Orleans, and the naval successes on Lake Erie and Lake Champlain. In this way, a certain mythology developed that transformed the War of 1812, in the public mind and memory, from a negative event in American history, a military defeat, into a victory over Great Britain—a second successful War of Independence! Even Ripley's withdrawal did not obscure the glorious picture of Americans fighting the British to a standstill at Lundy's Lane. After the War of 1812, Americans talked and sang about the "Star-Spangled Banner" of Fort McHenry, at Baltimore, forgetting about the capture of Washington and the burning of the Capitol. Everybody remembered USS *Constitution* (Old Ironsides), but who remembered that the British navy, despite defeats in duels with individual ships, dominated the oceans during the whole of the war years? In this way there grew up the American tradition of success in the War of 1812 that, despite its shaky foundation in historical fact, has served to stimulate an American sense of national identity, national pride and national unity.

The new pride in military achievement brought about the demise of the Federalist party in New England, as opposition to America's successful war became equated with disloyalty. Federalists had refused to support the war effort, they had dealt clandestinely with the British and the Canadians, they had even threatened to break up the union. Who now would or could trust the traitorous Federalists? And when prosperity returned to New England, after the conclusion of peace, the Federalists were deprived of the economic arguments they had formerly advanced in favour of peace with Great Britain. The Federalist party soon disappeared, even in its former stronghold of Massachusetts, extinguished by the war-stimulated wave of patriotism. It is evidence of the postwar popularity of the war that four of the presidents who succeeded Madison were men whose names were intimately associated, politically or militarily, with the War of 1812: James Monroe (1817–25), John Quincy Adams (1825–29), Andrew Jackson (1829–37) and William Henry Harrison (1841).

THE EVENTS OF 1812 to 1815 also left an imprint on British North America. The steady stream of immigrants that had moved into Upper Canada from the United States ceased abruptly at the beginning of hostilities and did not pick up the same momentum after the war. Prospective settlers no longer found the

friendly atmosphere of earlier years; and the old laws governing naturalization, which decreed that aliens had to live in
Upper Canada seven years before becoming entitled to hold
land, were now enforced with rigour. In November 1817, an
order from the Colonial Office stated that all persons holding
land illegally in the province should be dispossessed. Here was
a definite break in the old welcome-everybody settlement policy
and the adoption of a deliberate effort to control the composition of the Upper-Canadian population and strengthen its British quality. American immigration was to be discouraged and
British immigration encouraged. The settlement of disbanded
soldiers in Upper Canada and the promotion of Scottish and
English immigration schemes would ensure that it remained a
British province. In 1815 an announcement appeared in the
Edinburgh press offering free transportation, 100 acres of land
and rations for eight months to each prospective settler, provided he was of good character and deposited £18 as security
that he would remain in Canada at least two years. Other
schemes followed. They did not bring large numbers of people
to Upper Canada, for those anxious to emigrate tended to go
to the United States until the mid 1820s, when a more persis-
tent movement of people to Upper Canada began. But the policy
was politically successful in the long run, and the British imprint
remained on Upper Canada, on both the ethnic composition
of the province and the nature of its institutions.

Equally significant was the development of an Upper-
Canadian historical mythology. A little less than a generation
before Madison's declaration of war in June 1812, the Loyalists, the men and women who supported the Crown against
republicanism and democracy, had lost a seven years' civil war
in the Thirteen Colonies and had, in consequence, been driven
out of their homes in the United States and forced to seek refuge
in the wilderness of British North America—in the Maritimes
and in what became known as Upper Canada. Then, a second
time, they were faced with the same threat, the same need to
defend their new homes against the same enemies. Memories
of the Revolutionary War were renewed and intensified by the
War of 1812. But this time the Loyalists won; the enemy was
hurled back, not only by British regular troops, but by the virile
response of the old Loyalists and their sons and those who
shared the Loyalist tradition. The role of the Loyalists during
the war has been exaggerated, for Upper Canadians, no less
than Americans, have been inclined to see themselves as larger

106. Some War of 1812 veterans photographed in 1861 on a lawn in Rosedale, Toronto

than they really were. But what is true is not as important as what people believe to be true. And the conviction that the Loyalists stood up to and defeated the American invaders became fact to many Canadians as did its corollary, that the British–Canadian victory was one of loyalty, political integrity and liberty over the imperialistic continentalism of a foreign power. For some years after the war, the Loyalist tradition grew in virility. It also became exclusive, not in the social sense, but in the sense that the Loyalist tradition was not one that could be shared by the American settlers in the country; neither could it be shared by the Irish, nor the radical elements who came to the province from the British Isles after the war. Loyalism became a common bond holding together the diverse elements that made up the governing party, the so-called Family Compact, and made it possible for them to govern the province for almost twenty years. Weakened in its influence by the political reforms of the mid-century, the Loyalist tradition nevertheless remained the historical source of the anti-American feeling that occasionally surfaces in Canada's dealings with the United States. Five generations and more have not entirely obliterated the memories of the Revolution and the War of 1812.

The War of 1812 also tended to give Upper Canadians their own distinctive sense of identity. Just as it did in the United States, the war encouraged the growth of a national idea in Canada, not in the same sense that it made Americans more self-consciously American and strengthened the idea of the American union, but in tending to make Upper Canadians more British and anti-American. The war gave Upper Canadians a new focus of cohesion by providing them, for the first time, with a history. A land of refuge for the Loyalist exodus, Upper Canada had been a political entity since only 1791. It was scarcely more than twenty-one years of age when war broke out in 1812. But within three years Upper Canada had acquired a history, just as Lower Canada and Newfoundland, and perhaps Nova Scotia (Acadia), had a history. Not merely a history of trapline, axe and log cabin, or a history of physical endurance in an unfriendly climate, but the history of the survival of a people, a political idea, a political principle—the Crown—against ideas and principles of republicanism. Few towns along the St. Lawrence, the Lake Ontario strand, the Niagara River, the Lake Erie shore, the Thames, were untouched, were not scarred by the fighting between 1812 and 1814. The stories of battles, raids, burning and looting became the folklore of the province and provided Upper Canadians with a new appreciation of themselves and of their history and identity.

The feeling of confidence and identity engendered by the war among Upper Canadians was probably the only good thing that could be said for it. According to John Howison, the British traveller who spent two and a half years in Upper Canada, the war had had "a most pernicious effect upon the morals of the people". Responsibility for this moral decline, he attributed to the bad example set by the invading troops:

> Most of the American private soldiers were entirely destitute of moral principle, or any sense of decency, and often exhibited a wanton and unblushing profligacy, which in Europe would have received chastisement from the law. A good deal of this was communicated to the peasantry of Upper Canada, and the influence of the infection is not yet entirely destroyed.[8]

There was nothing unusual about a decline in morality during wartime. Theft, drunkenness, brutality, rape and murder are the usual accompaniments of war and invasion. But whether, as Howison implied, the American soldiers were principally responsible for stimulating an increase in the social immoralities in Canada is debatable. There is no denying, however, that theirs was a tradition that placed a premium on liberty and freedom from restraint, especially when that restraint was imposed by an English government or an English king. The libertarian

107. Matthew W. Stanley, of Mille Roches, served with the 1st Regiment Stormont Militia in the War of 1812

rhetoric of the Revolutionary War had by no means disappeared in 1812, even if it was less strident, and moral considerations seem to have had little restraining influence upon men like Andrew Westbrook and John B. Campbell.

THE WAR OF 1812 gave a fillip to the economy of British North America, particularly to that of Upper Canada. In the early years of the nineteenth century, all the provinces depended a great deal upon the markets for produce and labour provided by the British military garrisons. Without the military and naval establishments, the people of British North America would have found it much harder to make ends meet. Few of them had any capital and few were familiar with the problems of making a living in a raw, undeveloped land. But because they were able to sell their produce and their labour to the soldiers and sailors the British government sent to North America after the Revolutionary War, the people of the Maritime Provinces and the two Canadas were able to maintain a comparatively satisfactory standard of living. However, that standard had begun to decline in the years just before the War of 1812. The drop in the prices received for flour, potash and lumber, the principal products of colonial industry in 1810 and 1811, was reversed only by Mr. Madison's declaration of war in June 1812.

Throughout the war, military supplies of every kind rose in price. Admittedly, the fur trade suffered from the interruption the war imposed on the movement of furs from the West to Montreal, but this had little impact on the economy generally since men and boats found ready employment moving soldiers and supplies from Lower Canada to the military stations in Upper Canada. With full employment available in either the militia or the transport service and an effective medium of exchange in the form of Army Bills to supplement the limited supply of specie, Canadians enjoyed what might be termed a booming economy. Farmers, merchants and labourers alike received good prices, good profits and good wages throughout the war years.[9]

The Americans also profited from the war. Unable to purchase their arms abroad, they were compelled to develop their own armaments industry, thus providing the impetus for an industrial economy that carried over after the war. Following the signing of the Treaty of Ghent, the United States entered a period of geographical, economic and technological expansion.

In British North America the wartime prosperity did not carry over into the postwar period. According to Howison, the economic stimulus of the war was not an unmixed blessing. In Howison's view it was

> the main cause of the present embarrassed and unpromising state of Upper Canada, and produced this effect in three different ways: first it was the means of withdrawing the minds of its inhabitants from their usual pursuits and occupations; next it extinguished that steadiness and spirit of industry which had formerly characterized them; and, lastly, it created a temporary wealth in the Province, which induced the people to be lavish in every respect, and contract debts that were altogether disproportionate to their means of payment.[10]

With the cessation of hostilities came a reduction in British military expenditures. The British regiments either returned home or were disbanded in Canada, thus easing the burden on the British taxpayer but creating economic problems in Canada. The deflationary effect of withdrawing the Army Bills hit Upper Canadians hard, particularly as the slack was not taken up by any large-scale immigration into the province for some years after the war. Americans were not welcome after 1814, and the British, the English in particular, were not disposed to emigrate; when they did, many of them simply used Canada as a doorway to the United States, a movement that is not always apparent in the official statistics of the day.[11] Despite official encouragement, British settlers did not come in any numbers to British North America until the 1830s.[12] Some relief was afforded by the continued presence of British regular garrisons in North America, and by the great civil and military works undertaken in the postwar years, including the Lachine, Rideau and Welland canals and the great fortifications at Kingston, Quebec and Halifax. The establishment of Canada's first banks, including the Bank of Montreal, the Bank of Upper Canada and the Halifax Banking Company, helped to stimulate the circulation of money. Even so, economic stagnation persisted for some years after the war, providing fertile ground for the seeds of political unrest. The initial complaints after the conclusion of peace, regarding war pensions, militia land grants and compensation for property damage, were but the first indications of the troubles that were to lead to the rebellions of 1837–38 in Upper and Lower Canada.

To the Maritimes the war had brought prosperity, but wartime prosperity has always been deceptive. The return of peace in 1815 was accompanied by the prompt suspension of military building and ship repair, the reduction of the fleet, and the return to England of troops and government officials, speculators and camp followers. Halifax became a place of empty barracks and crumbling forts. During the war, Halifax and Saint John, as well as Quebec, had been filled with merchant ships carrying lumber openly to Great Britain and surreptitiously to the United States. But by 1818 the timber trade was falling apart, and the price of white pine—a wood favoured by the Admiralty for masts and spars owing to its straight grain—dropped between 1818 and 1824 from a high of 107s per load to 69s.[13] Great Britain was once again buying her lumber from the Baltic states, and British North America reverted to its familiar role as a standby source of lumber in time of war. Even the Halifax Dock Yard declined in importance as most of its employees were discharged and others moved to Bermuda. Not until fourteen years after the Treaty of Ghent did Halifax begin to show signs of economic vigour, when Gustavus Nicolls undertook to rebuild the Citadel, with a view to making it proof against the climate as well as against enemy shot and shell in the event of another war with the United States.[14]

FROM THE MILITARY standpoint, the most interesting aspect of the war, aside from politics and general strategy, was the role of the citizen soldier. The United States, despite the lessons of the Revolutionary War, began the War of 1812 still believing in the minuteman tradition. The government preferred the militiaman to the regular soldier, who was thought to be costly and poorly motivated. Since he was held in poor esteem, who would want to be a regular soldier? Given the chance of enlisting in the regular army or serving in the militia, the average American preferred the latter. Thus, even as late as 1814, when Congress finally accepted a regular army as a military necessity and authorized an establishment of 62 000, only 38 000 could be found in the ranks by September. It was not an impressive total; obviously the American people still chose to rely to a great extent on the state militias, with their inadequate training and incompetent officers. Yet, the need for a regular army had become obvious by 1814, and was reinforced by the events on the Niagara that year. It was the regulars, trained by Winfield Scott, who won the victory over Riall at Chippawa and made such a strong showing at Lundy's Lane; the American militia contributed little or nothing. Early operations had witnessed a disposition in the militia to either run away or refuse to cross the state line. Even at Plattsburg, in 1814, where the militia put on a better face, it was Macdonough's naval aggressiveness and Prevost's timidity on land, rather than the ferocity or determination of Macomb's militia, that secured the American victory. Broadly speaking, the record of the American militia during the War of 1812 was dismal and not to the credit of American arms. But if the militia could not be relied upon, neither could the volunteer, and ultimately the United States has, in wartime, resorted to conscription to build up its military strength.

In Canada, the situation was different. Here the Canadian regiments, fencibles and embodied militia worked in close collaboration with the British regular establishment. The fencibles were provincial units raised for service in North America.

They were recruited in Newfoundland, Nova Scotia, New Brunswick and the two Canadas. To all intents and purposes, they were colonial regular units, and took part in most of the battles of the war. Moreover, British regular officers frequently served in the fencibles for varying periods. The result was to give these corps the advantage of the best military professionalism available, and also to familiarize regular officers with colonial attitudes. For example, senior officers such as Colonel Edward Baynes, the adjutant general of the forces, served not only with the Nova Scotia Fencibles but also with the Glengarry Light Infantry; and Noah Freer, who was Prevost's military secretary, served at different times with the Nova Scotia Fencibles, the Canadian Fencibles and the New Brunswick Fencibles. Prevost also included provincial officers among his aides-de-camp, among them John Macdonell, Nathaniel Coffin, Christopher Hagerman and Allan McLean. Similarly, provincial aides were attached to the staff of the various general officers, including Brock, Sheaffe, Drummond and Procter. The senior officer of the Upper Canada militia was Major General Aeneas Shaw, a former member of the Queen's Rangers; the quartermaster general was Lieutenant Colonel Robert Nichol of the 2nd Regiment Norfolk Militia.

In addition to the fencible regiments there were battalions of embodied militia. The Volunteer Incorporated Militia Battalion, organized in Upper Canada in 1813, was staffed largely by officers drawn from county militia units from Lincoln, Norfolk, York, Northumberland, Leeds and Grenville. In Lower Canada, the adjutant general of the militia was Colonel François Vassal de Monviel, and the quartermaster general was Lieutenant Colonel Louis-Joseph Fleury Deschambault. The eight battalions of Milice d'Élite Incorporée and the Frontier Light Infantry were formed entirely by embodying companies of county militia. These embodied units were full-time units and were trained like regulars. Usually they were commanded by experienced Canadian officers who had seen service in the British army, such as Fleury Deschambault, Patrick Murray, Salaberry, and Thomas-Pierre-Joseph Taschereau; the first three had served with the 60th and the last with the Royal Canadian Volunteers, a fencible unit organized in 1796 and disbanded in 1802. The same was true in Upper Canada, where Neil McLean had served with the 84th and "Red George" Macdonell with the 8th. Thus, in the Canadian militia there existed a core of professionalism that the American battalions lacked.

In addition to the full-time militia soldiers were the men who belonged to the specially trained companies known as the flank companies; these were the companies that for the most part turned out when militiamen were required for operational purposes. Members of the battalion companies served from time to time as guards and escorts, performing tasks essential to the successful operation of any military force; while functioning on a part-time basis, they were easily and quickly integrated into the military establishment as paymasters, surgeons, provincial Royal Artillery drivers, light dragoons, rangers, judge advocates, chaplains, commissaries of transport, voyageurs, and town majors.

Fighting and working alongside the fencibles and militia were the officers and interpreters of the Indian Department, commanded by Lieutenant Colonel William Claus in Upper Canada and Colonel Sir John Johnson in Lower Canada. Their role was of great importance to Canada during the War of 1812.

In emphasizing the participation of the militia in the military structure of British North America the purpose is not to overplay their contribution to the Canadian War of 1812, but to establish the point that, as far as the two Canadas were concerned, the war was a national military effort, which involved the British, Canadians and Indians alike, and also to suggest that the integration of regular, fencible and militia troops achieved a considerable degree of success. Any Canadian familiar with the history of warfare will agree that experienced soldiers are superior to raw recruits and that courage is no substitute for training. Any Canadian familiar with the War of 1812 will acknowledge that, without the British regulars, Canada would probably have been rapidly overrun by the enemy. That this did not happen was largely owing to the employment of trained men, British and Canadian alike, and to the coordination of the efforts of regular and citizen soldiers—the kind of integration and coordination that was lacking in the United States.[15] On the British side, there was also a much closer collaboration, on the Great Lakes and Lake Champlain, by the Provincial Marine and Royal Navy forces with the land forces, particularly at the command level, than existed among the Americans. How Jacob Brown must have cursed inter-service rivalry as he stood on Queenston Heights in 1814, looking in vain for the sails of Chauncey's vessels, whose presence might have ensured his success. In a defensive war, fought on the Canadian frontier, there was no place for such rivalry. And there is no place for it in the Canadian armed forces today.

FOURTEEN YEARS after the Canadian War of 1812 ended, the Duke of Wellington, who had been unwilling to come to North America in 1814, was still wondering how it was that the British had come out of the war as well as they had. He concluded that the British had not won the war; the Americans had lost it. To a select committee of the House of Commons discussing defence expenditures in Canada, he said:

> I have never been in that country, but I must add that I have been astonished that the officers of the army and navy employed in that country were able to defend those provinces last war; and I can attribute their having been able to defend them as they did only to the inexperience of the officers of the United States in the operations of war.[16]

The Duke of Wellington was not very generous in his assessment of the Americans. Never, during his lifetime, was he willing to concede that there were any other troops to equal the infantry regiments that fought under his command in Spain. But Canadian and American infantry could fight well too when they were competently led, a fact the stiff-necked Iron Duke might have discovered for himself had he seized the opportunity to come to North America.

More to the point were Wellington's comments on war in general. To his friend Lady Frances Shelley he wrote:

> It is a bad thing to be always fighting. While in the thick of it, I am too much occupied to feel anything; but it is wretched just after. It is quite impossible to think of glory. Both mind and feelings are exhausted. I am wretched even at the moment of victory, and I always say that, next to a battle lost, the greatest misery is a battle gained. . . . I never wish for any more fighting.[17]

Appendix I

Honours and Awards

IN ADDITION to the usual knighthoods and memberships in chivalric orders conferred upon British officers who played a distinguished role in the Napoleonic wars and the War of 1812 (for example, Sir Isaac Brock and Sir Roger Sheaffe), medals were also issued "in commemoration of the brilliant and distinguished events in which the success of His Majesty's arms has received the royal approbation".[1] However, in view of the "considerable inconvenience having been found to attend the increased number of medals that have been issued", the Horse Guards announced on 7 October 1813 that only one medal "shall be borne by each officer recommended for such distinction" and that, in place of successive medals, each individual entitled to them would carry "a gold clasp attached to the ribbon to which the medal is suspended, and inscribed with the name of the battle, or siege, to which it relates". Should there be a legitimate claim to a fourth mark of distinction, "a cross shall be borne by each officer, with the name of the four battles, or sieges inscribed thereupon." Additional distinctions would take the form of a clasp to be worn on the ribbon of the cross. General officers were entitled to wear their medal or cross suspended by a red ribbon "the colour of the sash, with a blue edge, round the neck"; commanding officers of battalions or corps equivalent thereto, officers who succeeded to actual command during an engagement, chiefs of military departments and their deputies and assistants (having the rank of field officers), and other officers specially recommended were to wear their medals attached by a ribbon of the same colour "to the buttonhole of their uniform".

The gold cross is a straight-armed cross paty (known in Austria as the cannon cross) having, in the centre, a British lion statant. In each limb of the cross is inscribed the name of a battle. The cross is edged with laurel leaves and is attached by an ornamental ring to the top

108. General Officers' Gold Medal (obverse). It was hung round the neck by a crimson ribbon edged in blue.

swivel. The gold medal has on the obverse the figure of Britannia seated on a globe and wearing a helmet. In her right hand is a laurel wreath and in her left a palm branch. To Britannia's right is the head of a British lion, and her left hand rests on an oval shield charged with the crosses of the Union. The reverse carries, within a wreath of laurel, the name of the engagement for which the medal was awarded. The medal was struck in two sizes, 53 and 33 mm in diameter.[2]

On 28 January 1814, the Horse Guards issued a directive that "officers who have been most distinguished in the last two campaigns" in the Canadas "against very superior numbers of the enemy" and were recommended by Sir George Prevost were to be eligible to receive the appropriate medals. The battles that were considered "as giving a just claim to such distinctions, on the part of the officers engaged," were the capture of Detroit, 16 August 1812; the defeat of Hampton at Châteauguay, 26 October 1813; and the defeat of Wilkinson at Crysler's Farm, 11 November 1813.[3] That Ogdensburg, 22 February 1813, was not considered as a battle honour explains why "Red George" Macdonell did not receive recognition for this engagement.

109. Field Officers' Gold Medal (obverse) is of the same design as the larger General Officers' Medal, but was worn hanging from the buttonhole on a ribbon.

The officers[4] who received the above medals included:

GENERAL OFFICERS' GOLD MEDAL—FORT DETROIT
Major General Sir Isaac Brock

FIELD OFFICERS' GOLD MEDAL
FORT DETROIT
Lieutenant Colonel Matthew Elliott, 1st Essex; Superintendent of the Indian Department, Upper Canada
Lieutenant Colonel John Macdonell, Provincial Aide-de-Camp, Upper Canada Militia
Lieutenant Colonel Robert Nichol, 2nd Norfolk; Quartermaster General, Upper Canada Militia
Lieutenant Colonel Thomas St. George, Inspecting Field Officer, Upper Canada Militia
Captain John B. Glegg, 49th Foot, Aide-de-Camp
Captain Peter Chambers, 41st Foot
Captain M.C. Dixon, Royal Engineers

Captain Adam Muir, 41st Foot
Captain Joseph Tallon, 41st Foot
Lieutenant Felix Troughton, Royal Artillery

CHÂTEAUGUAY
Lieutenant Colonel George Macdonell, Glengarry Light Infantry;
   Inspecting Field Officer, Lower Canada Militia
Lieutenant Colonel Charles-Michel d'Irumberry de Salaberry, Volti-
   geurs; Inspecting Field Officer, Lower Canada Militia

CRYSLER'S FARM
Lieutenant Colonel John Harvey, 6th Garrison Battalion; Deputy
   Adjutant General
Lieutenant Colonel Joseph W. Morrison, 89th Foot
Lieutenant Colonel Thomas Pearson, 23rd Foot; Inspecting Field
   Officer of Upper Canada Militia at Prescott (received the clasp to
   his Albuera medal)
Lieutenant Colonel Charles Plenderleath, 49th Foot
Major Miller Clifford, 89th Foot
Major Frederick George Heriot, Voltigeurs
2nd Captain Henry G. Jackson, Royal Artillery

In addition to these medals and clasps, a special medal to signalize
distinguished service during the Canadian War of 1812 was struck by
the Loyal and Patriotic Society of Upper Canada, an organization
formed in the early months of the war for the dual purpose of reliev-
ing wartime distress and commemorating conspicuous bravery. The
specifications of the medal as determined by the directors in January
1813 were as follows:[5]

> Two inches and one half in diameter. In a circle formed by a wreath of
> laurel, the words FOR MERIT. Legend, PRESENTED BY A GRATE-
> FUL COUNTRY. On the reverse. A streight between two lakes, on the
> north side a Beaver (emblem of peaceful industry), the ancient armorial
> bearing of Canada. In the background an English lion slumbering. On
> the south side of the streight, the American eagle planeing in the air, as
> if checked from seizing the Beaver by the presence of the Lion. Legend,
> UPPER CANADA PRESERVED.

The recipients were to be recommended by "officers commanding
corps of militia", and their names were to be forwarded to the lieutenant governor. Unfortunately, the number of "subjects" recommended
exceeded the number of medals available and no awards were made.
From time to time questions were asked in the legislature about the
disposition of the medals. After an investigation in 1840, a select committee of the legislature recommended that the medals "should be distributed according to the original intention, among the militia entitled to them and who are now living, and the children of such as are
dead, that they may be retained as a distinguished memorial of the
gallantry and loyalty of the brave and patriotic men for whom they

110. Upper Canada Preserved Medal (obverse and reverse)

111. General Service Medal with the Châteauguay clasp (obverse and reverse)

were designed." At that date there were extant 61 gold and 548 silver medals. One gold and 2 silver medals of the original number struck were apparently missing. The directors of the Loyal and Patriotic Society of Upper Canada, resenting the intrusion of the legislature into what they regarded as a private matter, did not distribute the medals, but sold them for bullion for the benefit of the Toronto General Hospital.

Several years later, in 1847, Queen Victoria established the Military General Service Medal, with clasps, for distribution to other ranks as well as officers in recognition of the service of her soldiers. Aged veterans who forwarded applications received the medal in belated recognition of their services at Fort Detroit, Châteauguay and Crysler's Farm. Those who survived the bitterly fought actions of Queenston Heights and Lundy's Lane went unrewarded. This General Service Medal carries the head of Queen Victoria on the obverse and, on the reverse, the erect figure of the Queen standing on a dais and extending a wreath of laurel over the head of the Duke of Wellington, who kneels before her. The legend reads, "To the British Army/1793–1814." The ribbon is crimson edged with blue. The 911 medals that were issued for service in Canada were distributed as follows:[6]

	Upper Canada Militia	Lower Canada Militia	Indians	41st Foot	49th Foot	89th Foot	Royal Artillery	Royal Newfoundland Fencibles	Other	TOTAL
Fort Detroit	230		18	56	64		6	4		378
Châteauguay	1	251	82				4		1	339
Crysler's Farm	28	35	11			65	5	2	2	148
Fort Detroit and Châteauguay			3							3
Fort Detroit and Crysler's Farm	1	1	3		1		1	1		8
Châteauguay and Crysler's Farm		2	1							3
3 Bars: Fort Detroit Châteauguay Crysler's Farm		2	1							3
Fort Detroit and others				6			1			7
Châteauguay and others									1	1
Crysler's Farm and others						20	1			21
TOTAL	260	291	119	62	65	85	18	7	4	911

In addition to medals and awards, collective honours were given to various companies and regiments, including the 100th Regiment and the grenadier companies of the Royal and 41st Regiments, for the capture of Fort Niagara, 19 December 1813; and to the 1st Battalion of the Royals, the 1st Battalion of the 8th (King's), the 2nd Battalion of the 89th, the 103rd, the Glengarry Light Infantry, the flank companies of the 41st, Major Robert Lisle's squadron of the 19th Light Dragoons and detachments of the Royal Artillery for their service at Lundy's Lane, 25 July 1814. These regiments and companies were given the right to bear the word *Niagara* upon their colours and appointments, "as a testimony of their good conduct" on the occasions cited.[7] In November 1815, the 104th Regiment was also awarded this honour. Battle honours, including those for Detroit, Queenston and Miami (Maumee), are borne on the colours of the Welsh Regiment, which perpetuates the 41st Regiment of Foot.

Appendix II

Canadian Uniforms

IN UPPER CANADA, the militia wore green jackets faced with red in 1813, and with yellow in 1814; their trousers were blue. The Incorporated Militia wore red jackets with green facings in 1813 and grey trousers; in 1814 the facings were blue.

In Lower Canada, the several battalions of the embodied militia were authorized to wear scarlet jackets and blue trousers. The facings varied according to the unit; in 1813, they were blue for the 1st Battalion, light green for the 2nd, yellow for the 3rd, dark green for the 4th, and black for the 5th and 6th Battalions. Owing to the shortage of scarlet jackets, green ones were substituted in some battalions.

The fencible regiments were clothed in a manner similar to the British regulars, that is, they wore scarlet jackets. The Voltigeurs were an exception in that they wore grey jackets with black collar and cuffs, grey trousers, and a light bearskin cap in 1812–13 but a shako afterwards. The Glengarrians wore green.

Caldwell's Rangers, who fought alongside the Indians in Upper Canada, wore plain dark-green jackets, grey trousers, and a shallow bucket hat. Captain Thomas Coleman's Canadian Light Dragoons wore blue jackets with red cuffs and collar, felt helmets with a bearskin crown, grey trousers, and leather half-boots laced in front.[8]

Appendix III

British and Swiss Infantry and Canadian Fencible and Militia Regiments that Served in the Canadian War of 1812

BRITISH REGULAR INFANTRY REGIMENTS THAT SERVED IN THE CANADAS, WITH THE DATES OF THEIR ARRIVAL

1st, or Royal Scots, 1812
3rd (Buffs), 1814
5th (Northumberland), 1814
6th (Warwickshire), 1814
8th (King's), 1810
9th (East Norfolk), 1814
13th (First Somersetshire), 1813
16th (Bedfordshire), 1814
27th (Inniskilling), 1814
37th (North Hampshire), 1814
39th (Dorsetshire), 1814
41st Regiment, 1799
49th (Hertfordshire), 1802
57th (West Middlesex), 1814
58th (Rutlandshire), 1814
70th (Glasgow Lowland), 1813
76th Regiment, 1814
81st Regiment, 1814
82nd (Prince of Wales's Volunteers), 1814
88th (Connaught Rangers), 1814
89th Regiment, 1813
90th (Perthshire Volunteers), 1814
97th Regiment, 1814

100th (Dublin), 1805
101st (Duke of York's Irish), 1813
103rd Regiment, 1812

BRITISH REGULAR INFANTRY REGIMENTS THAT SERVED IN THE ATLANTIC REGION, WITH THE DATES OF THEIR ARRIVAL

4th (King's Own), 1814
8th (King's), 1810
21st (Royal North British Fuzileers), 1814
29th (Worcestershire), 1814
44th (East Essex), 1814
60th (Royal American), 1814
62nd (Wiltshire), 1814
85th (Bucks Volunteers), 1814
98th Regiment, 1814
99th (Prince of Wales's Tipperary), 1814
102nd Regiment, 1814

BRITISH GARRISON REGIMENTS

10th Royal Veteran Battalion, 1807

BRITISH NORTH AMERICAN FENCIBLE AND PROVINCIAL CORPS, WITH THE DATES OF THEIR FORMATION[9]

104th Regiment of Foot (originally New Brunswick Fencible Infantry), 1803
Royal Newfoundland Fencible Infantry, 1803
Nova Scotia Fencible Infantry, 1803
Canadian Fencible Infantry, 1803
Glengarry Light Infantry Fencibles, 1812
New Brunswick Fencible Infantry, 1812
Provincial Corps of Light Infantry (Voltigeurs), 1812
Michigan Fencibles, 1814

SWISS CORPS IN BRITISH SERVICE THAT SERVED IN THE CANADAS

Le Régiment de Meuron (Neuchâtel), 1813
Le Régiment de Watteville (Erlach), 1813

LOWER CANADA MILITIA (COMPRISING ONLY THOSE ACTUALLY ENGAGED)[10]

Frontier Light Infantry
Canadian Light Dragoons
Corps of Canadian Voyageurs
1st Battalion Select Embodied Militia (La Milice d'Élite Incorporée)
2nd Battalion Select Embodied Militia
3rd Battalion Select Embodied Militia

Canadian Chasseurs
2nd Battalion Beauharnois Militia

UPPER CANADA MILITIA (COMPRISING ONLY THOSE ACTUALLY ENGAGED)

1st Battalion Incorporated Militia
Cameron's Incorporated Artillery Company
Troop of Provincial Royal Artillery Drivers
1st Regiment Glengarry Militia
2nd Regiment Glengarry Militia
1st Regiment Stormont Militia
1st Regiment Dundas Militia
1st Regiment Grenville Militia
2nd Regiment Grenville Militia
1st Regiment Leeds Militia
2nd Regiment Leeds Militia
1st Regiment York Militia
2nd Regiment York Militia
3rd Regiment York Militia
Niagara Light Dragoons, Troop of Provincial Dragoons
1st Regiment Lincoln Militia
1st Lincoln Militia Artillery
Captain Runchey's Company of Coloured Men
2nd Regiment Lincoln Militia
3rd Regiment Lincoln Militia
4th Regiment Lincoln Militia
5th Regiment Lincoln Militia
1st Regiment Norfolk Militia
2nd Regiment Norfolk Militia
1st Regiment Oxford Militia
1st Regiment Middlesex Militia
1st Regiment Essex Militia
2nd Regiment Essex Militia
1st Regiment Kent Militia
Western (Caldwell's) Rangers

THE INDIAN COUNTRY

Mississippi Volunteers
Mississippi Volunteer Artillery
Dease's Mississippi Volunteers
Green Bay Militia

NOTE: It is to be regretted that no Canadian regiment of the present day, regular or reserve (militia), is authorized to carry any of the battles or engagements of the Canadian War of 1812 as "battle honours" on their colours. A case could be made for designating some existing militia units as perpetuating units of those which took part in the principal battles of the war.

Appendix IV

The Medical Services

LITTLE ATTENTION has been paid to the medical aspects of the War of 1812, perhaps because of the technical nature of the subject and the relative insignificance of the war by European standards. The casualties are said to have totalled 8774 British and Canadians and 7738 Americans.[11] Contemporary accounts tell us how sickness and wounds were treated, and how the medical services were organized in the contending armies. The American experience is told in James Mann, *Medical Sketches of the Campaigns of 1812, 1813, 1814 . . .*; and Dr. William "Tiger" Dunlop's *Recollections of the American War, 1812-14* describes the conditions in the British army in North America.[12] Recent work by Dr. Charles G. Roland of McMaster University is of interest to students of the War of 1812, in particular his articles "War Amputations in Upper Canada"[13] and "Medical Aspects of the War in the West, 1812-1813", written in 1980 but as yet unpublished.

In the British army, medical services were provided by general hospitals staffed by physicians, surgeons, apothecaries and purveyors who were part of the military establishment. The principal hospitals were in Quebec, Montreal, Kingston and York. Other medical services were the responsibility of the regimental surgeons. A regiment of 500 men was authorized to have one surgeon and two assistant surgeons, although, in actual fact, few regiments managed to have a full complement, owing to illness, transfer, resignation or death. The sub-staff included a sergeant, an orderly and a nurse, the latter being part of the regimental establishment, often in the capacity of laundress. Few such nurses possessed any real skill, but each was entitled to be paid a shilling a day.

433

Surgery was limited to trepanation, probing for bullets, drawing pus and amputating limbs. Anaesthesia was unknown and patients were usually plied with alcohol, often a mixture of brandy and pepper. Sometimes opium was used to deaden pain. While undergoing an amputation a soldier was usually strapped to a table or held forcibly by his companions. Antisepsis was also unknown, and little attention was paid to the cleanliness of either buildings or persons. In these circumstances it is hardly surprising that the reported mortality rate for simple fractures was nine per cent, and for compound or open fractures as much as forty-two per cent. Death from gunshot wounds was sometimes as high as fifty per cent.[14] Maggots were a dreadful problem during the heat of summer, but, surprisingly enough, hospital gangrene and tetanus were rare in Upper Canada. Disabled veterans were not wholly abandoned; a bounty, temporary assistance from the Loyal and Patriotic Society of Upper Canada, a small pension or a grant of land might be available. However, no provision was made for rehabilitation.

In the mind of the military historian, the question arises as to how far the course of the war was influenced by the health factor. It would seem obvious that in 1813 Major General James Wilkinson's troops suffered grievously from the inclement weather and the absence of suitable winter clothing. The American surgeon James Mann said that, of one small corps of 160 men, 75 were sick; there were 39 cases of diarrhoea and dysentry, 13 of pneumonia and 6 of typhus, and 12 men suffered paralysis of the extremities, some being "attended with mortification of the toes and feet".[15] Similar conditions caused the large number of deaths at French Mills during the winter of 1813–14 and the 450 cases of illness in the hospital at Malone. The standard remedies —laudanum, calomel, bleeding and blistering—were ineffectual. The use of sugar of lead was too frequently attended with fatal results. Dr. Charles Roland suggests, not without justification, that Hull's surrender of Detroit in August 1812 may be explained by the large number of American sick and wounded, the loss of medical supplies and a surgeon's mate, the capture by the British of the packet *Cuyahoga*, and the death of Hull's principal medical officer, Dr. Jonah Foster.[16] Were malaria and ague as important factors in the War of 1812 as guns and bullets? Perhaps. It is to be hoped that a thorough analysis of the medical history of the War of 1812 will yet be undertaken.

Notes

CHAPTER 1—THE DECLARATION OF WAR

1 Irving Brant, *James Madison*, 6 vols. (Indianapolis, 1941–61), vol. 5, *The President, 1809–1812* (1956), 463.
2 Ibid., 472.
3 Ibid., 473.
4 Ibid., 477.
5 Ibid., 478.
6 Benson J. Lossing, *The Pictorial Field-Book of the War of 1812; or, Illustrations, by Pen and Pencil, of the History . . . of the Last War for American Independence* (New York, 1869), 367. See also A. D. Crooks, "Recollections of the War of 1812. From Manuscript of the late Hon. James Crooks", *Women's Canadian Historical Society of Toronto, Transactions* 13 (1914): 13. The schooners were the *Lord Nelson, Ontario* and *Niagara*.
7 William Kirby, *Annals of Niagara* (Welland, Ont., 1896), 157. It may be that Kirby, a well-known novelist who lived at Niagara (now Niagara-on-the-Lake), was repeating local tradition. A more prosaic version of this story is given by John Richardson, quoting an American source:

> The news of war reached the British at (Niagara) Fort George the 24th by express, two days before it was received at our military station. General Brock, the British governor, arrived at Fort George the 25th. Several American gentlemen were there on a visit, who were treated very politely by the Governor, and sent under the protection of Captain Glegg, his aide, to Fort Niagara with a flag. The news of war was very unwelcome on both sides of the river. (John Richardson, *Richardson's War of 1812*, with notes and a life of the author by Alexander Clark Casselman [Toronto, 1902], 11.)

8 René Thomas Verchères de Boucherville, "The Chronicles of Thomas Verchères de Boucherville", in *War on the Detroit . . .*, ed. Milo Milton Quaife (Chicago, 1940), 77.
9 Ibid., 78.
10 Canada, Public Archives, RG 8, C 676: Brock to Prevost, 3 July 1812; Roberts to Brock, 12 July 1812 (hereafter cited as PAC). See also Robert

Christie, *The Military and Naval Operations in the Canadas during the Late War with the United States* (Quebec, 1818), 63.

11 PAC, MG 11, A 21, NB: Hunter to Liverpool, 27 June 1812.

12 Ibid.: Smyth to Liverpool, 4 July 1812.

13 *Gazette* (Montreal), 13 July 1812.

CHAPTER 2—THE UNITED STATES

1 H. L. Keenleyside, *Canada and the United States* (New York, 1929), 42. In 1777 John Van Cortlandt, a member of the New York Convention, said, "The Tories are plotting from New Hampshire to Carolina. . . . A thousand of them must in 2 or 3 months be hanged and then all will be peace." (Charles W. Royster, *A Revolutionary People at War* [Chapel Hill, N. C., 1979], 106.)

2 George F. G. Stanley, "The Six Nations and the American Revolution", *Ontario History* 56, no. 4 (Dec. 1964): 229.

3 J. B. McMaster, "The Struggle for Commercial Independence (1783–1812)", *The Cambridge Modern History*, vol. 7, *The United States* (1903), 327.

4 Harry F. Landon, *Bugles on the Border: The Story of the War in Northern New York* (Watertown, N. Y., 1954), 11.

5 Ibid., 12.

6 A. L. Burt, *The United States, Great Britain and British North America: From the Revolution to the Establishment of Peace after the War of 1812* (New Haven, Conn., 1940), 212.

7 Ibid., 116.

8 Ibid., 246.

9 PAC, *Annual Report, 1896* (Ottawa, 1897), 29: Grant to James Green, 7 Aug. 1807.

10 Julius W. Pratt, *Expansionists of 1812* (New York, 1925), 25.

11 Burt, *United States*, 246.

12 Charles and James C. Thomas, "Reminiscences of the First Settlers in the County of Brant", *Ontario Historical Society Papers and Records* 12 (1914): 66.

13 According to Carl Klinck, the orthography of the name is "Tecumthà", rather than the common spelling employed here to conform to familiar usage. See Carl F. Klinck, ed., *Tecumseh: Fact and Fiction in Early Records* (Englewood Cliffs, N. J., 1961), 12n. For biographies, see Benjamin Drake, *Life of Tecumseh and of His Brother The Prophet* (Cincinnati, 1841), and Glenn Tucker, *Tecumseh: Vision of Glory* (Indianapolis, 1956). Poetic interpretations of Tecumseh include Charles Mair, *Tecumseh, a Drama, and Canadian Poems* (Toronto, 1926), and Wallace H. Robb, *Tecumtha: Shawnee Chieftain, Astral Avatar* (Kingston, Ont., 1958). The name "Lolawauchika" is sometimes given as "Laulewasikau" and sometimes as "Elskwatawa". He was generally known as "The Prophet".

14 O. H. Smith, *Early Indian Trials and Sketches* (Cincinnati, 1858), 228. See also Benson J. Lossing, *The Pictorial Field-Book of the War of 1812* (New York, 1869), 192, and Tucker, *Tecumseh*, 161.

15 Drake, *Tecumseh and The Prophet*, 142. See also Flora Warren Seymour, *The Story of the Red Man* (London, 1929), 98.

16 Lossing, *Pictorial Field-Book*, 195.

17 Robert B. McAfee, *History of the Late War in the Western Country* (1816; reprint ed., Bowling Green, Ohio, 1919), 43. For a British account see E. A. Cruikshank, ed., *Documents Relating to the Invasion of Canada and the Surrender of Detroit, 1812*, Publications of the Canadian Archives, no. 7 (Ottawa, 1912), 6–8: Elliott to Brock, 12 Jan. 1812. This letter gives the Indian casualties as 25, with the Kickapoo losing the largest number.

18 Burt, *United States*, 22.

19 Henry Adams, *History of the United States of America during the Second Administration of Thomas Jefferson*, 2 vols. (1890; reprint ed., New York, 1962), 2: 36.

20 Burt, *United States*, 267.

21 Ibid. See also Merrill D. Peterson, *Thomas Jefferson and the New Nation: A Biography* (New York, 1970), 877.

22 Pratt, *Expansionists of 1812*, p. 58.

23 Patrick C. T. White, *A Nation on Trial: America and the War of 1812* (New York, 1965), 66.

24 Henry Clay, *The Papers of Henry Clay*, ed. James F. Hopkins and Mary W. M. Hargreaves, 5 vols. (Lexington, Ky., 1959–73), vol. 1, *The Rising Statesman, 1797–1814* (1959), 842.

25 Glenn Tucker, *Poltroons and Patriots: A Popular Account of the War of 1812*, 2 vols. (Indianapolis, 1954), 1: 56.

26 Ibid.

27 Ibid.

28 Ibid.

29 Burt, *United States*, 305.

30 Bradford Perkins, ed., *The Causes of the War of 1812: National Honor or National Interest?* (New York, 1962), 108. See also his *Prologue to War: England and the United States, 1805–1812* (Berkeley, Calif., 1961).

31 Rufus King, *The Life and Correspondence of Rufus King*, ed. Charles R. King, 6 vols. (New York, 1898), vol. 5, *1807–1816*, p. 177.

32 White, *Nation on Trial*, 63.

33 Tucker, *Poltroons and Patriots*, 1: 41.

34 Irving Brant, *James Madison*, 6 vols. (Indianapolis, 1941–61), vol. 5, *The President, 1809–1812* (1956), 390.

35 Ibid., 392–3.

36 Ibid., 391.

37 Ibid., 393.

38 Ibid., 396.

39 Ibid., 412.

40 E. A. Cruikshank, *The Political Adventures of John Henry: The Record of an International Imbroglio* (Toronto, 1936), 42. For an account of the financial side of this transaction see Tucker, *Poltroons and Patriots*, 1: 366, n. 20.

41 Tucker, *Poltroons and Patriots*, 1: 77.

42 Ibid.

43 Alden Bradford, *History of Massachusetts for Two Hundred Years, from the Years 1620 to 1820* (Boston, 1835), 382n. The votes on the petition were 406 for and 240 against.

44 Maryland went Federalist in the next election as a result of riots in Baltimore by the republican mob against the anti-war attitude of Alexander Hanson, who published the *Federal Republican*. During the riots the aged Revolutionary War veteran, James Lingan of Georgetown, was beaten to death; General Henry (Light-Horse Harry) Lee, "one of General Washington's favourite subordinates", was injured so severely that he never recovered; and other citizens were assaulted. For a firsthand account of the riot, see Henry Lee's pamphlet, *A Correct Account of the Conduct of the Baltimore Mob, by . . . One of the Sufferers* (Winchester, Va., 1814). See also Tucker, *Poltroons and Patriots*, 1: 136–44.

45 Burt, *United States*, 308. The South was the part of the United States most dependent upon the markets controlled by Napoleon; hence its sympathy for France and its antagonism towards Great Britain.

46 Margaret L. Coit, *John C. Calhoun: American Portrait* (Boston, 1950), 80.

47 J. R. Jacobs, *The Beginning of the U.S. Army, 1783–1812* (Princeton, N. J., 1950), 80.

48 Brant, *James Madison*, 5: 357.

49 Ibid., 358.

50 Raymond Walters, *Albert Gallatin: Jeffersonian Financier and Diplomat* (New York, 1957), 247. A few weeks later, Congress at least granted Gallatin's request to be allowed to plan an eleven-million-dollar loan to carry the United States through the first year of the war, if it should come.

51 C. W. Elliott, *Winfield Scott, the Soldier and the Man* (New York, 1937), 47.

52 Brant, *James Madison*, 5: 396.

CHAPTER 3—BRITISH NORTH AMERICA

1 Michael Smith, *A Geographical View of the British Possessions in North America: Comprehending Nova Scotia, New Brunswick, New Britain, Lower and Upper Canada* (Baltimore, 1814), iii–iv.

2 PAC, *Annual Report, 1892* (Ottawa, 1893), 21: Anglican Bishop of Quebec, 6 June 1803.

3 Smith, *British Possessions in North America*, 62–3.

4 PAC, *Annual Report, 1892*, p. 38.

5 Richard Cartwright, *Life and Letters of the Late Hon. Richard Cartwright*, ed. C. E. Cartwright (Toronto, 1876), 97.

6 Christian Schultz, *Travels on an Inland Voyage through the States of New York, Pennsylvania, etc., Performed in the Years 1807 and 1808 . . .*, 2 vols. (New York, 1810), 2: 55. See also Fred Landon, *Western Ontario and the American Frontier* (Toronto, 1941), 21.

7 E. A. Cruikshank, ed., *The Documentary History of the Campaign upon the Niagara Frontier in the Year 1812* (Welland, Ont., n.d.), pt. 1, p. 39: Brock to Baynes, 12 February 1812. See also Matilda (Ridout), Lady Edgar, *General Brock*, rev. by E. A. Cruikshank, Makers of Canada Series, vol. 4 (London, 1926), 184.

8 Fred Landon, *Western Ontario*, 30.

9 Cruikshank, *Niagara Frontier . . . 1812*, pt. 1, pp. 45: Baynes to Brock, 10 Mar. 1812.

10 William Wood, ed., *Select British Documents of the Canadian War of 1812*, 4 vols., Champlain Society Publications, nos. 13–15, 17 (Toronto, 1920–28), vol. 1 (1920), 396: Brock to Baynes, 29 July 1812. See also Cruikshank, *Niagara Frontier . . . 1812*, pt. 1, pp. 152–3.

11 Lady Edgar, *General Brock*, 217–18.

12 PAC, RG 8, C 676: Brock to Prevost, 28 July 1812.

13 William M. Weekes, "The War of 1812: Civil Authority and Martial Law in Upper Canada", *Ontario History* 48, no. 4 (autumn 1956): 149.

14 PAC, RG 8, C 676.

15 Gustave Lanctôt, "Le Québec et les colonies américaines, 1760–1820", in *Les Canadiens français et leurs voisins du sud . . .*, ed. Gustave Lanctôt (Montreal, 1941), 131 (my translation).

16 Ibid., 132. See also Denis-Benjamin Viger, *Considérations sur les effets qu'ont produit en Canada, la conservation des établissemens du pay, les moeurs, l'éducation, etc. de ses habitans . . .* (Montreal, 1809).

17 'Philalethes', "General Correspondence", *Colburn's United Service Magazine and Naval and Military Journal*, pt. 1 (London, 1848), 430. This account was written by Lieutenant Colonel "Red George" Macdonell of Glengarry, who says that he was informed of Craig's orders by officers in Quebec.

18 Robert Christie, *The Military and Naval Operations in the Canadas during the Late War with the United States* (Quebec, 1818), 50.

19 Ibid., 61–2. See also Charles-Marie Boissonnault, *Histoire politico-militaire des Canadiens-Français, 1763–1945* (Trois-Rivières, Que., 1967), 97–8; Fernand Ouellet, *Lower Canada, 1791–1840*, transl. Patricia Claxton (Toronto, 1979), 113.

20 J. M. Hitsman, *Safeguarding Canada, 1763–1871* (Toronto, 1968), 80.

21 48 George III, c. 1.

22 D. G. Creighton, *The Commercial Empire of the St. Lawrence, 1760–1850* (Toronto, 1937), 175.

23 PAC, RG 8, C 256: Glegg to Dickson, 27 Feb. 1812. See also George F. G. Stanley "British Operations in the Amrican North-West, 1812–1815", *Journal of the Society for Army Historical Research* 22, no. 87 (autumn 1943): 93.

24 Creighton, *Commercial Empire of the St. Lawrence*, 177–8.

25 George F. G. Stanley, "The Significance of the Six Nations Participation in the War of 1812", *Ontario History* 55, no. 4 (Dec. 1963): 230.

26 PAC, RG 8, C 688A: Thomas Talbot to Brock, 27 July 1812. See also John Norton, *The Journal of Major John Norton, 1816*, eds. Carl F. Klinck and James J. Talman, Champlain Society Publication, no. 46 (Toronto, 1970), 295, n. 10.

27 Edward J. Devine, *Historic Caughnawaga* (Montreal, 1922), 321–2.

28 Fernand Ouellet, *Histoire économique et sociale du Québec, 1760–1850* (Ottawa, 1966), 218.

29 The shortage of grain and the necessity of conserving supplies led to the first liquor legislation in Canada, when in 1813 the distillation of whisky was prohibited in Upper Canada. See Fred Landon, *Western Ontario*, 41.

30 Glenn A. Steppler, "A Duty Troublesome Beyond Measure: Logistical Considerations in the Canadian War of 1812" (Master's thesis, McGill University, 1974), 25. This is the only thorough study of logistical problems during the war on the Canadian side.

31 John Strachan, *The John Strachan Letter Book, 1812–1834*, ed. George W. Spragge (Toronto, 1946), 28: Strachan to Captain Cameron, 7 Dec. 1812.

32 The Americans had a gun foundry at Pittsburgh, but the two little foundries in Upper Canada, at Lyndhurst and in Norfolk County, were not equipped to bore cannon. The Forges Saint-Maurice in Lower Canada had made guns during the French regime, but no longer did so.

33 Harry F. Landon, *Bugles on the Border: The Story of the War in Northern New York* (Watertown, N. Y., 1954), 2. See also PAC, RG 8, C 119: Peter Turquand to Kent, Biggar, et al., 5 Dec. 1814; and Smith, *British Possessions in North America*, 24–5.

34 W. Austin Squires, *The 104th Regiment of Foot (the New Brunswick Regiment), 1803–1817* (Fredericton, N.B., 1962), 118–36. See also George F. G. Stanley, "The New Brunswick Fencibles", *Canadian Defence Quarterly* 16, no. 1 (Oct. 1938): 39–53; and H. F. Pullen, *The March of the Seamen*, Maritime Museum of Canada, Occasional Paper No. 8 (Halifax, 1961).

35 Marjorie Wilkins Campbell, *McGillivray, Lord of the Northwest* (Toronto, 1962), 193.

36 PAC, RG 8, C 373: William H. Robinson to Prevost, 29 June 1814. Crews numbered from 5 to 10 men for each bateau. In 1812 some 1315 men were needed to man the fleet of bateaux, and in 1815 the total was 3500 men for the bateaux and the Durham boats. In 1812, the service possessed 263 bateaux at Quebec, Trois-Rivières, William Henry, Montreal, Kingston, York, Niagara, Amherstburg and St. Joseph Island, and additional craft were stationed at Île aux Noix, La Prairie and Lachine in August 1812. For 1815, the proposed establishment included 150 Durham boats, the bulk of them to be located at Fort Wellington and Kingston, and 700 bateaux, of which 500 were to be stationed at Montreal, Lachine and Kingston. See PAC, RG 8, C 1223; and Steppler, "Logistical Considerations", app. XVIII. See also George F. G. Stanley, *Conflicts and Social Notes: The War of 1812–14; The Patriot War, 1837–38*, Island Insights, no. 7 (Parks Canada, Ottawa, 1976), 15–21.

37 Strachan, *Letter Book*, 34.

38 Hitsman, *Safeguarding Canada*, 70.

39 Ibid., 84.

40 E. A. Cruikshank, "Record of the Services of Canadian Regiments in the War of 1812, Part XIII, The Militia of the Eastern District: The Counties of Glengarry, Stormont and Dundas", *Transactions of the Canadian Military Institute, 1913–15*, Selected Papers, no. 21 (Toronto, 1916), 84.

41 PAC, RG 8, C 680: Return of R. A. Ordnance, Batteries and Blockhouses at Kingston, 9 Oct. 1813. See also J. O. Dendy, "The Fortifications of Kingston, 1790–1850: Plans and Commentary" (Hon. B.A. thesis, Royal Military College of Canada, 1964).

42 Hitsman, *Safeguarding Canada*, 90.

CHAPTER 4—THE DETROIT FRONTIER, 1812

1 Irving Brant, *James Madison*, 6 vols. (Indianapolis, 1941–61), vol. 6, *Commander in Chief, 1812–1836* (1961), 49.

2 Ibid., 50.

3   Ibid., 67. The prospect of war between Great Britain and the United States was alarming to the British army in Spain, which was in large measure dependent on American shipping and American supplies. Major General Robert B. Long, in a letter to his brother, wrote from Villa Franca on 3 August 1812, expressing satisfaction at the withdrawal of the British Orders in Council:

> "I see America is growing very angry. I am pleased we gave in before the gauntlet of defiance was thrown down. We cannot live here without her, therefore peace, I say, with her upon almost any terms." (Robert Ballard Long, *Peninsular Cavalry General, 1811–13: The Correspondence of Lieutenant-General Robert Ballard Long*, ed. T. H. McGuffie [London, 1951], 214.)

4   Brant, *James Madison*, 6: 67.

5   Ibid., 68.

6   Henry Adams, *History of the United States of America during the First Administration of James Madison*, 2 vols. (1890; reprint ed., New York, 1962), 2: 360–61.

7   Ibid.

8   On 8 August 1812, Dearborn wrote to Eustis, "Till now I did not consider the Niagara frontier as coming within the limits of my command." This was an astonishing confession by the senior officer who had drafted the original plan, following two months of correspondence with the Secretary of War. See Benson J. Lossing, *The Pictorial Field-Book of the War of 1812* . . . (New York, 1869), 381.

9   A. R. Gilpin, *The War of 1812 in the Old Northwest* (Toronto, 1958), 40.

10 Ibid., 48.

11 [James Foster], "The Capitulation, by an Ohio Volunteer", in *War on the Detroit* . . . ed. Milo Milton Quaife (Chicago, 1940), 209.

12 Thomas Worthington, "Thomas Worthington and the War of 1812", transcribed by Richard C. Knopf, Document Transcriptions of the War of 1812 in the Northwest, vol. 3, mimeographed (Columbus, Ohio: Anthony Wayne Parkway Board, Ohio State Museum, 1957), 96.

13 Lossing, *Pictorial Field-Book*, 260–61. See also [Foster], "The Capitulation", 221.

14 Gilpin, *War of 1812*, p. 72.

15 Worthington, "War of 1812", p. 89: Cass to Worthington, 19 May 1812.

16 Ibid, 106: McArthur to Worthington, 7 July 1812.

17 Gilpin, *War of 1812*, p. 73.

18 [Foster], "The Capitulation", 229–30.

19 Ibid., 226.

20 Ernest J. Lajeunesse, ed., *The Windsor Border Region, Canada's Southernmost Frontier; a Collection of Documents*, Champlain Society, Ontario, ser. 4 (Toronto, 1960), xxvii–cxxix.

21 John Richardson, *Richardson's War of 1812*, with notes and a life of the author by Alexander Clark Casselman (Toronto, 1902), 34.

22 Ibid., 36.

23 E. A. Cruikshank, ed., *The Documentary History of the Campaign upon the Niagara Frontier in the Year 1812* (Welland, Ont., n.d.), pt. 1, pp. 135–8: Brock's Proclamation, 22 July 1812. See also David B. Read, *Life and Times of Major-General Sir Isaac Brock, R. B.* (Toronto, 1894), 130–33.

24 E. A. Cruikshank, "Record of the Services of Canadian Regiments in the War of 1812, Part XI, The Militia of Norfolk, Oxford and Middlesex", *Transactions of the Canadian Military Institute, 1907*, Selected Papers, no. 15 (Toronto, 1908), 47.

25 C. O. Ermatinger, *The Talbot Regime, or, The First Half Century of the Talbot Settlement* (St. Thomas, Ont., 1904), 50.

26 Ibid., 52.

27 Ibid., 54. Macdonell wrote his letter of 10 August 1812 at Port Talbot.

28 Thomas H. Raddall, *The Path of Destiny: Canada from the British Conquest to Home Rule, 1763–1850*. Canadian History Series, vol. 3 (Toronto, 1957), 200.

29 Richardson, *War of 1812*, p. 50. Brock's demand for surrender and Hull's reply are reproduced there.

30 René Thomas Verchères de Boucherville, "The Chronicles of Thomas Verchères de Boucherville", in *War on the Detroit . . .*, ed. Milo Milton Quaife (Chicago, 1940), 108–9.

31 Richardson, *War of 1812*, p. 51.

32 Ibid., 56.

33 Verchères de Boucherville, "Chronicles", 110.

34 Gilpin, *War of 1812*, p. 106.

35 Ibid., 111–12.

36 Ibid., 118.

37 Reginald Horsman, *Matthew Elliott, British Indian Agent* (Detroit, 1964), 197.

38 Hull's letter is printed in its entirety in Richardson's *War of 1812*, pp. 70–76.

39 Americans of the time, such as Robert McAfee, blamed the British for the fighting at Fort Dearborn. On page 116 of his *History of the Late War in the Western Country* (1816; reprint ed., Bowling Green, Ohio, 1919), McAfee wrote:

> "What must we think of the British government and its agents, who could thus instigate the sanguinary savage of the forest to deeds of ingratitude, perfidy and murder? How low we must estimate the civilization of those who could court the alliance of these barbarians in war."

40 Gilpin, *War of 1812*, p. 139.

41 Richardson, *War of 1812*, p. 93.

42 Ibid., 97.

43 Verchères de Boucherville, "Chronicles", 113.

CHAPTER 5—THE NIAGARA FRONTIER, 1812

1 Benson J. Lossing, *The Pictorial Field-Book of the War of 1812* (New York, 1869), 381.

2 Ibid.

3 E. A. Cruikshank, ed., *The Documentary History of the Campaign upon the Niagara Frontier in the Year 1812* (Welland, Ont., n.d.), pt. 1, p. 227.

4 Henry Adams, *History of the United States of America during the First Administration of James Madison*, 2 vols. (1890; reprint ed., New York, 1962), 2: 343.

5 Ibid., 345.

6 Ibid., 346.

7   Cruikshank, *Niagara Frontier . . . 1812*, pt. 2, p. 65: Brock to Procter, 11 or 12 Oct. 1812.

8   H. A. Fay, ed. *Collection of the Official Accounts, in Detail, of All the Battles Fought by Sea and Land, between the Navy and Army of the United States, and the Navy and Army of Great Britain, during the Years 1812, 13, 14, and 15* (New York, 1817), 34: Van Rensselaer to Dearborn, 14 Oct. 1812. This letter also appeared in the *Halifax Journal*, 9 Nov. 1812, copied from Washington's *National Intelligencer*.

9   Lossing, *Pictorial Field-Book*, 389, n. 2.

10 Matilda (Ridout), Lady Edgar, *General Brock*, rev. by E.A. Cruikshank, Makers of Canada Series, vol. 4 (London, 1926), 225.

11 Cruikshank, *Niagara Frontier . . . 1812*, pt. 1, p. 187: *New York Statesman*, 25 Aug. 1812, from a correspondent at Lewiston, N. Y.

12 Ibid., 279: General Brock to Savery Brock, 18 Sept. 1812.

13 Ibid., 243: Brock to Prevost, 7 Sept. 1812.

14 Cruikshank, *Niagara Frontier . . . 1812*, pt. 2, p. 64: Brock to Prevost, 11 Oct. 1812.

15 Ibid., 64–5.

16 Lady Edgar, *General Brock*, 302.

17 William Kaye Lamb, *The Hero of Upper Canada* (Toronto, 1962), 27.

18 Cruikshank, *Niagara Frontier . . . 1812*, pt. 2, p. 115: a letter from Upper Canada, dated 15 Oct. 1812, printed in the *Quebec Mercury* of 27 Oct.

19 Charles Winslow Elliott, *Winfield Scott, the Soldier and the Man* (New York, 1937), 61.

20 Cruikshank, *Niagara Frontier . . . 1812*, pt. 2, p. 83: Glegg to William Brock, 14 Oct. 1812.

21 Lady Edgar, *General Brock*, 306.

22 Cruikshank, *Niagara Frontier . . . 1812*, pt. 2, p. 106.

23 Ibid., 147. The figure of 958 for the number of American prisoners is from Elliott's *Winfield Scott*, 67; but Major Thomas Evans, the British brigade major, put the total at 925 (see Cruikshank, *Niagara Frontier . . . 1812*, pt. 2, pp. 73–4).

24 Cruikshank, *Niagara Frontier . . . 1812*, pt. 2, p. 82: Van Rensselaer to Eustis, 14 Oct. 1812.

25 Ibid., 140: Smyth to Eustis, 20 Oct. 1812.

26 Ibid., 194.

27 Ibid., 152: Dearborn to Smyth, 21 Oct. 1812.

28 Ibid., 168: 28 Oct. 1812.

29 Ibid., 172: Smyth to Dearborn, 30 Oct. 1812.

30 Ibid., 180: *New-York Evening Post*, 11 Nov. 1812.

31 Ibid., 195.

32 Ibid., 238: letter dated 25 Nov. 1812.

33 Ibid., 216–17.

34 Ibid., 239.

35 Ibid.: Smyth to Porter, 27 Nov. 1812.

36 Ibid., 141: District General Order, 20 Oct. 1812

37 Ibid., 212: Militia General Order, 14 Nov. 1812

38 Ibid., 270–71: Smyth to McClure, Birdsall, et al., 3 Dec. 1812.

39 Ibid., 301: 13 Dec. 1812.

40 Glenn Tucker, *Poltroons and Patriots: A Popular Account of the War of 1812* (Indianapolis, 1954), 1: 204.

41 Irving Brant, *James Madison*, 6 vols. (Indianapolis, 1941–61), vol. 6, *Commander in Chief, 1812–1836* (1961), 120.

42 Tucker, *Poltroons and Patriots*, 1: 204.

CHAPTER 6—THE ERIE FRONTIER, 1813

1 Irving Brant, *James Madison*, 6 vols. (Indianapolis, 1941–61), vol. 6, *Commander in Chief, 1812–1836* (1961), 175.

2 John Richardson, *Richardson's War of 1812*, with notes and a life of the author by Alexander Clark Casselman (Toronto, 1902), 134.

3 Ibid., 136.

4 Thomas Worthington, "Thomas Worthington and the War of 1812", transcribed by Richard C. Knopf, Document Transcriptions of the War of 1812 in the Northwest, vol. 3, mimeographed (Columbus, Ohio: Anthony Wayne Parkway Board, Ohio State Museum, 1957), 169: Cass to Worthington, 4 Feb. 1813. Cass wrote, "It is an astonishing and unaccountable business."

5 Charles P. Lucas, *The Canadian War of 1812* (Oxford, 1906), 74.

6 Richardson, *War of 1812*, p. 146. Winchester's and Harrison's letters are printed there in full.

7 Ibid., 159.

8 William Wood, ed., *Select British Documents of the Canadian War of 1812*, 4 vols., Champlain Society Publications, nos. 13–15, 17 (Toronto, 1920–28), vol. 2 (1923), 35. See also PAC, RG 8, C 678.

9 PAC, RG 8, C 678: Procter to McDouall, 14 May 1813.

10 Ibid.: 19 June 1813.

11 Ibid.: Procter to Prevost, 14 May 1813.

12 Ibid.: Procter to McDouall, 14 May 1813.

13 Reginald Horsman, *Matthew Elliott, British Indian Agent* (Detroit, 1964), 205–6.

14 Wood, *Select British Documents*, 2: 28–30.

15 After capturing Detroit, Brock proclaimed the continuation of existing laws in Michigan Territory until further notice. When Brock left Amherstburg, Procter appointed himself civil governor and named an American, Judge Augustus Woodward, as his secretary. Fearing seditious activity after the battle on the River Raisin, Procter ordered several American civilians to leave Michigan. Public protest delayed the expulsion, but Woodward resigned and Procter proclaimed martial law in Michigan. His purpose was to expel "some of the more turbulent characters", who he sent off as prisoners to Fort George. Procter wanted as many of the inhabitants of Detroit as possible to take the oath of allegiance; he required confirmed United States citizens to take the oath of neutrality. See PAC, RG 8, C 678: Procter to Sheaffe, 4 Feb. 1813.

16 Ibid.: Procter to McDouall, 16 June 1813.

17 Wood, *Select British Documents*, 2: 253–4.

18 Richardson, *War of 1812*, p. 179.

19 Ibid.

20 Shadrach Byfield, "A Common Soldier's Account", in *Recollections of the War of 1812: Three Eyewitnesses' Accounts*, ed. John Gellner (1828–54; reprint ed. Toronto, 1964), 21.

21 Ibid., 23.

22 Wood, *Selected British Documents*, 2: 45.
23 Ibid., 46–7.
24 Gabriel Franchère, *A Voyage to the Northwest Coast of America*, ed. Milo Milton Quaife (Chicago, 1954), 121–2.
25 Ibid., 142. The *Isaac Todd* did not reach Astoria until the following year, on 22 April 1814.
26 Ibid., 143.
27 The date given by Franchère for the purchase of Fort Astoria, 23 October, is incorrect. My source is Gordon Charles Davidson, *The North West Company*, University of California, Publications in History, vol. 7 (Berkeley, Calif., 1918), 138. Davidson took the date from the bill of sale in the Foreign Office records. For a discussion of this episode see T. C. Elliott, "Sale of Astoria, 1813", *Oregon Historical Quarterly* 33, no. 1 (Mar. 1932): 44.
28 Franchère, *Voyage*, 151.

CHAPTER 7—THE NIAGARA FRONTIER, 1813

1 *Kingston Gazette*, 17 Nov. 1812.
2 P. Finan, "An Onlooker's View", in *Recollections of the War of 1812: Three Eyewitnesses' Accounts*, ed. John Gellner (1828–54; reprint ed., Toronto, 1964), 81–2.
3 Ibid., 87.
4 Ibid., 87–8.
5 E. A. Cruikshank, ed., *The Documentary History of the Campaign upon the Niagara Frontier in the Year 1813*, pt. 1, *January to June 1813* (Welland, Ont., 1902), 187: Sheaffe to Prevost, 5 May 1813.
6 Finan, "An Onlooker's View", 89.
7 Cruikshank, *Niagara Frontier . . . 1813*, pt. 1, pp. 194–5: Chewett, Allan, Cameron and Smith to Strachan, Woods and Baldwin, 8 May 1813.
8 Ibid., 195.
9 Finan, "An Onlooker's View", 91.
10 Cruikshank, *Niagara Frontier . . . 1813*, pt. 1, pp. 34–8: Glegg, 10 Jan. 1813—Notes on the Conduct of Major General Sheaffe and Major General Vincent, by W. D. Powell. See also the 1812 volume, pt. 2, p. 327: Nichol to Talbot, 18 Dec. 1812.
11 For more information on the looting at York, see C. P. Stacey, *The Battle of Little York* (Toronto, 1977), 16–22; also Charles W. Humphries, "The Capture of York", *Ontario History*, 51, no. 1 (winter 1959): 12–21.
12 Cruikshank, *Niagara Frontier . . . 1813*, pt. 1, pp. 199–200: Chewett, Allan, Cameron and Smith to Strachan, Woods and Baldwin, 8 May 1813; see also W. D. Powell's "Narrative of the Capture of York", ibid., 204.
13 Finan, "An Onlooker's View", 93.
14 Ibid., 98.
15 Cruikshank, *Niagara Frontier . . . 1813*, pt. 1, p. 229: Dearborn to Armstrong, 13 May 1813.
16 Ibid., 237.
17 Ibid., 243.
18 Ibid., 235: Talbot to Vincent, 18 May 1813.
19 Ibid., 265: Dearborn to Tompkins, 29 May 1813.

20 Harry F. Landon, *Bugles on the Border: The Story of the War in Northern New York* (Watertown, N. Y., 1954), 26.

21 Cruikshank, *Niagara Frontier . . . 1813*, pt. 1, pp. 298–9: Vincent to Baynes, 4 June 1813.

22 Ibid., pt. 2, *June to August 1813* (n.d.), 7: Harvey to Baynes, 6 June 1813.

23 Ibid., 13, 15: FitzGibbon to Somerville, 7 June 1813.

24 Ibid., 50–51: Letter of an American officer to the *United States Gazette*, 22 June 1813.

25 Ibid., 14: FitzGibbon to Somerville, 7 June 1813.

26 Ibid., 23: Burn to Dearborn, n.d.

27 Ibid., 56: Evans to Vincent.

28 Norman C. Lord, "The War on the Canadian Frontier, 1812–14. Letters Written by Sergt. James Commins, 8th Foot", *Journal of the Society for Army Historical Research* 18, no. 72 (winter 1939): 205.

29 Cruikshank, *Niagara Frontier . . . 1813*, pt. 2, p. 62: Evans to Harvey, 10 June 1813.

30 Ibid., 55.

31 E. A. Cruikshank, *The Fight in the Beechwoods: A Study in Canadian History*, 2nd ed. (Welland, Ont., 1895), 7.

32 Donald E. Graves, "The Canadian Volunteers, 1813–1815", *Military Collector and Historian* 31, no. 3 (fall 1979): 113.

33 Cruikshank, *Fight in the Beechwoods*, 9.

34 Ducharme was assisted by J.-B. de Lorimier, Gédéon Gaucher, Louis Langlade, Évangeliste St-Germain and Isaac Leclair. These officers were experienced in dealing with Indians; for several generations men in their families had led Indians in battle.

35 Cruikshank, *Fight in the Beechwoods*, 16.

36 William Wood, ed., *Select British Documents of the Canadian War of 1812*, 4 vols., Champlain Society Publications, nos. 13–15, 17 (Toronto, 1920–28), vol. 2 (1923), 163.

37 Cruikshank, *Niagara Frontier . . . 1813*, pt. 2, pp. 140–41: Boerstler to Dearborn, 25 June 1813.

38 Cruikshank, *Fight in the Beechwoods*, 32.

39 Ibid., 19. Some of Boerstler's officers also considered that he was "frightened". See Cruikshank, *Niagara Frontier . . . 1813*, pt. 2, p. 148: Journal of Major Isaac Roach.

40 Cruikshank, *Niagara Frontier . . . 1813*, pt. 2, p. 123: Notes by Captain W. H. Merritt.

41 Ibid., 120–21: FitzGibbon to Kerr, 30 March 1818.

42 Ibid., 123.

43 Ibid., 126–9: Laura Secord's Narrative; G. B. Secord to the editor of the *Church*, 11 April 1845.

44 Ibid., 130: FitzGibbon certificate, 23 Feb. 1837. For a discussion of the controversial aspects of the Laura Secord story see J. S. Moir's two articles, "An Early Record of Laura Secord's Walk", *Ontario History* 51, no. 2 (spring 1959): 105–8, and "Laura Secord Again", *Ontario History* 54, no. 3 (Sept. 1962): 190; also W. S. Wallace, *The Story of Laura Secord: A Study in Historical Evidence* (Toronto, 1932). The last word rests with the biographical note Ruth McKenzie supplied for the *Dictionary of Canadian Biography*, 9: s. v. Ingersoll, Laura (Secord).

45 Cruikshank, *Niagara Frontier . . . 1813*, pt. 2, p. 230: James Sloan's recollections of the attack on Black Rock.

46 Ibid., 209.

47 Ibid., 283.

48 Irving Brant, *James Madison*, 6 vols. (Indianapolis, 1941–61), vol. 6, *Commander in Chief, 1812–1836* (1961), 203.

49 Ibid., 208.

CHAPTER 8—MORAVIANTOWN

1 E. A. Cruikshank, ed., *The Documentary History of the Campaign upon the Niagara Frontier in the Year 1813*, pt. 2, *June to August 1813* (Welland, Ont., n.d.), 181–2.

2 Ibid., 17–18.

3 Ibid., 317.

4 Ibid., pt. 3, *August to October 1813* (1905), 21.

5 Ibid., 121.

6 Ibid.

7 Benson J. Lossing, *The Pictorial Field-Book of the War of 1812* (New York, 1869), 549.

8 William F. Coffin, *1812; the War and Its Moral: A Canadian Chronicle* (Montreal, 1864), 227.

9 Norman C. Lord, "The War on the Canadian Frontier, 1812–14. Letters Written by Sergt. James Commins, 8th Foot", *Journal of the Society for Army Historical Research* 18, no. 72 (winter 1939): 206.

10 John Richardson, *Richardson's War of 1812*, with notes and a life of the author by Alexander Clark Casselman (Toronto, 1902), 209.

11 William Wood, ed., *Select British Documents of the Canadian War of 1812*, 4 vols., Champlain Society Publications, nos. 13–15, 17 (Toronto, 1920–28), vol. 2 (1923), 340: Procter to Rottenburg, 16 November 1813. See also C. O. Ermatinger, *The Talbot Regime, or, The First Half Century of the Talbot Settlement* (St. Thomas, ·Ont., 1904), 63.

12 Richardson, *War of 1812*, p. 232: Bullock's letter dated 6 December 1813. Bullock commanded a detachment of the 41st at Moraviantown under Major Adam Muir.

13 Harrison Bird, *War for the West, 1790–1813* (New York, 1971), 249.

14 John Richardson, *Westbrook the Outlaw; or, The Avenging Wolf: An American Border Tale* (Montreal, 1973), 9. This novel was originally published in the *Sunday Mercury*, New York, in 1851.

15 Glenn Tucker, *Tecumseh: Vision of Glory* (Indianapolis, 1956), 309.

16 Ibid., 319. See also Richardson, *War of 1812*, p. 212. Johnson may or may not have killed Tecumseh, but he was not above turning the story to his own political advantage. During his successful campaign for the vice-presidency, his supporters chanted:

> Rum ti tiddy and a
> Rumsey, dumsey,
> Colonel Johnson
> Killed Tecumseh.

17 PAC, RG 8, C 680. See also Wood, *Select British Documents*, 2: 321.

18 Cruikshank, *Niagara Frontier . . . 1813*, pt. 3, pp. 184–5: McClure to the militia, as reported in the *Buffalo Gazette*, 5 Oct. 1813.

19 Cruikshank, *Documentary History of the Campaign upon the Niagara Frontier in 1812–4*, vol. 9, *December 1813 to May 1814* (Welland, Ont., 1908), 9: Rogers, Wilson and Fraser to the *Buffalo Gazette*, 21 Dec. 1813.

20 Donald E. Graves, "The Canadian Volunteers, 1813–1815", *Military Collector and Historian* 31, no. 3 (fall 1979): 114.

21 Cruikshank, *Niagara Frontier in 1812–4*, vol. 9, p. 50: "General McClure to the Public".

22 Glenn Tucker, *Poltroons and Patriots: A Popular Account of the War of 1812*, 2 vols. (Indianapolis, 1954), 2: 418.

23 William Kirby, *Annals of Niagara* (Welland, Ont., 1896), 182.

24 Cruikshank, *Niagara Frontier in 1812–4*, vol. 9, p. 4: Harvey to Murray, 17 Dec. 1813.

25 Shadrach Byfield, "A Common Soldier's Account", in *Recollections of the War of 1812: Three Eyewitnesses' Accounts*, ed. John Gellner (1828–54; reprint ed., Toronto, 1964), 30.

26 Cruikshank, *Niagara Frontier in 1812-4*, vol. 9, p. 17: Deposition of Robert Lee.

27 Ibid., 45: McClure to the Secretary of War, 25 Dec. 1813. In the same letter McClure also blamed Lieutenant Colonel Cyrenius Chapin for American misfortunes in the Niagara region:

> "To him in a great measure ought all our disasters to be imputed. His publications in the *Buffalo Gazette* that the enemy had abandoned Burlington I fear had the desired effect. I have found him an unprincipled disorganizer. Since dismissing him and his maurauding corps he has been guilty of the most outrageous acts of mutiny if not of *treason*."

28 Cruikshank, *Niagara Frontier in 1812–4*, vol. 9, p. 13: Murray to Drummond, 19 Dec. 1813.

29 James Hannay, *History of the War of 1812 between Great Britain and the United States of America* (Halifax, 1901; reprint ed., Toronto, 1905), 230. See also Cruikshank, *Niagara Frontier in 1812–4*, vol. 9, p. 16: quoted from the *Canadian Courant* (Montreal), 28 Dec. 1813.

30 Cruikshank, *Niagara Frontier in 1812–4*, vol. 9, p. 24.

31 Ibid., 26: McClure to Tompkins, 20 Dec. 1813.

32 Ibid., 54: 26 Dec. 1813.

33 Ibid., 60–61: District General Order, 28 Dec. 1813.

34 Ibid., 71–2: Riall to Drummond, 1 Jan. 1814.

35 Byfield, "A Common Soldier's Account", 40–41.

36 Cruikshank, *Niagara Frontier in 1812–4*, vol. 9, pp. 93–6: 6 Jan. 1814.

CHAPTER 9—MONTREAL, 1813

1 E. A. Cruikshank, "From Isle aux Noix to Chateauguay. A Study of Military Operations on the Frontier of Lower Canada in 1812 and 1813", *Transactions of the Royal Society of Canada*, vol. 8, ser. 3 (June 1941): 25–102.

2 'Philalethes', "General Correspondence", *Colburn's United Service Magazine and Naval and Military Journal*, pt. 1 (London, 1848), 433.

3 Ibid., 436–7.

4 Harry F. Landon, *Bugles on the Border: The Story of the War in Northern New York* (Watertown, N. Y., 1954), 33. See also George F. G. Stanley, *Conflicts and Social Notes: The War of 1812–14; The Patriot War, 1837–38*, Island Insights, no. 7 (Parks Canada, Ottawa, 1976), 24–34.

5 Ibid., 34.

6 'Philalethes', "General Correspondence", 438.

7 Ibid., 439.

8 For a contemporary account of Goose Creek see Robert Christie, *The Military and Naval Operations in the Canadas during the Late War with the United States* (Quebec, 1818), 124–5. See also Franklin B. Hough, *A History of Jefferson County in the State of New York . . .* (Watertown, N. Y., 1854), 494.

   Lieutenant Colonel Thomas Pearson conducted a small punitive expedition against the river privateers, visiting Goose Creek with a detachment of the 100th Regiment, but only found where the Americans had buried their dead, "and from appearances they must have been numerous". (William Wood, ed., *Select British Documents of the Canadian War of 1812*, 4 vols., Champlain Society Publications, nos. 13–15, 17 [Toronto 1920–28], vol. 2 [1923], 433: Pearson to Baynes, 22 Aug. 1813.) See also Stanley, *Conflicts and Social Notes*, 36–9.

9 Both metaphors have been attributed to a contemporary historian, Elihu Shepard, who lived near Henderson's Harbor. See Landon, *Bugles on the Border*, 44.

10 E. A. Cruikshank, ed., *The Documentary History of the Campaign upon the Niagara Frontier in the Year 1813*, pt. 1, *January to June 1813* (Welland, Ont., 1902), 280: 30 May 1813.

11 Landon, *Bugles on the Border*, 45.

12 Cruikshank, *Niagara Frontier . . . 1813*, pt. 1, p. 281: Brenton to Freer, 30 May 1813.

13 Ibid., 282.

14 Ibid., 283: Brown to Tompkins, 29 May 1813.

15 PAC, CO 42/157: 27 Aug. 1814.

16 PAC, RG 8, C 679: Taylor to Stovin, 3 June 1813.

17 Ibid.: Everard Report, 3 Aug. 1813. See also Cruikshank, "From Isle aux Noix to Chateauguay", 56.

18 James Wilkinson, *Memoirs of My Own Times*, 3 vols. (Philadelphia, 1816), 3: Appendix 1.

19 Henry Adams, *History of the United States during the Second Administration of James Madison*, 3 vols. (1891; reprint ed., New York, 1962), 1: 181.

20 Ibid., 182.

21 Ibid., 184.

22 F. F. Van de Water, *Lake Champlain and Lake George* (Indianapolis, 1946), 249–50.

23 I am not suggesting that there was plenty of water. Hampton obviously had too few water wagons with him, for he had to send his animals back to Champlain to be watered. Nevertheless, water was reportedly plentiful farther north, had Hampton but had the stomach to push ahead. See Cruikshank, "From Isle aux Noix to Chateauguay", 71.

24 Ibid.

25 PAC, RG 8, C 680: Sheaffe to Freer, 13 Oct. 1813. See also E. A. Cruik-

shank, "Record of the Services of Canadian Regiments in the War of 1812, Part VIII, The Frontier Light Infantry", *Transactions of the Canadian Military Institute*, Selected Papers, no. 12 (Toronto, 1902), 14.

26 Cruikshank, "From Isle aux Noix to Chateauguay", 76.

27 Ibid., 77.

28 Charles J. Ingersoll, *Historical Sketch of the Second War between the United States of America and Great Britain* . . ., 2 vols. (Philadelphia, 1845, 1849), vol. 1, *Embracing the Events of 1812–13* (1845), 297.

29 Benjamin Sulte, *Histoire de la milice canadienne-française, 1760–1897* (Montreal, 1897), 33; Salaberry's map of the troop dispositions is on p. 35.

30 W. E. Lighthall, *An Account of the Battle of Chateauguay* (Montreal, 1889), 22.

31 Robert Sellar, *The Tragedy of Quebec: The Expulsion of Its Protestant Farmers*, 4th ed. (Toronto, 1916), 105.

32 Cruikshank, "From Isle aux Noix to Chateauguay", 89–90.

33 Irving Brant, *James Madison*, 6 vols. (Indianapolis, 1941–61), vol. 6, *Commander in Chief, 1812–1836* (1961), 224.

34 Adams, *Second Administration of James Madison*, 1: 199.

35 Wilkinson, *Memoirs*, 3: Appendix 24.

36 Benson J. Lossing, *The Pictorial Field-Book of the War of 1812* (New York, 1869), 653.

37 C. W. Elliott, *Winfield Scott, the Soldier and the Man* (New York, 1937), 131.

38 To whom this book is dedicated, and whose father, Matthew Wyn Stanley, was a member of the 1st Regiment Stormont Militia.

39 Williamstown, the Manse, Church papers: Bethune to Reid, 20 April 1814.

40 Elliott, *Winfield Scott*, 135.

41 Lossing, *Pictorial Field-Book*, 655, n. 1.

42 William Dunlop, *Recollections of the American War, 1812–14*, 2nd ed. (Toronto, 1908), 13–14. The tower referred to is of course the Tower of London, where British ordnance stores were housed. Such stores, including muskets, were stamped with the word *Tower*. Subsequently the ordnance stores were moved to Woolwich and Enfield, although the Board of Ordnance kept an office in the Tower of London.

43 PAC, RG 8, C 681: Drummond to Riall, 29 Dec. 1813.

CHAPTER 10—WESTERN UPPER CANADA, 1814

1 E. A. Cruikshank, ed., *The Documentary History of the Campaign upon the Niagara Frontier in 1812–4*, vol. 9, *December 1813 to May 1814* (Welland, Ont., 1908), 100: 7 Jan. 1814.

2 PAC, RG 8, C 373: Robinson to Prevost, 29 June 1814.

3 Matilda (Ridout), Lady Edgar, *Ten Years of Upper Canada in Peace and War, 1805–1815, Being the Ridout Letters with Annotations by Matilda Edgar* (Toronto, 1890), 268–70, 282, 318–19.

4 PAC, RG 8, C 682: 25 April 1815.

5 PAC, RG 8, C 1222: 5 Jan. 1814.

6 For the plans of the Detroit operations see PAC, RG 8, C 682: Drummond to Prevost, 21 Jan. 1814.

7 Ibid.: 3 Feb. 1814.

8   Ibid.: Foster to Riall, 21 Feb. 1814. See also Cruikshank, *Niagara Frontier in 1812–4*, vol. 9, pp. 193–4.

9   PAC, RG 8, C 682: Butler to Riall, 5 March 1814.

10 Ibid.: Drummond to Prevost, 8 Feb. 1814.

11 Cruikshank, *Niagara Frontier in 1812–4*, vol. 9, pp. 208–9: Drummond to Prevost, 5 March 1814. Subsequent quoted passages in this paragraph are from the same source.

12 Ibid., 225: Holmes to Butler, 10 March 1814.

13 Ibid., 205: Stewart to Riall, 5 March 1814.

14 E. A. Cruikshank, "The County of Norfolk in the War of 1812", *Ontario Historical Society Papers and Records* 20 (1923): 30–31.

15 Cruikshank, *Niagara Frontier in 1814* (n.d.), pt. 1, p. 398: Ingersoll to Merritt, 20 May 1814.

16 Glenn Tucker, *Poltroons and Patriots: A Popular Account of the War of 1812*, 2 vols. (Indianapolis, 1954), 2: 422–3.

17 Cruikshank, *Niagara Frontier in 1814*, pt. 2, p. 287: Bostwick to the officer commanding at Long Point, 3 Nov. 1814.

18 Cruikshank, "County of Norfolk", 38.

19 Ibid.

20 "Eight Men Were Sentenced To Be 'Hanged-Drawn-Quartered' ", *Cuesta*, Niagara Escarpment Commission Publication, spring 1981, p. 31.

    The eyewitness was John Ryckman, whose reminiscences were published years later in the Hamilton *Spectator*. The execution was carried out near the present site of Dundurn Castle, Hamilton, but the sentence "hanged-drawn-quartered" was not carried out. The presiding judge wrote, "In point of fact, this sentence is never exactly executed, the Executioner invariably taking care not to cut the body down until the criminal is dead—but the sentence of the law . . . is always pronounced."

21 W. E. Riddell, "The Ancaster 'Bloody Assize' of 1814", *Ontario Historical Society Papers and Records* 20 (1923): 107 ff.

22 PAC, *Annual Report, 1887* (Ottawa, 1888), civ: McDouall to Drummond, 16 July 1814.

23 George F. G. Stanley, "British Operations in the American North-West, 1812–1815", *Journal of the Society for Army Historical Research* 22, no. 87 (autumn 1943): 98.

24 PAC, *Annual Report, 1887*, cvi: McKay to McDouall, 27 July 1814.

25 Ibid.

26 Ibid., cvii.

27 Ibid., cix: McKay to McDouall, 29 July 1814.

28 Ibid.

29 Ibid., cviii.

30 Robert S. Allen, "Canadians on the Upper Mississippi", *Military Collector and Historian* 31, no. 3 (fall 1979): 120. See also Thomas G. Anderson, "Anderson's Journal at Fort McKay, 1814", *Collections of the State Historical Society of Wisconsin* 9 (1882): 207–61.

31 PAC, Andrew Bulger Papers, 30: Bulger to McDouall, 7 Sept. 1814.

32 Allen, "Canadians on the Upper Mississippi", 120.

33 Ibid.

34 PAC, Bulger Papers, 194–7: Proceedings of Court Martial, 2 Jan. 1815.

35 Ibid., 266: Bulger to McDouall, 15 Jan. 1815.

36 Ibid., 146–7: McDouall to Bulger, 1 March 1815.

CHAPTER 11—LUNDY'S LANE

1   Henry Adams, *History of the United States of America during the Second Administration of James Madison*, 3 vols. (1891; reprint ed., New York, 1962), 2: 28.

2   Ibid., 27.

3   Ibid., 28.

4   E. A. Cruikshank, ed., *The Documentary History of the Campaign upon the Niagara Frontier in 1814* (Welland, Ont., n.d.), pt. 2, p. 452: Report of Hospital Surgeon Lovell.

5   C. W. Elliott, *Winfield Scott, the Soldier and the Man* (New York, 1937), 149.

6   PAC, RG 8, C 682: Drummond to Prevost, 14 March 1814.

7   Ibid.: 24 March 1814.

8   Ibid.: Harvey to Riall, 23 March 1814.

9   PAC, RG 8, C 683: Drummond to Prevost, 26 April 1814.

10 George F. G. Stanley and Richard A. Preston, *A Short History of Kingston as a Military and Naval Centre* (Kingston, n.d.), 15. Hewett was grandfather of the first commandant of the Royal Military College of Canada.

11 A. T. Mahan, *Sea Power in Its Relations to the War of 1812*, 2 vols. (London, 1905), 2: 285.

12 Harry F. Landon, *Bugles on the Border: The Story of the War in Northern New York* (Watertown, N. Y., 1954), 59.

13 J. P. Merritt, *Biography of the Hon. W. H. Merritt, M.P., . . . Compiled Principally from His Original Diary and Correspondence* (St. Catharines, Ont., 1875), 33.

14 Elliott, *Winfield Scott*, 162.

15 "Recollections of the War of 1812 by George Hay, Eighth Marquis of Tweeddale", contributed by Lewis Einstein, *American Historical Review* 32: 73.

16 Merritt, *Biography*, 33.

17 Official accounts of the Battle of Chippawa can be found in Cruikshank, *Niagara Frontier in 1814*, pt. 1, pp. 35–6.

18 Several of these incidents are noted in Niles's *Weekly Register*. See also Cruikshank, *Niagara Frontier in 1814*, pt. 1, p. 64, where the following excerpt describing such an attack on the Americans is quoted:

> On Friday last several wagons in the employ of the United States were taken by the enemy near St. Davids, four miles from Queenston. Seth Cotton of Buffalo and his team were among the captured. On Saturday night last a party of the enemy, said to be Indians, surprised our picket at Fort Erie, consisting of eight men, two of whom were killed and the rest taken.

19 Cruikshank, *Niagara Frontier in 1812*, pt. 1, p. 64.

20 Merritt, *Biography*, 34.

21 Cruikshank, *Niagara Frontier in 1814*, pt. 1, p. 73.

22 Ibid., 72: Extract from the Memorial of David Secord to the Legislative Assembly.

23 Ibid., 82: Harvey to Riall, 23 July 1814.

24 Ibid., 83.

25 Ibid., 87.

26 Ibid., 88: Drummond to Prevost, 27 July 1814.

27 Merritt, *Biography*, 35.

28 Cruikshank, *Niagara Frontier in 1814*, pt. 1, p. 88: Drummond to Prevost, 27 July 1814.

29 Ibid.

30 Elliott, *Winfield Scott*, 175.

31 Cruikshank, *Niagara Frontier in 1814*, pt. 1, p. 89: Drummond to Prevost, 27 July 1814.

32 Ibid., 89–90.

33 Norman C. Lord, "The War on the Canadian Frontier, 1812–14. Letters Written by Sergt. James Commins, 8th Foot", *Journal of the Society for Army Historical Research* 18, no. 72 (winter 1939): 209.

34 Cruikshank, *Niagara Frontier in 1814*, pt. 1, p. 120: Tucker to Conran, 4 Aug. 1814.

35 Ibid., 131: Scott to his brother, 12 Aug. 1814.

36 William Dunlop, *Recollections of the American War, 1812–14*, 2nd ed. (Toronto, 1908), 64.

37 Cruikshank, *Niagara Frontier in 1814*, pt. 1, p. 140: Harvey, secret instructions, 14 Aug. 1814.

38 Charles P. Lucas, *The Canadian War of 1812* (Oxford, 1906), 188.

39 William Wood, ed., *Select British Documents of the Canadian War of 1812*, 4 vols., Champlain Society Publications, nos. 13–15, 17 (Toronto, 1920–28), vol. 3, pt. 1 (1926), 190: Drummond to Prevost, 16 Aug. 1814.

40 Cruikshank, *Niagara Frontier in 1814*, pt. 1, p. 142: Drummond to Prevost, 15 Aug. 1814.

41 Dunlop, *Recollections*, 85.

42 Cruikshank, *Niagara Frontier in 1814*, pt. 1, p. 132.

43 Anna Brownell Jameson, *Winter Studies and Summer Rambles in Canada* (Toronto, 1965), 57. The book was originally published in London in 1838.

44 Wood, *Select British Documents*, vol. 3, pt. 1, p. 189: 16 Aug. 1814.

45 Ibid., 180.

46 Lucas, *The Canadian War of 1812*, pp. 189–90.

47 Cruikshank, *Niagara Frontier in 1814*, pt. 2, p. 225: Drummond to Prevost, 21 September 1814.

48 Ibid.

49 Ibid., 256: 16 October 1814.

50 Ibid., 299: 8 November 1814.

CHAPTER 12—THE BRITISH OFFENSIVE, 1814

1 PAC, MG 11, A 151, Nova Scotia: Sherbrooke to Bathurst, 28 Sept. 1814.

2 J. M. Hitsman, *The Incredible War of 1812: A Military History* (Toronto, 1965), 208.

3 Glenn Tucker, *Poltroons and Patriots: A Popular Account of the War of 1812*, 2 vols. (Indianapolis, 1954), 1: 301.

4 *Diplomatic Correspondence of the United States: Canadian Relations, 1784–1860*, comp. William R. Manning, 4 vols. (1940–45; reprint ed., Millwood, N. Y., 1975), vol. 1, *1784–1820*, p. 624.

5 *New-York Spectator*, 27 Aug. 1814.

6 Hitsman, *Incredible War of 1812*, p. 209.

7 Irving Brant, *James Madison*, 6 vols. (Indianapolis, 1941–61), vol. 6, *Commander in Chief, 1812–1836* (1961), 292.

8 Tucker, *Poltroons and Patriots*, 2: 541. See also G. R. Gleig, *A Narrative of the Campaigns of the British Army at Washington and New Orleans . . . in the Years 1814 and 1815* (London, 1821).

9 Tucker, *Poltroons and Patriots*, 2: 550.

10 *National Intelligencer* (Washington), 31 Aug. 1814. See also Brant, *James Madison*, 6: 306. Charles J. Ingersoll wrote in 1849:

> After incendiarism had done its worst, both at the President's house, and the navy yard, indiscriminate pillage closed the scene; less by the British soldiers, who were restrained by their officers, than by negroes, vagrants, and caitiffs of various kinds and hues, freed from all restrictions on their proneness to steal and drink, consume and waste. (*Historical Sketch of the Second War between the United States of America and Great Britain. . .*, 2 vols. [Philadelphia, 1845, 1849], vol. 2, *Embracing the Events of 1814* [1849], 187.)

11 Tucker, *Poltroons and Patriots*, 2: 742.

12 Henry Adams, *History of the United States of America during the Second Administration of James Madison*, 3 vols. (1891; reprint ed., New York, 1962), 2: 99.

13 William Kingsford, *The History of Canada*, 10 vols. (Toronto, 1887–98), vol. 8, *1808–1815* (1895), 532n. See also Hitsman, *Incredible War of 1812*, p. 220.

14 Hitsman, *Incredible War of 1812*, p. 220.

15 William Wood, ed., *Select British Documents of the Canadian War of 1812*, 4 vols., Champlain Society Publications, nos. 13–15, 17 (Toronto, 1920–28), vol. 3, pt. 1 (1926), 358: Macomb to the Secretary of War, 15 Sept. 1814.

16 Ibid., 352: Prevost to Bathurst, 11 Sept. 1814.

17 Hitsman, *Incredible War of 1812*, p. 226.

18 Benson J. Lossing, *The Pictorial Field-Book of the War of 1812* (New York, 1869), 874.

19 Tucker, *Poltroons and Patriots*, 2: 749, n.16.

20 Ibid., 636.

21 Wood, *Select British Documents*, vol. 3, pt. 1, p. 367: Yeo to Croker, 24 Sept. 1814.

22 Adams, *Second Administration of James Madison*, 2: 112.

23 Wood, *Select British Documents*, vol. 3, pt. 1, p. 365: Prevost to Bathurst, 22 Sept. 1814.

24 Adams, *Second Administration of James Madison*, 2: 113.

25 Wellington is referring here to Prevost's enforcement of dress regulations, mentioned earlier in this chapter. An officer of the 88th wrote that Wellington

> never harassed us with reviews, or petty annoyances, which, so far from promoting discipline, or doing good in any way, have a contrary effect. A corporal's guard frequently did duty at Headquarters, and every officer who chose to purchase a horse might ride on a march. Provided we brought our men into the field well appointed, and with sixty rounds of ammunition each, he never looked to see whether their trowsers were black, blue or grey, and as to ourselves [that is, the officers] we might be rigged out in all the colours of the rainbow if we fancied it. (Hitsman, *Incredible War of 1812*, pp. 219–20.)

26 Adams, *Second Administration of James Madison*, 2: 113.
27 Simeon E. Baldwin and John S. Barry, "The Hartford Convention: Protests against the War of 1812", in *The Great Events, by Famous Historians*, vol. 15, ed. Rossiter Johnson, Charles F. Horne, John Rudd and Walter F. Austin (New York, 1926), 327.
28 Ibid., 332.
29 James Truslow Adams, *New England in the Republic, 1776–1850* (1926; reprint ed., Gloucester, Mass., 1960), 259.
30 Ibid., 260.
31 Tucker, *Poltroons and Patriots*, 2: 654–5.
32 Theodore Dwight, *History of the Hartford Convention, with a Review of the Policy of the United States Government Which Led to the War of 1812* (New York, 1833).
33 Adams, *Second Administration of James Madison*, 2: 300–01.
34 Ibid., 292.
35 Dwight, *Hartford Convention*, 353–5.
36 Ibid., 365–6.
37 PAC, MG 11, A 151, Nova Scotia: 20 Nov. 1814.

CHAPTER 13—THE CASTINE EXPEDITION

1 "Secret Reports of John Howe, 1808", pt. 1, contributed by D. W. Parker, *The American Historical Review* 17: 90.
2 Ibid., pt. 2, p. 349.
3 Richard J. Young, "Blockhouses in Canada, 1749–1841: A Comparative Report and Catalogue", *Canadian Historic Sites: Occasional Papers in Archaeology and History* 23: 93, 96–7.
4 Joseph Gubbins, *New Brunswick Journals of 1811 and 1813*, ed. Howard Temperley (Fredericton, 1980), 45.
5 New Brunswick Museum Archives, Saint John: Scott to Sherbrooke, 10 May 1823; and PAC, C 1456: Barry to Couper, 7 Nov. 1823. See also J. C. Medcof, *Blockhouse at St. Andrews, New Brunswick, 1812* (St. Andrews, N. B., n.d.).
6 Gubbins, *New Brunswick Journals*, 3, 7, 9, 19.
7 W. O. Raymond, ed., *The Winslow Papers*, A.D. *1776–1826* (Saint John, N.B., 1901), 691.
8 Gubbins, *New Brunswick Journals*, 65. Throughout most of the eighteenth century, the personal salute consisted of raising the hat. Just before the American Revolution, however, certain British regiments introduced the salute that called for touching the headdress with the hand. The engineer officer at Fort Cumberland was of the old school! With regard to saluting, see E. C. Russell, *Customs and Traditions of the Canadian Armed Forces* (Ottawa, 1980), 5.
9 Alden Nowlan, *Campobello: The Outer Island* (Toronto, 1975), 58.
10 PAC, MG 11, A 23, New Brunswick: Joint Address, 3 March 1814, signed by J. W. Odell. See also New Brunswick, *Journal of the House of Assembly*, 1814, p. 39.
11 PAC, MG 11, A 23, New Brunswick: Lutwyche to Bathurst, 15 June 1814.

12 Public Archives of Nova Scotia, 52, Doct. 120: Bathurst to Sherbrooke, 6 June 1814. See also George F. G. Stanley, "British Operations on the Penobscot in 1814", *Journal of the Society for Army Historical Research* 19, no. 75 (autumn 1940): 168.

13 Alden Bradford, *History of Massachusetts for Two Hundred Years, from the Years 1620 to 1820* (Boston, 1835), 395.

14 *New-Brunswick Courier* (Saint John), 8 April 1813.

15 PAC, MG 11, A 151, Nova Scotia: letter from Thomaston, 23 June 1814.

16 *Halifax Journal*, 11 July 1814.

17 PAC, MG 11, A 151, Nova Scotia: Sherbrooke to Bathurst, 9 July 1814. Bathurst had authorized the Passamaquoddy expedition on 28 April 1814 in a letter that reached Sherbrooke on 30 June.

18 Ibid.

19 Nowlan, *Campobello*, 60.

20 Benson J. Lossing, *The Pictorial Field-Book of the War of 1812* (New York, 1869), 890, n.4.

21 PAC, MG 11, A 151, Nova Scotia.

22 Ibid.: Sherbrooke to Bathurst, 18 Aug. 1814.

23 Ibid.: 26 Aug. 1814.

24 My account of the battle is drawn largely from Lieutenant Colonel Henry John's report to Sherbrooke, written at Bangor, Maine, on 3 September 1814. This report and other documents relating to Castine can be found in PAC, MG 11, A 151, Nova Scotia. See also Sherbrooke to Bathurst, 18 Sept. 1814, and Barrie to Griffith, 3 Sept. 1814, both of which are quoted in William James, *A Full and Correct Account of the Military Occurrences of the Late War between Great Britain and the United States of America*, 2 vols. (London, 1818), 2: 475, 487. See also William D. Williamson, *The History of the State of Maine, from Its First Discovery, A.D. 1602, to the Separation, A.D. 1820*, 2 vols. (Hallowell, Me., 1832); see particularly vol. 2, pp. 642–51.

25 PAC, MG 11, A 151, Nova Scotia: John to Sherbrooke, 3 Sept. 1814.

26 Leavitt's journal, quoted in Barry J. Lohnes, "The War of 1812: the British Navy, New England and the Maritime Provinces of Canada" (Master's thesis, University of Maine at Orono, 1971), 233.

27 Apparently Barrie allowed his sailors to loot at will, but John kept his men under tighter discipline. Private property to the value of about $6000 was stolen from the townspeople (ibid., 237).

28 PAC, MG 11, A 151, Nova Scotia: Pilkington to Sherbrooke, 14 Sept. 1814. The American officer who commanded in the Machias region was Brigadier General John Brewer, of whom Joseph Gubbins wrote in his 1813 journal: "Militia titles do not convey great ideas of rank or respectability in this quarter of the world. General Brewer . . . keeps an ale house opposite St. Andrews." (*New Brunswick Journals*, 84.) Brewer was, nevertheless, one of the leading figures in southeastern Maine. He was a staunch Federalist, and after the war was accused by his political opponents of having supplied information to the British. See Harold A. Davis, *An International Community on the St. Croix, 1604–1930* (Orono, Me., 1950), 90, 104 (n. 13), 111, 167 (n. 34).

29 PAC, MG 11, A 151, Nova Scotia: Pilkington to Sherbrooke, 14 Sept. 1814.

30   Ibid.: Sherbrooke to Bathurst, 10 Sept. 1814.

31   Ibid.: 24 Sept. 1814.

32   Irving Brant, *James Madison*, 6 vols. (Indianapolis, 1941–61), vol. 6, *Commander in Chief, 1812–1836* (1961), 360.

33   PAC, MG 11, A 154, Nova Scotia: Sherbrooke to Bathurst, 15 March 1815.

34   *New-Brunswick Courier* (Saint John), 13 Aug. 1814. See also *The Times* of London, 14 Aug. 1814.

CHAPTER 14—THE TREATY OF GHENT

1   A. L. Burt, *The United States, Great Britain and British North America: From the Revolution to the Establishment of Peace after the War of 1812* (New Haven, Conn., 1940), 347.

2   Frank A. Updyke, *The Diplomacy of the War of 1812* (1915; reprint ed, Gloucester, Mass., 1965), 178–9.

3   Ibid., 182.

4   E. A. Cruikshank, ed., *The Documentary History of the Campaign upon the Niagara Frontier in 1812-4*, vol. 9, *December 1813 to May 1814* (Welland, Ont., 1908), 195: Platt to Merritt, 21 Feb. 1814.

5   *Diplomatic Correspondence of the United States: Canadian Relations, 1784–1860*, comp. William R. Manning, 4 vols. (1940–45; reprint ed., New York, 1975), vol. 1, *1784–1820*, pp. 675–6: Proposed article for a treaty of peace, enclosed in Gambier *et al* to the American ministers, 8 Oct. 1814.

6   Ibid., 680: Adams *et al* to the British ministers, 13 Oct. 1814.

7   Algernon Cecil, *British Foreign Secretaries, 1807–1916: Studies in Personality and Policy* (London, 1927), 24. See also A. J. Grant and Harold Temperley, *Europe in the Nineteenth Century (1789–1914)* (London, 1927), 174n.

8   Arthur Wellesley Wellington, *Supplementary Despatches, Correspondence, and Memoranda*, ed. by his son, the Duke of Wellington, 15 vols. (London, 1858–72), vol. 9, *South of France, Embassy to Paris and Congress of Vienna (April 1814 to March 1815)* (1862), 425–6.

9   W. S. MacNutt, *New Brunswick, a History: 1784–1867* (Toronto, 1963), 161.

10   Wellington, *Supplementary Despatches*, vol. 9, pp. 278–9, 385: Liverpool to Castlereagh, 23 Sept., 28 Oct. 1814.

11   Raymond Walters, *Albert Gallatin: Jeffersonian Financier and Diplomat* (New York, 1957), 286.

12   Ibid.

13   William Wood, ed., *Select British Documents of the Canadian War of 1812*, 4 vols., Champlain Society Publications, nos. 13–15, 17 (Toronto, 1920–28), vol. 3, pt. 1 (1926), 516: Treaty of Ghent, article 1.

14   Ibid., 525: article 10.

15   Walters, *Albert Gallatin*, 287.

16   Irving Brant, *James Madison*, 6 vols. (Indianapolis, 1941–61), vol. 6, *Commander in Chief, 1812–1836* (1961), 49.

17   Burt, *United States*, 385.

18   Updyke, *Diplomacy*, 461–2.
19   T. L. Brock, "H. M. Dock Yard, Kingston, under Commissioner Robert Barrie, 1819–1834", *Historic Kingston* 16 (Jan. 1968): 12.

CHAPTER 15—CONCLUSION

 1   William Dunlop, *Recollections of the American War, 1812–14*, 2nd ed. (Toronto, 1908), 63–4.
 2   Ibid., 48.
 3   Ibid., 63.
 4   Ibid., 26.
 5   C. F. Klinck, "Some Anonymous Literature of the War of 1812", *Ontario History* 49, no. 2 (spring 1957): 49–60. But he was mistaken in saying that the 5th Regiment arrived in Canada in 1813; it was 1814.
 6   Karl von Clausewitz, *The Living Thoughts of Clausewitz, Presented by Lt.-Col. Joseph I. Greene, U.S.A.* (London, 1945), 2.
 7   Quoted in Harold Underwood Faulkner, *American Political and Social History*, 4th ed. (New York, 1946), 231.
 8   John Howison, *Sketches of Upper Canada, Domestic, Local and Characteristic . . .* (1821; reprint ed., Coles Canadiana Collection, Toronto, 1970), 83.
 9   Adam Shortt, "The Economic Effect of the War of 1812 on Upper Canada", *in* Morris Zaslow and Wesley B. Turner, eds., *The Defended Border: Upper Canada and the War of 1812* (Toronto, 1964), 299–300.
10   Howison, *Sketches of Upper Canada*, 81–2.
11   Aileen Dunham, *Political Unrest in Upper Canada, 1815–1836* (Toronto, 1963), 22. T. R. Preston, in his *Three Years' Residence in Canada, from 1837 to 1839* (London, 1840, vol. 2, p. 39), when comparing conditions north and south of the international boundary, says that moving from Upper Canada to New York is like plunging "from a stagnant pool into a vivifying stream".
12   Dunham, *Political Unrest*, 22.
13   Arthur R. M. Lower, *Great Britain's Woodyard: British America and the Timber Trade, 1763–1867* (Montreal, 1973), 68.
14   Thomas H. Raddall, *Halifax, Warden of the North* (Toronto, 1948), 168, 176.
15   During the Second World War, the German command structure was complex and fragmented, like that of the American in 1812–14. It appears to have fought the war with a Prussian army, an Imperial navy, and a National Socialist air force. According to General Alfred Jodl, Hitler put it this way, "I have a reactionary army, a Christian navy . . . and a National Socialist air force." (*Trial of the Major War Criminals before the International Military Tribunal*, vol. 15 [Nuremberg, Germany, 1948], 294.) The Americans would have done better in 1812–14 if the lake fleet had been assigned the role of supporting the land forces.
16   J. M. Hitsman, *The Incredible War of 1812: A Military History* (Toronto, 1965), 240.
17   Frances, Lady Shelley, *The Diary of Frances, Lady Shelley*, ed. Richard Edgcumbe, 2 vols. (London, 1912–13), vol. 1, *1787–1817* (1912), 102.

APPENDICES

1   William Wood, ed. *Select British Documents of the Canadian War of 1812*, 4 vols., Champlain Society Publications, nos. 13–15, 17 (Toronto, 1920–28), vol. 3, pt. 2 (1928), 769–71: Colonel Torrens, Horse Guards, 7 Oct. 1813.

2   H. Taprell Dorling and L. F. Guill, *Ribbons and Medals: The World's Military and Civil Awards*, enl. ed., rev. and ed. by Francis K. Mason (London, 1974), 90–1.

3   Wood, *Select British Documents*, vol. 3, pt. 2, p. 768: Horse Guards to Prevost, 28 Jan. 1814.

4   Ross W. Irwin, comp., *A Guide to the War Medals and Decorations of Canada*, 2nd ed. (Guelph, Ont., 1971), 3.

5   The quoted passages in this paragraph and the next are from Hamilton Craig, "The Loyal and Patriotic Society of Upper Canada and Its Still-Born Child—the 'Upper Canada Preserved' Medal", *Ontario History* 52, no. 1 (March 1960): 31–52.

6   Irwin, *Guide to the War Medals*, 8.

7   Wood, *Select British Documents*, vol. 3, pt. 2, pp. 771–2: Drummond to Prevost, 24 Nov. 1814.

8   L. Homfray Irving, *Officers of the British Forces in Canada during the War of 1812–15* (Welland, Ont., 1908), 250–1. See also Eric I. Manders and René Chartrand, "Lower Canada Select Embodied Militia Battalions, 1812–1815", *Military Collector and Historian* 31, no. 3 (fall 1979): 127; and José M. Bueno and René Chartrand, "Upper Canadian Militia and Provincials, 1812–1815", *Military Collector and Historian* 28, no. 1 (spring 1976): 14–16.

9   The order of precedence is based on the British Army List of 1814.

10 The militia units of Lower and Upper Canada are arranged in the order given in Irving's *Officers of the British Forces in Canada*.

11 William Jay, comp., "Table of the Killed and Wounded in the War of 1812, Compiled during the War", *New York Historical Society, Collections*, 2nd ser., vol. 2 (1849): 447.

12 Mann's book was published in Dedham, Mass., in 1816, and the second edition of Dunlop's recollections in Toronto in 1908.

13 *Archivaria* 10 (summer 1980): 73–85.

14 Owen H. Wangensteen and Sarah D. Wangensteen, "Successful Pre-Listerian Antiseptic Management of Compound Fracture: Crowther (1802), Larrey (1824), and Bennion (ca. 1840)", *Surgery* 69, no. 6 (June 1971): 819. Cited in Charles G. Roland, "War Amputations in Upper Canada", *Archivaria* 10 (summer 1980): 76.

15 *Medical Sketches of the Campaigns of 1812, 1813, 1814* . . . (Dedham, Mass., 1816), 119.

16 "Medical Aspects of the War in the West, 1812–1813". Typescript, pp. 9–10.

Select Bibliography

THE PURPOSE of this bibliography is to provide readers interested in the history of land operations during the War of 1812 with a guide to the basic source materials, both primary and secondary. For a more detailed bibliography of secondary sources, readers are advised to consult John C. Fredriksen's *Resource Guide for the War of 1812* (Los Angeles: Subia, 1979), probably the most complete bibliography available on the war.

Primary Sources

The great bulk of manuscript materials will be found in the national archives of Canada, the United States and Great Britain. The C and MG 11 series in the Public Archives of Canada in Ottawa contain the largest collection of manuscript material on the war, expressing the Canadian and British points of view. Many of these documents are copies of originals in the CO 42, CO 188 and CO 217 series in the Public Record Office in London. In addition to the CO series, the other British sources to consult include the WO 1/96 and WO 17 series. For American material the student should go to the RG 107 papers in the National Archives in Washington, D. C.

Individual items and small collections of documents of the period 1812–14 are to be found in various provincial, state and university libraries and in the libraries of some historical societies. In Canada, the most important collections outside Ottawa are those in the Archives of Ontario and the Toronto Public Library. Individual items will be found in the libraries of the Royal Military College of Canada, the New Brunswick Museum and the University of British Columbia. In the United States, the logbook of HM Sloop-of-War *Racoon* will be found in the Bancroft Library, University of California, Berkeley; letters by Pike and Van Rensselaer are in the library of Yale University; and the Boston Public Library has letters by Pike, Chandler and Dearborn. A collection of Peter B. Porter papers is in the possession of the Buffalo and Erie County Historical Society at Buffalo, N. Y.; the Parish letters are in the Library of St. Lawrence University, Canton, N. Y.; various Meigs letters belong to the Ohio Historical Society, Columbus; a selection of Winchester and Jackson papers are in the Tennessee State Library; and one box of Lewis Cass papers and four volumes (photocopies) of Duncan McArthur papers are in the Burton Historical Collection, Detroit Public Library.

Published documents in official depositories:

BRANNAN, JOHN (COMP.) *Official Letters of the Military and Naval Officers of the United States, during the War with Great Britain in the Years 1812, 13, 14 and 15; with Some Additional Letters and Documents Elucidating the History of That Period.* Washington, D. C.: Way & Gideon, 1823.

COYNE, J. H. (ED.) "The Talbot Papers". In *Proceedings and Transactions of the Royal Society of Canada*, 3rd. ser., vol. 1, pp. 15–210. Ottawa, 1907.

CRUIKSHANK, E. A. (ED.) *The Documentary History of the Campaign upon the Niagara Frontier in the [Years 1812 to 1814].* 9 vols. Welland, Ont.: Lundy's Lane Historical Society, [1896]–1908.

————. *Documents Relating to the Invasion of Canada and the Surrender of Detroit, 1812.* Publications of the Canadian Archives, no. 7. Ottawa, 1912. Reprint ed., New York: Arno Press, 1971.

Diplomatic Correspondence of the United States: Canadian Relations, 1784–1860. Selected and arranged by William R. Manning, 4 vols. Washington, D. C.: Carnegie Endowment for International Peace, 1940. Reprint ed., Millwood, N. Y.: Kraus Reprint Co., 1975.

Documents Legislative and Executive of the Congress of the United States, *American State Papers: Military Affairs*, 1 (1832).

FAY, H. A. (ED.) *Collection of the Official Accounts, in Detail, of All the Battles Fought by Sea and Land, between the Navy and Army of the United States, and the Navy and Army of Great Britain, during the Years 1812, 13, 14 and 15.* New York: E. Conrad, 1817.

HARRISON, WILLIAM HENRY. *Messages and Letters of William Henry Harrison.* Edited by Logan Esarey. 2 vols. Ca. 1922. Reprint ed., New York: Arno Press, 1975.

McKAY, WILLIAM. "Capture of Fort McKay, Prairie du Chien, in 1814". *Public Archives of Canada Annual Report, 1887*, pp. civ–cix. Ottawa, 1888.

STRACHAN, JOHN. *The John Strachan Letter Book, 1812–1834.* Edited by George W. Spragge. Toronto: Ontario Historical Society, 1946.

WOOD, WILLIAM (ED.) *Select British Documents of the Canadian War of 1812.* 4 vols. Champlain Society Publications, nos. 13–15, 17. Toronto, 1920–28.

Other published works containing primary source materials:

BROCK, SIR ISAAC. *The Life and Correspondence of Major-General Sir Isaac Brock. . . .* Edited by Ferdinand Brock Tupper. London: Simpkin, Marshall, 1845.

COBBETT, WILLIAM. *Letters on the Late War between the United States and Great Britain. . . .* New York: J. Belden, 1816.

EDGAR, MATILDA (RIDOUT), LADY. *Ten Years of Upper Canada in Peace and War, 1805–1815; Being the Ridout Letters with Annotations by Matilda Edgar.* Toronto: W. Briggs, 1890.

HOUGH, FRANKLIN B. *A History of Jefferson County in the State of New York.* . . . Watertown, N. Y.: Sterling & Riddell, 1854.

JAMES, WILLIAM. *A Full and Correct Account of the Military Occurrences of the Late War between Great Britain and the United States of America.* 2 vols. London: Printed for the author, 1818.

SPECTATOR [JOHN ARMSTRONG ?]. *An Enquiry Respecting the Capture of Washington by the British.* . . . Washington, D. C., 1816.

Book-length accounts by participants:

ARMSTRONG, JOHN. *Notices of the War of 1812.* 2 vols. New York: Wiley & Putnam, 1840.

DUNLOP, WILLIAM. *Recollections of the American War, 1812–14.* 2nd ed. Toronto: Historical Publishing Co., 1908.

FRANCHÈRE, GABRIEL. *A Voyage to the Northwest Coast of America.* Edited by Milo Milton Quaife. Chicago: Lakeside Press, 1954. The original French edition was published in 1820.

GLEIG, G. R. *The Campaigns of the British Army at Washington and New Orleans, 1814–1815.* New edition. London: J. Murray, 1827.

————. *A Subaltern in America; Comprising His Narrative of the British Army at Baltimore, Washington, etc.* . . . Philadelphia: Carey & Hart, 1833.

GUBBINS, JOSEPH. *New Brunswick Journals of 1811 and 1813.* Edited by Howard Temperley. New Brunswick Heritage Publications, no. 1. Fredericton, N.B., 1980.

McAFEE, ROBERT B. *History of the Late War in the Western Country.* Lexington, Ky., 1816. Reprint ed., Bowling Green, Ohio: Historical Publications Co., 1919.

NORTON, JOHN. *The Journal of Major John Norton, 1816.* Edited by Carl F. Klinck and James J. Talman. Publications of the Champlain Society, no. 46. Toronto, 1970.

Recollections of the War of 1812: Three Eyewitnesses' Accounts. Edited by John Gellner. Toronto: Baxter, 1964. The accounts were originally published between 1828 and 1854.

[REYNOLDS, JAMES ?] *Journal of an American Prisoner at Fort Malden and Quebec in the War of 1812.* Edited by George Moore Fairchild, Jr. Quebec: F. Carrel, 1909. The author of the journal is believed to be Surgeon's Mate James Reynolds, who was captured on the *Cuyahoga.*

RICHARDSON, JOHN. *Richardson's War of 1812.* Edited by Alexander Clark Casselman. Toronto: Historical Publishing Co., 1902.

VERCHÈRES DE BOUCHERVILLE, RENÉ THOMAS. "The Chronicles of Thomas Verchères de Boucherville". In *War on the Detroit.* Edited by Milo Milton Quaife. Chicago: Lakeside Press and R. R. Donnelley & Sons, 1940.

WILKINSON, JAMES. *Memoirs of My Own Times.* 3 vols. Philadelphia: Abraham Small, 1816.

Article-length accounts by participants:

ANDERSON, THOMAS G. "Narrative of Captain Thomas G. Anderson, 1800–28". *Collections of the State Historical Society of Wisconsin* 9 (1909): 137–261. Reprint of 1882 edition.

ASKIN, JOHN. "Extracts from the Diary of John Askin". *Michigan Pioneer and Historical Society, Historical Collections* 32 (1903): 468–73.

BOYLEN, J. C. "Strategy of Brock Saved Upper Canada: Candid Comments of a U.S. Officer Who Crossed at Queenston". *Ontario History* 58, no. 1 (March 1966): 59–60.

DUNCAN, ENNIS, JR. "The Journal of Ennis Duncan, Junior, Orderly Sergeant, 16th Regiment, Kentucky Militia Detached". Transcription and preface by Richard C. Knopf. Mimeographed. Columbus, Ohio: Anthony Wayne Parkway Board, Ohio State Museum, 1956.

GAUGREBEN, BARON DE. "Baron de Gaugreben's Memoir on the Defence of Upper Canada". Edited by H. R. Holmden. *Canadian Historical Review* 1 (March 1921): 58–68.

HAY, GEORGE. "Recollections of the War of 1812 by George Hay, Eighth Marquis of Tweeddale. Contributed by Lewis Einstein. *American Historical Review* 32: 69–78.

LORD, NORMAN C. "The War on the Canadian Frontier, 1812–14. Letters Written by Sergt. James Commins, 8th Foot". *Journal of the Society for Army Historical Research* 18, no. 72 (winter 1939): 199–211.

MERRITT, WILLIAM HAMILTON. *Journal of Events Principally on the Detroit and Niagara Frontiers, during the War of 1812.* St. Catharines, Ont.: St. Catharines Historical Society, 1863.

'PHILALETHES'. "The Last War in Canada". *Colburn's United Service Magazine and Naval and Military Journal*, 1848, pt. 2: 271–83.

PINGUET, CHARLES. "Une Voix de 1813: Deux lettres écrites dans les tentes de Châteauguay". *Les Soirées canadiennes* 4 (1864): 91–96.

[VIGER, JACQUES?]. *Reminiscences of the War of 1812–13, Being Portions of the Diary of a Captain of the "Voltigeurs Canadiens" while in Garrison at Kingston, etc.* Translated by J. L. Hubert Neilson. Kingston: Privately printed, 1895.

WORTHINGTON, THOMAS. "Thomas Worthington and the War of 1812". Transcribed by Richard C. Knopf. Document Transcriptions of the War of 1812 in the Northwest, vol. 3. Mimeographed. Columbus, Ohio: Anthony Wayne Parkway Board, Ohio State Museum, 1957.

Contemporary newspapers and magazines:

A great body of information is obtainable from newspapers published in British North America, Great Britain and the United States during the war. Much of this material was simply reprinted from official reports since newspapers did not maintain war correspondents in the field, but participants in the war sometimes wrote to the newspapers to air grievances against the politicians or their senior officers. The newspapers of the day were highly politicized and expressed the views of the parties they supported; partisanship was especially virulent in the United States.

The most thorough coverage of the war will be found in the pages of H. Niles's *Weekly Register*, which was published in Baltimore. The Library of the Royal Military College of Canada, Kingston, Ontario, has a complete set of this newspaper. Other publications, such as the *Annual Register* (London) and the *Gentleman's Magazine* (New York), contain material relating to the war.

Secondary Sources

General histories of the war are legion, as are books dealing with various aspects of the war, political, military, economic, biographical, social and regional. The books selected here should all be available in Canadian and American libraries.

ADAMS, HENRY. *History of the United States of America [during the Administrations of Thomas Jefferson and James Madison]*. 9 vols. New York: Scribner's, 1889–91. Reprint ed., New York: Antiquarian Press, 1962.

AUCHINLECK, GILBERT. *A History of the War between Great Britain and the United States in the Years 1812, 1813, and 1814*. Toronto: Maclear, 1855.

BABCOCK, LOUIS L. *The War of 1812 on the Niagara Frontier*. Buffalo, N.Y.: Buffalo Historical Society, 1927.

BEIRNE, FRANCIS F. *The War of 1812*. New York: Dutton, 1949.

BERTON, PIERRE. *The Invasion of Canada, 1812–1813*. Toronto: McClelland & Stewart, 1980.

————. *Flames Across the Border, 1813–1814*. Toronto: McClelland & Stewart, 1981.

BIRD, HARRISON. *War for the West, 1790–1813*. New York: Oxford University Press, 1971.

BOISSONNAULT, CHARLES-MARIE. *Histoire politico-militaire des Canadiens-Français, 1763–1945*. Trois-Rivières, Que.: Éditions du Bien public, 1967.

BRANT, IRVING. *James Madison*. 6 vols. Indianapolis: Bobbs-Merrill, 1941–61. Vol. 6, *Commander in Chief, 1812–1836*. 1961.

BURT, A. L. *The United States, Great Britain and British North America: From the Revolution to the Establishment of Peace after the War of 1812*. New Haven, Conn.: Yale University Press, 1940.

CHRISTIE, ROBERT. *The Military and Naval Operations in the Canadas during the Late War with the United States*. Quebec and New York, 1818.

COFFIN, WILLIAM F. *1812; the War and Its Moral: A Canadian Chronicle*. Montreal: John Lovell, 1864.

CRAIG, GERALD M. *Upper Canada: The Formative Years, 1784–1841*. Canadian Centenary Series, vol. 7. Toronto: McClelland & Stewart, 1963.

CRUIKSHANK, E. A. *The Political Adventures of John Henry: The Record of an International Imbroglio*. Toronto: Macmillan, 1936.

CULLUM, GEORGE W. *Campaigns of the War of 1812–15, against Great Britain, Sketched and Criticised; with Brief Biographies of the American Engineers*. New York: J. Miller, 1879.

DAVID, LAURENT O. *Le héros de Châteauguay*. 2nd ed. Montreal: Cadieux et Derome, 1883.

DWIGHT, THEODORE. *History of the Hartford Convention, with a Review of the Policy of the United States Government, Which Led to the War of 1812*. New York: N. & J. White, 1833.

EDGAR, MATILDA (RIDOUT), LADY. *General Brock*. Revised by E. A. Cruikshank. Makers of Canada Series, vol. 4. London: Oxford University Press, 1926.

ELLIOTT, C. W. *Winfield Scott, the Soldier and the Man*. New York: Macmillan, 1937.

FITZGIBBON, MARY AGNES. *A Veteran of 1812: The Life of James Fitz-Gibbon*. 2nd ed. Toronto: William Briggs, 1898.

FORTESCUE, SIR JOHN WILLIAM. *A History of the British Army*. Vols. 7–10. London: Macmillan, 1912–20.

GILPIN, A. R. *The War of 1812 in the Old Northwest*. Toronto: Ryerson, 1958.

HAMIL, FREDERICK C. *Michigan in the War of 1812*. Lansing, Mich.: Michigan Historical Commission, 1960.

_____. *The Valley of the Lower Thames, 1640–1850*. Toronto: University of Toronto Press, 1951.

HANNAY, JAMES. *History of the War of 1812 between Great Britain and the United States of America*. Collections of the Nova Scotia Historical Society, 1899 and 1900, vol. 11. Halifax, 1901. Reprint ed., Toronto: Morang, 1905.

HEITMAN, FRANCIS B. (COMP.) *Historical Register and Dictionary of the United States Army, from Its Organization, September 29, 1789, to March 2, 1903*. 2 vols. Washington, D. C.: Government Printing Office, 1903. Reprint ed., Urbana, Ill.: University of Illinois Press, 1965.

HITSMAN, J. M. *The Incredible War of 1812: A Military History*. Toronto: University of Toronto Press, 1965.

HORSMAN, REGINALD. *The War of 1812*. New York: Knopf, 1969.

INGERSOLL, CHARLES J. *Historical Sketch of the Second War between the United States of America and Great Britain*. . . . 2 vols. Philadelphia: Lea & Blanchard, 1845, 1849.

IRVING, L. HOMFRAY. *Officers of the British Forces in Canada during the War of 1812–15*. Welland, Ont.: Canadian Military Institute, 1908.

KELLOGG, LOUISE PHELPS. *The British Regime in Wisconsin and the Northwest*. Madison, Wis.: State Historical Society of Wisconsin, 1935.

KINGSFORD, WILLIAM. *The History of Canada*. 10 vols. Toronto: Rowsell & Hutchison, 1887–98. Vol. 8, *1808–1815*. 1895.

LANCTÔT, GUSTAVE (ED.) *Les Canadiens français et leurs voisins du sud*. . . . Montreal: B. Valiquette, 1941.

LANDON, FRED. *Western Ontario and the American Frontier*. Toronto: Ryerson, 1941.

LANDON, HARRY F. *Bugles on the Border: The Story of the War in Northern New York*. Watertown, N. Y.: Watertown Daily Times, 1954.

LOSSING, BENSON J. *The Pictorial Field-Book of the War of 1812; or, Illustrations, by Pen and Pencil, of the History . . . of the Last War for American Independence*. New York: Harper & Brothers, 1869. Reprint ed., Glendale, N. Y.: Benchmark Publishing, 1970.

LUCAS, CHARLES P. *The Canadian War of 1812*. Oxford, England: Clarendon Press, 1906.

MCMASTER, J. B. *A History of the People of the United States, from the Revolution to the Civil War*. 5 vols. New York: D. Appleton, 1883–1900.

MAHAN, A. T. *Sea Power in Its Relations to the War of 1812*. 2 vols. London: Low, Marston, 1905. Reprint ed., New York: Greenwood Press, 1968.

MASON, PHILIP P. *After Tippecanoe: Some Aspects of the War of 1812*. East Lansing, Mich.: Michigan State University Press, 1963.

MERRITT, J. P. *Biography of the Hon. W. H. Merritt, M.P., . . . Compiled Principally from His Original Diary and Correspondence*. St. Catharines, Ont.: Leavenworth, 1875.

PERKINS, BRADFORD. *Prologue to War: England and the United States, 1805–1812*. Berkeley, Calif.: University of California Press, 1961.

PRATT, JULIUS W. *Expansionists of 1812*. New York: Macmillan, 1925.

RADDALL, THOMAS H. *The Path of Destiny: Canada from the British Conquest to Home Rule, 1763–1850*. Canadian History Series, vol. 3. Toronto: Doubleday, 1957.

SAPIO, VICTOR A. *Pennsylvania and the War of 1812*. Lexington, Ky.: University Press of Kentucky, 1970.

SQUIRES, W. AUSTIN. *The 104th Regiment of Foot (the New Brunswick Regiment), 1803–1817*. Fredericton, N. B.: Brunswick Press, 1962.

STANLEY, GEORGE F. G. *Canada's Soldiers: The Military History of an Unmilitary People*. 3rd ed. Toronto: Macmillan, 1974.

SULTE, BENJAMIN. *La Bataille de Châteauguay*. Quebec: R. Renault, 1899.

————. *Histoire de la milice canadienne-française, 1760–1897*. Montreal: Desbarats, 1897.

SUMMERS, JACK L., AND CHARTRAND, RENÉ. *Military Uniforms in Canada, 1665–1970*. Canadian War Museum Historical Publication No. 16. Ottawa: National Museum of Man, National Museums of Canada, 1981.

THOMPSON, DAVID. *History of the Late War between Great Britain and the United States of America; with a Retrospective View of the Causes. . . .* Niagara, U. C.: T. Sewell, 1832.

TUCKER, GLENN. *Poltroons and Patriots: A Popular Account of the War of 1812*. 2 vols. Indianapolis: Bobbs-Merrill, 1954.

————. *Tecumseh: Vision of Glory*. Indianapolis: Bobbs-Merrill, 1956.

UPDYKE, FRANK A. *The Diplomacy of the War of 1812*. Baltimore: Johns Hopkins Press, 1915. Reprint ed., Gloucester, Mass.: Peter Smith, 1965.

WHITE, PATRICK C. T. *A Nation on Trial: America and the War of 1812*. New York: Wiley, 1965.

WILLIAMS, J. S. *History of the Invasion and Capture of Washington and of the Events Which Preceded and Followed*. New York: Harper Brothers, 1857.

YOUNG, RICHARD J. "Blockhouses in Canada, 1749–1841: A Comparative Report and Catalogue". *Canadian Historic Sites: Occasional Papers in Archaeology and History* 23: 5–116.

ZASLOW, MORRIS, and TURNER, WESLEY B. (EDS.) *The Defended Border: Upper Canada and the War of 1812*. Toronto: Macmillan, 1964.

Periodicals

It may seem unusual to omit the periodical literature dealing with the War of 1812, to make little mention of the contributions to our knowledge and understanding of what happened between 1812 and 1815 by such historians as C.-M. Boissonnault, E. A. Cruikshank, Brereton Greenhous, F. C. Hamil, J. M. Hitsman, C. W. Humphries, J.-J. Lefebvre, J. S. Martell, J. S. Moir, M. M. Quaife, P.-G. Roy, C. P. Stacey, W. S. Wallace, J.-P. Wallot and others in the *Bulletin des recherches historiques*, *Canadian Historical Review*, *Ontario History*, *Journal of the Society for Army Historical Research*, *Revue d'histoire de l'Amérique française*, and elsewhere. They are simply too numerous to mention and are, in any event, to be found in Fredriksen's *Resource Guide*, cited at the beginning of this bibliography, and in Claude Thibault's *Bibliographia Canadiana* (Don Mills, Ont.: Longman, 1973).

Manuscript Theses

A number of unpublished university theses are worth examining. The most pertinent are:

BOWLER, REGINALD A. "Propaganda in Upper Canada: A Study of the Propaganda Directed at the People of Upper Canada during the War of 1812". Master's thesis, Queen's University, 1965.

CHALOU, GEORGE C. "The Red Pawns Go to War: British–American–Indian Relations, 1810–1815". Ph.D. dissertation, Indiana University, 1971.

GRAVES, DONALD E. "Joseph Willcocks and the Canadian Volunteers: An Account of Political Disaffection in Upper Canada during the War of 1812". Master's thesis, Carleton University, 1982.

HYATT, A. M. J. "The Defence of Upper Canada in 1812". Master's thesis, Carleton University, 1961.

LOHNES, BARRY J. "The War of 1812: The British Navy, New England, and the Maritime Provinces of Canada". Master's thesis, University of Maine at Orono, 1971.

STEPPLER, GLENN A. "A Duty Troublesome Beyond Measure: Logistical Considerations in the Canadian War of 1812". Master's thesis, McGill University, 1974.

SUTHERLAND, IRA M. "The Civil Administration of Sir George Prevost, 1811–1815: A Study in Conciliation". Master's thesis, Queen's University, 1959.

WAY, RONALD L. "Defences of the Niagara Frontier, 1764–1870". Master's thesis, Queen's University, 1938.

Illustration Credits

1   Portrait by J. W. L. Forster, ca. 1897–98. Courtesy Government of Ontario Art Collection.
2   Engraving by David Edwin, 1810, after T. Sully. Courtesy Library of Congress.
3   Watercolour by Charles Stadden, 1978. Courtesy Parks Canada.
4   Reprinted from Benson J. Lossing, *The Pictorial Field-Book of the War of 1812* (New York, 1869), 785.
5   Portrait painted by an unknown artist before 1813. Courtesy Field Museum of Natural History, Chicago.
6   Courtesy Library of Congress.
7   Portrait by John Wesley Jarvis, 1811. Courtesy New-York Historical Society.
8   Portrait by Matthew Jouett, ca. 1818. Courtesy Library of Congress.
9   Engraving by T. B. Welch after J. B. Longacre. Courtesy Library of Congress.
10   Courtesy University of Maine at Orono.
11   Portrait by Walter M. Brackett, 1873, after an earlier likeness. United States Army photograph 94150.
12   Portrait by Jean-Baptiste Roy-Audy, 1824. Courtesy Château Ramezay, Montreal.
13 and 14   Collection of the Canadian War Museum.
15   Courtesy McCord Museum, Montreal.
16 and 17 *top and lower left:*   Collection of the Canadian War Museum.
17 *lower right:*   Courtesy New Brunswick Museum.
18 and 19   Collection of the Canadian War Museum.
20   Portrait by Thomas Phillips. Courtesy His Grace the Duke of Northumberland.
21   Collection of the Canadian War Museum.
22   Portrait by William von Moll Berczy. Courtesy McCord Museum, Montreal.

23   Watercolour by J. P. Cockburn, ca. 1830. Courtesy Public Archives of Canada.

24   Courtesy Metropolitan Toronto Library Board.

25   Engraving by St. Memin, 1805. Courtesy Library of Congress.

26   Watercolour by Gerry Embleton. Courtesy Parks Canada.

27   Portrait by John Trumbull, 1792. Courtesy Yale University Art Gallery.

28   Courtesy Detroit Public Library.

29   Taken from the negative of an oil painting whose location is unknown. Courtesy Hiram Walker Historical Museum, Windsor, Ontario.

30   Watercolour by Margaret Reynolds, whose father was a British officer at Fort Malden. Courtesy Fort Malden National Historic Site.

31   Courtesy Mr. Harrison Bird.

32   Courtesy Public Archives of Canada.

33   Engraving by T. Sutherland, 1836. Courtesy Public Archives of Canada.

34   Collection of the Canadian War Museum.

35   Lithograph by J. T. Bowen, 1838, after Ralph Tremblay. Courtesy Public Archives of Canada.

36   Portrait by Rembrandt Peale. Courtesy Francis Vigo Chapter, DAR, Vincennes, Indiana.

37   Drawing by S. Henley Phillips. Courtesy Library of Congress.

38   Courtesy Anne S. K. Brown Military Collection, Brown University Library.

39   Reprinted from Gabriel Franchère, *A Voyage to the Northwest Coast of America* (New York, 1854), frontispiece. Photograph courtesy Oregon Historical Society.

40   Watercolour by Lieutenant Sempronius Stretton, 1804. Courtesy Public Archives of Canada.

41   Watercolour by Gerry Embleton. Courtesy Parks Canada.

42   Courtesy Historic Fort York, Toronto Historical Board.

43   Courtesy Archives of Ontario.

44   Reprinted from A. N. Bethune, *Memoir of the Right Reverend John Strachan, D.D., LL.D., First Bishop of Toronto* (Toronto and London, 1870), 46. Photograph courtesy Public Archives of Canada.

45   Courtesy United States Naval Academy Museum.

46   Reprinted from Charles H. Smith, *Costume of the Army of the British Empire* (London, 1815).

47   Courtesy Public Archives of Canada.

48   Courtesy New York State Library.

49   Etching by A. Buck engraved by H. R. Cook and published in 1810. Courtesy Public Archives of Canada.

50   Painting by Hugh Charles McBarron, Jr. Courtesy Parks Canada.

51   Lithograph by J. H. Lynch from a drawing by Stephen Pearce. Courtesy Public Archives of Nova Scotia.

52   Drawing by C. W. Jefferys. Courtesy Public Archives of Canada.

53 and 54   Courtesy Metropolitan Toronto Library Board.

55 Photographed from a daguerreotype taken in 1836. Courtesy Public Archives of Canada.

56 Reprinted from DeCost Smith, *Martyrs of the Oblong and Little Nine* (Caldwell, Idaho, 1948), facing p. 297.

57 Courtesy McCord Museum, Montreal.

58 Courtesy Public Archives of Canada.

59 Watercolour by R. J. Marrion; reprinted from Jack L. Summers and René Chartrand, *Military Uniforms in Canada, 1665–1970* (Ottawa, 1981), 73.

60 Courtesy Baron John M. Parish von Senftenberg.

61 Reprinted from John Richardson, *Richardson's War of 1812* (Toronto, 1902), facing p. 272.

62 Published in 1818. Courtesy Metropolitan Toronto Library Board.

63 Engraving by J. and C. Walker after Colonel J. Bouchette, 1815. Courtesy Public Archives of Canada.

64 An early-twentieth-century watercolour by an unidentified artist. Courtesy Mariners Museum, Newport News, Virginia.

65 Courtesy National Portrait Gallery, Smithsonian Institution.

66 Reproduced from a negative in the Burgerbibliothek Berne. Courtesy Mr. Gérard de Watteville, Pully, Switzerland.

67 Watercolour by Gerry Embleton. Courtesy Parks Canada.

68 Portrait by Donald Guthrie McNab. Courtesy Château Ramezay, Montreal.

69 Watercolour by Eugène Lelièpvre. Courtesy Parks Canada.

70 Painted by H. de D. Holmfeld. Courtesy Château Ramezay, Montreal.

71 Watercolour by Thomas Burrowes, 1830. Courtesy Archives of Ontario.

72 Detail of a mural painted by A. Sherriff Scott and displayed at Crysler Farm Battlefield Park, Ontario. Courtesy St. Lawrence Parks Commission.

73 Courtesy Archives of Ontario.

74 Reprinted from Benson J. Lossing, *The Pictorial Field-Book of the War of 1812* (New York, 1869), 658.

75 Portrait by George Berthon. Courtesy Government of Ontario Art Collection.

76 Portrait attributed to James B. Wandesford, ca. 1850. Courtesy Lawson Memorial Library, University of Western Ontario.

77 Reprinted from Benson J. Lossing, *The Pictorial Field-Book of the War of 1812* (New York, 1869), 267.

78 Courtesy Mr. George E. Thorman.

79 Courtesy Archives of Ontario.

80 Courtesy Château Ramezay, Montreal.

81 Engraving by Richard Dillon, 1813. Courtesy McCord Museum, Montreal.

82 Portrait by George Catlin. Courtesy National Portrait Gallery, Smithsonian Institution.

83 Painting by Peter Rindisbacher, ca. 1823. Courtesy Amon Carter Museum, Fort Worth, Texas.

84 Courtesy Library of Congress.

85 Reprinted from Colonel Congreve, *The Details of the Rocket System* . . . (London, 1814), pls. 11 and 5 (fig. 2).

86 Drawing by Captain Steele, published in 1817. Courtesy McCord Museum, Montreal.

87 Courtesy Thousand Islands State Park Commission, Alexandria Bay, New York.

88 Engraving by W. G. Armstrong from a painting by C. Ingham. Courtesy National Portrait Gallery, Smithsonian Institution.

89 Portrait by Lars G. Sellstedt, 1873, after a miniature by Anson Dickinson, 1815. Courtesy Buffalo and Erie County Historical Society, Buffalo, New York.

90 Painting by Charles McBarron, Jr. Courtesy of the artist.

91 Courtesy Public Archives of Canada.

92 Watercolour by C. W. Jefferys, 1909. Collection of the Corporation of the City of Toronto.

93 Collection of the Canadian War Museum.

94 Engraving published ca. 1815. Courtesy New-York Historical Society.

95 Courtesy Library of Congress.

96 Reprinted from *Canadian Illustrated News* 15 (23) 9 June 1877: 357. Photograph courtesy Public Archives of Canada.

97 Engraving by Benjamin Nutting from a drawing by Alicia Ann Jeffery; published 1836. Courtesy Nova Scotia Museum.

98 Lithograph from a drawing by W. Hunt. Courtesy Public Archives of Canada.

99 Courtesy Diana Pine. Photograph, New Brunswick Heritage Publications.

100 Engraving by Robert Field. Courtesy Public Archives of Canada.

101 Courtesy University of King's College, Halifax.

102 Painting by Sir Amédée Forestier, 1914. Courtesy National Collection of Fine Arts, Smithsonian Institution; gift of Sulgrave Institution of the United States and Great Britain.

103 Engraving by Joshua Gleadah from a drawing by James Gray, 1828. Courtesy Royal Ontario Museum.

104 Painting by E. E. Vidal, July 1815. Courtesy Royal Military College of Canada.

105 Portrait by F. W. Lock. Courtesy Public Archives of Canada.

106 Courtesy Archives of Ontario.

107 The author.

108 and 109 Collection of the Canadian War Museum.

110 Courtesy Royal Ontario Museum.

111 Collection of the Canadian War Museum.

Index

Abenakis, 89
Ackley, Joel, 243
Adams, Henry, 299
Adams, John, 12, 30
Adams, John Quincy, 353, 382, 398, 409
Adams, William, 384–85, 386
Adams (renamed *Detroit*), 93, 120, 124
Adams, USS, 370, 372, 373, 374, 375
Adet, Pierre, 15–16
Albany, N.Y., 83, 85, 86, 87, 272
Alexander I, Tsar, 381, 382, 390
Algonquins, 89
Allan, Ebenezer, 96
Allan, William, 174, 175
Allen, John, 145, 146
Alwood, Reuben, 276
American Revolutionary War, 12–13,
    21, 29, 61, 66–67, 162, 213, 336, 352,
    357, 365, 370, 413, 414, 416
Amherst, Jeffrey, 83, 225, 244–45
Amherstburg, U.C., 23, 28, 65, 76, 95,
    97, 98, 99 pl, 102, 106, 111, 115, 116,
    145, 147, 148, 150, 153, 160, 201, 203,
    208, 271, 285; fortifications at, 76, 98
    (*see also* Fort Malden); Procter's with-
    drawal from, 204–7; supply lines of,
    70, 120, 155–56, 186, 202–3, 204
Ancaster, U.C., 212, 283, 302; Bloody
    Assize, 286–87
Anderson, Thomas Gummersall, 290,
    292, 295–96
Annapolis Royal, N.S., 358

Armstrong, John, 139, 143, 148, 156,
    167, 168, 179, 199–200, 214, 299–300,
    319, 331, 340, 343, 344; and burning
    of Niagara, 218, 222; and St. Law-
    rence campaign, 225–26, 243, 245–46,
    249, 251, 253, 255, 259
Army, British, 61–64, 63 pl, 335, 337,
    343, 344, 354, 369, 417, 418, 429–30,
    433–34, 455 n.8; Centre Division, 161,
    201; Right Division, 154, 156, 157,
    212, 404; 19th Light Dragoons, 223,
    251, 280, 426; Royal Artillery, 169,
    240, 242, 372, 426. *See also* Militia,
    British North American
Regular infantry units:
1st Regiment, or Royal Scots (Royals),
    180, 219, 220, 221, 223, 234, 237,
    274, 275, 277, 278, 309, 313, 321,
    322, 329, 426
4th Regiment, 337
6th Regiment, 314, 330
8th (King's) Regiment, 170, 170 pl,
    172, 177, 180, 183, 188, 193, 195,
    216, 223, 234, 237–38, 310, 321,
    322, 326, 328, 417, 426
13th Regiment, 242, 335
21st Regiment, 369
29th Regiment, 369, 372, 374
41st Regiment, 6, 98, 101, 103, 105,
    106, 122, 150, 152, 154, 180, 201,
    204, 210, 219, 220, 221, 233, 274,
    321, 322, 325, 326, 330, 426

44th Regiment, 337
49th Regiment, 61 pl, 122, 127, 137, 180, 183, 188, 259, 261
60th (Royal American) Regiment, 253, 372, 373, 417
62nd Regiment, 369, 372
82nd Regiment, 314, 330
84th Regiment, 417
85th Regiment, 337
89th Regiment, 223, 259, 261, 263, 268, 274, 277, 278, 314, 317, 321, 322, 326, 328, 335, 426
97th Regiment, 331
98th Regiment, 369, 372, 373
99th Regiment, 369
100th Regiment, 219, 220, 233, 234, 237–38, 240, 242, 274, 278, 310, 313, 326, 426, 449 n.8
103rd Regiment, 242, 243, 268, 283, 302, 317, 321, 322, 326, 330, 426
104th Regiment of Foot, 61 pl, 71, 180, 192, 193, 195, 234, 237–38, 314, 317, 322, 325, 326, 360, 363, 426
Garrison regiments:
10th Royal Veteran Battalion, 7, 7 pl
North American fencible and provincial corps, 62, 69, 416–17, 427
Canadian Fencible Infantry, 60 pl, 242, 251, 256, 260, 265, 268, 417
Glengarry Light Infantry Fencibles (Glengarrians), 63, 169, 172, 180, 183, 230, 231 pl, 234–35, 303, 306, 317, 318, 321, 417, 426, 427
King's New Brunswick Regiment, 61
Michigan Fencibles, 289, 290, 296
New Brunswick Fencible Infantry, 62, 360–61, 417
19th Light Dragoons, 223, 251, 280, 426
Nova Scotia Fencible Infantry, 62 pl, 417
Provincial Corps of Light Infantry (Voltigeurs), 63, 88 pl, 89, 234, 247, 251, 253, 256, 257 pl, 260, 261, 427
Queen's Rangers, 61, 417
Royal Canadian Volunteers, 61, 417
Royal Newfoundland Fencible Infantry, 169, 172, 180, 183, 289, 294
Royal Nova Scotia Regiment, 61
Swiss corps:
Régiment de Meuron, 251
Régiment de Watteville, 61 pl, 256, 303, 305–6, 314, 325, 326, 328, 330, 335

Army, U.S., 44–47, 86, 91, 118, 168, 187 pl, 209, 267 pl, 268, 312, 332, 408–9, 416; Army of the Centre, 118, 122, 134; Northern Army, 83, 86, 87, 331; North Western Army, 90, 114, 143, 145. *See also* Militia, U.S. *Regular infantry units:*
1st Regiment, 322
11th Regiment, 321
13th Regiment, 125
14th Regiment, 195
21st Regiment, 322–23
22nd Regiment, 321
23rd Regiment, 322
25th Regiment, 263, 321
Arnold, Benedict, 29, 46
Arnold's mill, 203, 207
Aroostook River, 389
Aroostook War, 396
Ashburton, Lord, 396
Askin, Charles, 197
Astor, John Jacob, 162, 383–84
Astoria. *See* Fort Astoria
Atlantic Coast, 336, 337, 338, 357

Baby, François, 275
Baby, James (Jacques), 96, 97 pl, 105
Bacchante, 372
Bacon, Constant, 303
Bagot, Sir Charles, 398
Bald Head Cove, 373
Baldoon, U.C., 282
Ball's farm, 199
Baltimore, 134, 338, 342, 409, 438 n.44
Baltimore Whig, 134
Bangor, Maine, 372, 373, 375
Barclay, Robert Heriot, 160, 201, 202, 203
Baring, Alexander, 392
Barney, Joshua, 341
Bar Point, 208, 274
Barrie, Robert, 367, 372–73, 374–75, 400, 456 n.27
Bartlett, Enoch, 369
Basden, James, 278–79
Bathurst, Lord, 180, 240, 336, 350, 351, 355, 362, 364, 365, 369, 377, 378, 388, 456 n.17
Bayard, James A., 382
Baynes, Edward, 52, 53, 86, 186, 234 pl, 235, 237, 239, 417
Beauharnois, L.C., 266
Beaujeu, Louis de, 256
Beaver Dams, U.C. (Thorold, Ont.), 184; Battle of, 193–97, 199, 271

Beekmantown Road, 345
Belfast, Maine, 372
Belvidera, 4–5
Benedict, Md., 338
Beresford, 237
Bethune, Angus, 163
Bethune, Rev. John, 263–64
Birbeck, Morris, 408
Bisshopp, Cecil, 136, 137–38, 174, 184, 193, 196, 197, 198–99
Black, W., 165
Blackbird, 112, 114
Black Creek, 331
Black Hawk, 296, 297 pl, 408
Black Rock, N.Y., 136, 137, 180, 184, 224, 308, 326, 331; attacks on, 197–98, 222–23, 325
Black Swamp, 91
Bladensburg, Md., 338; Battle of, 340–41, 354, 388, 408
Blake, John, 373–74, 375
Bloomfield, Joseph, 47, 87–88, 133
Bodley, Thomas, 31
Boerstler, Charles G., 136–37, 193–96, 446 n.39
Bois Blanc Island, 98, 397
Bonaparte, Napoleon. *See* Napoleon
Boston, 363, 367, 369, 372, 377, 378
Boston Gazette, 366
Boston Messenger, 249
Bostwick, Henry, 105, 106, 276, 280, 282, 283, 284 pl, 284–85
Bostwick, John, 280, 282
Boucher de Boucherville, Pierre-René, 265
Boucher de La Bruère, Pierre-René, 256
Boucherville, Thomas Verchères de. *See* Verchères de Boucherville
Boulton, D'Arcy, 286
Bourchier, William, 397
Boyd, John, 27, 182, 192, 193, 245, 246, 260–61, 263
Brant, John, 130 pl, 196
Brant, Joseph, 13, 21, 65
Brent, Richard, 38
Brenton, Edward, 235, 237, 238
Brewer, John, 456 n.28
Bridge (Chimney) Island, 79
Brisbane, Thomas, 344–45, 346, 348
Brisebois, Antoine, 290
Brock, Sir Isaac, frontispiece, 6, 8, 64, 65, 66, 79–80, 105, 112, 120, 122, 139, 140, 149, 169, 174, 211, 213, 403, 406, 417, 423, 435 n.7, 444 n.15; and administration of Upper Canada, 51–54; on Detroit frontier, 106–8, 110; proclamation of, 104–5; at Queenston Heights, 124–28, 126 pl, 131
Brockville, Ont. *See* Elizabethtown, U.C.
Broke. See Eagle (U.S. sloop)
Brooke, Arthur, 342
Brown, Jacob, 19, 246, 273, 280, 301 pl; at Fort Erie, 330, 331, 343, 352; invades Niagara peninsula, 299–301, 310, 315–16, 317, 318–19, 418; at Lundy's Lane, 323–24; at Sackets Harbor, 235, 237, 239; on St. Lawrence, 260–61
Brown's Point, 124, 127
Brownstown, Michigan Terr., 97, 102, 106, 145–46, 147
Brownstown Creek, 101
Brownville, N.Y., 19
Bruère, Pierre-René Boucher de La. *See* Boucher de La Bruère
Brunswicker, 363
Brush, Henry, 101–2, 109, 110, 114
Bruyère, Joseph-Bernard, 256, 257
Bruyères, Ralph Henry, 73, 78
Buck, Thomas, 308–9
Bucks Harbor, 375
Bucksport, Maine, 372
Buffalo, N.Y., 83, 118, 121, 134, 138, 220, 221, 222, 274, 299, 300, 303, 309, 315, 319, 325, 326, 332; attack on, 222–23, 224
Buffalo Gazette, 216, 217 pl, 448 n.27
Bulger, Andrew, 294, 295, 296–98, 298 pl, 395
Bullock, Richard, 210, 221, 447 n.12
Bulwark, 377
Burford, U.C., 282, 283
Burgoyne, John, 21, 29, 111, 351, 365
Burlington, Vt., 86, 241, 243, 246, 249, 250, 334
Burlington Heights (U.C.), 184, 186, 197, 201, 206, 212, 213, 214, 215, 216, 219, 274, 276, 282, 284, 300, 302–3, 316, 318, 336, 448 n.27
Burn, James, 190, 191
Burtonville, U.C., 89, 333
Burwell, Mahlon, 105
Burwell, William, 32
Butler, John, 13–14
Butler's Rangers, 21, 155
Byfield, Shadrach, 159, 160, 220, 223–24

Cabot, George, 352, 354
Cabot, Jean-Baptiste, 106
Caldwell, William, 155, 211–12, 278
Caledonia, 120, 124

Calhoun, John C., 3, 33, 35, 36 pl, 44
California, 408
Campbell, J. H., 91
Campbell, John, 292
Campbell, John B., 279, 280, 413
Campbell, William, 286
Campobello Island, 363, 368, 396
Canard River, 99, 101, 106, 107
Canning, George, 34
Carleton, Guy, 21, 29
Carleton Point, 359
Cartwright, Richard, 51
Cass, Lewis, 91, 168, 208, 209, 214,
  397; on Detroit frontier, 94, 95, 99,
  101, 103–4, 107, 109–11
Castine, Maine, 355, 357, 375, 389, 396;
  capture of, 342, 370, 372, 373, 376,
  377, 388
Castlereagh, Viscount, 39, 75, 357, 385,
  386, 387–88, 390, 398, 401
Cataraqui River, 239
Caughnawaga, L.C., 249, 251, 252,
  265; reserve, 66
Caughnawaga Indians, 266
Cedars (Les Cèdres), L.C., 267
Chambers, Peter, 66, 105, 151, 285, 423
Chambly, L.C., 76, 225
Champlain, Lake, 179, 200, 240, 242–43,
  245, 246, 268, 334, 346, 348, 398, 409,
  418; as invasion route, 83, 225, 342–43
Champlain, N.Y., 89, 247, 343, 344, 349
Chandler, John, 182, 186, 188, 192
Chapin, Cyrenius, 91, 138, 193–94, 222,
  448 n.27
Charlotte, Vt., 243
Charlotte County, N.B., 358
Charlotteville, U.C. (Turkey Point,
  Ont.), 278, 280
Charwell, 326
Chateaugay, N.Y. *See* Four Corners,
  N.Y.
Châteauguay, L.C., 89, 267
Châteauguay, Battle of, 254–58, 258 pl,
  265, 271, 408, 422, 424, 426
Châteauguay River, 247, 249, 250–51,
  253–54, 256
Chatham, U.C., 206, 276
Chauncey, Isaac, 179, 184, 185–86, 215,
  233–34, 239, 299, 300, 315, 316 pl,
  317, 319, 330, 331, 418; at Fort
  George, 182, 183; and Sackets Harbor
  blockade, 306–7; at York, 168, 170,
  173, 175, 176
Chaussegros de Léry, Louis-René, 256
Chazy, N.Y., 243, 247, 333, 344
Cherokees, 408

Cherry Valley, N.Y., 21
Chesapeake, 17, 20–21, 23, 30, 35, 38,
  51, 363
Chesapeake Bay, 338
Chester, N.S., 358
Cheves, Langdon, 35–36
Chewett, William, 174, 175
Chickasaws, 408
Chimney Island. *See* Bridge Island
Chippawa, U.C., 129, 136, 137, 184,
  191, 192–93, 303, 309–10, 315, 318,
  324, 325, 331
Chippawa, Battle of, 309–13, 312 pl,
  327, 409, 416
Chippawa (Welland) River, 282, 310,
  311
Chippewas, 212, 214
Choctaws, 408
Christie, Robert, 406
Chrystie, John, 121
Cincinnati, 148, 214
Clark, Isaac, 249
Clark, Thomas, 197
Clark, William, 44, 162, 288, 289, 290
Clarke, Isaac, 71
Claus, William, 418
Clausewitz, Karl Von, 406–7
Clay, Green, 150, 152, 153, 157–58
Clay, Henry, 31, 32, 34 pl, 35–36,
  43–44, 111, 134, 147, 199, 383, 387,
  388, 392
Clifford, Miller, 424
Cochrane, Sir Alexander, 337–38, 342,
  365
Cockburn, Sir George, 338, 341
Coffin, John, 360–61
Coffin, Nathaniel, 417
Coleman, Thomas, 275, 427
Collins Landing, N.Y., 19
Columbian Centinel (Boston), 353
Columbia River, 162, 384, 395
Commins, James, 191, 207, 325
Confiance, 348
Connecticut, 84, 352, 355
Connecticut Courant, 84
Constitution, 409
Conway, 367
Cooks Mills, U.C., 332
Cooper, James Fenimore, 307, 406
Cornwall, U.C., 73, 78, 260, 265, 267
Coteau-du-Lac, L.C., 73, 78, 78 pl, 266,
  272
Couche, Edward, 203
Covington, Leonard, 246, 263, 265
Craig, Sir James, 23, 30–31, 38, 55–57,
  75, 139, 226, 350, 358, 406

Crawford, William Harris, 139
Creek Indians, 408
Crillon, Comte Édouard de. *See* Soubiron, Paul-Émile
Croghan, George, 158–59, 292–93
Crysler, John, 260
Crysler Island, 260
Crysler's Farm, Battle of, 260–64, 264 pl, 265, 271, 408, 422, 424, 426
Cumberland Head, 243, 247, 343, 345, 346, 350
Cuyahoga, 6, 79, 91, 93, 106, 434
Cuyahoga River, 22

Dalhousie College, 396
Daly, Charles, 256, 257
Dana, Josiah, 369
Dance, Edward, 303
Dane, Nathan, 354
Darroch, Duncan, 369
Dearborn, Henry, 46–47, 85 pl, 90, 139, 168, 175, 176, 233–34, 300, 382; and armistice, 85–86, 110, 118, 122, 381; and Montreal offensive, 83–89, 342; and Niagara frontier, 117, 118–20, 132, 133, 179, 182, 184, 186, 192, 193, 196, 199–200, 441 n.8
Dease, Francis Michael, 288, 289
Debartzch, Dominique, 256
Decatur, Stephen, 317
Decatur, 375
De Cou (DeCew) Falls, 319
De Cou's (DeCew's), 194
DeHaren, P. V., 193, 194–95
Delaware, U.C., 275, 277, 278
Delaware Indians, 207
Delaware Township, U.C., 97, 105
Dennis, James, 125 pl, 128, 260
Deschambault, Louis-Joseph Fleury. *See* Fleury Deschambault
Desha, Joseph, 30, 39
Des Moines River, 296
Detroit, 4, 6, 23, 66, 83, 85, 91, 93, 94 pl, 96, 98, 101, 102, 104, 113, 145, 154, 155, 274–75, 286, 292, 293, 303, 336; capture of, 107–11, 120, 122, 127, 213, 408, 422, 423, 426, 434, 444 n.15; reoccupation of, 114, 133, 145, 206, 208, 213, 214, 288
Detroit. See *Adams*
Detroit frontier, 69, 90, 106, 120, 154, 186, 336, 381
Detroit River, 6, 65, 95, 96, 98, 99, 101, 102, 152, 186, 204, 208, 274–75, 336
Dickson, Robert, 65, 296, 298

Dickson, Mrs. William, 219
Digby, N.S., 358
Diligence, 367
Disappointment, Cape, 165
Dixon, M. C., 423
Dobbs, Alexander, 326
Dolson, Matthew, 208–9
Dolson's, 96, 206, 207, 208
Douglas, William, 372
Douglass Battery, 328
Dover, 98
Dover Mills, U.C., 180
Downie, George, 346, 348, 350, 354
Doyle, Edward, 226
Dragon, 372, 373
Drummond, Sir Gordon, 267, 268, 273 pl, 274–75, 277–78, 282, 286, 289, 301–3, 332, 395, 404, 406, 417; at Fort Erie, 325–26, 327, 329–31; at Lundy's Lane, 319, 321, 323, 324; on Niagara frontier, 219, 222, 272–73, 309, 311–12, 313, 318; and raid on Oswego, 303–5
Drummond of Kelty, William, 317–18, 326, 328, 329, 404, 406
Drummond Island, 294
Ducharme, Dominique, 89, 193, 196
Dudley, William, 150–51, 152
Dudley Island (now Treat Island), 396
Dudley Island. *See* Frederick Island
Duke of Gloucester, 169
Dunlop, William "Tiger", 266 pl, 266–67, 403–4, 433; at Fort Erie, 326, 328–29; as writer, 404, 406
Dupuis, La Serre, 296–97
Dwight, Theodore, 354

Eagle (U.S. brig), 348
Eagle (U.S. sloop; renamed *Broke*, then *Finch*), 240–41, 242 pl
Eastern Townships, 54
Eastport, Maine, 8, 363, 367, 368, 369, 370, 396
Edwards, Ninian, 156
Eel River, 360
Eisenhower, Peter, 268
Eleanor, 98
Elizabethtown, U.C. (Brockville, Ont.), 6, 73, 229
Elliott, Alexander, 101
Elliott, Jesse, 120
Elliott, Matthew, 28, 107, 155, 423
Embargo Act, 18 pl, 18, 19, 50, 66–67, 353, 358
Embargo Road, 19

Erie, Lake, 95, 98, 99, 116, 120, 136, 186, 223, 274–75, 383, 412; naval superiority on, 111, 143, 157, 167, 201–2, 204, 288, 336, 409

Erie, Penn. *See* Presque Isle, Penn.

Erie frontier, 143, 149, 154, 161, 167, 200, 271

Erskine, David Montagu, 30–31, 34

Essex, 17

Eustis, William, 46 pl, 47, 86, 91, 93–94, 95, 111, 114, 117, 132, 139, 226, 441 n.8

Evandale, N.B., 359

Evans, Thomas, 190–91

Everard, Thomas, 242, 243

Fairfield, U.C., 207

Fallen Timbers, Battle of, 14, 21, 25, 91, 148

Federalists, 14, 15–16, 35, 37, 38–39, 45, 134, 139, 353, 355–56, 378, 409, 438 n.44

Fencibles. *See under* Army, British

Ferguson, George R., 256

Finan, P., 169, 170, 172, 173, 177, 178

Finch, Titus, 280

Finch. See Eagle (U.S. sloop)

Findlay, James, 91

Finlay, John, 71

Fischer, Victor, 306, 326, 327, 328

FitzGibbon, James, 87, 195 pl, 318, 329; at Beaver Dams, 193–97; at Stoney Creek, 188, 189–90

Fleury Deschambault, Louis-Joseph, 266, 417

Florida, 43, 408

Forsyth, Benjamin, 86, 172, 182, 229, 230

Fort Armstrong, 396

Fort Astoria (renamed Fort George), 162–65, 163 pl, 383–84, 389, 395, 445 nn.25, 27

Fort Beauséjour. *See* Fort Cumberland

Fort Bowyer, 394

Fort Brown, 345

Fort Chouaguen. *See* Oswego, N.Y.

Fort Covington. *See* French Mills, N.Y.

Fort Crawford, 396

Fort Cumberland (Fort Beauséjour), 8, 358, 361

Fort Dearborn, 111–12, 396, 442 n.39

Fort Defiance, 115

Fort Detroit. *See* Detroit

Fort Drummond, 358

Fort Erie, 51, 106, 136, 137, 180, 184, 191, 192, 201, 215, 284, 302, 303, 308–9, 324, 325, 332, 343, 352, 389; siege of, 325–31

Fort Findlay, 91

Fort Frederick, 359

Fort George, Maine, 377

Fort George, Oregon Terr. *See* Fort Astoria

Fort George, U.C., 6, 99, 104, 111, 122, 124, 131, 135–36, 156, 191, 192–93, 197, 199, 216, 218, 274, 302, 303, 309–10, 314, 315–16, 317, 318, 319, 332, 382, 435 n.7; U.S. attacks on, 120, 133, 156, 167, 182 pl, 182–84, 183 pl, 199, 201, 203, 233, 234, 250, 271, 409

Fort Gratiot, 288, 289

Fort Harrison, 27, 28, 113

Fort Henry, 401

Fort Howard, 396

Fort Howe, 359

Fort Île aux Noix (Fort Lennox), 242, 247. *See also* Noix, Île aux

Fort Lennox, 401. *See also* Fort Île aux Noix

Fort McArthur, 91

Fort McHenry, 342, 409

Fort McKay, 292, 295, 296, 297–98, 298 pl. *See also* Fort Shelby

Fort Madison, 113, 156

Fort Malden, 6, 93, 94, 95, 96, 98, 99 pl, 274, 288, 336, 389, 395. *See also* Amherstburg, U.C.

Fort Meigs, 148, 151 pl; sieges of, 149–153, 154, 157–58, 160

Fort Miami, 150

Fort Michilimackinac. *See* Michilimackinac

Fort Mississauga, 315

Fort Moreau, 345

Fort Niagara, 6, 118, 122, 128, 136, 179, 180, 183, 215, 218, 222, 223, 224, 245, 274, 302, 303, 309, 315–16, 318, 319, 435 n.7; capture of, 219–20, 271, 330, 389

Fort O'Brien, 375

Fort Pike, 235, 238 pl,

Fort Portage, 91

Fort Presque Isle, 360, 364

Fort Schlosser, 197, 221, 318, 319

Fort Scott, 345

Fort Shelby, 288, 290, 292. *See also* Fort McKay; Prairie du Chien

Fort Sherbrooke. *See* Fort Sullivan

Fort Snelling, 396

Fort Stephenson, 158–60, 161 pl, 293

Fort Sullivan (renamed Fort Sherbrooke) 368

Fort Tipperary, 359

Fort Tompkins, 235, 237, 238 pl

Fort Wayne, 111, 113, 114, 115, 148

Fort Wellington, 68, 78, 228, 230, 259, 261 pl. *See also* Prescott, U.C.

Fort William, 165

Forty Mile Creek (Grimsby, Ont.), 184, 190, 191, 193, 216

"Forty Thieves", 193–94

Foster, Augustus John, 4

Foster, Jonah, 434

Four Corners (Chateaugay), N.Y., 247, 249, 251, 253, 254, 258, 268

Fox Indians, 292

Fox River, 290, 396

France, 16–20, 334–35; U.S. relations with, 15–16, 35, 37

Franchère, Gabriel, 162, 165, 445 n.27

Frankfort, Maine, 373

Franklin, Benjamin, 30

Fraser, Alexander, 188

Frederick, Point, 79, 400

Frederick Island (now Dudley Island), 396

Fredericton, N.B., 8, 361

Freer, Noah, 235, 272, 417

Frenchman Creek, 136, 137, 174

French Mills (Fort Covington), N.Y., 265, 268, 299, 336, 434

French River, 213, 288

Frenchtown, Michigan Terr. (Monroe, Mich.), 91, 115, 144–45; Battle of, 146–48

Frend, Richard, 221, 223

Front Road, 73, 79

Gaines, Edmund Pendleton, 263, 273, 326, 328

Gales, Joseph, 342

Gallatin, Albert, 45, 382, 386, 392, 394, 438 n.50

Gambier, James, Lord, 384–85, 386

Gananoque, U.C., 87, 229, 233

Gansevoort, Peter, 47

Gaucher, Gédéon, 446 n.34

Gaugreben, Frederic de, 220

Gazette (Montreal), 9

General Hunter, 98, 99 pl

General Pike, 185

General Smyth, 363

Genesee River, 193

Genêt, Edmond, 15

Georgian Bay, 213, 288

German Flatts, N.Y., 21

Ghent, Holland, 378, 385, 386; peace negotiations at, 385–92; Treaty of, 298, 392–95, 393 pl, 396, 408, 414, 416

Gibraltar Point, 169, 170

Giles, William, 37

Gilmor, Robert, 203, 206

Givins, James, 137

Glegg, John B., 107, 108, 110, 127, 423, 435 n.7

Gleig, George R., 341

Glengarry House, 78

Goose Creek, 233, 449 n.8

Gordon, John, 223, 313

Gore, Francis, 51–52

Gosselin, Gerard, 369, 372, 377, 396

Goulburn, Henry, 384–85, 386, 388, 408

Governor Clark, 290, 291–92

Graham, Duncan, 295–96

Grand Falls, N.B., 360, 364

Grand Island, 138

Grand Magazine, 173, 174 pl

Grand Manan Island, 396

Grand River, 206, 276, 283–84, 285

Grand River Reserve, 66, 129

Granger, Erastus, 65

Grant, Jasper, 23

Gray, Andrew, 73

Gray, Hugh, 51

Great Lakes, 213, 225, 288, 397, 408, 418; disarmament on, 386–87, 394, 398; naval superiority on, 140, 351, 383, 388, 391–92, 398, 401; trading posts, 13, 64–65. *See also* individual lakes

Great Miami River, 22

Green, Billy, 187

Green Bay, 101, 288, 396

Greenville, Treaty of, 21–23, 25, 26, 384

Grenadier Island, 246, 259

Griffith, Edward, 365, 370, 372, 375, 376, 377

Grimsby, Ont. *See* Forty Mile Creek

Griswold, Roger, 84, 352

Grosse Ile, 397

Grosvenor, Abel, 134

Grosvenor, Thomas, 134

Growler (renamed *Shannon*), 240–41, 242 pl

Grundy, Felix, 32, 35, 37

Gubbins, Joseph, 359, 360, 361, 362 pl, 456 n.28

Guysborough, N.S., 358, 361

Hagerman, Christopher, 417
Haldimand, Sir Frederick, 14, 21
Halifax, 4, 8, 75–76, 337, 342, 358,
  359 pl, 360, 362, 363, 365, 369, 377,
  394, 415, 416; Citadel, 358, 401, 416
Hall, Amos, 222–24
Hamilton, Alexander, 14
Hamilton, Henry, 21
Hamilton, Paul, 47
Hamilton, Ont., 451 n.20
Hampden, Maine, 372, 373, 375
Hampton, Wade, 47, 243, 244–45, 246,
  265, 449 n.23; and invasion of Lower
  Canada, 247–59
Handcock, Richard B., 333
Hanks, Porter, 108
Hanson, Alexander, 438 n.44
Hardy, Sir Thomas, 368, 369
Harmar, Josiah, 14
Harper, John, 3, 32, 35, 37
Harrison, William Henry, 23, 47,
  113–14, 133, 143, 144 pl, 147, 148,
  154, 156, 160, 167, 206, 409; at Fort
  Meigs, 149–53, 158; and invasion of
  Upper Canada, 207–10, 213–14; and
  Tecumseh, 26–27; at Tippecanoe,
  27–28
Hartford, Conn., 352, 354
Hartford Convention, 354–55, 378
Harvey, John, 183, 187–89, 189 pl, 260,
  261, 272, 396, 406, 424
Haviland, William, 225, 245
Heald, Mrs., 113 pl
Heald, Nathan, 112
Hemmingford, L.C., 251
Hemmingford Township, L.C., 54
Henderson's Bay, 246
Hendrick, Joseph, 175
Henry, John, 38–39, 358
Henry the younger, Alexander, 165
Henry, Point, 79
Heriot, George, 73, 424
Herkimer, Nicholas, 21
Hertel de Rouville, J.-B., 256
Hewett, John, 306, 452 n.10
Hindman, Jacob, 324
Holmes, A. H., 278–79
Hoople Creek, 260
Hopkins, Timothy, 221–22
Hopkinton, N.Y., 268
Horse Island, 235, 237
Howe, John, 358
Howison, John, 412, 414
Hudson's Bay Company, 289, 395
Hull, William, 28, 47, 53, 65, 90 pl,
  117, 118, 119; on Detroit frontier, 6,

69, 87, 90–102, 104, 109–10, 111–12;
  proclamation of, 95–96, 102, 104; and
  surrender of Detroit, 106–8, 110–11,
  113, 434
Hunter, Martin, 8
Huron, Lake, 95, 186, 275, 293, 295,
  399; naval superiority on, 288
Huron River, 160

Illinois River, 114
Indiana Territory, 24, 113, 336
Indian Department, 23, 65, 155, 160,
  196, 290, 296, 418
Indians, 154, 155, 156–57, 203, 206,
  207, 208, 224, 296–97, 403, 418,
  446 n.34; British relations with, 8,
  13–14, 64–66, 83, 112, 122, 288–89,
  295, 298, 336, 383, 384, 385–86, 388,
  394–96, 407; U.S. policy towards,
  21–24, 26, 28–29, 37, 42, 93, 104,
  288, 382, 385, 388, 394, 395–96, 408;
  at Beaver Dams, 194, 196; at Detroit,
  95–96, 97, 98, 101–3, 107, 109, 110,
  111; at Fort Meigs, 150–53, 157–58; at
  Fort Stephenson, 159–60; at Frenchtown, 144, 145–46, 147; and the
  Governor Clark, 291–92; at Moraviantown, 209, 211–12; at Michilimackinac,
  7, 65, 293, 294, 295; at Queenston
  Heights, 129, 130, 131; at Tippecanoe,
  27–28; at other battles, 112, 113, 115,
  146–47, 172, 191, 199, 221, 223, 254,
  256, 258, 260, 261, 278–79, 290, 296,
  307–8, 310, 325, 452 n.18. See also
  individual tribes
Ingersoll, Charles, 280
Ingersoll, Charles J., 199, 454 n.10
Iroquois, 65–66, 193, 225, 283
Irumberry de Salaberry, Charles-Michel
  d'. See Salaberry
Isaac Todd, 163, 445 n.25
Izard, George, 168, 273, 331–32, 343–44,
  345, 352; at Châteauguay, 253, 254,
  256, 257

Jackson, Andrew, 45, 273, 408, 409
Jackson, Francis James, 34–35
Jackson, Henry G., 424
James, William, 405
Jameson, Anna, 329
Jay, John, 14, 162
Jay's Treaty, 14–15, 98, 162, 382, 384
Jefferson, Thomas, 15, 16, 17–19, 21,
  26, 29, 30, 32, 33, 43, 44, 352

Jenkins, John, 230
Jenkins, Penelope, 361
Jesup, Thomas, 321, 378
Joes Point, 359
John, Henry, 372–73, 374–75, 456 n.27
Johnson, Sir John, 13, 418
Johnson, Richard M., 32, 35, 37, 156, 208; at Moraviantown, 209, 212, 213 pl, 214, 447 n.16
Johnston, David, 279
Johnston's Point, 359
Jones, Dunham, 5–6
Juchereau Duchesnay, J.-B., 256
Juchereau Duchesnay, M.-L., 256
Julia, 397

Keating, James, 296
Kedron Stream, 360
Kempenfelt Bay, 289
Kennebec River, 389
Kentucky, 113, 134, 143, 150
Kerr, William Johnson, 196
Kickapoos, 292, 397
King, Capt. William, 137
King, Maj. Gen. William, 378
King, William Rufus, 35
King's Road, 261
Kingston, U.C., 51, 70, 73, 74, 86, 117, 154, 156, 168, 173, 177, 186, 200, 213, 228, 229, 239, 243, 244, 245–46, 250, 253, 259, 272, 274, 299–300, 302, 314, 316, 336, 343, 400; fortifications at, 79, 415; hospitals at, 215, 433; as naval base, 79, 167, 185, 233, 234, 306, 330, 398–400
Kingston Dock Yard, 399 pl, 400, 400 pl
Klinck, Carl, 436 n.(2)13
Kosciuszko, Tadeusz, 44

L'Acadie, L.C., 89, 247, 251, 265
Lachine, L.C., 58, 60, 71, 228, 233, 249, 267, 343, 399
Lachine Canal, 415
Lachine Rapids, 71
Lacolle, L.C., 89, 334
Lacolle River, 89, 333
Lady Prevost, 98
Lalanne, Léon, 226
Lamont, Thomas, 137
Lamothe, J.-M., 256, 258
Langlade, Louis, 446 n.34
Lansdowne, Marquis of, 398
La Prairie, L.C., 76, 251
Larocque, Joseph, 163

Laurens, Henry, 30
Lawe, John, 199
Leander, 17
Le Breton, John, 151
Leclair, Isaac, 446 n.34
L'Écuyer, Benjamin, 256
Lee, Henry, 438 n.44
Lee, Robert, 220
Leonard, Nathaniel, 220
Leopard, 17, 23
Lewis, Meriwether, 44, 162
Lewis, Morgan, 246
Lewis, William, 145, 146
Lewiston, N.Y., 221, 224, 309
Lewiston Heights, 121
Lingan, James, 438 n.44
Linnet, 348, 350
Lisle, Robert, 426
Liverpool, Lord, 8, 55, 76, 387–88, 390, 391
Liverpool, N.S., 358
Liverpool Packet, 363
Logan, Chief, 102, 111
Lolawauchika (the Prophet), 23–26, 25 pl, 28, 436 n.(2)13
London region, U.C., 105, 206
Long, Robert B., 441 n.3
Longmore, George, 406
Long Point, 136, 161, 203, 204, 274, 276, 277–78, 288, 302
Long Sault Rapids, 71, 260, 261
Longtin, J.-M., 256
Longwood, U.C., 278–79
Lord Nelson, 435 n.6
Lorimier, J.-B. de, 446 n.34
Louis XVIII, 334, 390
Louisiana, 15, 353
Louisiana Purchase, 16
Lowell, John, 354
Lower Canada, 56–58, 302, 333, 337, 381, 383, 407, 412, 414, 427; Americans in, 54–56, 58, 59 pl, 180, 182; defence of, 58, 60, 74–75, 76, 78, 226, 250–51, 417; food supplies in, 68–69, 240, 272; Hampton's invasion of, 247–59, 271; population of, 49–50; transport and communications in, 70–74, 76; and U.S. border, 337, 383, 389. *See also under* Militia, British North American
Lower Cove, 359
Lowndes, William, 35, 37
Loyalists, 12–13, 49–51, 95, 104, 410–11, 412
Loyal and Patriotic Society of Upper Canada, 424–25, 434

Lundy's Lane, 319, 321, 324; Battle of, 319–25, 322 pl, 327, 409, 416, 426
Lunenburg, N.S., 358
Lutwyche, Edward G., 364–65
Lyndhurst, U.C., 440 n.32
Lynn River. *See* Patterson's Creek

McAfee, Robert, 442 n.39
McArthur, Duncan, 90–91, 168, 208, 282, 283 pl, 283–86, 288; on Detroit frontier, 94, 101, 103–4, 109–10, 111
McClure, George, 215–16, 217 pl, 220, 221–22, 300, 448 n.27; and burning of Niagara, 218–19, 222
McCrae, Thomas, 276, 286
McDonald, John ("Le Bras croche"), 165
Macdonell, Rev. Alexander, 63, 230
Macdonell, John, 106, 417; at Detroit, 107, 108, 110, 423; at Queenston Heights, 124, 127, 131
Macdonell, "Red George", 228 pl, 417; and raid on Ogdensburg, 228–33, 422; at Châteauguay, 250, 256, 424
Macdonough, Thomas, 349, 350, 416
McDouall, Robert, 154, 155, 202, 289, 290, 296, 297–98; at Michilimackinac, 293–95, 395
McDougall, Duncan, 163–65
McFarland, Daniel, 317
McGill, James, 251
McGillivray, John, 202
McGillivray, Joseph, 71
McGillivray, William, 71, 72 pl, 89, 395
McGlassin, George, 346
McGregor Creek, 207, 209
McGregor's mill, 96, 203, 206–7
Machesney, John, 121
Machias, Maine, 370, 375–76, 389, 456 n.28
McKay, William, 89, 289, 290–91, 292
McKee, Alexander, 21
McKenzie, Donald, 162, 163
Mackinac Island, 293, 298. *See also* Michilimackinac
Maclean, Allan, 13–14
McLean, Allan, 417
McLean, Donald, 172
McLean, George, 68
McLean, Neil, 417
McMicking, Peter, 221
McMullen, Alexander, 279, 280
McNeale, Neal, 172
Macomb, Alexander, 246, 260, 333; at Plattsburg, 343, 344, 345, 350, 416
McTavish, John George, 163, 165

McTavish, Simon, 202
Madawaska Settlement, 364
Madison, Dolley, 4
Madison, James, 3–4, 5 pl, 8, 11, 21, 23–24, 27, 33–35, 37–39, 44–45, 46–47, 84, 86, 89, 111, 114, 139, 199–200, 214, 337, 340, 342, 353, 354, 378, 381–82, 393, 409
Madrid, N.Y., 268
Magaguadavic River, 360
Maguaga, Michigan Terr., 103, 106
Mailhot, Pierre, 256
Mailloux, Joseph Saint-Valier, 247
Maine, 337, 354, 357, 358, 363, 365, 366, 370, 377–78, 387, 389, 396; and New Brunswick border, 357, 364–65, 384, 389–90, 392, 396
Malcolm's mills, 282, 284, 285
Mallory, Benajah, 192, 215, 221, 224, 276, 317
Malone, N.Y., 268, 434
Manchester (Niagara Falls), N.Y., 221
Mann, James, 433, 434
Manning, David, 254
Maritime Provinces, 337, 357, 358, 363, 367, 369, 394, 410, 414, 415; and boundary with Maine, 14, 364–65; food supplies of, 363; population of, 49
Markle, Abraham, 215, 280, 286, 288, 302
Marpot, 111
Marsh Bay, 372
Mary, 203
Maryland, 438 n.44
Massachusetts, 84, 337, 353, 355, 365, 369, 372, 377–78, 409
Massey, Hart, 19
Matchedash Bay, 275, 289, 292
Matthews, George, 43
Maumee Bay, 145
Maumee Rapids, 114, 115, 147, 148
Maumee River, 114, 115, 138, 143; sieges of Fort Meigs on, 148, 150, 157–58, 160, 426
Medcalf, Henry, 276, 280, 286
Meductic, N.B., 364
Meigs, Return J., 90, 101, 109
Memphremagog, Lake, 54, 337
Menominis, 65, 101, 293
Merritt, William Hamilton, 180, 184, 193, 196, 199, 317, 321; at Chippawa, 310, 313
Metternich, 390
Miami Indians, 214
Michigan, Lake, 7, 289, 383

Michigan Territory, 93, 138, 149, 156, 202, 203, 214, 286, 336, 396, 444 n.15
Michilimackinac, 13, 213, 274, 288–89, 292, 294 pl, 384, 389, 395; British capture of, 6–8, 65, 79, 102, 108, 111, 112; U.S. attack on, 292–95
Micmacs, 358
Midland district, U.C., 302
Militia, British North American, 61, 69–70, 101, 403, 416–18, 431
  Lower Canada, 58, 60, 64, 72, 252 pl, 253, 256, 266–67, 417, 427, 430–31
  Units:
    Canadian Light Dragoons, 275, 427
    Frontier Light Infantry, 247, 249, 251, 417
    Provincial Commissariat Voyageurs (Corps of Canadian Voyageurs), 71, 89
    Select Embodied Militia
      1st Battalion (Milice d'Élite Incorporée), 56 pl, 61 pl, 89, 242, 251, 417
      2nd Battalion, 251, 256
      3rd Battalion, 251
      4th Battalion, 247, 249
      Canadian Chasseurs (5th Battalion), 57 pl, 89, 265, 268
    Sedentary Militia
      2nd Battalion Beauharnois, 251, 256, 265–66
      Boucherville, 251, 256
      Châteauguay, 251
      Eastern Townships, 251
      Longueuil, 251
      Montreal, 251
      Montreal Volunteers, 251
      Verchères, 251
  New Brunswick, 64, 360, 361
  Nova Scotia, 64, 357–58, 361–62
  Prince Edward Island, 64
  Upper Canada, 52, 58, 60, 64, 69, 70 pl, 79, 105, 122, 129, 136, 137, 149, 150, 153, 155, 180, 184, 191, 261, 302, 315, 317, 417, 427, 431
  Units:
    Incorporated Militia, 180, 427
      Caldwell's Rangers, 278, 427
      Provincial Light Dragoons, 180
      Provincial Royal Artillery Drivers, 179, 179 pl, 418
      Volunteer Incorporated Militia Battalion, 314, 318, 321, 327 pl, 417
    Sedentary Militia
      Essex, 144, 154, 155

      Glengarry, 78, 268
      Grenville, 78
      Kent, 145, 154, 155, 276, 277, 278
      Leeds, 73
      Lincoln, 122, 197, 250, 310
      Long Point, 53, 105, 136
      Middlesex, 105, 136, 276, 281
      Norfolk, 105, 106, 136, 281, 417
      Oxford, 105, 136, 281, 282
      Stormont, 78, 260, 268
      York, 69, 106, 127, 136, 169
    Captain Runchey's Company of Coloured Men, 129
    Mississippi Volunteer Artillery, 288, 296
Militia, U.S., 43–45, 47, 84, 86, 91, 117, 134, 135, 138, 195, 224, 300, 317, 338, 341, 345, 376, 416
  Illinois, 295
  Kentucky, 43–44, 114, 207–8, 209, 212, 214, 282
  Michigan, 93, 110
  New York State, 118, 131–32, 133–34, 215, 216, 217 pl, 353, 344
  Ohio, 90–91, 96, 101, 108, 111, 114, 292
  Pennsylvania, 310, 311
  Canadian Volunteers, 192, 215, 216, 218, 221, 224, 317
Miller, James, 91, 102, 103; at Lundy's Lane, 322–23, 324
Mille Roches Rapids, 71, 260
Milne, David, 377
Minnesota River, 396
Miramichi River, 358
Missisquoi Bay, 54, 249, 333
Mississauga Point, 274
Mississippi River, 32, 288, 384, 392, 395, 396; upper, 289, 292, 295, 298, 408
Mohawks, 66, 129, 196
Molson, John, 71
Monguagon. *See* Maguaga, Michigan Terr.
Monroe, James, 3, 37, 38, 139, 143, 338, 378, 382, 383–84, 387, 398, 409
Monroe, Mich. *See* Frenchtown, Michigan Terr.
Montgomery, Richard, 29, 83–84, 225
Montreal, 30, 110, 229, 241, 242, 250, 256, 336, 343, 370, 433; as communications centre, 70–71, 73, 156, 226, 288, 337, 357, 414; defence of, 76, 226, 251, 266, 272; strategic importance of, 225–26; U.S. offensives against, 83, 85–89, 117, 133, 200, 215, 243–44, 245–46, 259–60, 265, 383

Montreal, 305

Monviel, François Vassal de. *See* Vassal de Monviel

Moose Island, 367, 368, 369, 396

Moraviantown, U.C., 207, 282

Moraviantown, Battle of, 207, 209–13, 213 pl, 214, 263, 271, 274, 288, 351, 409, 447 n.12

Morris, Charles, 373, 374

Morrison, Joseph W., 259–60, 313–14, 317; at Crysler's Farm, 261–64, 265, 424

Morristown, N.Y., 229

Mowry, Jabez, 369

Muir, Adam, 98, 101, 103, 115–16, 151, 283, 424, 447 n.12

Mulcaster, William, 260, 261, 306

Murney Point, 79

Murray, John, 216, 218, 219, 220, 242, 243, 330

Murray, Patrick, 417

Myers, Christopher, 183

Nancy, 293

Nanticoke Creek, 276

Napoleon, 9, 11, 16, 17, 37, 104, 271, 300, 334, 382, 386, 390, 407

National Intelligencer (Washington), 45, 253–54, 342

Navy Bay, 399

Newark. *See* Niagara, U.C.

New Brunswick, 8, 363, 365, 368, 369, 370, 378, 407; defence of, 357, 358–60, 367; population of, 49; and U.S. border, 14, 337, 364–65, 384, 389–90, 396. *See also under* Militia, British North American

New-Brunswick Courier, 366, 370

Newcastle district, U.C., 302

New England, 337, 370, 376; defence of, 84, 354, 355, 378; opposition to war in, 365–66, 409; separatist movement in, 352–56, 378; and trade with Maritimes, 68, 358, 363

New Hampshire, 352, 354

New Jersey, 352

New Mexico, 408

New Orleans, 30, 168, 354, 355, 356, 394, 409

New Orleans, 399

New York (state), 134, 168, 216, 226, 343, 352, 387, 458 n.11; defence of, 131, 308; and trade with the Canadas, 68, 240, 272, 337, 354

New-York Evening Post, 133, 343

Niagara, U.C. (previously Newark; now Niagara-on-the-Lake, Ont.), 51, 76, 86, 117, 122, 131, 136, 182 pl, 184, 435 n.7; burning of, 218–19, 221, 271

Niagara, 305, 435 n.6

Niagara Falls, N.Y. *See* Manchester, N.Y.

Niagara Falls, 319

Niagara frontier, 167, 168, 191–92, 200, 201, 202, 215–16, 222, 245, 299, 317, 336, 381, 383, 448 n.27; Dearborn's offensive on, 83, 85, 86, 90, 117–18, 441 n.8; defence of, 136, 154, 179–80, 224, 242, 271, 272, 276, 281, 302, 308, 313–14, 384

Niagara-on-the-Lake, Ont. *See* Niagara, U.C.

Niagara River, 116, 118, 122, 129, 136, 167, 179, 182, 191, 197, 199, 216, 221, 222, 223, 245, 271, 274, 318, 319, 325, 384, 412; U.S. crossings of, 87, 120, 121, 131–32, 133, 135, 136, 184, 273, 300, 302, 308, 331

Nichol, George, 282

Nichol, Robert, 105, 106, 191, 274, 276, 280, 303, 326, 417, 423

Nicolls, Gustavus, 368, 372, 416

Noix, Île aux, 76, 240, 241 pl, 243, 247, 251, 333, 399. *See also* Fort Île aux Noix

Non-Importation Act, 18

Non-Intercourse Act, 19, 66–67

Norfolk County, U.C., 440 n.32

North American Naval Station, 337

North West Company, 65, 98, 120, 156, 162–65, 201, 213, 288, 289, 293, 395

Norton, John, 66, 67 pl, 196, 199, 283

Nor'Westers, 71, 164–65, 395

Nottawasaga, U.C., 289

Nottawasaga River, 289, 293

Nottingham, Md., 338

Nova Scotia, 4, 30, 31, 343, 363, 364; defence of, 355, 357, 358, 361–63, 369; population of, 49. *See also under* Militia, British North American

Nova-Scotia Royal Gazette, 8–9

Odelltown, L.C., 247, 333

Ogdensburg, N.Y., 6, 19, 68, 87, 253, 302; raid on, 229–30, 422

Ogilvie, James, 183, 223

Ohio, 24, 113, 143, 150, 274

Ohio, 326

Ohio River, 22

Ohio Valley, 4, 14, 30

Ojibwas, 291

Oneida, 5
Ontario, Lake, 5–6, 99, 167, 184–86, 191, 215, 225, 244, 303, 315, 342–43, 412; naval superiority on, 120, 156, 186, 202, 234, 306, 330, 336, 398, 401
Ontario, 435 n.6
Ontario Repository (Canandaigua, N.Y.), 218
Orders in Council, 17–19, 34, 39, 43, 85, 381, 441 n.3
Oriskany, N.Y., 21
Oshawana, 211 pl, 212
Osnabruck, U.C., 78
O'Sullivan, Michael, 256
Oswald, Richard, 30
Oswego, N.Y., 13, 179, 304; raid on, 303–8, 305 pl
Oswego Falls, 306, 308
Oswego River, 306
Otis, Harrison, 354
Ottawa River, 213, 288
Owen, David, 368
Owen, Sir Edward, 397
Oxford, U.C. (Woodstock, Ont.), 274, 277, 278, 279, 282

Pacific Coast, 384
Pacific Fur Company, 162, 164, 384
Pacific Ocean, 162
Pagan, Robert, 359
Pakenham, Sir Edward, 356
Panet, Philippe, 256
Paris, Treaty of, 12–13, 21, 30, 384
Parish, David, 68, 230, 232 pl
Parker, Hyde, 375
Parrsboro, N.S., 358, 360 pl, 361
Partridge Island, 359, 360 pl
Passamaquoddy Bay, 365, 367, 376, 377; British expedition to, 368–69, 456 n.17; islands of, 364, 367, 368, 384, 389, 396
Patterson's Creek (Lynn River), 279
Patuxent River, 338
Pearson, Thomas, 228–29, 310, 424, 449 n.8
Penetanguishene, U.C., 275, 289, 399
Peninsula, Point, 306
Pennsylvania, 42
Penobscot Bay, 367, 369, 370, 373, 396; British expedition to, 369–77
Penobscot River, 342, 357, 365, 369, 370, 372, 376, 377, 389, 390
Peoria, Illinois Terr., 156
Penoyer's Road, 73
Perkins, Joseph, 288, 290

Perrault, Joseph-François, 89, 247
Perrot, Île, 253
Perry, Oliver H., 203–4, 208
Perry brothers, 254
Petry, Jean-Baptiste, 394
Philipsburg, L.C., 249
Phoebe, 163
Pickering, Timothy, 352, 353, 354
Pictou, N.S., 358
Pigeon Roost Creek, 113
Pike, Zebulon, 168, 172, 173
Pike's Cantonment, 348
Pilkington, Andrew, 363, 369, 375–76
Pinckney, Thomas, 47
Pins, Pointe aux, (Rondeau Provincial Park, Ont.), 274
Plattsburg(h), N.Y., 86, 87, 89, 240, 241–43, 246, 259, 268, 333, 343, 344, 345, 349, 351, 357; Battle of, 304 pl, 334, 345–50, 349 pl, 352, 355, 356, 390, 409, 416
Plattsburg(h) Bay, 346
Pleasant, Point, 358
Plenderleath, Charles, 188–89, 424
Plumer, William, 3, 352, 353
Pointe-Claire, L.C., 58
Pontiac, 408
Popham, Stephen, 307–8
Porlier, Jacques, 290
Portage Road, 315, 319, 321, 332
Port Dover, U.C., 106, 276, 278, 279–80, 285
Porter, Peter B., 35–37, 45, 134, 135, 138, 199, 308, 311 pl, 315, 317, 378; at Chippawa, 310, 311; at Lundy's Lane, 322
Portland, Maine, 363, 369, 372
Port Ryerse, U.C., 279
Port Talbot, U.C., 106, 276, 280
Potawatomis, 112, 214
Pothier, Toussaint, 290, 291 pl
Powell, Thomas, 327
Powell, William Dummer, 286
Power, Manley, 344, 345
Prairie du Chien, Illinois Terr., 156, 288, 289–90, 293, 295, 296, 297, 389, 395, 396. See also Fort Shelby
Prescott, U.C., 78, 79, 228, 229, 231, 233, 260, 265, 272. See also Fort Wellington
Presque Isle (Erie), Penn., 156, 157, 160, 201, 202, 204
Preston, James P., 184
Prevost, Sir George, 6, 52, 54, 55 pl, 57–58, 68, 124, 149, 154, 155, 157, 180, 201, 240, 256, 267, 275, 289,

292, 303, 313, 314, 329, 330, 331, 334, 335, 336, 342, 395, 403–4, 406, 417, 422; and armistice, 85–86, 110, 118, 122, 381; and defence of the Canadas, 58, 60, 63–64, 76, 79–80, 139, 214–15, 226, 228, 250, 253, 272, 302, 369; at Plattsburg, 342, 344, 345–46, 348–52, 354, 356, 392, 394, 416; and raid on Ogdensburg, 229–32; at Sackets Harbor, 233–35, 237–40; Wellington's assessment of, 351, 352, 454 n.25

Prince Regent, 175

Prince of Wales Tower, 359 pl

Pring, Daniel, 242, 243

Procter, George, 406

Procter, Henry, 99 pl, 101–2, 104, 115, 120, 122, 145–46, 147, 148, 154, 155–56, 161, 186, 187, 201–3, 204, 263, 276, 351, 417, 444 n.15; at Fort Stephenson, 158–60; at Moraviantown, 210–13; at sieges of Fort Meigs, 149–53, 156–58; withdrawal of, from Amherstburg, 204–7, 208–9, 214

Prophet, the. *See* Lolawauchika

Prophet's town, 27, 28

Provincial Marine, 98, 107, 145, 167, 169, 175, 203, 233, 242, 418

Psyche, 70

Purdy, Robert, 255–58

Put-in-Bay, 274; Battle of, 203–4, 288, 351

Putnam, Perley, 368

Quebec (city), 29, 57, 70–71, 111, 226, 241, 242, 253, 272, 365, 415, 433; defence of, 30–31, 58, 75–76, 225, 401, 415; expulsion of Americans from, 58, 59 pl

Queen Charlotte, 98, 99 pl, 107

Queenston, U.C., 120, 121, 124, 125, 126, 127, 128, 191, 193, 194, 221, 309, 315, 318, 319

Queenston Heights, Battle of, 106, 125 pl, 125–32, 135, 138, 408, 426

Quincy, Josiah, 35, 39, 139, 352, 353

Racoon, 165

Raisin, River (Michigan Terr.), 91, 93, 101, 104, 109, 115, 145, 147–48, 154; Indian massacre at, 147, 210

Raisin River (U.C.), 78

Raleigh Township, U.C., 276

Ramillies, 368

Randolph, John, 32, 33 pl, 37, 47

Rapelje, Abraham, 280

Raymond, Hyacinthe, 256

Regiments. *See under* Army, British; Army, U.S.

Reiffenstein, John C., 210–11

Retaliation, 363

Rhea, John, 32

Rhode Island, 84, 352, 355, 365

Riall, Sir Phineas, 221, 222–24, 267, 277, 302, 303, 308, 314–15, 318–19, 416; at Chippawa, 309–13; at Lundy's Lane, 319, 321

Richard, 17

Richardson, John, 103, 107, 108, 109, 146, 209, 211, 405 pl, 435 n.7; at sieges of Fort Meigs, 150, 151, 152–53, 157–58, 159; as writer, 404, 406

Richelieu River, 225, 240

Richibucto River, 358

Rideau Canal, 401, 415

Ridout, George, 130

Ridout, Thomas, 272

Rifleman, 370

Ripley, Eleazer Wheelock, 308, 310; at Lundy's Lane, 322–23, 324, 326, 409

Roberts, Charles, 6–8, 79, 108, 289, 293

Robertson, James, 348

Robinson, Frederick, 344, 345, 346, 348, 350

Robinson, John Beverley, 175, 286, 287 pl

Robinson, William Henry, 69, 272

Rock Island, 396

Rock Island Rapids, 288, 292, 295–96

Rockport, U.C., 233

Rock River, 156

Roland, Charles G., 433, 434

Rolette, Charles Frédéric, 6, 79, 93, 120, 290

Rolette, Joseph, 290

Rome, N.Y., 179, 308

Rondeau district, U.C., 276

Rondeau Provincial Park, Ont. *See* Pins, Pointe aux

Ross, John, 230

Ross, Robert, 337, 338, 340, 341–42, 354

Rottenburg, Baron Francis de, 76, 156–57, 197, 201, 203, 204, 206, 213, 214, 230, 240, 253, 272, 278, 344

Rouge, River, 93

Roundhead, 146

Rouses Point, 240

Royal George, 167

Royal Marines, 267
Royal Military College of Canada, 399,
    400, 452 n.10
Royal Navy, 20, 43, 76, 185, 233, 267,
    364, 369, 409, 418
Rush, Richard, 398
Rush–Bagot Agreement, 398, 400–401
Russell, Jonathan, 383
Russia, 381, 382, 384, 390
Ryckman, John, 451 n.20
Ryerse, Samuel, 279, 280
Ryerson, Joseph, 105, 106
Ryland, Herman, 56, 58

Sacket, Augustus, 19
Sackets Harbor, 19, 83, 86, 90, 168, 179,
    200, 215, 230, 238 pl, 244, 245, 259,
    299, 303, 304, 307 pl, 308, 331, 336,
    343; attack on, 185, 233–40; as naval
    base, 74, 118, 120, 167, 168, 244,
    306, 399.
St. Andrews, N.B., 8, 359, 367
St. Catharines, Ont. *See* Twelve Mile
    Creek
St. Clair, Arthur, 14
St. Clair, Lake, 282, 397
St. Clair River, 282
Saint-Constant, L.C., 89
St. Croix River, 364, 396
St. Davids, U.C., 193, 194, 215, 219,
    317, 318, 452 n.18
Sainte-Geneviève, L.C., 58
Saint-François River, 54
St. George, Thomas, 93, 94, 96, 98, 99,
    423
St. George, Maine, 367
St-Germain, Évangeliste, 446 n.34
Saint-Jean, L.C., 76, 225, 247, 251, 333
Saint John, N.B., 8, 358, 360, 361 pl,
    363, 367, 415
Saint John River, 358, 364, 370, 389
St. Joseph Island, 6, 8, 65, 76, 288, 293,
    395
St. Lawrence, 330, 331, 336, 399
St. Lawrence River, 30, 32, 65, 71–72,
    79, 87, 200, 225, 233, 247, 253, 259,
    268, 336, 343, 383, 384, 401, 412
St. Leger, Barrimore, 21
St. Louis, 290, 292, 295, 296, 298
Saint-Maurice, Forges, 440 n.32
St. Petersburg, Russia, 382, 383
Saint-Philippe (-de-Laprairie), L.C., 88,
    89, 251, 265
Saint-Pierre, L.C., 251, 265

Saint-Régis, L.C., 87, 251, 261
St. Regis, N.Y., 259, 265
Salaberry, Charles-Michel d'Irumberry
    de, 88–89, 247, 255 pl, 417; at
    Châteauguay, 253, 254–57, 265, 424
Salmon River, 78, 265, 272
Sanborn Cove, 375
Sandusky, Ohio, 157, 208
Sandusky River, 22, 158, 160
Sandwich, U.C. (Windsor, Ont.), 53,
    95, 96, 98, 99, 106, 107–8, 206, 208,
    271, 274, 285
Sandy Creek, 307, 308
Saranac River, 345, 346, 350
Saratoga, N.Y., 111, 351
Sauk Indians, 288, 292, 296
Saumarez, Sir Thomas, 364
Scajaquada Creek, 223
Schultz, Christian, 51
Scioto River, 91
Scorpion, 293–95, 296
Scott, Christopher, 359
Scott, Hercules, 266, 268, 317, 321, 322,
    326, 328, 329
Scott, Thomas, 286
Scott, Walter, 406
Scott, Winfield, 118, 182, 183, 260, 273,
    300, 308, 309 pl, 396, 416; at Chip-
    pawa, 310–13; at Lundy's Lane, 319,
    321, 322, 323; at Queenston Heights,
    129, 130
Secord, David, 317
Secord, Laura Ingersoll, 196–97, 198 pl
Selkirk Settlement, 282
Seminoles, 408
Sénécal, Hypolite, 297
Sérurier, Louis, 37
Sewell, Jonathan, 55, 56, 58
Shannon. See *Growler*
Shannon, HMS, 363
Shaw, Aeneas, 417
Shawnees, 26
Sheaffe, Roger, 135, 136, 177, 177 pl,
    178, 180, 202, 241, 250, 251, 417; at
    Queenston Heights, 128–29; at York,
    172–75, 176
Shelburne, N.S., 358, 361
Shelburne Bay, 243
Shelby, Isaac, 207, 208
Shelley, Frances, Lady, 419
Shepard, Elihu, 449 n.9
Sherbrooke, Sir John Coape, 63, 337,
    342, 354, 355, 357, 361, 362, 365,
    366 pl, 367, 368, 378, 406, 456 n.17;
    and Penobscot Bay expedition, 369–72,
    376–77

Sim, Lieut., 121
Simcoe, John Graves, 50, 206
Simcoe, Lake, 275, 289
Sioux, 65, 212, 291, 296
Sir Isaac Brock, 174
Sir John Sherbrooke, 363
Six Nations Indians, 13–14, 65, 105, 122, 193, 196, 283
Sloan, James, 96
Smith, Michael, 50
Smuggler Brown's Road, 19
Smyth, Alexander, 47, 87, 118, 120–21, 131, 133–35, 137, 138, 174; proclamation of, 132–33
Smyth, George S., 8
Snake Hill, 327
Snake Island, 79
Solomon's Town, Ohio, 91
Somers, 326
Sorel, Que. *See* William Henry, L.C.
Soubiron, Paul-Émile, 37–38
Spain, 408, 441 n.3
Spilsbury, Francis B., 307
Split Log, 111
Split Rock Rapids, 71
Spokane, 162
Stanley, Matthew W., 413 pl, 450 n.38
Stewart, Alex, 279
Stewart, Alexander, 165
Stone, Isaac, 317
Stoney Creek, Battle of, 187–91, 190 pl, 192, 201
Stoney (Stony) Island, 306
Stoney (Stony) Point, 306
Stonington, Maine, 369
Stony Creek (Michigan Terr.), 146
Stony Creek (N.Y.), 307
Stovin, Richard, 241, 251
Strachan, Rev. John, 73, 174, 175, 176 pl
Street, Mrs. Samuel, 310
Street's Creek, 310, 311, 313, 331
Street's mill, 324
Strong, Caleb, 39, 42 pl, 84, 378
Stuart, James, 226
Superior, Lake, 156, 201
Sutherland, William, 276
Swanton, Vt., 86
Swartwout, Robert, 246, 263, 378
Sweden, 382, 384
Swiftsure, 71

Tabusintac River, 358
Talbot, Thomas, 105, 180, 206, 281, 281 pl
Talbot Settlement, 274

Talleyrand, Charles Maurice de, 16, 394
Tallon, Joseph, 424
Tartarus, 4
Taschereau, Thomas-Pierre-Joseph, 417
Taylor, George, 240–41
Taylor, Zachary, 295, 296
Tecumseh, 24 pl, 25–28, 65, 66, 97, 99 pl, 102, 106, 107, 108, 111, 112, 206, 207, 404, 436 n.(2)13, 447 n.16; at Moraviantown, 211–12, 213 pl; at sieges of Fort Meigs, 149, 151, 153, 157–58
Tennessee, 24, 113
Texas, 408
Thames, 98
Thames River, 96, 99, 186, 203, 204, 206, 207, 209, 274, 275, 276, 277, 278, 282, 336, 412
Thomas, John, 24–25
Thomaston, Maine, 367
Thompson, David, 405
Thorold, Ont. *See* Beaver Dams, U.C.
Thousand Islands, 6, 233
Tigress, 293–95
Times, The (London), 335, 350
Tippecanoe, Battle of, 27–28, 65, 112
Tippecanoe River, 26
Tompkins, Daniel D., 117, 118, 222, 224, 239, 245
Tonawanda Creek, 221
Toronto, Ont. *See* York, U.C.
Toussaint Island, 87
Tower of London, 267, 450 n.42
Towson, Nathan, 327
Tracy, Uriah, 352
Treat Island. *See* Dudley Island
Troughton, Felix, 424
Troy, N.Y., 87
Tucker, J. G. P., 321
Tupper, Edward, 114
Turkey Point, Ont. *See* Charlotteville, U.C.
Turkey Point, 99, 182, 186, 278, 279
Turreau, Louis-Marie, 30
Tweeddale, Marquis of, 310, 313
Twelve Mile Creek, 193, 194–95, 216, 318
Twenty Mile Creek, 193, 197, 216, 315
Two Mile Creek, 183

Upper Canada, 186, 201, 214, 224, 226, 274, 299, 301–2, 316, 336, 342, 382, 399, 410–12, 413–15, 417, 427, 434, 458 n.11; Americans in, 50–51, 94, 95, 139, 180, 288, 409–10; defence of, 76, 79, 154, 239, 267, 271, 272, 395; food supplies in, 68–69, 230–31, 272, 302; population of, 49–50; transport and communications in, 70–75, 74 pl, 226, 278, 295; U.S. offensives against, 83, 85, 86, 119, 154, 167, 213, 214, 253, 268, 338, 407; U.S. raids in western, 272, 275–76, 278–83, 286; war service medal in, 424–25, 425 pl. *See also under* Militia, British North American

Upper Marlboro, Md., 338

Upper Sandusky, Ohio, 148

Urbana, Ohio, 101

U.S. Navy, 43, 45, 76, 167, 234

Utica, N.Y., 179

Vancouver Island, 395

Van Horne, Thomas, 101–2, 103

Van Rensselaer, Solomon, 121, 138

Van Rensselaer, Stephen, 47, 87, 117–21, 119 pl, 124, 131–32, 133, 135, 300

Vassal de Monviel, François, 417

Verchères de Boucherville, Thomas, 6, 103, 107, 109, 116

Vermont, 68, 240, 247, 337, 352, 354

Vidal, Alexander, 397

Viger, D.-B., 54

Villatte, Charles de, 327

Vincennes, Ind., 26, 27, 28

Vincent, John, 180, 183–84, 186, 187, 189, 190, 192–93, 201, 212, 213, 214–15, 216, 234, 239, 276

Virginia Resolutions, 355

Vrooman's Point, 125, 128

Wabash River, 22, 26, 27

Walk-in-the-Water, 111

Warburton, Augustus, 207, 212

War Hawks, 4, 35, 36–39, 43, 57, 113, 337, 353, 381

Warren, John Borlase, 337–38, 381

Washington, George, 12, 14, 29

Washington, 398; raid on, 338–42, 340–41 pl, 357, 409, 454 n.10

Wasp, 242

Watson, Simon Zelotes, 96, 105

Watteville, Louis de, 250 pl, 256

Wayne, Anthony, 14, 21, 22

Webster, Daniel, 396

Welland Canal, 415

Welland River. *See* Chippawa River

Wellington, Duke of, 312, 344, 390–92, 391 pl, 398, 419; assesses Prevost, 351, 352, 454 n.25

Wells, Samuel, 145

Westbrook, Andrew, 96–97, 275, 279, 280, 413

Westminster Township, U.C., 97

Westmorland County, N.B., 360

Weston, Jonathan D., 369

Wilkinson, James, 47, 168, 229, 244 pl, 268, 333–34, 338, 343, 434; and invasion of Lower Canada, 200, 243–46, 249, 251, 253, 255–56, 259, 260–61, 265, 266, 267, 342

Willcocks, Joseph, 52, 192, 215–16, 218, 286, 302, 317, 330

William Henry, L.C. (Sorel, Que.), 71

Williams, Capt., 127

Williams, William, 350

Williamstown, U.C., 263

Winchester, James, 47, 114–15, 143, 145, 146–48

Winder, William H., 136–37, 168, 182, 186, 188, 192; and raid on Washington, 338, 340, 341

Windsor, N.S., 358

Windsor, Ont. *See* Sandwich, U.C.

Winnebagos, 65, 112, 291, 296

Winslow, Edward, Jr., 361

Wisconsin region, 288, 292

Wisconsin River, 290

Wolfe, 235, 237

Wood, Calvin, 287

Wood, Jacob, 282

Woodstock, Ont. *See* Oxford, U.C.

Woodward, Augustus, 444

Wool, John, 125, 127

Woolsey, Melancthon T., 307

Worsley, Miller, 294–95

Worthington, Thomas, 91

Wyandots, 214

Wyoming Valley, Penn., 21

Yarmouth, N.S., 358, 361

Yeo, Sir James, 185 pl, 185–86, 191, 193, 202, 245, 305, 330, 331, 350; at Oswego, 303, 305, 306–8; at Sackets Harbor, 233–35, 237, 239

York, U.C. (Toronto, Ont.) 70, 73, 99, 122, 184, 186, 213, 215, 218, 274, 288, 289, 300, 302, 316, 332, 382, 433; attack on, 156, 167, 168–77, 174 pl, 178 pl, 233, 271; fortifications at, 76, 169, 169 pl; legislature at, 52–53

York Battery, 131

Young, Robert, 212

Youngstown, N.Y., 220, 221, 318

EASTERN THEATRE

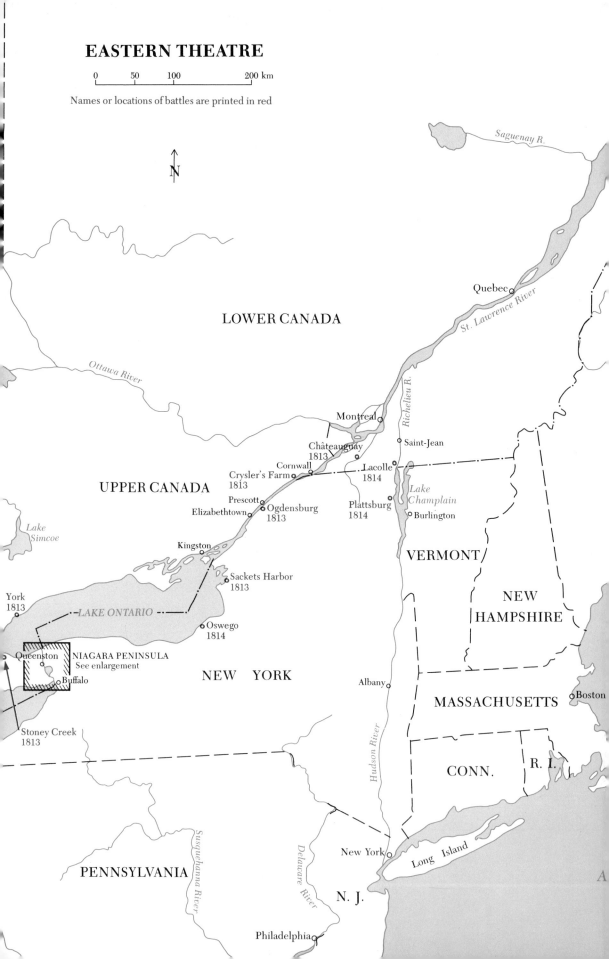

0 50 100   200 km

Names or locations of battles are printed in red

N

Saguenay R.

Quebec

LOWER CANADA

St. Lawrence River

Ottawa River

Montreal

Richelieu R.

Saint-Jean

Châteauguay
1813

Cornwall

Lacolle
1814

Crysler's Farm
1813

UPPER CANADA

Prescott

Ogdensburg
1813

*Lake
Champlain*

Elizabethtown

Plattsburg
1814

Burlington

*Lake
Simcoe*

Kingston

VERMONT

Sackets Harbor
1813

York
1813

LAKE ONTARIO

NEW
HAMPSHIRE

Oswego
1814

Queenston

NIAGARA PENINSULA
See enlargement

NEW   YORK

Albany

MASSACHUSETTS

Boston

Buffalo

Stoney Creek
1813

Hudson River

CONN.

R. I.

PENNSYLVANIA

Susquehanna River

Delaware River

New York

Long   Island

N. J.

A

Philadelphia